W0246423

Transforming Health in Turkey

Turkey's Health Transformation Programme (H.T.P.) has been instrumental in reshaping the country's healthcare landscape, aiming at enhancing accessibility, efficiency, and quality of services. Despite generating significant academic and policy interest, there remains a gap in consolidated scholarly resources. This book addresses this need, synthesizing the existing research to provide a comprehensive overview and critical analysis of the H.T.P.'s impacts from multiple perspectives.

Structured into five main sections, the book delves into the H.T.P.'s policy changes, theoretical framework, and intended outcomes since its inception in 2003. It then assesses its effects through various lenses: From the government's strategic planning and economic considerations to healthcare providers' experiences and institutional dynamics and, finally, from the users' perspective, evaluating access, quality, and social implications. Additionally, a comparative analysis with similar reforms worldwide offers lessons and future directions.

Targeting academics, healthcare professionals, policymakers, and students interested in health economics and policy analysis, this book aims to fill a critical gap in the literature, providing insights for ongoing and future reforms not only in Turkey but also in comparable global contexts.

Dr. Dilek Başar received a bachelor's degree in economics from Hacettepe University (Ankara, Turkey) in 2006 and was awarded a master's degree in economics by Hacettepe University in 2008. She received a Doctor of Philosophy degree in economics from the University of Sheffield in 2012. Her field of interests include health economics, labour economics, and gender economics. Dr. Başar is currently Professor at Hacettepe University, Ankara, Turkey. Dr. Başar is on the board for Hacettepe University Health Economics and Health Policy Research and Application Center.

Dr. Selcen Öztürk completed her undergraduate education at Gazi University Department of Economics in 2006 and her master's degree at Hacettepe University Department of Economics in 2008. Dr. Öztürk completed her Ph.D. in the field of Economics at the University of Sheffield in 2012. Since 2012, she has been working at Hacettepe University, where her field of interests include gender economics, regional economics, labour economics, and health economics. Dr. Öztürk is currently a professor at Hacettepe University, Ankara, Turkey. Dr. Öztürk is on the board for Hacettepe University Health Economics and Health Policy Research and Application Center.

Transforming Health in Turkey

An Evaluation of Two Decades of Reform

Edited by Dilek Başar and Selcen Öztürk

Routledge
Taylor & Francis Group

A PRODUCTIVITY PRESS BOOK

Designed cover image: Shutterstock

First published 2025
by Routledge
605 Third Avenue, New York, NY 10158

and by Routledge
4 Park Square, Milton Park, Abingdon, Oxon, OX14 4RN

Routledge is an imprint of the Taylor & Francis Group, an informa business

ISBN: 978-1-032-88835-4 (hbk)
ISBN: 978-1-032-88523-0 (pbk)
ISBN: 978-1-003-53989-6 (ebk)

DOI: 10.4324/9781003539896

Typeset in Garamond
by Apex CoVantage, LLC

Contents

Contributors

Berna Tuncay Alpanda
Graduate School of Health Sciences
Koç University
İstanbul, Turkey

Dilek Başar
Department of Economics
Hacettepe University
Ankara, Turkey

Nüket Örnek Büken
Faculty of Medicine, Department of History
    of Medicine and Ethics
Hacettepe University
Ankara, Turkey

Jesse B. Bump
Department of Global Health and Population
Harvard T.H. Chan School of Public Health
Boston, United States

İsmail Çakmak
Department of Management and
    Organization
Ordu University
Ordu, Turkey

Zafer Çalışkan
Department of Economics
Hacettepe University
Ankara, Turkey

Asena Caner
Department of Economics
TOBB University of Economics and
    Technology
Ankara, Turkey

Kübra Coşar
Department of Econometrics
Ankara Hacı Bayram Veli University
Ankara, Turkey

Eren Gürer
Department of Economics
Middle East Technical University
Ankara, Turkey

Deniz Karaoğlan
Department of Economics
Gebze Technical University
Gebze, Turkey

Aziz Küçük
Turkish Ministry of Health
Ankara, Turkey

Osman Küçükşen
Department of Economics
Hacettepe University
Ankara, Turkey

Alper Mortaş
Turkish Ministry of Health
Ankara, Turkey

Zeynep Güldem Ökem
Department of International Entrepreneurship
TOBB University of Economics and
    Technology
Ankara, Turkey

Fatih Cemil Özbuğday
Department of Economics
Ankara Yıldırım Beyazıt University
Ankara, Turkey

İlhan Can Özen
Department of Economics
Middle East Technical University
Ankara, Turkey

Selcen Öztürk
Department of Economics
Hacettepe University
Ankara, Turkey

Didem Pekkurnaz
Department of Economics
Başkent University
Ankara, Turkey

Işın Kortan Saraçoğlu
Department of Economics
Ordu University
Ordu, Turkey

Sıtkıcan Saraçoğlu
Department of Economics
Ankara Hacı Bayram Veli University
Ankara, Turkey

Susan Powers Sparkes
Health Financing and Economics
World Health Organization
Geneva, Switzerland

Seher Nur Sülkü
Department of Econometrics
Ankara Hacı Bayram Veli University
Ankara, Turkey

Abdullah Tirgil
Department of Economics
Ankara Yıldırım Beyazıt University
Ankara, Turkey

Yağmur Tokatlıoğlu
Department of Econometrics
Ankara Hacı Bayram Veli University
Ankara, Turkey

Zeynep Öztürk Yaprak
Department of Economics
Yozgat Bozok University
Yozgat, Turkey

Gülbiye Yenimahalleli Yaşar
Department of Health Management
Ankara University
Ankara, Turkey

Introduction

Dilek Başar and Selcen Öztürk

Turkey's Health Transformation Programme (H.T.P.) has played a pivotal role in reshaping the country's healthcare setting, with a focus on enhancing accessibility, efficiency, and the quality of services. Intended for a diverse audience, including academics, healthcare professionals, policy-makers, and students with an interest in health economics and policy analysis, this book provides a comprehensive evaluation of Turkey's health reforms. This work aims to fill a critical gap in the literature, offering insights that are relevant not only to Turkey but also to other countries under-going or contemplating similar healthcare transformations.

This groundbreaking book represents the first comprehensive analysis of Turkey's health reforms under the H.T.P. Drawing on the expertise of leading scholars and practitioners, it assesses the programme's impact on public health outcomes, healthcare delivery, economic efficiency, and social equity. Organised into five main sections, the book provides an in-depth examination of the H.T.P., assesses its impact from multiple perspectives, and includes a comparative analysis with similar reforms globally. The insights and recommendations offered here are invaluable for future research and reform efforts.

The Healthcare System in Turkey before the H.T.P.

To fully appreciate the significance of the H.T.P., it is essential to understand the historical context of Turkey's health system, which can be divided into four distinct periods: 1923 to 1939, 1940 to 1980, 1980 to 2003, and 2003 to present.

1923–1939: Foundation and Early Development

In the aftermath of the War of Independence, Turkey embarked on the monumental task of nation-building, which included the establishment of a national health system. This period marked the foundation and early development of health institutions and services, with a primary focus on controlling infectious diseases and developing public health infrastructure. The efforts during this time were aligned with Turkey's broader goals of constructing a planned economy and modernising the state. The foundation laid during these years was key in setting the stage for future expansions in health services.

DOI: 10.4324/9781003539896-1

1940–1980: Centralisation and Expansion

The era from 1940 to 1980 was characterised by the centralisation of health services, reflecting the government's commitment to extending healthcare across the nation. This period saw significant efforts to expand access to medical care, particularly through the establishment of a comprehensive primary healthcare network and the expansion of hospital services. The centralisation policy aimed to ensure that healthcare resources were distributed more evenly across the country, addressing the disparities that had emerged during the earlier years.

1980–2003: Fragmentation and the Need for Reform

Following the economic liberalisation of the 1980s, Turkey's health system entered a period of fragmentation. The shift from a planned to a market economy introduced new challenges, as the health system struggled to adapt to the changing economic landscape. The fragmentation of services, coupled with growing inefficiencies and inequities, underscored the urgent need for comprehensive reform. Limited access to quality care, especially in rural areas, and the lack of coordination among different levels of care emerged as critical issues. This era highlighted the shortcomings of the existing system and set the stage for the transformative changes that would come with the H.T.P.

2003 to Present: The Health Transformation Programme

In recent years, the term "reform" has become increasingly significant in the field of health, referring to efforts aimed at improving and restructuring health systems. The World Health Organization (WHO) defines health reform as activities aimed at changing health policies and institutions, often driven by planned, top-down political initiatives. Globally, health reforms have become a focus of attention, particularly in health economics, as nations grapple with rising costs, increasing expectations, and limited financial capacity.

Since the early 1980s, health reform initiatives have emerged in both developed and developing countries, generally categorised into two models: The "market-based" approach, supported by the World Bank and the I.M.F., which links health services to the market economy and the "social model", endorsed by W.H.O. and U.N.I.C.E.F., which views health services as a basic need. Additionally, a hybrid model combining these approaches has also gained attention.

The driving factors behind these global health reforms include escalating healthcare costs, rising public expectations, and financial constraints that challenge governments to balance demand with economic realities. These reforms often share common features such as restructuring social security systems, increasing patient choice, decentralising services, and encouraging competition among service providers.

Turkey's Health Transformation Programme aligns closely with these global reform trends. The following chapters of this book will delve into the specifics of Turkey's health reform and its implications. The H.T.P. introduced several key reforms, including:

■ **Universal Health Insurance**: Aimed at ensuring equitable access to healthcare for all citizens, this reform has been a cornerstone of the H.T.P., helping to reduce disparities in healthcare access.

- **Primary Care Strengthening**: The role of family physicians was enhanced, making them the gatekeepers of the healthcare system. This shift was designed to improve the efficiency of care delivery and ensure that patients receive appropriate care at the right level.
- **Hospital Reform**: The H.T.P. sought to improve the efficiency and quality of hospital services through the introduction of public–private partnerships and performance-based financing models. These reforms aimed to increase the accountability of hospitals and enhance patient outcomes.
- **Human Resources Development**: Recognizing the importance of a well-trained healthcare workforce, the H.T.P. invested heavily in the education and training of healthcare professionals. This investment has been critical in addressing the shortages of skilled personnel in the health sector.
- **Health Information Systems**: The strengthening of data management and utilisation for evidence-based decision-making was another key component of the H.T.P. The development of robust health information systems has enabled better planning, monitoring, and evaluation of health services.

The H.T.P. has had a profound impact on the Turkish health system, leading to significant improvements in access, quality, and efficiency of care. However, challenges remain, such as the sustainability of the system, regional disparities in the quality of care, and the rising costs of healthcare. Despite these challenges, the H.T.P. represents a necessary and transformative step in addressing Turkey's healthcare challenges, and its ongoing evolution continues to shape the future of health in the country.

By examining the historical evolution of Turkey's health system, it becomes clear that the H.T.P. was not just a response to immediate needs but also a conclusion of decades of developments, challenges, and reforms. This programme has fundamentally altered the trajectory of health in Turkey, setting new standards and expectations for the future.

Main Goals of the H.T.P.

The H.T.P. is structured around eight key themes:

- Ministry of Health as Planner and Supervisor: Strengthening the Ministry's role in planning and oversight.
- General Health Insurance (G.H.I.): Unifying the population under a single health insurance system.
- Accessible and Patient-Friendly Health Services: Enhancing primary healthcare services, establishing an effective referral system, and creating financially and administratively autonomous health enterprises.
- Skilled and Motivated Healthcare Workforce: Developing a knowledgeable and dedicated healthcare workforce.
- Supportive Educational and Scientific Institutions: Building institutions that support the health system through education and research.
- Quality and Accreditation: Ensuring high-quality and effective healthcare services through accreditation.
- Rational Drug Use and Material Management: Establishing a national pharmaceuticals agency and a medical devices agency.
- Health Information System: Improving access to data for informed decision-making.

In 2007, three additional themes were introduced, following the establishment of a new government:

■ Health Promotion for a Better Future: Initiatives for healthy living.
■ Multi-Dimensional Health Responsibility: Encouraging inter-sectoral collaboration and mobilising stakeholders.
■ Cross-Border Health Services: Enhancing the country's influence in international health services.

Finally, in 2017, the government announced that the "Second Phase" of the H.T.P. has started. In this phase, the government focused on building "City Hospitals" with Public–Private Partnerships (P.P.P.). This second phase had three main objectives:

■ Supporting and enhancing the strategic planning of Ministry of Health (MoH).
■ Conducting a pilot study on output-based financing for preventive health services.
■ Increasing the capacity of the Social Security Institution (S.S.I.).

Milestones of the H.T.P.

Table 0.1 provides information regarding the milestones of the H.T.P. chronologically between 2003 and 2024.

Table 0.1 Milestones of H.T.P.

Year	Milestone
2003	Announcement of the H.T.P.
2003	A law was adopted to introduce contract-based employment with the aim of increasing the number of health staff in areas where recruitment and retention are challenging.
2003	Performance-based Supplementary Payment (P.B.S.P.) system piloted in ten MoH hospitals
2004	Law on pilot implementation for family medicine
2004	Individual P.B.S.P. system implemented in MoH institutions
2004	Reference pricing follow-up system
2004	Green Card holders covered for outpatient services
2004	Reimbursement Commission established
2005	Pilot implementation of family medicine in Düzce province
2005	Green Card holders covered for outpatient prescription drugs and co-payment introduced

Table 0.1 (*Continued*) Milestones of H.T.P.

Year	Milestone
2005	S.I.I. hospitals transferred to MoH, S.I.I. pharmacies closed, private facility access allowed
2006	Implementation of family medicine in seven provinces
2006	Global budget implemented for MoH hospitals
2006	Establishment of the S.S.I.
2006	P.P.P. in Turkey begins
2007	Implementation of family medicine in 14 provinces
2007	Draft law on the pilot implementation of Public Hospital Associations (P.H.A.)
2007	Removal of referral requirement (gatekeeper system) for university hospitals, new bundled payment systems, reporting through MEDULA required
2008	Implementation of family medicine in 22 provinces
2008	Social Insurance (S.I.) and General Health Insurance (G.H.I.) Act passed, making the financial coverage universal
2009	Implementation of family medicine in 33 out of 81 provinces
2010	Implementation of family medicine in the whole country
2011	Turkish Medicines and Medical Devices Agency was established, Refik Saydam Public Health Institute was closed, Turkish Public Hospitals Institution was established, and Public Hospital Union was established under the same Act
2011	The first P.P.P. initiative
2012	The Universal Health Coverage (U.H.C.) legislation which was announced in 2006 was put into force
2014	Health Institutes of Turkey were established
2017	The organisational structure of MoH was changed
2017	"Second Phase" of the H.T.P.
2020	Prevention of Violence in Health Sector Act
2022	"White Reform" in health to improve the working conditions of health workers
2023	"Second White Reform" in health including malpractice law and fighting violence in law more effectively

Chapter Summaries and Key Insights

The book is organised into five main parts; each dedicated to a thorough exploration of the H.T.P.'s policy changes, theoretical framework, and intended outcomes.

Part I: Sculpting Health: From the Government's Perspective and Impact on Turkey's Health Transformation Programme

The performance of the H.T.P. in reaching its objectives has been evaluated from various perspectives; yet, a thorough analysis of its impact on economic well-being remains absent. The first chapter titled "Implications of The Health Transformation Programme on Consumption Inequality" by Osman Küçükşen and Eren Gürer offers an in-depth examination of the redistributive effects of the H.T.P., aiming to address this gap. The authors explain the need to examine the issue for the following reasons. First, the H.T.P. introduces fundamental changes in premiums, contributory payments, and coverage, which could significantly impact healthcare expenditures and potentially exacerbate consumption inequality if these effects are unevenly distributed. Second, by influencing healthcare utilisation, the H.T.P. may alter the distribution of earning capacity across the population. Their findings indicate that, despite the equity goals of the H.T.P., its overall impact on consumption inequality is insignificant. The authors claim that although the F.M.P. has improved certain mother–child health indicators, regional disparities in service provision and usage limit its potential redistributive gains. Additionally, chronic issues in the Turkish labour market – such as high unemployment, a large informal sector, and high minimum wage take-up rates – diminish the incentives to use public healthcare services, further reducing the H.T.P.'s redistributive impact. They suggest that addressing these labour market problems through targeted policies, particularly those improving access to education and reducing the informal sector, is crucial for achieving the programme's equity objectives.

"Enhancing Health and Health System Outcomes: Exploring the Interplay between Health Expenditures, Access to Health Services, Utilization of Health Services, and Health Status" by Zeynep Öztürk Yaprak explores the relationships among health expenditures, access to health services, utilisation of health services, and health status within the framework of the H.T.P. utilising data spanning from 2003 to 2021. The author, who employs the Vector Autoregressive Model for this analysis, also enhances the study by incorporating Impulse-Response Functions, Variance Decomposition, and Historical Variance Decomposition methodologies. The findings demonstrate that enhancements in patient satisfaction under the H.T.P. have contributed to a 36% increase in life expectancy at birth, while improvements in the rate of doctor consultations have led to a 20% reduction in infant mortality rates. These results underscore the multifaceted impact of health services improvements – pertaining to expenditures and access – on health status indicators, with varying effects in different dimensions.

With the implementation of H.T.P., significant changes were introduced not only in the organisation of healthcare delivery but also in drug pricing and reimbursement mechanisms. Prior to 2004, drug pricing in Turkey adhered to a cost–benefit model; however, the pricing decree of 2004 established a reference pricing system. Additionally, the drug reimbursement process became more reliant on pharmacoeconomic evaluations. Nevertheless, as the demand for healthcare services grew, new treatment needs emerged, resulting in challenges related to the availability and accessibility of medications. The third chapter for this part, written by Zafer Çalışkan titled "The Pharmaceutical Pricing and Reimbursement Policies with Health Transformation Programme in Turkey" examines the H.T.P. process, investigates the current status of drug pricing and reimbursement, identifies the main problems, and suggests potential solutions. The author emphasises that the goal of ensuring rational drug use and efficient pharmaceutical budget management during the H.T.P. has not been fully met. While most prescription medications are covered, prioritising domestic production is important to reduce the reliance on imports. Local manufacturing would help secure supply, lower the current account deficit, and support the economy. There is also a need for more investment in R&D, especially for biologic medicines, biosimilars, and biotechnology products. In the short term, additional funding should go to the pharmaceutical sector. The pricing and reimbursement processes must be updated to handle the rising costs of innovative treatments like biological therapies.

Part II: Voices from the Frontlines: From the Supply Side Perspective

The first chapter of this section is titled "Strangers in a New Land: Evaluating the Diagnostic Effectiveness of the Turkish Health System in the Context of Syrian Refugees" by İlhan Can Özen and Berna Tuncay Alpanda. This chapter analyses factors contributing to underdiagnosis among Syrian refugees during their initial integration into Turkey's healthcare system, using over 10 million electronic health records. The study finds that underdiagnosed patients faced significantly worse health outcomes later on. It highlights the need for timely and accurate diagnosis, especially for refugees, and calls for improved healthcare resources, provider training, and systemic reforms to enhance diagnostic accuracy and equity in healthcare delivery in Turkey's healthcare system.

While equity in accessing healthcare services is a crucial concern, the type of healthcare services utilised and the efficiency of hospitals within this context are equally significant. The number of private hospitals in Turkey has doubled between 2002 and 2022, reflecting the significant growth trend in the global private healthcare market in recent years. The H.T.P. has played a major role in this expansion. However, despite this increase and emphasis, most of the existing literature emphasises public sector efficiency and leaves the private sector underexplored. In this context, "Efficiency of Private Hospitals under the Health Transformation Programme" by Seher Nur Sülkü, Yağmur Tokatlıoğlu, Aziz Küçük, and Alper Mortaş investigates the technical efficiency of outpatient and inpatient care services of private hospitals in Turkey using Stochastic Frontier Analysis. Their findings indicate that private hospitals in Turkey have significant potential to improve their efficiency, with technical efficiencies averaging 46% for inpatient services and 60% for outpatient services. Efficiency does not vary much across years, regions, hospital types, or sizes. Healthcare staff play a key role in service delivery, with nurses and other personnel acting as substitutes in private hospitals. Additionally, this chapter demonstrates that private hospitals experience diminishing returns to scale as they grow beyond their management capacity. These findings offer valuable guidance for hospital managers and policymakers in shaping the sector.

Part III: Empowering Health: Insights into Healthcare Users' Experiences and Perceptions within Turkey's Health Transformation Programme

The authors of the first chapter, titled "Examining Trends and Predictors of Satisfaction with Healthcare Providers in Turkey: Exploring the Impact of the Health Transformation Programme (2006–2022)" in the third part, which examines the demand side of the H.T.P., are Abdullah Tirgil and Fatih Cemil Özbuğday. Using data from Life Satisfaction Surveys, a regression model is estimated for the predictors of healthcare service satisfaction in this chapter. Results show a general satisfaction with public hospitals, unchanged satisfaction with university hospitals, and a slight decline in satisfaction with private providers since 2007. Overall, 73% of respondents are satisfied with healthcare services. The authors emphasise that the H.T.P. significantly boosted patient satisfaction, especially in public and private hospitals. Key factors influencing satisfaction include age, gender, employment status, marital status, education, income, personal health satisfaction, and insurance coverage. However, the authors assert that new policies are required to sustain and enhance the initial gains and satisfaction levels achieved at the outset of the H.T.P.

One of the most widely debated issues in the demand dimension of the H.T.P. is health expenditures. "Determinants of Household Health Expenditures in the Era of the Health Transformation Programme in Turkey" by Işın Kortan Saraçoğlu investigates the factors influencing household health expenditures during the H.T.P., with a focus on individual and household characteristics using data from the Life in Transition Survey. The findings of this chapter suggest that as individuals age, their likelihood of incurring out-of-pocket (O.O.P.) health expenses decreases. In contrast, factors such as being female, living in larger households, lacking formal education, residing in urban areas, and possessing a moderate level of wealth increase the probability of incurring O.O.P. health expenditures.

One of the most pivotal expansions introduced by the H.T.P. is the digitisation of health. The third chapter of this part titled "Healthcare Users' Experience with E-Health: Benefits, Drawbacks, and the Future" by Zeynep Güldem Ökem and Didem Pekkurnaz explores the awareness and usage of e-health applications among healthcare users in Turkey. The authors highlight that the H.T.P. has supported the growth of e-health practices. When creating or updating e-health technologies, it is important to consider demographic and socio-economic differences. They stress that addressing data security and regulatory challenges is key for sustainable development. To improve Universal Health Coverage (U.H.C.) and health outcomes, Turkey needs a secure and inclusive digital health environment. This requires cooperation among healthcare providers, policymakers, technology developers, and users.

The final chapter of this part, in turn, addresses another topic of significant importance from a demand perspective. "Evaluation of the Health Transformation Programme from the Perspective of Effectiveness and Satisfaction" by İsmail Çakmak specifically focuses on effectiveness of the H.T.P. and individuals' perceived satisfaction. This chapter underscores a notable advancement in infant and child mortality rates, a key focus of the programme. However, it seems that the programme did not actively drive this positive trend. Furthermore, the research shows a substantial increase in both satisfaction with drug pricing and overall satisfaction with healthcare services compared to the period before the programme. Despite this, there has been a noticeable decline in these satisfaction measures, especially after the mid-2010s.

Part IV: Charting the Course: Exploring Healthcare Utilization Patterns and Trends in Turkey's Health Transformation Programme

The first chapter of this part, which focuses on healthcare utilisation, concentrates on inequality in the context of primary healthcare utilisation among young children in the context of the H.T.P. "Does Health Reform Reduce Inequalities? Primary Healthcare Utilization of Young Children in Turkey" by Asena Caner, Deniz Karaoğlan, and Gülbiye Yenimahalleli Yaşar. The authors examine whether the family medicine system helped equalise healthcare utilisation between young children from low- and high-resource households using Health Survey data from 2008, 2010, and 2012. The results of the difference-in-differences analysis show that, when using "being taken to a health institution" as the measure, there is no evidence of a positive differential effect on children from low-resource households. However, when considering "being taken to a health institution when not sick", the reform appears to have benefited children from lower-resource households more than their better-off counterparts.

The second chapter titled "Socio-Economic Determinants of Public Healthcare Utilization in the Aftermath of the Health Transformation Programme in Turkey" by Sıtkıcan Saraçoğlu explores the socio-economic determinants of public healthcare utilisation, following the implementation of the H.T.P. within the framework of the Behavioural Model using the probit regression estimation method. The author utilises nationally representative data from three rounds of the Life in Transition Survey and finds that predisposing factors, such as age and the highest level of educational attainment, consistently have statistically significant effects on public healthcare utilization across all years analysed, while enabling and need factors are statistically significant only for 2006.

In recent years, rising indicators and needs related to mental health have shifted the focus of research towards this area. In line with this, the concluding chapter of this part addresses the unmet healthcare needs in accessing mental health services in Turkey. Kübra Coşar's study, titled "Unmet Need for Mental Healthcare: A Comprehensive Prevalence and Determinants Investigation for Turkey", explores the prevalence of unmet mental health needs and identifies high-risk groups using the probit model and Health Survey data. The findings show a decline in unmet mental health needs in 2022 compared to 2014, though vulnerable populations – such as women, low-income individuals, the uninsured, and those with health problems – remain particularly at risk.

Part V: Power, Policy, and Progress: Unravelling the Political Economy and Ethics of Turkey's Health Transformation Programme

The final part of the book is dedicated to the political economy and ethical issues related to the H.T.P. The first chapter titled "A Political Economy Analysis of Turkey's Health Transformation Programme" by Jesse B. Bump and Susan Powers Sparkes addresses key political economy challenges central to health reform and examines the strategies employed by the Minister of Health and the senior leadership team to navigate them. Instead of assessing the reform's effects on health indicators or outcomes, this analysis centers on the strategies employed by the Ministry of Health's leadership to address these intricate challenges. Particular attention is given to examining these challenges through a political economy framework, highlighting the interplay between political and economic dynamics in influencing the allocation of health resources. The second chapter titled "Capital Accumulation and the Restructuring of the Turkish Health System" by Aziz Küçük explores the H.T.P.'s impact through the lens of capitalist state theories since the recent reforms are largely driven by the goal of capital accumulation.

Medical ethics are critical for the allocation of limited resources, maintaining physician integrity, fostering professional solidarity, and ensuring optimal service delivery. While health policy aspects like financing, organisation, and management appear politically driven, they are rooted in moral choices and reflect ethical considerations. In this regard, the final chapter titled "Evaluation of Turkey's Health Transformation Programme in Terms of Medical Ethics" by Nüket Örnek Büken discusses ethical issues and stresses that healthcare should be funded through general taxes within a framework of social justice, as privatisation risks increasing inequality in access to care.

Chapter 1

Implications of the Health Transformation Programme on Consumption Inequality

Osman Küçükşen and Eren Gürer

Contents

1.1 Introduction

The Health Transformation Programme (H.T.P.) of Turkey, initiated in 2003 and implemented gradually, includes a series of significant reforms aimed at restructuring the healthcare system. These reforms encompass the harmonization and expansion of separate health insurance schemes, various efforts to achieve Universal Health Coverage (U.H.C.), implementation of family medicine system, digitalization of health records, improvements in health infrastructure, and the introduction of the performance-based payment system for physicians among others. According to a policy report by the former Health Minister, the H.T.P. was undertaken with the moral understanding that all citizens should have equitable access to primary healthcare services (Akdağ, 2011, p. 30).

DOI: 10.4324/9781003539896-2

Since the implementation of these reforms, their equity implications on access to healthcare have been a subject of debate. It is argued that reforms have been particularly instrumental in enhancing healthcare access and improving health outcomes, such as reducing infant mortality rates, among disadvantaged groups (Atun et al., 2013). However, counterarguments suggest that various obstacles may have led to the persistence of inequities (Yenimahalleli-Yasar & Ugurluoglu, 2011), or that existing inequities have transformed into a different shape rather than being eliminated (Yilmaz, 2013). Moreover, some recent studies find that the utilization of health services has become more regressive over the course of the implementation of the H.T.P. (Cinaroglu & Çalışkan, 2022).

While the literature on the equity effects of the H.T.P. on access to health is growing, there is a lack of systematic investigation into its redistributive effects on economic well-being. Such redistributive effects of the H.T.P. require careful consideration by policymakers for two main reasons. First, the H.T.P. introduces fundamental changes in premiums, contributory payments, and coverage. These changes can significantly impact healthcare expenditures, potentially exacerbating consumption inequality, especially if the effects are unevenly distributed. Second, by influencing health utilization, the H.T.P. may alter the distribution of earning capacity across the population.

In this chapter, we define economic well-being as consumption inequality excluding health expenditures, but for convenience, we mostly refer to it simply as consumption inequality. This exclusion is justified by the perspective that higher spending on health does not necessarily equate to improved economic well-being. Instead, it may simply represent the financial burden of healthcare on individuals. We consider health expenditures as necessary costs for maintaining health rather than discretionary spending that enhances economic satisfaction. Similar measures are employed in several studies on consumption inequality.[1]

The H.T.P. may affect our definition of consumption inequality via three main channels. First, the H.T.P. includes fundamental changes in the finances and benefits of the public and private health services, which can impact individuals' health expenditures through their effects on the perceived prices of medical services and changes in public and private health insurance expenditures. Second, as health status is a primary determinant of labour income, increased insurance coverage and more equitable access to health can mitigate the existing consumption inequalities. Third, insurance coverage can alter individuals' behaviour regarding medical expenditures and labour supply decisions. These behavioural responses can be amplified or mitigated by the design of the health insurance system. Additionally, since public health expenditures are partially financed by the general government budget, any change in the burden of the health system on the government budget can induce an indirect redistribution mechanism through the progressive tax-and-transfer system.

This chapter goes beyond the existing literature by conducting a comprehensive analysis of the direct and indirect redistributive effects of the H.T.P. Our focus is to uncover the primary mechanisms related to the three dimensions outlined before and provide theoretical foundations and empirical evidence for these mechanisms, which we argue have significant implications for the distribution of consumption. Specifically, we discuss the implications of the H.T.P. on health and non-health expenditures and labour earnings in detail. We then explain the primary sources of behavioural responses induced by the H.T.P.

The rest of the chapter is organized as follows. The next section introduces a parsimonious framework that serves as a workhorse model. In Section 1.3, we analyse the ways in which the H.T.P. might have altered health expenditures and their relevance for consumption inequality. Section 1.4 starts with a summary of the theoretical foundations of the health-income relationship. We then discuss how various stages of the H.T.P. might have influenced the distribution of labour income and its implications for consumption inequality. Finally, in Section 1.5, we highlight several behavioural channels that have been altered or introduced by the H.T.P. and their potential redistributive impacts. The chapter concludes with a discussion of our primary findings and their policy implications.

1.2 Analytical Framework

The H.T.P. is a large-scale reform that spans over an extended period of time (2002–13). Identifying its causal impact on consumption inequality is virtually impossible, as there are numerous potential direct and indirect channels at play, possibly more than what we discuss later in the chapter. Moreover, there is very limited data available, especially concerning the period before the reform. Therefore, we would like to emphasize that the aim of our analyses is mainly to provide the reader with a structured way of thinking, which is outlined in this section, about the possible channels through which the H.T.P. may have affected consumption inequality. We strive to support our arguments empirically with this limited data, as well as with theoretical discussions.

Let the gross earnings of a household per month be denoted by Y. The household pays taxes T, public health insurance premiums H, and other social security contributions R, out of their gross earnings. The remaining budget can be used for consumption and savings, denoted as S. For our purposes, it is fruitful to distinguish between three separate types of consumption expenditures. The first item is the out-of-pocket health expenditures, C_H. We define this item consistently with the United Nations' Classification of Individual Consumption According to Purpose (C.O.I.C.O.P.). It includes "Medicines and health products", "Outpatient care services", and "Inpatient care services". We define the second item as private health insurance spending, C_I. The third item, C_O, consists of all the other expenses except for out-of-pocket health expenditures and private health insurance spending.

Our main focus is on inequality in the third item, C_O, which is all the consumption expenses except for out-of-pocket health expenditures and private health insurance spending. This item can be expressed as:

$$C_O = Y - (T + H + R) - S - (C_H + C_I) \tag{1.1}$$

In the rest of this chapter, the term "consumption inequality" refers to the inequality in C_O. Any reform brought about by the H.T.P. that affects variables on the right-hand side would alter our definition of consumption inequality. The discussions of our prioritized channels below are grounded in this equation, which serves to structure discussions.

We distinguish between the effects of the H.T.P. on consumption inequality via expenditures and behavioural responses. Effects that work through expenditures alter H, R, C_H, and C_I. Behavioural responses, on the other hand, generally affect labour income, Y. We choose to evaluate the implications of the H.T.P. on Y triggered by asymmetric information, that is, adverse selection and moral hazard, in a separate section.

1.3 Redistributive Effects through Expenditures

This section discusses the channels via which the H.T.P. may have had an impact on our definition on consumption inequality through expenditures. We analyse three avenues: (i) changes in out-of-pocket health expenditures, (ii) adjustments in public health insurance contributions, (iii) utilization of private healthcare services.

1.3.1 Out-of-Pocket Health (O.O.P.) Expenditures

The H.T.P. contains several policy reforms that may have altered such O.O.P. expenditures. These reforms encompass a reduction in V.A.T. on drugs, increased public health insurance coverage, expanded scope of public health services, and changes in drug co-payments among others. While the reforms were initiated in 2003, the extensive reforms did not start until a year after, 2004. Thus, the years before 2004 are mainly considered as the pre-reform period. If the H.T.P. caused a systematic variation in the pattern of O.O.P. health expenditures, C_H, across the distribution, our definition of inequality in consumption without health expenditures (defined in Equation (1.1)), may be affected. The purpose of this section is to investigate whether the changes in the progressivity of O.O.P. health expenditures were sizeable enough to alter consumption inequality.

The impact of the H.T.P. of Turkey on O.O.P. health expenditures across the distribution is explored in the related literature from two distinct but related perspectives outlined later in the chapter. The first perspective, which aligns more closely with our objective, examines the progressivity of such expenditures as the share of total household expenditure.

Findings from this literature generally propose that the H.T.P. decreased the progressivity of O.O.P. health expenditures. Erus and Aktakke (2012) use the subsample of households with non-zero O.O.P. health expenditures and illustrate that the share of such O.O.P. health expenditures went down to 4% in 2006 (post-reform) from 5% to 6% in 2003 (pre-reform) for affluent households. During the same period, O.O.P. health expenditure share, if anything, increased for the poorest households. Yardim et al. (2014) examine the O.O.P. health expenditure shares of households in total expenditure minus subsistence expenditure (referred to as capacity-to-pay) and determine a steep increase in this share for the poorest expenditure quintile. Cinaroglu and Baser (2019), Cinaroglu (2021) (for the period 2003–15), and Cinaroglu (2024) (for the period 2015–19) investigate the same theme, calculating changes in the Kakwani index. This index compares the difference between inequality in capacity-to-pay and O.O.P. health expenditures. These studies find that over time, O.O.P. health expenditures become regressive, meaning that the share of O.O.P. health expenditures increases within the capacity-to-pay of poorer households relative to richer households.

The findings of the literature that employs this perspective provide valuable insights into the impact of the H.T.P. on O.O.P. expenditures across the distribution. At the same time, restricting the analysis to a subsample of households with non-zero health expenditures or using capacity-to-pay as a measure of total household consumption expenditure limits the relevance of these findings for our purpose. To accurately assess changes in consumption inequality excluding health expenditures, there should be no restrictions on the analysis sample or the consumption baskets considered. Furthermore, the degree of O.O.P. health expenditure shares holds significance in our context, as minor changes in progressivity may not notably impact consumption inequality.

We utilize the publicly available data by TurkStat to examine the changes in the share of O.O.P. health expenditures within the total consumption expenditures across equivalized household income quintiles. Based on the C.O.I.C.O.P. classification utilized in household budget surveys, our definition of O.O.P. health expenditures includes spending on "Medicines and health products", "Outpatient healthcare services", and "Inpatient healthcare services", consistent with the related literature. While some studies additionally consider private health insurance spending as O.O.P. health expenditure, we opt to evaluate this item separately under Section 3.3.

As evident from Figure 1.1, O.O.P. health expenditure shares are not substantially different in the post-H.T.P. period (as of 2004) compared to pre-H.T.P. period (2002–03). The initial increase in the O.O.P. share of the poorest quintile, which also lends itself to Erus and Aktakke (2012) and Yardim et al. (2014), is offset in the following years. Eventually, there appears to be some reduction in the O.O.P.

health expenditure share of the poorest quintile over time, but the extent of this change is not large enough to arrive at a meaningful conclusion about the effect of the H.T.P. on consumption inequality. In fact, Figure 1.1 suggests that the share of health expenditures attributed to O.O.P. payments in Turkey is notably low, hovering around 2% for across the income distribution over the period of interest.

In Figure 1.2, we utilize the publicly available E.U. Household Budget Survey data and compare the O.O.P. health expenditure shares of Turkish households with that of some selected European countries. Figure 1.2 corroborates that O.O.P. health expenditure shares in Turkey consistently rank among the lowest. This is consistent with Aran and Hentschel (2012), who argue that the financial protection offered by the expansion of the Green Card Programme (G.C.P.) in Turkey over 2003–2008 was limited since O.O.P. payments were already restricted.

The second perspective considers the impoverishing effects of catastrophic health expenditures and examines whether H.T.P. reforms brought about adequate coverage and financial protection (Yardim et al., 2014; Narcı et al., 2015; Brown et al., 2014). While protection against catastrophic expenditures is a crucial aspect for health equity, such expenditures are already factored into Figures 1.1 and 1.2 and averaged out within quintiles. A more relevant aspect of this perspective for our purpose is the argument that the existing O.O.P. health expenditure share figures may

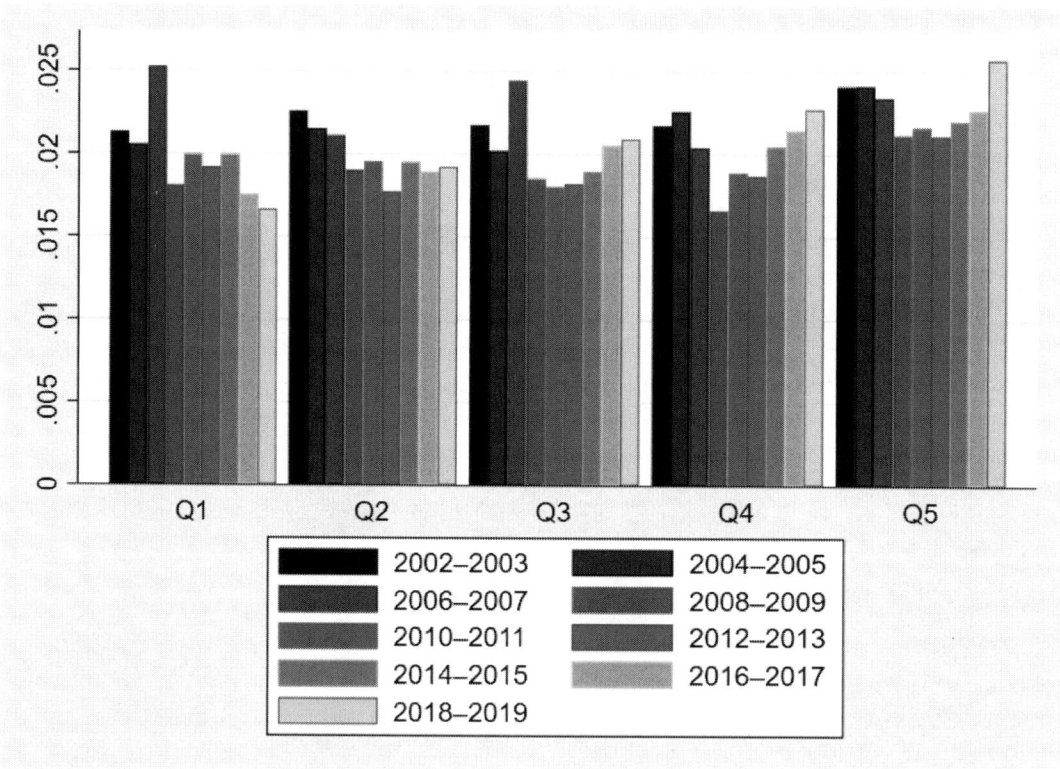

Notes: Authors' own calculations using publicly available TurkStat data on Household Budget Surveys (HBSs). Q1 to Q5 refer to equivalised household disposable income quintiles. OOP health expenditures include "Medicines and health products", "Outpatient healthcare services", and "Inpatient healthcare services", OOP health expenditure shares are averaged across the indicated periods.

Figure 1.1   Out-of-pocket health expenditures as fraction of total expenditure.

be misleading since poorer households may not seek healthcare simply because they are not able to afford it (Kisa et al., 2009; Brown et al., 2014). If there is a systematic change in healthcare-seeking behaviour across the distribution as a result of the H.T.P., this could show itself in labour market outcomes, that is, employment and earnings, and indirectly affect consumption inequality. This aspect is discussed in Section 1.4 in further detail.

In summary, our investigation does not provide sufficient evidence to conclude that the H.T.P. has resulted in a significant change in consumption inequality (excluding health expenditures) through direct changes in O.O.P. health expenditures.

1.3.2 Public Health Insurance Contributions

Prior to the H.T.P. reforms, Turkey's social insurance system, including public health insurance, was fragmented. In 2008, the health segments of various social insurance branches, which covered different parts of society, were unified under a single umbrella system: General Health Insurance (G.H.I.). This unification led to changes in the social insurance, and therefore health insurance contributions, H and R, in Equation (1.1), from different segments of the society. Once again, a systematic alteration of H across the distribution may affect consumption inequality.

Before the H.T.P., public health insurance was provided by three different organizations. *Sosyal Sigortalar Kurumu (S.S.K.)* covered private sector employees and blue-collar public workers. *Esnaf*

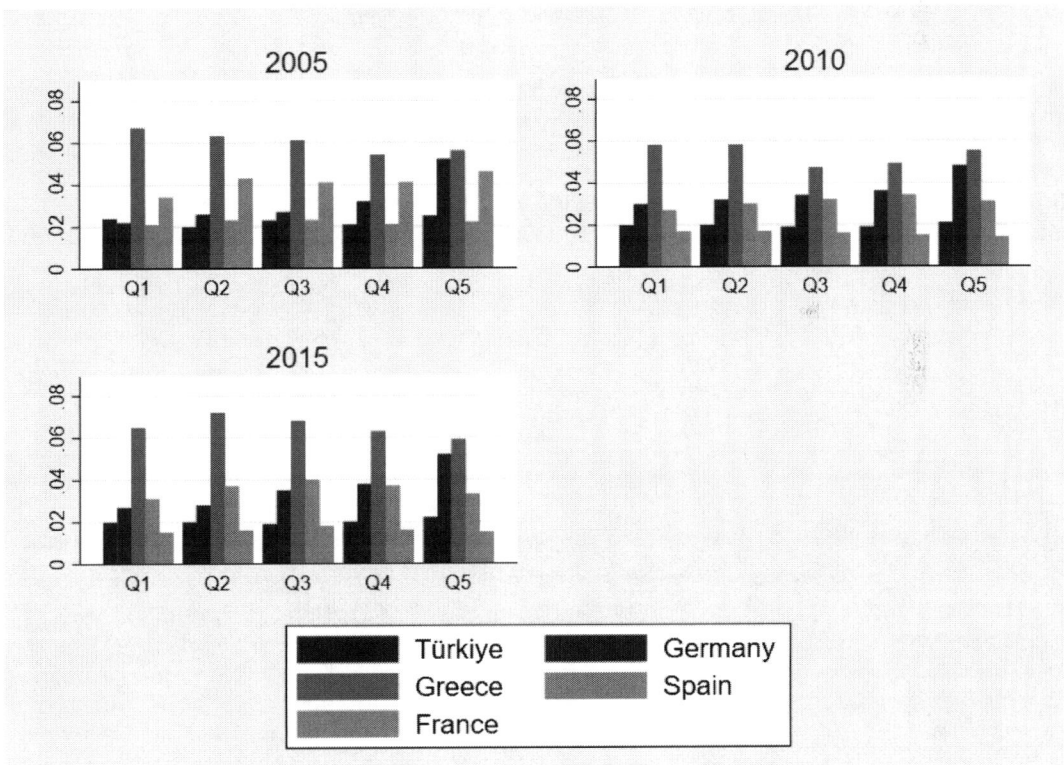

Notes: Authors' own calculations using publicly available Eurostat data on the EU Household Budget Surveys (HBSs). Q1 to Q5 refer to equivalised household disposable income quintiles. Out-of-pocket health expenditures include "Medicines and health products", "Outpatient healthcare services", and "Inpatient healthcare services".

Figure 1.2   Out-of-pocket health expenditures in Turkey versus selected European economies.

ve Sanatkârlar ve Diğer Bağımsız Çalışanlar Kurumu (*Bağ-Kur*) covered the self-employed. Emekli Sandığı covered white-collar public employees. The G.C.P., on the other hand, targeted poor individuals who were not covered by any social security scheme. It was a means-tested programme which provides public health services without any premium payment by the individuals in need.

An ideal dataset for investigating the impact of the H.T.P. on consumption inequality would include records of individuals' insurance payments along with their incomes. Unfortunately, such a dataset does not exist in Turkey.

We attempt to elaborate on the impact of the H.T.P. on consumption inequality through changes in social security premiums, which are summarized in Table 1.1. This attempt presents several challenges. First, although Green Card holders are likely the poorest, locations of individuals covered by *S.S.K.*, *Bağ-Kur*, and *Emekli Sandığı* along the income distribution are unclear. Beneficiaries of these three institutions likely span nearly every income bracket. Second, many individuals were insured by more than one social security institution, complicating the estimation of the number of beneficiaries for each institution (Atasever, 2014, p. 48). Third, numerous exceptions in social security premiums based on employment type, occupation, and income level add to the complexity. As a result, our short analysis given here should be merely viewed as an informed commentary.

According to Gürsel et al. (2009), Green Card holders constituted 14% of the population in 2006. This programme continued even after the introduction of the universal General Health Insurance programme. The criteria for admittance into the Green Card programme remained unchanged: having monthly earnings after taxes and premiums of less than one-third of the minimum wage per person in a household. Therefore, any possible increase or decrease in the number of Green Card holders would arise due to the alterations in the income distribution and not because of the H.T.P.

Statistical Yearbooks of the Social Security Institution of Turkey (S.G.K., 2007) indicate that the SSK covers the highest number of individuals. The sum of health and long-term insurance

Table 1.1 Social Insurance Premiums of Different Groups before and after the Introduction of G.H.I.

	(Gürsel et al., 2009)	(S.G.K, 2007)	Pre-G.H.I.		Post-G.H.I.	
	Coverage, %, 2006	Coverage, %, 2007	Health	Long-Term	Health	Long-Term
SSK	65% (SSK + *Bağ-Kur* + *Emekli Sandığı*)	47.91%	11%	22%	12.5%	20%
Bağ-Kur		21.28%	20%*	20%	12.5%	20%
Emekli Sandığı		15.05%	0%	36%	12.5%	20%
Green Card (G0)	14%	Not specified	0%	-	0%	-

Notes: "Health" indicates health insurance payments, and "Long-term" indicates insurance payments for old age (retirement), disability, and death. We assume that the incidence of employers' contributions also falls on the employees. Exceptions, caps, and floors typically found in insurance policies have been excluded from the comparison. Additionally, smaller insurance items such as unemployment insurance and short-term insurance have been omitted due to their potential variability, which may depend not only on occupation but also on factors such as income level, type of employment, and specific industry regulations. G0 is a term used for Green Card holders after the H.T.P. Pre-2008 figures are based on Sülkü (2011, pp. 21–22). Post-2008 figures can be found at ssk.gov.tr. *Participation in the health insurance scheme was not obligatory for *Bağ-Kur*. TÜSİAD (2004, p. 58) estimated the fraction of *Bağ-Kur* beneficiaries participating in the health insurance scheme as only 22%.

premiums for this group remained almost unaltered. Since the introduction of G.H.I. in 2008, *Bağ-Kur* beneficiaries have been required to pay a 12.5% premium on health insurance. Participation in the health insurance scheme was not obligatory and was, in fact, rather low at around 22% for Bağ-Kur beneficiaries prior to the G.H.I. (TÜSİAD, 2004, p. 58). Thus, the majority of *Bağ-Kur* beneficiaries were only obligated to pay a 20% premium on long-term insurance. At the same time, the total obligatory insurance premium payment for *Emekli Sandığı* beneficiaries was 36% before the H.T.P. As a result, there is a case to be made that the H.T.P. slightly benefited *Emekli Sandığı* (white-collar public employees) beneficiaries at the expense of *Bağ-Kur* beneficiaries (self-employed) through insurance payments. However, the implications of this for consumption inequality are not straightforward, as both groups are very heterogeneous in terms of the income levels of their members.

Due to the challenges mentioned earlier, the analysis of the impact of the H.T.P. on consumption inequality via changes in insurance premiums is largely inconclusive.

1.3.3 *Utilisation of Private Health Services*

A longstanding literature investigates the relationship between the expansion of public health sector and utilisation of private health services. If public and private healthcare are substitutes, expanding the scope of services and coverage among the population may attract more individuals to give up on private healthcare to benefit from free or low-cost public health services (Cutler & Gruber, 1996). At the same time, as the number of people benefiting from public services increase, leading to overcrowded hospitals and longer waiting times, particularly high income individuals may prefer increasingly relying on private health services (Besley et al., 1999). Relatedly, Sekhri and Savedoff (2005) argues that private health services can be used to supplement public health services, i.e., filling in the gaps of public system and meeting the increased health service demand in the phase of economic development. Finally, Liu and Chen (2002) and Finkelstein (2004) find no relationship between the demand for public and private health services. In summary, the literature is not conclusive and an expanded public health system may lead to an increase or a decrease in the demand for private health services.

The H.T.P. of Turkey unified a fragmented healthcare system, expanded the scope of public health services, and aimed to achieve universal health insurance coverage. According to Atun et al. (2013), health insurance coverage of the poorest decile increased from 24% in 2003 to 85% in 2013. Thus, as described in the related literature above, there may be implications for individuals' private health insurance spending, C_I from equation (1). If such implications are systematically different across the consumption expenditure distribution, our definition of consumption inequality may be affected.

As an addition to the G.H.I., the Supplementary (and Complementary) Health Insurance Program (S.P.H.I.), which organises (private) complementary health insurance policies that cover the additional payments not insured by the G.H.I., was implemented in 2013 (Başoğlu, 2021). While the S.P.H.I. programme primarily aims to enhance private healthcare and health insurance markets and alleviate the financial burden on the public health system (Attila & Gülay, 2022), it may have redistributive effects through its several effects on C_H and C_I. For example, the increasing coverage of the G.H.I. can diminish the quality of health services provided by the public health system. Therefore, the widened quality differences between private and public health providers can motivate demand for private health services, especially for the middle- and high-income individuals.[2] However, despite the increasing popularity of the S.P.H.I. program, the share of insurance expenditure in total expenditures is remains quite low in Turkey. [3] Therefore, the quantitative effect of the S.P.H.I. is expected to be, if there is any, small in terms of its effect on consumption inequality.

A causal analysis of the interplay between public and private health insurance spending is lacking in the context of Turkey's H.T.P., and we believe that this is a fruitful area for future research. Such an analysis is out of the scope of this chapter since our purpose is to provide a holistic view H.T.P.'s effect on consumption inequality. Nevertheless, we utilise Turkstat's publicly available data on Household Budget Surveys to provide some relevant stylized facts. Figure 1.3 illustrates the evolution of private insurance spending as a fraction of total budget for equivalised-income quintiles over the period of interest. An important limitation of Figure 1.3 is that the insurance spending encompasses life, accident, dwelling, and other insurances along with private health insurance. As a result, the evidence presented in Figure 1.3 is far from being conclusive. On the other hand, the changes in insurance spending fractions do not indicate a systematic alteration. Moreover, insurance spending as a fraction of total budget never exceeds 0.8% even for the richest household equivalised-income quintile.

Overall, we are unable to identify a substantial impact the of the H.T.P. on consumption inequality through the private health insurance spending channel.

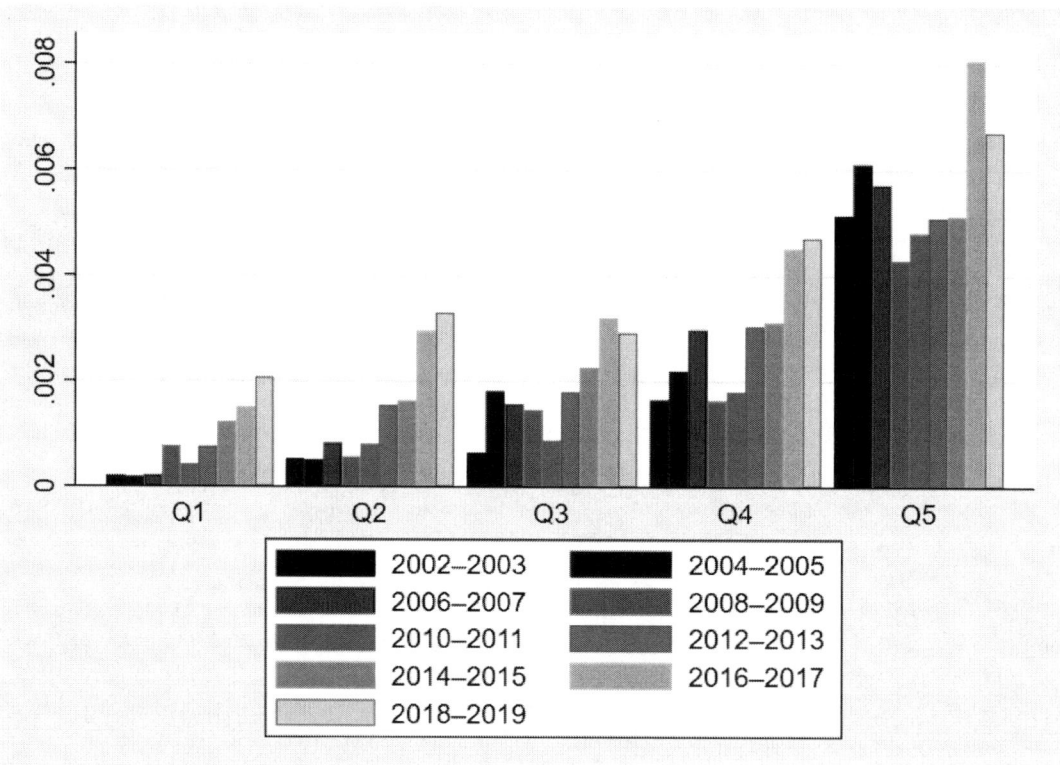

Notes: Authors' own calculations using publicly available TurkStat data on Household Budget Surveys (HBSs). Q1 to Q5 refer to equivalised household disposable income quintiles. The corresponding consumption expenditure item includes life, accident, dwelling and other insurances along with private health insurance. Insurance spending shares are averaged across the indicated periods.

Figure 1.3   Insurance spending as a fraction of total expenditure.

1.4 Redistributive Effects through Labour Income

Along with a direct negative impact of poor health on an individual's well-being, the demand for health insurance is also induced by the potential threats that poor health poses to the earning capacity of the individual, which determines Y of Equation (1.1). The term "earning capacity" is a multifaceted concept with health forming a distinct dimension within it. In this section, we first provide a brief review of the theoretical background on the relationship between health and labour income. We then discuss distributional consequences of the H.T.P., which operate through their impacts on labour supply decisions.

1.4.1 Theoretical Background

In the simplest form, the labour income has three main components: A (occupation-specific) wage rate (w), an individual-specific productivity component (ϵ), and working hours (h). Suppressing the time index, let us express these three components of labour income explicitly:

$$Y_{ij} = w_j \times \epsilon_{ij} \times h_{ij}, \tag{1.2}$$

where $i = 1, \ldots, I$ denotes a specific worker and $j = 1, \ldots, J$ identifies different occupations. In this formulation, the wage rate (w_j) represents the average wage rate for an occupation j, and, when combined with a worker's occupation-specific skills, it gives us the worker's wage rate in a specific occupation for a given unit of time which we denote by $w_{ij} \equiv w_j \times \epsilon_{ij}$. While w_j is determined by the labour market conditions, an individual's skill set in a particular occupation is the output of her "human capital" which can be accumulated over time.

Health has long been recognized as a distinct component of human capital, and Grossman (1972) is the first to model the demand for "health capital" which is referred as the "*Human Capital Model*" (HCM) (Grossman, 2000). Before the HCM, health status of an individual is considered as any other dimension of skills. In other words, health becomes one of the components of ϵ_{ij} in Equation (1.2). However, a distinct feature of health is that it determines the number of available resources (e.g. time) that can be used for market or nonmarket activities. Grossman argues "*that a person's stock of knowledge affects his market and nonmarket productivity, while his stock of health determines the total amount of time he can spend producing money earnings and commodities*" (Grossman, 2000, p. 350). In the model that he proposes, health does not only provide a direct utility to an individual as a *consumption good* but also serve as an *investment good* since she can invest in her health to increase the available resources. Moreover, "*an increase in the stock of health reduces the amount of time lost from these activities, and the monetary value of this reduction is an index of the return to an investment in health*" (Grossman, 2000, p. 350).

This monetary value of the time lost due to ill-health is positively correlated with w_{ij}, and, consequently, the demand for healthcare services becomes an increasing function of income. Additionally, as health status also determines the available time for productivity-enhancing activities, such as education and training, investment in health capital is complementary to investments in other types of human capital. Overall, these theoretical insights suggest a positive and bidirectional relationship between labour income and health. A vast body of literature confirms these insights by finding a positive relationship between health and other forms of human capital, in particular education (Grossman & Kaestner, 1997; Grossman, 2006). While the positive correlation is well-established, the direction of causality is an open debate (O'Donnell et al., 2015; Lenhart, 2019). There are three potential channels for the relationship between health and education: Health determines education,

education determines health, and, a third factor – such as risk aversion – determines both (Conti et al., 2010). In either case, we obtain a positive correlation between health and education.

The relationship between health and knowledge is present even after the formal education is completed. Involuntary departure from work due to bad health conditions can lead to disruptions in the accumulation of experience and thus may decrease future earnings (Blundell et al., 2022). On the other hand, such involuntary employment can have destructive effects on health outcomes (Schmitz, 2011).

The multidimensional nature and potential feedback mechanisms make the causal effect of health on labour earnings more complicated than it appears. Figure 1.4 summarizes main channels through which health and income are interconnected. As the figure depicts, a change in health status has *direct* impacts on earnings through altered occupational choices, deteriorated skills, and reduction in time available for work. As the figure depicts, there are also *indirect* effects that operate via feedback effects.[4]

Overall, the positive association between health and income is a well-documented phenomenon, whereas there are studies which estimate a negative impact of ill-health on wages, and, the literature finds a stronger negative effect on labour supply (Currie & Madrian, 1999). A growing strand of the empirical literature evaluates the role of specific mechanisms some of which we outline before. The handbook chapter by O'Donnell et al. (2015) provides a comprehensive review of such studies.

While the number of studies investigating the health–income and health–wage relationships in Turkey is limited, there are a few significant contributions. For example Brown et al. (2014) find a negative causal effect of poverty on catastrophic health expenditures. They argue that poor households are less likely to seek healthcare than non-poor households and to experience

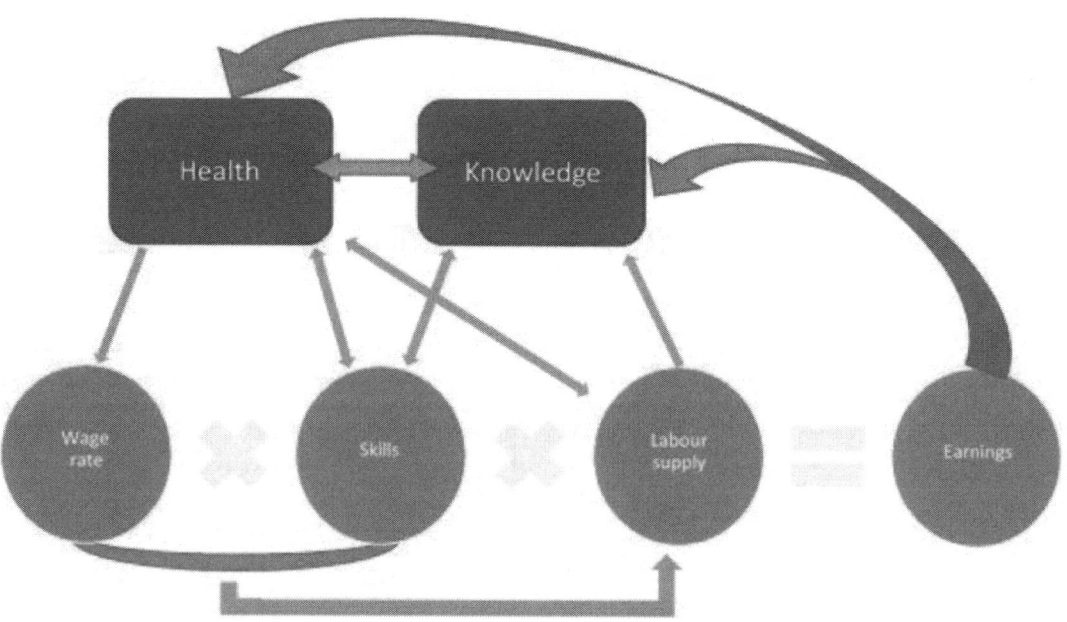

Figure 1.4   Health and Income.

catastrophic health expenditures (Brown et al., 2014, p. 216). A more recent study by Alcan and Özsoy (2020) confirms the negative effect of bad health on wages. To the best of our knowledge, there is no empirical study that attempts to estimate causal effects of the H.T.P. on income or income inequality, which constitutes an important gap in the literature.

1.4.2 The H.T.P., Labour Income, and Consumption Inequality

As outlined in the introduction to this book, the H.T.P. has been implemented at several stages since 2003. These regulations are designed to achieve certain policy objectives, including the provision of a *universal health coverage* and to expand access to health-care, especially for the poorest population groups (Atun et al., 2013). To this end, one of the major changes is *the unification of multiple social security schemes under one umbrella* (WHO, 2012). Although this unification seems to vanish inequalities in access and in the finances of health across occupational groups at the first sight, Yilmaz (2013) argues that it rather transforms the existing inequalities into a new dimension. More specifically, while H.T.P. reduces inequalities across occupational groups, inequities in access to health on the income dimension persist and are exacerbated (Yilmaz, 2013).

For the distribution of consumption, however, the implications are less clear. First, workers typically make their occupational choices based not only on the monetary benefits but also on the non-pecuniary benefits of a particular job and/or occupation (O'Donnell et al., 2015). As the monetary values of such non-pecuniary benefits are hard to quantify, we cannot assess how much of the labour income inequalities that existed before the H.T.P. can be associated with differential costs and benefits of the alternative health insurance schemes. Second, Atun et al. (2013) claim that the consolidation of the alternative schemes into a unified G.H.I. *"created a unified risk pool to more effectively share, across all income groups, the risks associated with health-care costs and catastrophic payments"* (Atun et al., 2013, p. 76). In this regard, it is plausible to think that the unification reduces the adverse selection problem that existed in the previous multi-optional social health provision system. However, the introduction of the S.P.H.I. has the potential to limit the extent of the reduction in the adverse selection problem: We may expect individuals with higher medical risk to opt for S.P.H.I. thereby increasing the average cost of the S.P.H.I. for the government. Moreover, when the quality of medical services differs across private and public institutions, the S.P.H.I. can amplify the existing consumption inequalities as the effective utilization of medical services will depend on the income levels. Additionally, the introduction of S.P.H.I. has become a part of collective bargaining provision (Erdoğan, 2020). Thus, the S.P.H.I. creates a new dimension of consumption inequality that operates through heterogeneity in pecuniary and non-pecuniary benefits of occupations.

A central issue that determines the redistributive effects of the H.T.P. is the link between the statutory minimum wage and threshold levels for the G.C.P. and contribution rates for the G.H.I.[5] Three features of the Turkish economy require a closer look at the role of the minimum wages in determination of the redistributive impacts of the transformation: Dramatic size of the informal sector, high unemployment rates, and unprecedented take-up rates for the minimum wage in the formal sector.[6,7,8] These three facts together make the minimum wage a significant, and also a complicated, policy tool because of its implications for the finances of the health system and the distribution of income/consumption. Due to this link we described earlier, an increase in the real minimum wage, along with its direct effects on the consumption inequality, has several indirect effects on the distribution of income. First, all else equal, a higher real minimum wage would lead to an increase in the contribution payments of the G.H.I. participants and increases the number of eligible individuals for the G.C.P. Second, as the cost of workers increases, we expect an increase in unemployment which reduces the amount of contributions. Third, the increase in the real minimum wage can also lead to an increase in the informal sector wages through a *"lighthouse effect"* thereby reducing total employment and hence the aggregate contributions (Pelek, 2015).

Another sort of informality can emerge in labour contracts: To reduce their labour costs, employers can offer a minimum wage contract with additional informal payments (Aslan, 2019). Thus, an increase in minimum wages can reduce incentives for such informal payments. Overall, the net effect of an increase in minimum wage rate on the health budget is determined by the relative strength of all these forces. But how does this burden affect consumption inequality? First of all, as we described in the first part of this chapter, the payroll taxes are unified through the H.T.P., and they are paid at a linear rate. If we ignore the indirect effects that we listed earlier, and, if the share of medical expenditures is constant along the income dimension, the linear payroll tax would not interact with consumption inequality. Unfortunately, estimating the causal relationship between income and health expenditures is quite difficult, and there are not many studies that attempt to do so with a few exceptions (Acemoglu et al., 2013). However, even if there is a linear relationship, since high-income individuals prefer private health services more often, the linear payroll taxes still imply a redistribution of disposable income. The scope of this redistribution is limited by the introduction of the subsidies under the S.P.H.I. programme.

The indirect effects of the H.T.P. on the distribution of labour income can emerge in different horizons. The most prominent aspect of the H.T.P. that can affect consumption inequality in the medium and long run is the introduction of the *family medicine programme* (F.M.P.). The main purpose of such systems is to provide medical consultancy and to practise outpatient and preventive healthcare (Akaydın & Baltacı, 2024). Another role that is played by the F.M.P. is the so-called *"referral system"*. When implemented nation-wide and efficiently, the family medicine programme can have substantial gains by reducing the burden on the secondary and tertiary health services and by extending the mother–child health services and monitoring of mother–child health. The F.M.P. has been argued to be contributing to the decreasing infant mortality rate and communicable (contagious) diseases (Akdağ, 2011). Although the efficiency of the programme has been criticized by others on several grounds, the indirect effects of family medicine programme on the distribution of income and consumption can be immense.[9] Such effects can emerge in the long run as skills developed at very early ages are important determinants of labour market outcomes, and the health component plays an important role for the accumulation of these skills (Currie & Madrian, 1999). Thus, the F.M.P. can play an important role in eliminating inequalities in health status of children, thereby reducing inequalities in labour income that originate from such differences.

Despite the fact that the universal and equitable health coverage is one of the prior objectives of the H.T.P., some argue that there is still a potential for increased access to health and to reduce quality differences across private and public health services (Yardim & Uner, 2018; Yetim & Çelik, 2020; Söyler & Çavmak, 2023). Yetim and Çelik (2020) find that the share of unmet medical needs of low-income individuals is higher compared to that of high-income individuals. Similarly, the study by Caner, Karaoglan, and Yenimahalleli-Yasar (in this book) finds a limited equalizing effect of the H.T.P. on the utilization of health services by young children. In addition, Başar et al. (2021) find that unmet healthcare needs are more prevalent among individuals with chronic diseases, who are considered as one of the most disadvantaged groups in the country. Overall, the effects of the H.T.P. on working hours of workers from various parts of the distribution are not straightforward. Existing studies underline counter-acting features of the H.T.P. on consumption inequality and a limited equalizing effect.

1.5 Redistributive Effects through Asymmetric Information and Behavioural Responses

According to the expected utility theory, the marginal utility of consumption decreases with the level of consumption for risk-averse individuals. As a result, individuals are better off by transferring income from good states of the world, that is, periods with higher income streams, to bad states, which is referred to as "consumption-smoothing" (Gruber, 2013). An adverse health shock, namely, an unexpected decrease in the health status, leads to a reduction in income and/or medical expenses, thereby reducing resources to be used for consumption. Thus, health insurance, either private or public, provides valuable consumption-smoothing benefits against such health shocks.

Unfortunately, private insurance markets suffer from various types of market failures. One of the most prominent sources of market failures in insurance markets is the *asymmetric information*. These information asymmetries can cause two sorts of inefficiencies: *Adverse selection* and *moral hazard*. "*Adverse selection occurs when persons with poor health tend to choose insurance with high benefits, and persons with good health tend to avoid such insurance because of high costs*" (Marquis & Phelps, 1987, p. 300). They argue that three criteria must be fulfilled for adverse selection to emerge: Undetectable and heterogeneous health risks among the insured, ability to assess self-risk, and price-responsiveness of demand for health insurance (Marquis & Phelps, 1987, p. 300). In such conditions, pooling individuals in the same insurance plan can reduce the average costs for the insurance provider by increasing the predictability of medical risks. As we discussed in the first part, the H.T.P. can mitigate the adverse selection problem by increasing the insurance coverage, but the S.P.H.I. has an opposite effect.

The moral hazard problem refers to *adverse behaviour that emerges from incentives altered by obtaining insurance against an unpredictable event,* and such cases can appear in numerous ways and at several stages of the healthcare services (Gruber, 2013).[10] The moral hazard problems regarding patient behaviour can be divided into two categories. The ex-*ante moral hazard* comes into play before an adverse health shock arrives. Individuals who obtain health insurance coverage may reduce their preventive efforts, thereby increasing the probability of ill-health. Moreover, health insurance policies are designed to decrease the anticipated cost of medical services. As the neoclassical demand theory suggests, we expect an increase in the quantity demanded as a response to a ceteris paribus change in the price of a commodity. Since health serves as a normal good according to the HCM, we expect an increase in the demand for medical services once an individual obtains health insurance (Feldstein, 1973). As this version of the moral hazard problem comes to existence after the health shock is received, it is labelled as the *ex-post moral hazard.*

A third type of moral hazard exists in public health insurance schemes that implement means-tested social insurance (Capatina et al., 2020). In the H.T.P. context, the *G.C.P.,* which aims to provide health insurance coverage for the poor, is a means-tested programme. On the one hand, because the eligibility is determined on the basis of the individuals' income and wealth, the G.C.P. can motivate some people to remain unemployed or to participate in the informal markets, which reduces the contributions to the G.H.I. and increases the burden for the workers in the formal labour market. On the other hand, since it provides health insurance coverage for the poor, the G.C.P. is expected to have considerable equity gains. Erus et al. (2015) find that although the G.C.P. covers about 15% of the population, the non-take-up rates among the eligible individuals are as high as 44%, and the O.O.P. expenditures for the uninsured are sizably higher compared to the individuals covered by the G.H.I. However, the H.T.P. has introduced contributory payments to the G.C.P. participants, too (Yenimahalleli-Yasar & Ugurluoglu, 2011). Overall, we conclude that the H.T.P. brings more stringent controls to the means-testing and contributory payments and, thereby, mitigates moral hazard costs and equity gains of the G.C.P. simultaneously.

Another aspect of the information asymmetry that emerges in healthcare is concerned with the behaviour of the physicians. As individuals possess imperfect information about their health status or the medical services required for a particular condition, the demand for healthcare is determined partially, if not fully, by the physicians. From the physician's perspective, the mapping between their practice and payments determines the scope and the size of the moral hazard problem. In the case of a social health system, the moral hazard problem concerning providers has two facets: First, the payments to physicians employed by the public health system and, second, the payments to private healthcare providers. Eventually, the design of these aspects of the social health system determines the significance of the moral hazard problem that emerges on the supply side of the medical services. For the former, Sülkü (2011) finds a positive effect of the performance-based payment to the physicians (P4P) on the productivity of the public health providers. However, she claims that the increase in productivity is primarily due to scale efficiencies and such productivity gains are not observed for less-developed regions. Thus, we infer that the P4P system does not contribute to equity in health services and consumption inequality.

To sum up, behavioural responses to the H.T.P. have the potential to induce additional costs to the public health system, and they may have counteracting effects on the distribution of consumption. Efforts to limit such inefficiencies, in the form of tightened controls on means-testing and contributory payments, can amplify the existing inequalities. Moreover, the financing of the public health provision can create further redistribution mechanisms as contributions are income-contingent and partially financed by the general government budget.[11] Consequently, aggregate redistributive effects of the excess burden are determined by the progressivity of the tax-and-transfer system.

1.6 Summary and Discussion

When it was launched in 2003, the H.T.P. set a number of ambitious goals, including the provision of equitable and universal access to health. Since then, the performance of the H.T.P. in achieving these goals has been examined on several grounds, but a comprehensive analysis of the H.T.P. on economic well-being is lacking. In this chapter, we pose the question: What is the impact of the H.T.P. on consumption inequality? We provide a comprehensive discussion of the redistributive effects of the H.T.P. in an attempt to answer this question. In doing so, our primary focus is to reveal potential mechanisms through which the H.T.P. can affect the distribution of consumption through its effects on labour income and individuals' expenditures.

Our analysis suggests that despite the equity objectives of the programme, the aggregate impact of the H.T.P. on consumption inequality is insignificant. Parallel to the existing literature, we identify various channels that the H.T.P. implies either positive or negative (or both) effects on consumption inequality. However, the data limitations prevent a thorough investigation of the isolated effects of these separate channels. In addition, the implementation of the H.T.P. does not facilitate the identification of causal effects. Provision of administrative data which covers socio-demographic indicators along with health outcomes and expenditures can substantiate further studies that explore the performance of the H.T.P. on several grounds.

The theoretical link between health and income suggests that the medium- and long-run effects of the F.M.P. can be substantial on consumption inequality. While the F.M.P. achieved a considerable improvement in certain indicators of mother–child health, the regional disparities in the provision and the utilization of such services reduce the potential redistributive gains of this policy.

Moreover, the chronic problems of the Turkish labour market, high levels of unemployment, prevalence of the informal sector, and high take-up rates of the minimum wage limit incentives to utilize public health services, thereby mitigating redistributive gains of the H.T.P. In the light of these discussions, these structural problems in the labour market constitute threats towards achieving equity objectives of the program. Therefore, the design and implementation of complementary policies that target these three aspects of the Turkish labour market appear to be crucial. Policies aimed at achieving equity in access to education can play a central role in this regard.[12] Finally, reducing the prevalence of the informal sector can reduce the burden on the public health system and provide resources for other redistributive policies. The optimal design of these policies, however, can be determined on the ground of quantitative significance of these several dimensions and the level of their interdependence. Therefore, the most vital improvement in the direction of evaluation of the H.T.P. and the design of future policies is the provision of comprehensive data that includes all these aspects.

Notes

1 See Meyer and Sullivan (2023) for a recent example.
2 For example, Yilmaz (2013) argues that by contributing to the "commodification" of health services, the S.P.H.I. strengthens the stratification of access in favour of middle- and high-income individuals (Yilmaz, 2013, p. 73).
3 See Figure 1.3, below.
4 There exist several extensive reviews on the relationship between health and income/inequality, which discuss other potential channels. See, for example, O'Donnell et al. (2015), Gruber (2000), and Currie and Madrian (1999).
5 For the G.H.I., the contribution rate is 3%, and the threshold level for G.C.P. is one-third of the gross minimum wage. The latter has become the statutory threshold level since 1992 and is not introduced as a part of the H.T.P. (Yenimahalleli-Yasar & Ugurluoglu, 2011).
6 The data from International Labour Organization (I.L.O.) shows that although the informal employment among Turkish workers has been declining since 2000, the share of informally employed workers in total employment is still about 28% in 2022.
7 The unemployment rates in Turkey have been around 9–10% over the 2000s with two exceptions: The unemployment rate has jumped over 13% in 2019 and 2020 due to the pandemic, and it reached 14% in 2009 due to the Great Recession.
8 In a previous study (Gürer & Küçükşen, 2023), we find that more than 21% of the full-time workers work at or below the minimum wage in 2020 – as opposed to an 8% average in OECD countries – and a recent report by one the largest labour union confederations, DİSK, finds that nearly the half of the Turkish labour force earns less than 110% of the minimum wage in 2021 (DİSK-AR, 2023).
9 See, for example, Yılık (2023) for an evaluation of the family medicine practice in Turkey.
10 For a comprehensive review of moral hazard problems in healthcare, see, for example, Zweifel and Manning (2000).
11 Health expenditures financed by the general government budget in Turkey between 2003 and 2020 constitute on average 25% of the total health expenditures, the share of social security contributions is about 50%, and the private health expenditures are about 25% of the total expenditures (TurkStat).
12 See, for example, Murvanidze (2017) on the regressivity of the education finances in Turkey.

References

Acemoglu, D., Finkelstein, A., & Notowidigdo, M. J. (2013). Income and Health Spending: Evidence from Oil Price Shocks. *The Review of Economics and Statistics*, 95(4), 1079–1095.

Akaydın, H., & Baltacı, A. (2024). The Effect of Physician-Patient Communication on Patient Satisfaction in Family Medicine Services. *Alanya Akademik Bakış*, 8(1), 15–33.

Akdağ, R. (2011). *Turkey Health Transformation Program Evaluation Report (2003–2010)*. T.C. Sağlık Bakanlığı Yayın No: 839. Retrieved from https://ekutuphane.saglik.gov.tr/Yayin/452

Alcan, S., & Özsoy, O. (2020). Relation Between Health and Wages in Turkey. *Panoeconomicus*, 67(1), 111–126.

Aran, M. A., & Hentschel, J. S. (2012). Protection in Good and Bad Times? The Turkish Green Card Health Program. World Bank Policy Research Working Paper, 6178.

Aslan, G. (2019). Türkiye'de Asgari Ücretli Çalışan Sayısı ve Ücret Seviyelerinin Değişimi (2003–2017 Hanehalkı İşgücü Anketleri Veri Analizi). *Sosyal Güvenlik Dergisi*, 9(1), 141–159.

Atasever, M. (2014). *Türkiye Sağlık Hizmetlerinin Finansmanı ve Sağlık Harcamalarının Analizi: 2002–2013 Dönemi*. T.C. Sağlık Bakanlığı Yayın No: 983. Retrieved from https://ekutuphane.saglik.gov.tr/Yayin/488

Attilla, İ., & Gülay, A. (2022). Türkiye'de Genel Sağlık Sigortası'nın Sürdürülebilirliği İçin Zorunlu Tamamlayıcı Sağlık Sigortası Modeli Önerisi. *Uygulamalı Bilimler Fakültesi Dergisi*, 4(1), 17-40.

Atun, R., Aydın, S., Chakraborty, S., Sümer, S., Aran, M., Gürol, İ., Nazlıoğlu, S., Özgülcü, Ş., Aydoğan, Ü., Ayar, B., Dilmen, U., & Akdağ, R. (2013). Universal Health Coverage in Turkey: Enhancement of Equity. *Health Policy*, 382, 65–99.

Başar, D., Dikmen, F. H., & Öztürk, S. (2021). The Prevalence and Determinants of Unmet Health Care Need in Turkey. *Health Policy*, 125, 786–792.

Başoğlu, B. (2021). Türkiye'de Tamamlayıcı Sağlık Sigortaları Primi Üretimi ve Özel Sağlık Sigortaları Sistemine Katkıları Açısından Değerlendirilmesi. *Selçuk Üniversitesi Sosyal Bilimler Dergisi*, 46, 108-123.

Besley, T., Hall, J., & Preston, I. (1999). The Demand for Private Health Insurance: Do Waiting Lists Matter? *Journal of Public Economics*, 72, 155-181.

Blundell, R., Britton, J., Dias, M. C., French, E., & Zou, W. (2022). The Dynamic Effects of Health on the Employment of Older Workers: Impacts by Gender, Country, and Race. Michigan Retirement and Disability Research Center Working Paper No: 2022–451.

Brown, S., Hole, A. R., & Kilic, D. (2014). Out-of-pocket Health Care Expenditure in Turkey: Analysis of the 2003–2008 Household Budget Surveys. *Economic Modelling*, 41, 211–218.

Capatina, E., Keane, M., & Maruyama, S. (2020). Health Shocks and the Evolution of Earnings over the Life-Cycle. UNSW Business School Research Paper 2018–14b.

Cinaroglu, S. (2021). Poverty Effects of Public Health Reforms in Turkey: A Focus on Out-of-pocket Payments. *Journal of Evaluation in Clinical Practice*, 27, 53–61.

Cinaroglu, S. (2024). Trends in Out-of-pocket Health Expenditure Inequality in Turkey under Comprehensive Health Reforms. *World Development Perspectives*, 34, 100583.

Cinaroglu, S., & Baser, O. (2019). Does the Unification of Health Financing Affect the Distribution Pattern of Out-of-pocket Health Expenses in Turkey? *International Journal of Social Welfare*, 28, 293–306.

Cinaroglu, S., & Çalışkan, Z. (2022). Distributive Pattern of Health Services Utilization Under Public Health Reform and Promotion in Turkey. *Health Policy Analysis*, 31, 25–33.

Conti, G., Heckman, J., & Urzua, S. (2010). The Education-Health Gradient. *American Economic Review: Papers & Proceedings*, 100, 234–238.

Currie, J., & Madrian, B. C. (1999). Health, Health Insurance and the Labor Market. In Ashenfelter, O., & Card, D. (Eds.), *Handbook of Labor Economics* (pp. 3309–3416). Elsevier.

Cutler, D. M., & Gruber, J. (1996). Does Public Insurance Crowd Out Private Insurance? *The Quarterly Journal of Economics*, 111(2), 391-430.

DİSK-AR. (2023). *Asgari Ücret Gerçeği 2023 Araştırması*. Türkiye Devrimci İşçi Sendikaları Konfederasyonu Araştırma Merkezi Raporu.

Erdoğan, C. (2020). *Expanding Supplementary Voluntary Private Health Insurance in Turkey: How and Why?* Bielefeld University Working Paper No: 5.

Erus, B., & Aktakke, N. (2012). Impact of Healthcare Reforms on Out-of-Pocket Health Expenditures in Turkey for Public Insurees. *The European Journal of Health Economics, 13*, 337–346.

Erus, B., Yakut-Cakar, B., Cal, S., & Adaman, F. (2015). Health Policy for the Poor: An Exploration on the Take-up of Means-Tested Health Benefit in Turkey. *Social Science & Medicine, 130*, 99–106.

Feldstein, M. S. (1973). The Welfare Loss of Excess Health Insurance. *Journal of Political Economy, 81*(2), 251–280.

Finkelstein, A. (2004). The Interaction of Partial Public Insurance Programs and Residual Private Insurance Markets: Evidence from the US Medicare Program. *Journal of Health Economics, 23*(1), 1-24.

Grossman, M. (1972). On the Concept of Health Capital and Demand for Health. *Journal of Political Economy, 80*(2), 223–255.

Grossman, M. (2000). The Human Capital Model. In Culyer, A. J., & Newhouse, J. P. (Eds.), *Handbook of Health Economics* (pp. 348–407). Elsevier.

Grossman, M. (2006). Education and Nonmarket Outcomes. In Hanushek, E. A., & Welch, F. (Eds.), *Handbook of Economics of Education* (pp. 578–633). Elsevier.

Grossman, M., & Kaestner, R. (1997). Effects of Education on Health. In Behrman, J. R., & Stacey, N. (Eds.), *The Social Benefits of Education* (pp. 69–124). University of Michigan Press.

Gruber, J. (2000). Disability Insurance Benefits and Labor Supply. *Journal of Political Economy, 108*(6), 1162–1183.

Gruber, J. (2013). *Public Finance and Public Policy* (4th ed.). Worth Publishers.

Gürer, E., & Küçükşen, O. (2023). Calculating Optimal Nonlinear Taxes Using Censored Income Data. *Fiscaoeconomia, 7*(2), 1721–1735.

Gürsel, S., Darbaz, B., & Karakoç, U. (2009). *Yeşil Kart: Türkiye'nin En Maliyetli Sosyal Politikasının Güçlü ve Zayıf Yanları*. Betam Araştırma Notu 09/39. Retrieved from https://betam.bahcesehir.edu.tr/2009/06/yesil-kart-turkiyenin-en-maliyetli-sosyal-politikasinin-guclu-ve-zayif-yonleri/

Kisa, A., Yilmaz, F., Younis, M. Z., Kavuncubasi, S., Ersoy, K., & Rivers, P. A. (2009). Delayed Use of Healthcare Services Among the Urban Poor in Turkey. *Education, Business and Society: Contemporary Middle Eastern Issues, 2*(3), 232–240.

Lenhart, O. (2019). The Effects of Health Shocks on Labor Market Outcomes: Evidence from UK Panel Data. *The European Journal of Health Economics, 20*, 83–98.

Marquis, M. S., & Phelps, C. E. (1987). Price Elasticity and Adverse Selection in the Demand for Supplementary Health Insurance. *Economic Inquiry, 25*(2), 299–313.

Meyer, B., & Sullivan, J. X. (2023). Consumption and Income Inequality in the United States since the 1960s. *Journal of Political Economy, 131*(2), 247–284.

Murvanidze, E. (2017). *It is Expensive to Be Poor: Equity in Financing Education in Turkey (2004–2012)*. Master's Thesis, University of Denver.

Narcı, H. Ö., Şahin, İ., & Yıldırım, H. H. (2015). Financial Catastrophe and Poverty Impacts of Out-of-Pocket Health Payments in Turkey. *The European Journal of Health Economics, 16*, 255–270.

Liu, T. C., & Chen, C. S. (2002). An Analysis of Private Health Insurance Purchasing Decisions with National Health Insurance in Taiwan. *Social Sciences & Medicine, 55*, 755-774.

O'Donnell, O., Van Doorslaer, E., & Van Ourti, T. (2015). Health and Inequality. In Atkinson, A. B., & Bourguignon, F. (Ed.), *Handbook of Income Distribution* (pp. 1419–1533). Elsevier.

Pelek, S. (2015). The Employment Effect of the Minimum Wage: An Empirical Analysis from Turkey. *Ekonomi-Tek, 4*(1), 49–68.

S.G.K. (2007). *Statistical Yearbook*. Social Security Institution of Turkey. https://www.sgk.gov.tr/Istatistik/Yillik/fcd5e59b-6af9-4d90-a451-ee7500eb1cb4/, accessed 2 June 2024.

Schmitz, H. (2011). Why are the Unemployed in Worse Health? The Causal Effect of Unemployment on Health. *Labour Economics, 18*, 71–78.

Sekhri, N., & Savedoff, W. (2005). Private Health Insurance: Implications for Developing Countries. *Bulletin of the World Health Organization, 83*(2), 127-134.

Söyler, S., & Çavmak, D. (2023). An Evaluation of Access to Healthcare Services in Türkiye. *Aurum Journal of Health Sciences, 5*(2), 69–76.

Sülkü, S. N. (2011). *Türkiye'de Sağlıkta Dönüşüm Programı Öncesi ve Sonrasında Sağlık Hizmetlerinin Sunumu, Finansmanı ve Sağlık Harcamaları.* T.C. Maliye Bakanlığı Strateji Geliştirme Başkanlığı Yayın No: 2011/414. Retrieved from https://ms.hmb.gov.tr/uploads/2019/09/Kitap-414.pdf

TÜSİAD. (2004). *Sağlıklı Bir Gelecek: Sağlık Reformu Yolunda Uygulanabilir Çözüm Önerileri.* Yayın No: TÜSİAD-T/2004-09/380. Retrieved from https://tusiad.org/tr/yayinlar/raporlar/item/3597-saglikli-bir-gelecek--saglik-reformu-yolunda-uygulanabilir-cozum-onerileri

WHO. (2012). *Successful Health System Reforms: The Case of Turkey.* World Health Organization.

Yardim, M. S., & Uner, S. (2018). Equity in Access to Care in the Era of Health System Reforms in Turkey. *Health Policy, 122*(6), 645–651.

Yardim, M. S., Cilingiroglu, N., & Yardim, N. (2014). Financial Protection in Health in Turkey: The Effects of the Health Transformation Programme. *Health Policy and Planning, 29*, 177–192.

Yenimahalleli-Yasar, G., & Ugurluoglu, E. (2011). Can Turkey's General Health Insurance System Achieve Universal Coverage? *International Journal of Health Planning and Management, 26*, 282–295.

Yetim, B., & Çelik, Y. (2020). Sağlık Hizmetlerine Erişim: Karşılanmamış İhtiyaçlar Sorunu. *Toplum ve Sosyal Hizmet, 31*(2), 423–440.

Yılık, P. (2023). Current Situation Analysis of the Family Medicine System in Türkiye and Recommendations. *Review of Socio-Economic Perspectives, 8*(3), 59–65.

Yilmaz, V. (2013). Changing Origins of Inequalities in Access to Health Care Services in Turkey: From Occupational Status to Income. *New Perspectives on Turkey, 48*, 55–77.

Zweifel, P., & Manning, W. G. (2000). Effects of Education on Health. In Culyer, A. J., & Newhouse, J. P. (Eds.), *Handbook of Health Economics* (pp. 410–459). Elsevier.

Chapter 2

Enhancing Health and Health System Outcomes: Exploring the Interplay between Health Expenditures, Access to Health Services, Utilization of Health Services, and Health Status

Zeynep Öztürk Yaprak

Contents

2.1 Introduction

Health Transformation Programme (H.T.P.), which was launched in Turkey in 2003, aims to increase the effectiveness, efficiency, and quality of the health system. It also aims to expand access to health services and ensure equality (The Ministry of Health, 2003). H.T.P. has accelerated the health reforms on Turkey's agenda since the 1980s and made these reforms implementable. Since 2003, the Turkish Health System has undergone significant changes to expand the scope and

DOI: 10.4324/9781003539896-3

depth of health insurance in Turkey and increase equality in access to health services (Gürsoy, 2015). Individuals, societies, and countries can overcome the severe problems they experience in the field of health with health reforms (Akkavak, 2018). The H.T.P. consists of a broad structure covering eight essential components of the health sector. These include strengthening the planning and supervisory role of the Ministry of Health, the introduction of a general health insurance system, a family medicine plan, and autonomous hospitals. In addition, developing human resources and reorganizing the provision of health services are among the important goals of the programme (Yasar, 2011).

Changing economic, political, and social conditions around the world force governments to make new regulations and seek opinions in the health systems. For this reason, health programs are developed by governments to improve health services and increase service quality (Ak, 2023). Under the names of reform or improvement in health services, various reform-oriented projects have been put forward in the healthcare sector in Turkey, as well as in England, the United States of America, and other countries, with the influence of global organizations such as the World Bank, World Health Organization, Economic Development and Cooperation Organization (O.E.C.D.), and International Monetary Fund (I.M.F.). The most comprehensive and latest example of these projects is the H.T.P. (Cansever, 2018). To improve the welfare and health status of individuals, health policies and practices have undergone many changes and transformations in parallel with globalization and technological developments. In this context, with the implementation of the H.T.P., Turkey has expanded the scope of health insurance and increased equality in access to health services (Aydın, 2022). It is also stated that health reforms and H.T.P. have generally received support from society due to the problems and inequalities experienced in providing health services (Erol and Özdemir, 2019).

Health policies have been one of the most important issues in countries. With different health policies implemented since 1923, efforts have been made to increase the quality of health services and the health level of society (Yılmaztürk, 2023). Although the practices and suggestions put forward over time vary according to the countries' political, historical, and cultural conjuncture, their institutional and economic problems are similar everywhere. The things that need to be done in the face of these problems that arise in health services can be listed as reducing costs, improving quality, ensuring equality, increasing the efficiency of consumers and service providers, and increasing satisfaction (Gülşen and Yıldıran, 2017). There is a strong relationship between health policy and health outcomes. Health policies provide the necessary ways for society to be welfare-friendly and healthy (Ceylan et al., 2023). In addition, health policy includes environmental and socioeconomic factors that directly or indirectly affect health, as well as health services. Health policy in its most general definition consists of all actions that affect the health system's institutions, services, and financing arrangements (İleri et al., 2016). In addition, the applied health policies determine indicators related to a country's health system (Yılmaztürk, 2023). Whether the implemented health policies are effective can be understood by looking at some health outcome indicators. Health outcome indicators of countries provide information about the health status (Ata and Eryer, 2021).

It is stated that the official health policy implemented in a country is the most important determinant of that country's health-related indicators (İleri et al., 2016). Health indicators are objective, standard, and quantitative values to obtain information about the health levels of countries and to make cross-country comparisons. Health indicators enable determining policies regarding essential health services, management and planning of health services, determining and meeting the demand in the field of health, detecting and solving health problems, and measuring the change of different dimensions of public health according to some factors such as age, gender, and population. Comparisons made with health indicators are very important in terms of revealing the success of the health service provided and taking the necessary precautions in the unsuccessful parts (Demirtaş and Metintaş, 2017). Factors such as increasing the health status of society, making efforts to maintain the health of individuals in society, and protecting individuals from diseases are among the objectives of health services (Sert, 2019). With the implementation of the H.T.P., these objectives were expanded, and it was observed that it improved primary health indicators (such as infant mortality rate and life expectancy at birth). However, although Turkey has achieved improvements in major health indicators in the last ten years, it remains behind the O.E.C.D. averages (Cansever, 2018). Health indicators are predicted to improve with the reforms (Erol and Özdemir, 2019). The joint effort of health policies in all developed and developing countries is to control health expenditures and ensure fair access to health services (Akbulut, 2015). Therefore, it is important to present a comprehensive analysis of the transformation in the Turkish health system by evaluating the results and effects obtained with the implementation of the H.T.P.

The Ministry of Health has identified three stages for the performance evaluation of H.T.P.: Health system functions, intermediate goals, and results. The results include elements aimed at the satisfaction of individuals receiving the service, protection from financial risks, and improving their health (Alpaslan and Çıraklı, 2024). At this point, this study aims to examine the effects of H.T.P. on health status, health expenditures, utilization of health services, and access to health services within the scope of the results.

2.2 Related Literature

It is seen that multifaceted investigations and scientific studies have been carried out on the effects of H.T.P. on the health system and to measure the effectiveness of the applications. First, the studies that have been examined using different methods within the scope of H.T.P. since the day it started are discussed. Subsequently, studies in the literature on health status, health expenditures, use of health services, and access to health services, which are the main variables of the study, were examined.

In the study conducted by Yasar (2011), although none of the components of the H.T.P. have been sufficiently implemented yet, there have been some improvements, but the Turkish people continue to face low health status and low levels of financial risk protection. Similarly, Tatar et al. (2011) study that Turkey's health system has undergone significant reforms since 2003, leading to improved health status and reduced infant mortality rates. However, it is stated that future challenges include reorganizing referral systems, increasing personnel supply, and improving patient rights. Bostan (2013) evaluates the program's success from the patient's perspective. From the data obtained by applying the survey method, information was obtained that the patients' opinions about the programme were generally positive, and the problems in the health system were partially solved. Atun et al. (2013), who conducted a detailed study on H.T.P., emphasized the 2003–2013 period. He mentions that the health system changes have been successfully implemented and that the programme has successfully provided universal health coverage, increased equality, and improved health outcomes, especially for socio-economically disadvantaged groups. The study of Horton and Lo (2013), which is similar to this study, also deals with the reforms in the health system in the 2003–2013 period. He mentions that the H.T.P. rapidly expands health insurance coverage and access to health services for all citizens, especially the poorest population groups, to achieve universal health coverage and helps eliminate inequalities in access to health services and health outcomes. According to Ökem and Çakar (2015), according to the results of empirical studies conducted after H.T.P. implementation, Turkey has made significant progress in improving the quality and efficiency of health services, but long-term financial sustainability has not been resolved due to structural problems in employment. Stokes et al. (2015), who analysed the impact of changes in the healthcare system on user satisfactions in logistic regression using data, for 2004–2012, state that H.T.P. significantly increased user satisfaction with healthcare services, leading to increased access and options to primary healthcare providers. According to Bener et al. (2019), Turkey achieved great success in health service provision equality and economic justice with decreased health costs and the population's satisfaction with the health system from 2003 to 2015. Bozdemir et al. (2021), who analysed the success, efficiency, and sustainability of the H.T.P. in two parts, measured the effectiveness of Turkey's health activities between 2003 and 2016 with the super efficiency (SE) model in the first part. They conclude that the 2003–2012 period was inefficient due to investments in technology, infrastructure, and employees. In the second part, we evaluate the efficiency of nine O.E.C.D. countries and of Turkey in the same period. When we look at all countries, it is seen that Turkey is efficient except for 2007, when it had the highest health expenditure and financing.

When we examine the relevant literature within the scope of H.T.P. in terms of health status, health expenditures, use of health services, and access to health services. In his study, Bağcı (2023) analysed the impact of health expenditures, the number of physicians, and H.T.P. on infant mortality with the Autoregressive Distributed Lag (A.R.D.L.) bounds test approach, using data from the period 1975–2018. It was concluded that health expenditures, the number of doctors, and H.T.P. reduce infant mortality rates in the long term. Similarly, Dhrifi (2020) stated that health expenditures reduce infant mortality rates. Shi et al. (2004) noted in their study that there is a negative relationship between the number of primary care physicians and infant mortality rates in the United States. İlgün et al. (2023) examined the impact of per capita income, annual inflation, and the health reform called H.T.P. on per capita health expenditure in Turkey. The study, covering the period 1985–2016, found a positive relationship between health expenditures and income and a negative relationship between them and health reform. This result reflects a downward trend in per capita health expenditures after implementing the H.T.P. Yardim et al. (2014), in their study aiming to evaluate financial protection in health during the health reform period between 2003 and 2009 in Turkey, analysed the probability and volume of out-of-pocket spending using the logistic and O.L.S. regression method. The results show that the probability and volume of out-of-pocket expenses gradually increased in publicly insured households between 2003 and 2009, but there was a decreasing trend in catastrophic health expenditures in Turkey during the considered period.

San (2020) aimed to analyse the impact of health reforms on satisfaction at the household level in Turkey. He conducted a statistical analysis using cross-sectional data from 2003 and 2012. The results show that men, those who are married, and older people were more likely to be satisfied with their healthcare in both years. In addition, because of the reforms, it is seen that the rate of complaints about essential health services decreased by approximately 20–25 points. According to these results, reforms in the field of health are interpreted as increasing access to health services and indirectly reducing health inequality.

Similarly, regarding patient satisfaction, Ugur and Tirgil (2018) state in their study that the society was satisfied with the innovations in health services between 2003 and 2016 and that there was an increase in the satisfaction of each social security group. Regarding the use of health services, in the study by Atılgan (2015), it is stated that the H.T.P. has dramatically changed the structure of the health system and that the structure of the demand for health services has, directly and indirectly, changed with the reforms implemented. In addition, there has been an increase in the demand for health services due to an increased access to health services and the removal of restrictions. With the increasing demand, health expenditures have also increased. Caner et al. (2018) conducted a logistic regression analysis with microdata collected by Turkey Health Research and concluded that Turkey has made progress toward universal health coverage with the H.T.P., but children living in households with low socioeconomic status still face obstacles in the use of health services. Caner and Cilasun (2019), who investigated the use and satisfaction of elderly people with healthcare services between 2006 and 2015, revealed in their study that the use of healthcare services increased and the percentage of patients preferring primary healthcare institutions increased with the introduction of the family medicine system. However, they concluded that general satisfaction increased only until 2011–2012. When the studies are carried out within the scope of H.T.P. and their results are examined, we can say that they are generally like the fundamental goals that the programme aims to achieve. It can be expressed as covering the entire society by gathering it under one roof with General Health Insurance (G.H.I.), improving health indicators, increasing the number of physicians and healthcare personnel, increasing the rate of admission to hospitals, increasing efficiency by reducing costs, reducing health inequalities, and increasing patient satisfaction.

2.3 Data and Methodology

Annual data for the period 2003–2021 was used in the study. Both data and variable specifications are shown in Table 2.1. The fact that the number of observations of the variables used in the study is within a limited time interval shows that they are below the desired number for a time series study. This situation constitutes the limitation of this study, which is considered within the scope of H.T.P.

The descriptive statistics of the variables used in the analysis and correlation matrix are presented in Table 2.2.

According to Table 2.2, the average values of the series are between 1.136 and 7.247. The variable with the highest median value belongs to the doctor consultation rate, and the lowest median value belongs to the infant mortality rate. The standard deviation values of the variables are between

Table 2.1 Data and Variables' Specification

Data and Variables' Specification			
Variables	*Specification*	*Symbols*	*Data Source*
Health Status Indicators	Life Expectancy at Birth (MODEL 1)	LnLifeex	World Bank
	Maternal Mortality Rates (MODEL 2)	Maternal	O.E.C.D.
	Infant Mortality Rates (MODEL 3)	Infant	O.E.C.D.
Utilization of Health Services	Doctor Consultation Rate (Per Capita)	Dcons	O.E.C.D.
Health Expenditures	Current Health Expenditures (% G.D.P.)	HexGDP	O.E.C.D.
Access to Health Services	Patient Satisfaction Rate (Satisfaction Rate)	Hcsat	TurkStat

Table 2.2 Descriptive Statistics and Correlation Matrix

	LnLifeex	Maternal	Infant	Dcons	Hcsat	HexGDP
Descriptive Statistics						
Mean	4,32303	1.284116	1.136703	7.247368	6.604794	4.683263
Median	4.326487	1.195899	1.133539	8.000000	7.037561	4.617000
Std. Dev.	0.019674	0.203560	0.162806	1.851236	1.032837	0.423789
Maximum	4.354553	1.785330	1.403121	9.800000	75.90000	5.494000
Minimum	4.288951	1.113943	0.886491	3.400000	39.50000	4.117000
Observations	19	19	19	19	19	19
Correlation Matrix						
	LnLifeex	Maternal	Infant	Dcons	Hcsat	HexGDP
LnLifeex	1					
Maternal	−0.17587	1				
Infant	−0.49045	0.151209	1			
Dcons	0.841502	−0.291929	−0.38149	1		
Hcsat	−0.15635	−0.024075	0.32665	−0.08993	1	
HexGDP	−0.25171	−0.162397	0.04223	−0.15738	−0.66025	1

Table 2.3 Econometric Models and Variables

Econometric Models and Variables	
Health Status Indicators	Utilization of Health Services Health Expenditures Access to Health Services
Model 1: V.A.R.(Lifeex)	Doctor consultation rate (per capita), current health expenditures (% G.D.P.), patient satisfaction rate (satisfaction rate)
Model 2: V.A.R.(Maternal)	Doctor consultation rate (per capita), current health expenditures (% G.D.P.), patient satisfaction rate (satisfaction rate)
Model 3: V.A.R.(Infant)	Doctor consultation rate (per capita), current health expenditures (% G.D.P.), patient satisfaction rate (satisfaction rate)

0.01 and 1.85. In the correlation matrix, according to our first model, there is a positive correlation between life expectancy at birth and doctor consultation rates and a negative correlation between life expectancy at birth and health expenditures and health services satisfaction level. It is seen that there is a negative correlation between maternal mortality rates, which we will consider in the second model, and doctor consultation rates, health expenditures, and satisfaction level with health services. In our third model, there is a negative correlation between infant mortality rate and doctor consultation rates and a positive correlation between infant mortality rate and health expenditures and healthcare satisfaction level. First, the variables to be used in the study were subjected to stationarity testing. According to the stationarity test results, three econometric models were estimated using the Vector Autoregressive Model (V.A.R.) model. The assumptions of all three V.A.R. models were tested with the E-Views 13 package program, and the findings of variance decomposition and impulse-response functions were presented in the study. The reason for establishing three separate models is to see in which direction and to what extent health status indicators respond to changes in health expenditures, doctor consultation rates, and satisfaction levels with health services. Table 2.3 includes the econometric models and variables used.

In the V.A.R. model, one of the most preferred methods in time series, all selected variables are considered together and analysed simultaneously. In the model, variables are not strictly divided into internal and external variables (Özgen and Güloglu, 2004). In this respect, it differs from simultaneous equation systems. This complexity is eliminated with the V.A.R. model developed by Sims (1980) to solve the complexity of simultaneous equation systems (Mucuk and Alptekin, 2008). Since the model is estimated by the "Simple Least Squares" method, there is no obstacle or problem, even if the time interval is low, unless there is a structural incompatibility (Koçyiğit et al., 2023). The stationary states of the series are used in the application of the V.A.R. method. However, their levels do not need to be the same (Sarıtaş et al., 2018). According to Table 2.4, since all the series used in the study are stationary at both levels and first differences, all variables were included in the model as they are. Three ways are used to get results in V.A.R. analysis. These ways are: Granger causality tests, variance decomposition, and impulse-response functions showing the interaction between variables (Özgen and Güloglu, 2004). Variance decomposition is used to determine which variable is most effective in explaining the dependent variable, and impulse-response functions are used to determine whether effective variables can be used as policy tools (Bayar and Öztürk, 2021). Before moving on to V.A.R. analysis, which we use to determine the direction and degree of the relationship between variables, it is necessary to determine whether the series used in the analysis are stationary. One of the most important conditions for a time series analysis to contain accurate and consistent results is that the series are stationary. Stationarity can also be expressed as no deviation in the mean and variance of the time series. Many econometric measurements are based on the assumption of stationarity (Samancı and Noyan, 2023). Due to the spurious regression problem encountered in models estimated with nonstationary time series, t and F statistics will lose their validity as the results obtained will not reflect the real relationship (Kesbiç and Salman, 2018). If all variables in the model are stationary, V.A.R. model analysis can be applied. In this study, the Augmented Dickey–Fuller (A.D.F.) test developed by Dickey and Fuller (1981) was used for unit root (stationarity) analysis of the series. The findings obtained are given in Table 2.4.

According to the A.D.F. unit root test results, it is seen that the series contain unit roots at their levels in the intercept and trend–intercept model and are not stationary, but when their first differences are taken, it is seen that all the series does not contain unit roots in the intercept and trend–intercept model, that is, they are stationary.

Table 2.4 A.D.F. Unit Root Test Results

	A.D.F. Unit Root Test					
	At Level I (0)			*At First Difference I (1)*		
Variables	*Intercept*	*Trend and Intercept*	*None*	*Intercept*	*Trend and Intercept*	*None*
LnLifeex	−1.8053	−0.8849	1.3175	−3.8538	−4.3379	−3.6818
	(0.3661)	(0.9357)	(0.9461)	(0.0107) **	(0.0165) **	(0.001) ***
Maternal	−6.1319	−5.8983	−0.7688	−4.9327	−2.1318	−6.106
	(0.0002) ***	(0.0012) ***	(0.3681)	(0.002) ***	(0.4935)	(0.0000) ***
Infant	−3.8217	0.5588	−1.8723	0.0735	−5.1019	−1.2515
	(0.0108) **	(0.9985)	(0.0601) *	(0.9526)	(0.0063) ***	(0.1848)
Dcons	−2.3369	−1.3178	0.8002	−4.2435	−5.8076	−3.9424
	(0.1720)	(0.8494)	(0.8766)	(0.0049) ***	(0.0012) ***	(0.0006) ***
Hcsat	−3.3048	−2.0704	0.8366	−4.9338	−6.6023	−4.7205
	(0.0301) **	(0.5264)	(0.883)	(0.0013) ***	(0.0003) ***	(0.0001) ***
HexGDP	−1.1503	−1.2346	−0.6000	−3.2273	−3.1212	−3.3100
	(0.6715)	(0.8711)	(0.4433)	(0.0360) **	(0.1328)	(0.0025) ***

Notes: (*) Significant at the 10%; (**) Significant at the 5%; (***) Significant at the 1%.

2.4 Results

2.4.1 V.A.R.(Lifeex) Model Results

After the unit root analysis, the optimal lag length must be determined to perform the V.A.R. analysis because the correct installation of the V.A.R. model depends on the appropriate lag length. Various information criteria are used in the literature to determine the lag length (Gujarati, 2004). The most used ones include the Likelihood Ratio Test (L.R.), Final Prediction Error (F.P.E.), Akaike Information Criterion (A.I.C.), Schwarz Information Criterion (S.C.), and Hannan–Quinn (H.Q.). As a result of the evaluation, the length with the most stars (*) is considered as the optimal lag length number. The optimal lag length is shown in Table 2.5.

According to Table 2.5., the optimal lag length (row with the most stars) was determined to be 1. Whether the model created with a lag length of 1 meets the stability condition was tested with the A.R. polynomial inverse roots graph. When the autoregressive A.R. polynomial inverse roots graph in Figure 2.1 is examined, it is seen that all roots are within the circle, and the model meets the stability condition.

When the analysis was continued with the V.A.R. model created after the lag length was determined, it was determined that there was no problem in the autocorrelation and heteroskedasticity testing, which are the other assumptions of the model. The compatibility test results of these assumptions are shown in Table 2.6.

Table 2.5 V.A.R.(Lifeex) – Lag Length

Lag Length	LogL	LR	FPE	AIC	SC	HQ
0	−90034947	NA	0.778002	11.09994	11.29599	11.11943
1	−1322735	108.8783*	0.000629*	3.909100*	4.889351*	4.006539*
2	0.064815	12.51028	0.001301	4.227669	5.992121	4.403059

Inverse Roots of AR Characteristic Polynomial

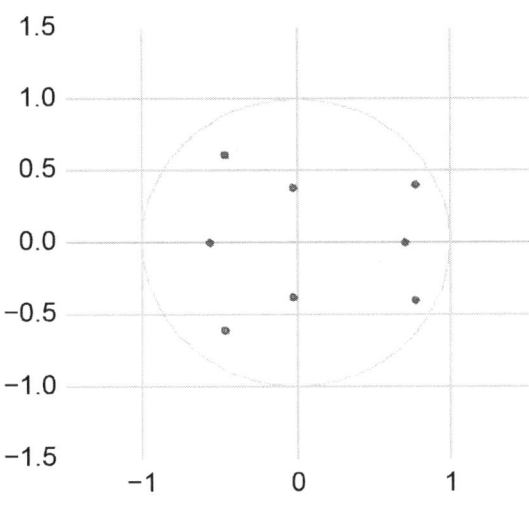

Figure 2.1   V.A.R.(Lifeex) – A.R. polynomial inverse roots.

Table 2.6 shows that the V.A.R. model created with the variables used in V.A.R.(Lifeex) does not contain autocorrelation and heteroskedasticity problems, and the series are normally distributed. Therefore, the V.A.R.(Lifeex) model can be expressed as stable and stationary with a lag length of 1. Impulse-response analysis was performed to examine the reaction of a one standard deviation shock to a variable on other variables in the system. Impulse-response functions of the variables of life expectancy at birth, health expenditures, utilization of health services, and access to health services are presented in Figure 2.2.

Figure 2.2 shows the effects on the Lnlifeex variable when a standard deviation shock is given to the Dcons, Hcsat, and HexGDP series. According to impulse–response analysis, a shock given to the Dcons variable positively affected the Lnlifeex variable. Since there was a positive relationship between them, it can be said that its effect lasted for many years. It is seen that the effect of a shock to the Hcsat variable on the Lnlifeex variable is positive until the fifth time interval but will exhibit a reverse trend after the fifth time interval. In short, the reaction of Lnlifeex to a shock in Hcsat is significantly positive. However, it is seen that a shock to the HexGDP variable creates an adverse reaction in the Lnlifeex variable for approximately five periods, and after the sixth period, the effect will disappear or become uncertain. Variance decomposition, which shows what percentage of a change in the variables used is due to itself

Table 2.6 V.A.R.(Lifeex) – Autocorrelation, Heteroscedasticity, and Normality Test Results

Autocorrelation Results (Autocorrelation LM Test)		
Lag	*F*-statistic	Probability
1	0.914537	0.610
2	2.117004	0.258
Heteroscedasticity Results (White Heteroskedasticity Tests)		
Chi-square	Probability	
88.105	0.250	
Normality test results in Jarque–Bera test (distribution of error term)		
Jarque–Bera	Probability	
10.652	0.222	

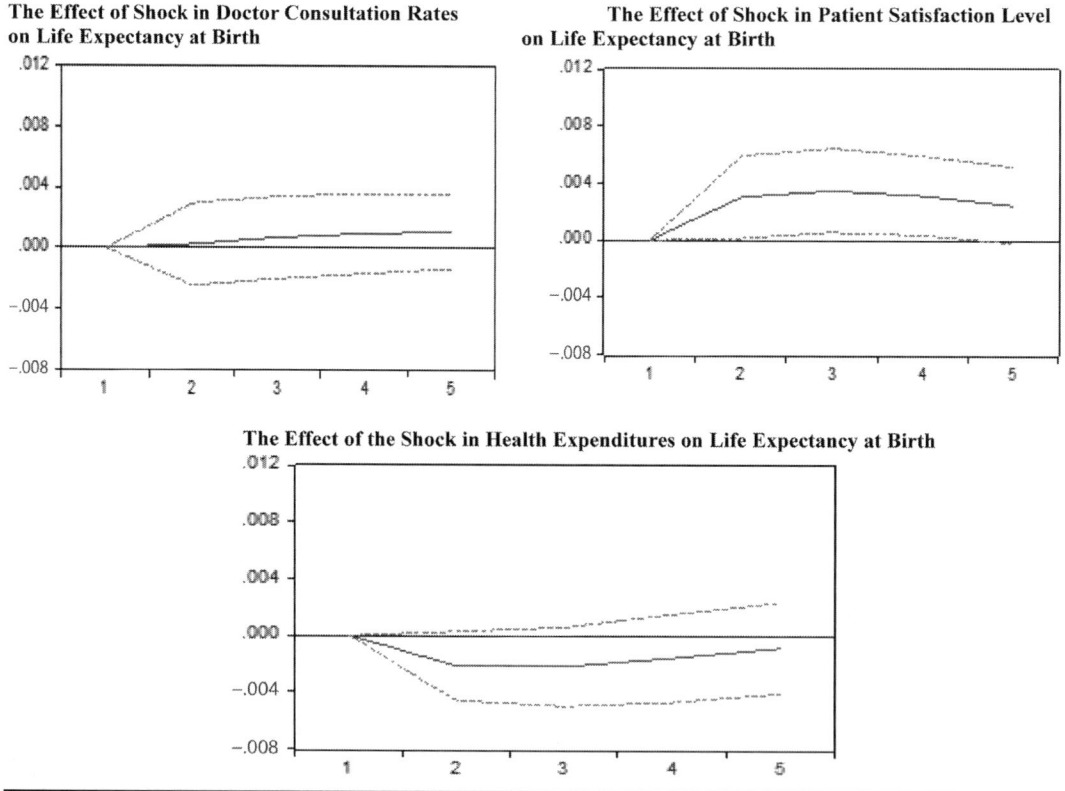

Figure 2.2 V.A.R.(Lifeex) – impulse response functions (I.R.F.s) of health expenditure, utilization of health services, and access to health services (response of life expectancy at birth).

and what percentage is due to other variables, is obtained from the moving averages section of the model (Sarıtaş et al., 2018). Variance decomposition results for the V.A.R.(Lifeex) model are given in Table 2.7 to interpret which of the variables of health status, health expenditures, utilization of health services, and access to health services is most effective.

According to the results of variance decomposition, which measures the explanatory power of variables on each other, 100% of the LnLifeex variable in the first period is explained by the variable itself. In other words, in the first period, it is 100% affected by the change. This result also shows that the LnLifeex variable is the most exogenous. In the second period, 76.9% is affected by the change. This rate decreases as the period increases. It is seen that the self-disclosure rate of the LnLifeex variable in the fifth period is 49.1%. In addition, when looking at the explanatory power of other variables for the LnLifeex variable, Hcsat ranks first with 36.3%, HexGDP ranks second with a share of 11.8%, and Dcons variable ranks third with 2.67%. Therefore, 49.1% of the change in the LnLifeex variable is due to itself, 36.3% is due to the Hcsat variable, 11.8% is due to the HexGDP variable and 2.6% is due to the Dcons variable.

The consequences of shocks in doctor consultation rates, patient satisfaction levels, and health expenditures on life expectancy at birth were revealed by the findings obtained from the V.A.R. model impulse–response analysis. It is also supported by the findings obtained with the historical decomposition technique and shown in Figure 2.3. With the historical decomposition method, shocks can be examined as a whole, and their effects on output can be observed throughout the entire period. If we look at it periodically, it can be seen that the contribution of all three variables was low in 2004–2008, and, therefore, life expectancy at birth was low. It is determined that the effect of health expenditures increased significantly in the 2008–2012 period, and the effect of doctor consultation rates and patient satisfaction levels was also positive. When we look at 2012–2016, we see an increase in health expenditures and patient satisfaction levels and a high contribution to the rate of doctor consultation. If we consider the last period of 2016–2021, we can say that the level of patient satisfaction increased very strongly with the reforms made. The impact of doctor consultation rates and health expenditures remains at the same levels as in the previous period. The increase in life expectancy at birth can be explained by the increase in patient satisfaction levels.

2.4.2 V.A.R.(Maternal) Model Results

The appropriate lag length of our second model in the study is determined as follows and shown in Table 2.8.

When Table 2.8 is examined, the optimal lag length (row with the most stars) was determined to be 1. Whether the model created with a lag length of 1 meets the stability condition

Table 2.7 V.A.R.(Lifeex) – Forecast Variance Decomposition (FVD) for Life Expectancy at Birth, Health Expenditure, Utilization of Health Services, and Access to Health Services

Period	S.E.	LnLifeex	Dcons	HexGDP	Hcsat
1	0.006082	100.0000	0.000000	0.000000	0.000000
2	0.007728	76.90811	0.114372	7.454761	15.52276
3	0.008952	60.98820	0.718714	11.38930	26.90378
4	0.009724	52.96435	1.621166	12.16429	33.25019
5	0.010163	49.12395	2.672765	11.81526	36.38803

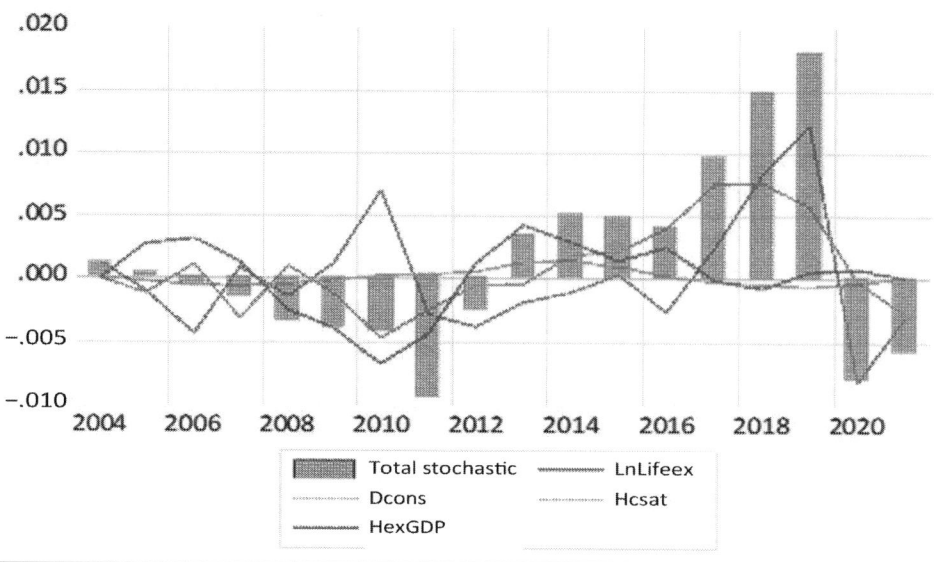

Figure 2.3 V.A.R.(Lifeex) – historical variance decomposition for life expectancy at birth, health expenditure, utilization of health services, and access to health services.

Table 2.8 V.A.R.(Maternal) – Lag Length

Lag Length	LogL	LR	FPE	AIC	SC	HQ
0	−53.86802	NA	0.010642	6.808002	7.004053	6.827490
1	−1127576	74.45710*	0.000152*	2.485597*	3.465848*	2.583036*
2	13.03403	13.32857	0.000283	2.701879	4.466331	2.877269

was similarly tested with the A.R. polynomial inverse roots graph. When the autoregressive A.R. polynomial inverse roots graph in Figure 2.4 is examined, it is seen that all roots are located within the circle, as in our first model, and this model also meets the stability condition.

When we look at the compatibility test results of the V.A.R.(Maternal) model, we find no problem with autocorrelation and heteroskedasticity testing. The results of these tests are given in Table 2.9.

According to the table, there is no autocorrelation or heteroscedasticity problem in our model, and the series are normally distributed. Impulse–response functions of the V.A.R.(Maternal) model, including maternal mortality rates, health expenditures, utilization of health services, and access to health services, are presented in Figure 2.5.

Figure 2.6 shows that the effects on the maternal variable when a standard deviation shock is given to the Dcons, Hcsat, and HexGDP series. According to the impulse–response analysis, a shock given to the Dcons variable had a positive effect on the maternal variable, like the function in the first model. A shock given to the Hcsat variable had a very strong and positive effect on the maternal variable for approximately five periods. However, it is seen that a shock to the HexGDP variable has a negative effect on the maternal variable for approximately five periods. It can be

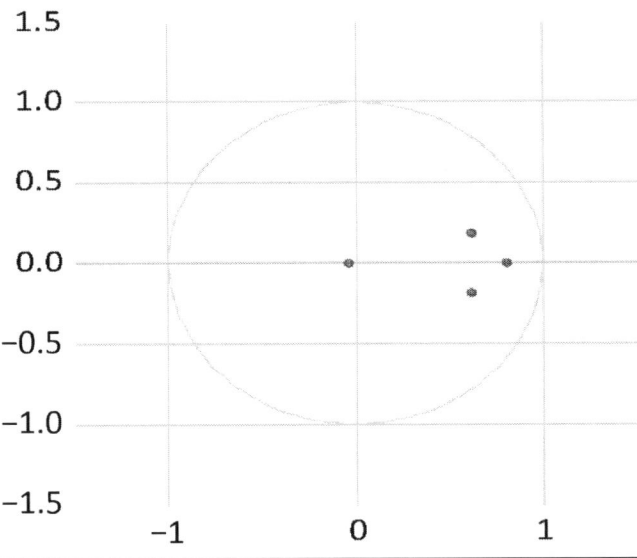

Figure 2.4   V.A.R.(Maternal) – A.R. polynomial inverse roots.

Table 2.9 V.A.R.(Maternal) – Autocorrelation, Heteroscedasticity, and Normality Test Results

Autocorrelation Results (Autocorrelation LM Test)		
Lag	F statistic	Probability
1	1.00915	0.4871
2	0.542097	0.9017
Heteroscedasticity results (white heteroskedasticity tests)		
Chi-Square	Probability	
153.8209	0.2005	
Normality test – Jarque–Bera test (distribution of error term)		
Jarque–Bera	Probability	
4.343639	0.8249	

stated that health expenditures had a strong and negative impact throughout the period. In this regard, maternal mortality rates react negatively to health expenditures and positively to patient satisfaction rates in all five periods. Variance decomposition results to find out which of the variables of maternal mortality rates, health expenditures, utilization of health services, and access to health services are most effective in the V.A.R.(Maternal) model are given in Table 2.10.

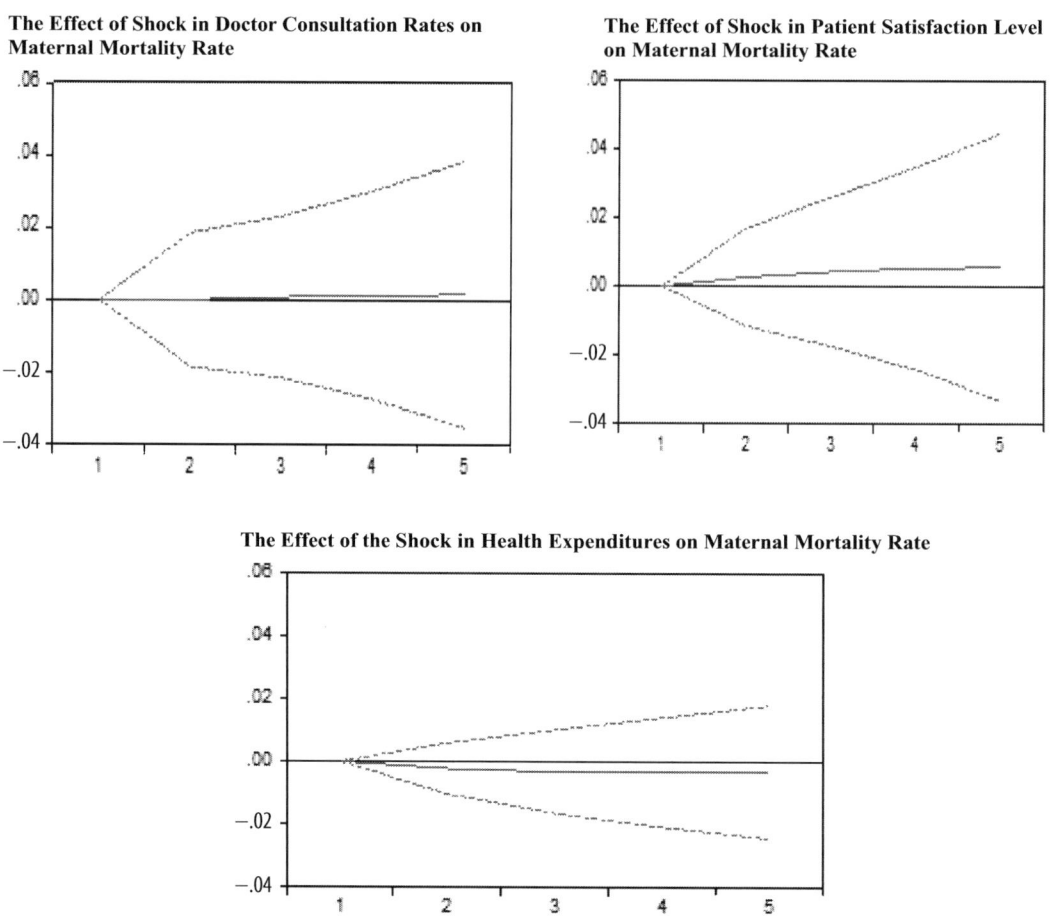

The Effect of Shock in Doctor Consultation Rates on Maternal Mortality Rate

The Effect of Shock in Patient Satisfaction Level on Maternal Mortality Rate

The Effect of the Shock in Health Expenditures on Maternal Mortality Rate

Figure 2.5   V.A.R.(Maternal) – impulse response functions (I.R.F.s) of health expenditure, utilization of health services, and access to health services (response of maternal mortality rate).

According to the variance decomposition results in Table 2.10, approximately 93.8% of a shock in maternal mortality rates at the end of the 5th period is explained by itself. The changes that may occur in this variable are explained next most by health expenditures, at a rate of approximately 4.06%. Patient satisfaction explains the changes in maternal mortality rates at a rate of 1.88%, and referral to a doctor explains it at the lowest rate, at 0.24%.

We can state that the results obtained because of the impulse–response analysis are like the results of historical variance decomposition, where maternal mortality rates are observed. In the period 2004–2008, doctor consultation rates, health expenditures, and patient satisfaction levels are at very low levels. It is seen that the contribution of all three variables did not change in the 2008–2012 period and remained at the same low levels. If we look at the period 2012–2016, it can be said that there was only an increase in the level of patient satisfaction. It is understood from the graph that the 2016–2021 period is like the previous period. When we compared it with the results of variance decomposition, it was determined that almost all the change in maternal mortality rates was explained by its dynamics and that this stability was like the results of historical variance decomposition.

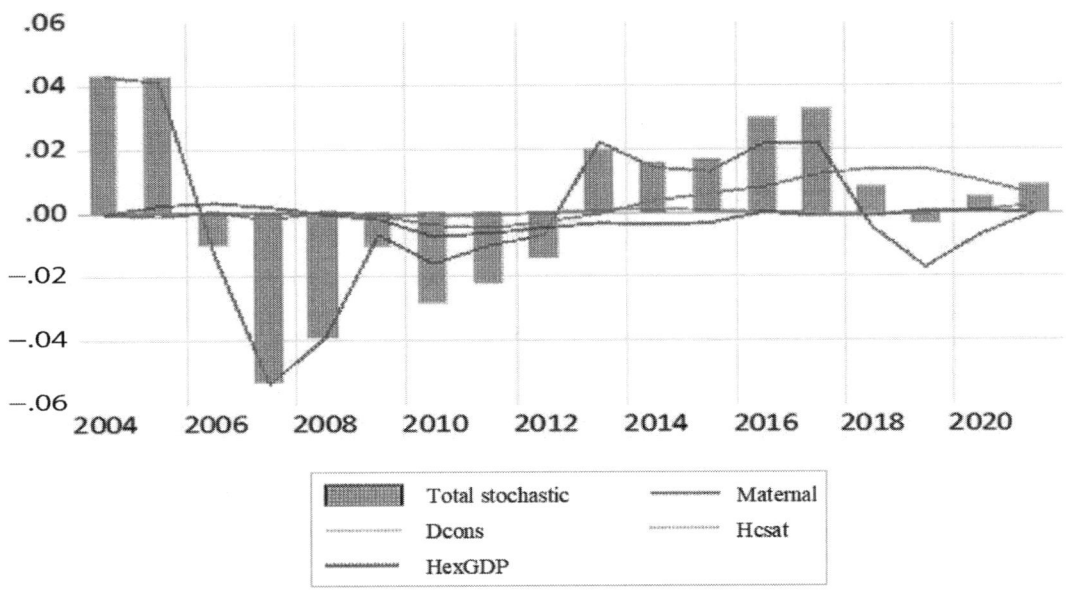

Figure 2.6 V.A.R.(Maternal) – historical variance decomposition for maternal mortality rate, health expenditure, utilization of health services, and access to health services.

Table 2.10 V.A.R.(Maternal) – Forecast Variance Decomposition (FVD) for Maternal Mortality Rate, Health Expenditure, Utilization of Health Services, and Access to Health Services

Period	S.E.	Maternal	Dcons	HexGDP	Hcsat
1	0.025749	100.0000	0.0000	0.0000	0.0000
2	0.034098	98.98655	0.0003	0.568985	0.44417
3	0.039327	97.35515	0.04116	1.593782	1.00991
4	0.042937	95.51747	0.12961	2.843261	1.50966
5	0.045491	93.81328	0.24096	4.064414	1.88134

2.4.3 V.A.R.(Infant) Model Results

Table 2.11 presents the results regarding the selection of the appropriate lag length of the V.A.R.(Infant) model, which was created to assess the effectiveness and comprehensiveness of health expenditures, utilization of health services, and access to health services in relation to infant mortality rates.

According to the table, we can say that the optimal lag length (row with the most stars) was determined to be 1. A.R. polynomial inverse roots are shown in Figure 2.7 to see whether the V.A.R.(Infant) model is stable with a lag length of 1. Like other models, we can state that all roots are located within the circle and the model meets the stability condition.

Table 2.11 V.A.R.(Infant) – Lag Length

Lag Length	LogL	LR	FPE	AIC	SC	HQ
0	–62.75865	NA	0.030288	7.853959	8.050009	7.873446
1	43.12503	149.4828*	8.31e-07*	–2.720592	–1.740341*	–2.623153
2	60.41265	16.2707	1.07E-06	–2.872077*	–1.107625	–2.696687*

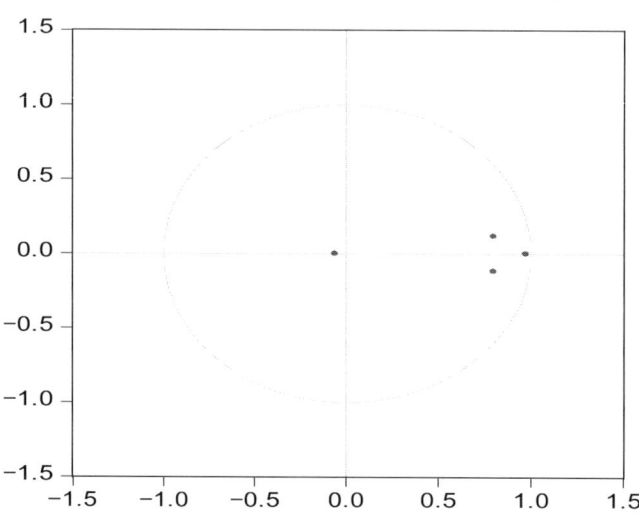

Figure 2.7   **V.A.R.(Infant) – A.R. polynomial inverse roots.**

Table 2.12 shows the V.A.R.(Infant) model's autocorrelation, heteroscedasticity, and normality test results. At a lag length of 1, the model is stable and stationary.

Impulse–response functions for model V.A.R.(Infant) are presented in Figure 2.8.

In the impulse–response analysis of the model, the effects on the Infant variable when a standard deviation shock is given to the Dcons, Hcsat, and HexGDP series are shown. Infant mortality rates react very strongly negatively to a shock to the Dcons variable. It shows that this effect will reduce infant mortality rates in the long term. With a shock to the Hcsat variable, infant mortality rates react positively for approximately two periods. Over time, this positive effect decreases and approaches zero. After the second period, the response of infant mortality rates to a shock in the Hcsat variable is negative. When a shock is applied to the HexGDP variable, the response of infant mortality rates is significantly positive. However, it can be said that this reaction will turn negative in the long run.

Table 2.13 shows how much variance decomposition infant mortality rates (Infant) are explained by the variables of healthcare utilization level (Dcons), healthcare expenditures (HexGDP), and healthcare satisfaction rate (Hcsat). In the first period, all (100%) of the change in infant mortality rates is due to internal factors. After the fourth period, the effect of the Dcons (15.9%) and HexGDP (3.2%) variables becomes more evident. Internal factors are the cause of 71.4% of the change in infant mortality rates in the fifth period, 19.7% is due to the Dcons

Table 2.12 V.A.R.(Infant) – Autocorrelation, Heteroscedasticity, and Normality Test Results

Autocorrelation results (autocorrelation LM test)		
Lag	*F* statistic	Probability
1	1.2136	0.3400
2	0.7602	0.7070
Heteroscedasticity results (white heteroskedasticity tests)		
Chi-Square	Probability	
94.70730	0.1250	
Normality test – Jarque–Bera test (distribution of error term)		
Jarque–Bera	Probability	
3.040889	0.9318	

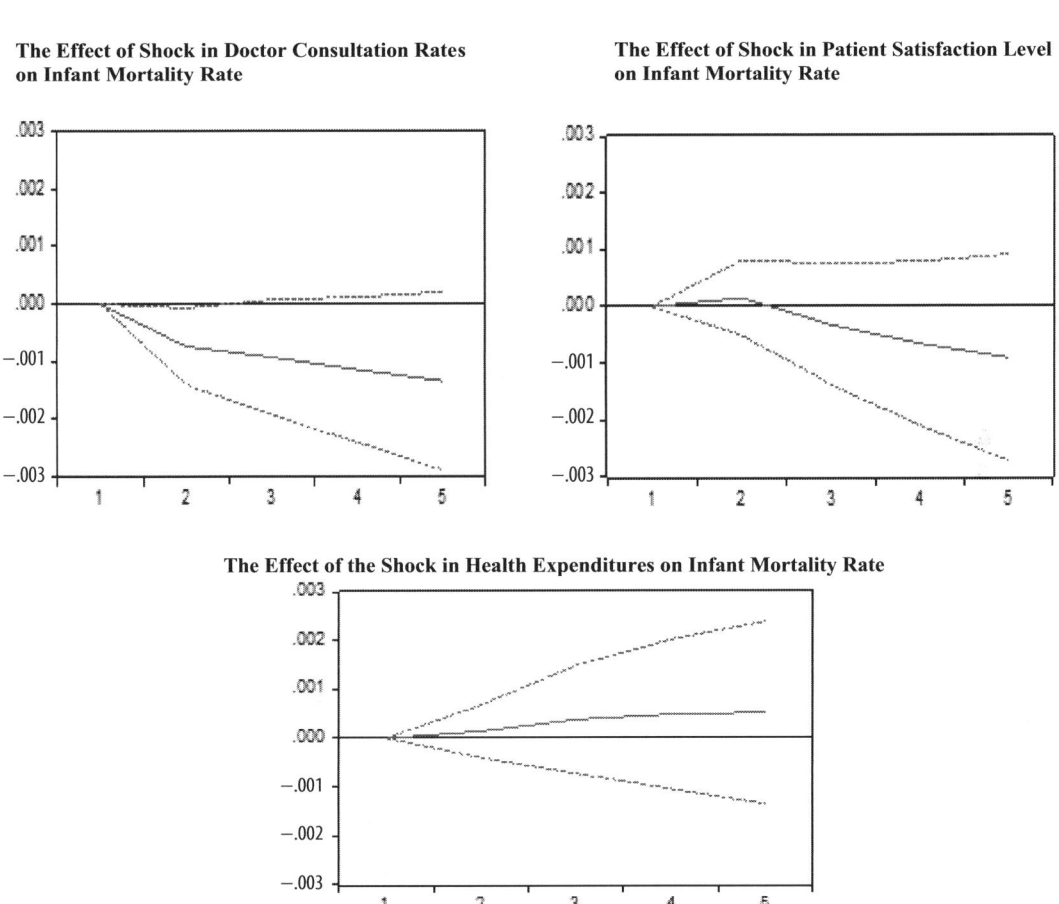

Figure 2.8 V.A.R.(Infant) – impulse response functions (I.R.F.s) of health expenditure, utilization of health services, and access to health services (response of infant mortality rate).

Table 2.13 V.A.R.(Infant) – Forecast Variance Decomposition (FVD) for Infant Mortality Rate, Health Expenditure, Utilization of Health Services, and Access to Health Services

Period	S.E.	Infant	Dcons	HexGDP	Hcsat
1	0.001643	100.0000	0.0000	0.0000	0.0000
2	0.002692	91.89645	7.542932	0.305284	0.255331
3	0.003451	85.72146	11.91525	1.063115	1.300182
4	0.004143	78.51794	15.98645	3.252231	2.243373
5	0.004807	71.45008	19.72994	6.006243	2.813741

variable, 6% is due to the HexGDP variable, and 2.8% is due to the Hcsat variable. There has been a significant increase in the impact of other variables. According to this table, it can be said that the level of utilization of health services and health expenditures have significant effects on infant mortality rates. It also appears that these factors will contribute more to changes in infant mortality rates over time.

The impulse-response functions and variance decomposition analysis of the infant mortality rates examined in the third model and the historical variance decomposition of the results are shown in Figure 2.9. With this graph, it is possible to see the effects of shocks in doctor consultation rates, patient satisfaction level, and health expenditures on the infant mortality rate in certain periods. If we divide the graph into certain periods, 2004–2008 covers the first years when the H.T.P. started to be implemented. Increases can be seen in doctor consultation rates, patient satisfaction levels, and healthcare expenditures. During this period, a downward trend in infant mortality rates is observed. The period 2008–2012 can be described as the period when the effects of the H.T.P. became evident. In this period, the increasing trend in variables seems to be greater. The decrease in infant mortality rates continues. In the third period, between 2012 and 2016, there appears to be a slowdown or stagnation in the rate of increase in doctor consultation rates and health expenditures. Patient satisfaction rate also remained high. The long-term effects of H.T.P. have emerged, and the downward trend continues. In the 2016–2021 period, the increase in doctor consultation rates continues as the demand for healthcare services increases. While the rate of health expenditures remained constant, patient satisfaction rates remained high during this period. The long-term positive effects of H.T.P. appear more clearly in this period.

2.5 Discussion and Conclusion

In this study, within the scope of H.T.P., which started to be implemented in Turkey in 2003, the relationship between health expenditures, utilization of health services, level of access to health services, and health status was examined. In this context, V.A.R. analysis was applied using data between 2003 and 2021. First, the A.D.F. unit root test determined whether the series were stationary. At the end of the analysis, it was determined that the variables were stationary at their first differences (Table 2.4). In the study, three separates V.A.R. models were created for the econometric data analysis. The appropriate lag length for V.A.R. analysis was determined as 1, and variance decomposition and impulse–response analyses were performed according to this lag length. In addition to these analyses, the results obtained using the historical variance decomposition

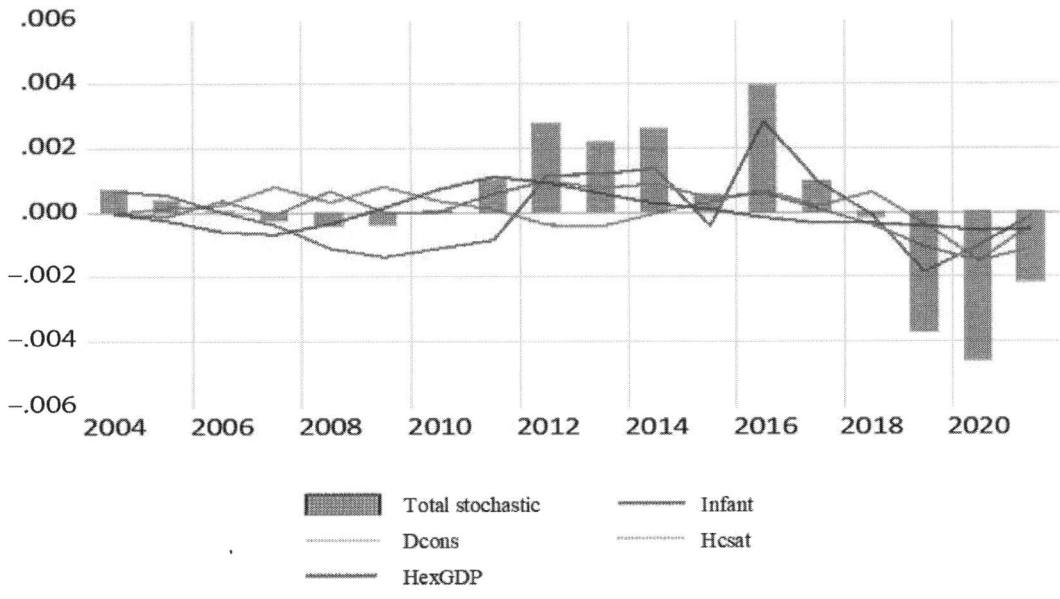

Figure 2.9 Historical variance decomposition for infant mortality rate, health expenditure, utilization of health services, and access to health services.

method were examined periodically. The results reveal a relationship of very different dimensions between health expenditures, level of utilization of healthcare services, level of access to health services, and health status indicators.

When the findings obtained from the variance decomposition results are examined (Table 2.7), it is determined that 49% and almost half of the change in life expectancy at birth at the end of the fifth period are affected by its dynamics, while 36% of the change in life expectancy at birth is due to the level of patient satisfaction. Therefore, life expectancy at birth changes and develops depending on patient satisfaction, which is one of the most important indicators of access to health services after its dynamics. This result is similar to the findings in the study of Hao et al. (2020). In addition, it has been determined that a shock in doctor consultation rates and patient satisfaction levels positively affects life expectancy at birth for approximately two periods, while a shock in health expenditures negatively affects life expectancy at birth. Studies that find a negative relation between health expenditures and life expectancy at birth emphasize that the main factors impacting this situation are poverty level, income inequality, education, infant mortality, and other socioeconomic factors (Morina et al., 2022). Similarly, it is seen that some countries spend more on healthcare, but life expectancy is shorter. The lack of a positive relationship between health expenditures and life expectancy may indicate that health resources must be allocated effectively. Therefore, this can be interpreted as increasing health expenditures does not guarantee any improvement in health services (Balkhi et al., 2021). In the results of variance decomposition of maternal mortality rates in Table 2.10, which we considered in the second model, almost all (93%) of the change in maternal mortality rates at the end of the fifth period is affected by its dynamics. It is seen that the change in maternal mortality rates was affected by health expenditures starting from the third period, and this reached 4% in the fifth period. However, patient satisfaction levels and doctor consultation levels also affect maternal mortality rates starting from the third period, although at very low rates.

In the impulse–response functions, it is seen that with a shock to the variables, the maternal mortality rates remain unresponsive and become uncertain after a certain period, and only health expenditures negatively affect the maternal mortality rates in the first period, and then they become uncertain in Figure 2.5. The negative relationship between health expenditures and maternal mortality rates, it is like the study by Owusu et al. (2021), in which they examined the impact of health expenditures on maternal and infant mortality rates in 177 countries. According to this study, health expenditures potentially reduce maternal and infant mortality in low- and middle-income countries. Likewise, Manyika et al. (2019) also concluded in their study that health expenditures should be increased to reduce maternal mortality rates in Zimbabwe. Rana et al. (2018) found that the relationship between increasing health expenditures and maternal deaths was insignificant at all income levels. In the variance decomposition results of the third V.A.R. model, in which infant mortality rates, one of the health status indicators, are analysed, all the change in infant mortality rates in the first period is due to their internal factors. It is seen that approximately 20% of this change in the fifth period was due to the increase in doctor consultation rates, and 6% was due to health expenditures in Table 2.13.

According to the impulse–response analysis findings of the study, life expectancy at birth reacts positively to doctor consultation rates and patient satisfaction levels and negatively to health expenditures. In the first model, health expenditures reduce life expectancy at birth. Therefore, health expenditures are not an effective policy tool for life expectancy at birth, one of the health status indicators. Likewise, the positive response of infant mortality rates in the third model tells us that health expenditures are ineffective policy tools for infant mortality rates. However, in the second model, the very low negative response of maternal mortality rates to a shock to health expenditures may indicate that health expenditures can reduce maternal mortality rates. In this context, it can be said that health expenditures are an effective policy tool on maternal mortality rates. It is stated that the relationship between health expenditures and health status indicators, such as that between life expectancy at birth and mortality rate, is complex. Research results also reveal different and contradictory results regarding this relationship. In addition, since it is not clear how and why health expenditures affect health outcomes, a causal link between the two has yet to be fully proven (Van Den Heuvel and Olaroiu, 2017). From impulse–response functions, it can be said that doctor consultation rates negatively affect infant mortality rates, while health expenditures have a positive effect. It was determined that the effect of a shock in patient satisfaction rates on infant mortality rates was positive in the first two periods, and then this effect continued to be negative. Kiross et al. (2021), is one of the studies examining that doctor consultation rates negatively affect infant mortality rates.

It has been concluded that the optimum use of maternal health-related services in health services in Ethiopia reduces infant mortality rates. Similarly, Wise et al. (1988), state that increases in infant mortality rates are due to inadequate use of maternal health services. The low effect of health expenditures on infant mortality rates is similar to the result obtained by Bhalotra (2007) in his study in India in which health expenditures are insignificant. Akinlo and Sulola's (2019) study, in which they concluded that health expenditures in Sub-Saharan African countries do not help reduce infant mortality rates and, therefore, there is a positive relationship between them, shows that they obtained the same result as this study. Another result of the study is that patient satisfaction rates positively affected and increased infant mortality rates for two periods, but in the following period, this effect changed negatively and decreased infant mortality rates. When the findings are considered thoroughly, increasing doctor consultation rates and patient satisfaction levels, which are variables other than health expenditures, increase life expectancy at birth and reduce infant mortality rates. The impact of doctor consultation rates and patient satisfaction levels on maternal mortality rates is not clear, as it was first negative and then unresponsive. Impulse–response functions and variance decomposition findings obtained from V.A.R. models support these results.

If we consider the historical variance decomposition results periodically (Figure 2.3, Figure 2.6, and Figure 2.9), in the initial period of the 2004–2008 H.T.P., the effects of all three variables on health status indicators were at very low levels, and their contributions were uncertain. The period 2008–2012 shows the years when the effects of H.T.P. began to become evident. It is a period when doctor consultation rates, health expenditure rates, and patient satisfaction levels begin to increase. During this period, life expectancy at birth and infant mortality rates began to show a positive trend. Since the effects of the variables on maternal mortality rates are very low and uncertain, their contribution is almost negligible. The period 2012–2016 is when H.T.P.'s applications became established, and its effects began to emerge. In this period when access to the health system increases, the level of patient satisfaction increases, the quality of health services improves, and investments in health services are sustained, improvements in health status indicators are also expected. Apart from maternal mortality rates, the positive effects on the other two health status indicators appear to continue. The 2016–2021 period represents a period in which the effects of the H.T.P. are fully felt, and the system becomes established. For this period, doctor consultation rates and health expenditure rates remained at high levels and became stagnant, while the patient satisfaction level increased, and its impact was significant. It can also be described as a period in which the long-term effects of H.T.P. can be seen.

As a result, this study found that the most important variable among the health status indicators that were found to be significant on life expectancy at birth was the patient satisfaction level. It has been determined that doctor consultation rates are the most effective and important variable on infant mortality rates. No variable is significant or very effective on maternal mortality rates. However, it can be said that a very low increase in health expenditures can reduce maternal mortality rates, but after a while, they will remain unresponsive and uncertain. One of the main components of the H.T.P. is to create a "common, easy-to-access and friendly health service system", and in this context, especially with the introduction of the "General Health Insurance" component, the H.T.P. is expected to contribute to access to health services. According to the results of the study, as access to healthcare and medicine becomes more accessible in Turkey because of H.T.P. applications, this situation is also reflected in patient satisfaction. Therefore, high patient satisfaction positively affects and increases life expectancy at birth. In addition, individuals who have easier access to health services will create an effective demand for health services, and there will be an increase in the rate of doctors consulting for health services. This can be interpreted as contributing to the decrease in infant mortality rates, one of the health status indicators.

References

Ak, S. (2023). Health transformation program in Turkish health system reforms and policy processes. *Journal of Health Sciences and Management, 3*(3), 71–78.

Akbulut, Y. (2015). Sağlık okuryazarlığının sağlık harcamaları ve sağlık hizmetleri kullanımı açısından değerlendirilmesi. İçinde: F. Yıldırım & A. Keser (Eds.), *Sağlık Okuryazarlığı*. Ankara: Ankara Üniversitesi Sağlık Bilimleri Fakültesi Yayın No: 3, 113–132.

Akinlo, A. E., & Sulola, A. O. (2019). Health care expenditure and infant mortality in sub-saharan Africa. *Journal of Policy Modeling, 41*(1), 168–178.

Akkavak, T. (2018). *Türkiye'de sağlık sisteminin gelişimi: Sağlıkta dönüşüm programı (2003–2011)* (Master's Thesis, Namık Kemal Üniversitesi).

Alpaslan, M. N., & Çıraklı, Ü. (2024). Sağlıkta Dönüşüm Programının Sağlık Hizmeti Kullanımına Etkisi: Ekonometrik Bir Analiz. *Süleyman Demirel Üniversitesi Vizyoner Dergisi*, *15*(41), 299–311.

Ata, A. Y., & Eryer, A. (2021). Sağlık Statüsü Üzerinde Sağlık Harcamaları ve Gelir Dağılımının Etkisi: MINT Ülkeleri Üzerine Bir İnceleme. *Karadeniz Ekonomi Araştırmaları Dergisi*, *2*(2), 32–49.

Atılgan, E. (2015). Sağlıkta dönüşüm programının Türkiye'de sağlık hizmetleri talebi üzerine etkileri. *Sosyal Güvenlik Dünyası Dergisi*, *18*(96), 8–23.

Atun, R., Aydın, S., Chakraborty, S., Sümer, S., Aran, M., Gürol, I., . . . & Akdağ, R. (2013). Universal health coverage in Turkey: Enhancement of equity. *The Lancet*, *382*(9886), 65–99.

Aydın, N. (2022). Historical perspective on the health transformation in Turkey. *Sağlık Bilimlerinde Değer*, *12*(1), 188–193.

Bağcı, H. (2023). Do healthcare reforms Affect health status? Türkiye practice. *Ankara Medical Journal*, *23*(3).

Balkhi, B., Alshayban, D., & Alotaibi, N. M. (2021). Impact of healthcare expenditures on healthcare outcomes in the Middle East and North Africa (MENA) region: A cross-country comparison, 1995–2015. *Frontiers in Public Health*, *8*, 624962.

Bayar, H. T., & Öztürk, M. (2021). Teknolojinin istihdam üzerine etkisi: VAR analizi. *Süleyman Demirel Üniversitesi İktisadi ve İdari Bilimler Fakültesi Dergisi*, *26*(2), 119–127.

Bener, A., Alayoglu, N., Çatan, F., Torun, P., & Yilmaz, E. S. (2019). Health services management in Turkey: Failure or success? *International Journal of Preventive Medicine*, *10*(1), 30.

Bhalotra, S. (2007). Spending to save? State health expenditure and infant mortality in India. *Health Economics*, *16*(9), 911–928.

Bostan, S. (2013). What has the health transformation program in Turkey changed for patients? *Hacettepe Sağlık İdaresi Dergisi*, *16*(2), 91–103.

Bozdemir, M. K. E., Avcı, S., & Aladağ, Z. (2021). Assessment of the Turkish health transformation program with data envelopment analysis. *IEEE Transactions on Engineering Management*, *70*(8), 2800–2808.

Caner, A., & Cilasun, S. M. (2019). Health care services and the elderly: Utilization and satisfaction in the aftermath of the Turkish health transformation program. *Gerontology and Geriatric Medicine*, *5*, 2333721418822868.

Caner, A., Karaoğlan, D., & Yaşar, G. (2018). Utilization of health-care services by young children: The aftermath of the Turkish health transformation program. *The International Journal of Health Planning and Management*, *33*(3), 596–613.

Cansever, İ. H. (2018). Devlet anlayışları ekseninde sağlık politikalarının değişimi ve analizi: Türkiye incelemesi. *Süleyman Demirel Üniversitesi Sosyal Bilimler Enstitüsü Dergisi*, *31*, 105–120.

Ceylan, B. K., Azizoğlu, F., & Mete, M. (2023). Sağlık Politikaları ve Türkiye'de Sağlık Politikalarının Dönüşümü. *Selçuk Üniversitesi Akşehir Meslek Yüksekokulu Sosyal Bilimler Dergisi*, *16*, 186–203.

Demirtaş, Z., & Metintaş, S. (2017). Türk Cumhuriyetlerinde Anne Çocuk Sağlığı Göstergelerinin Ekonomik ve Doğurganlık Özellikleri Açısından Değerlendirilmesi. *ESTÜDAM Halk Sağlığı Dergisi*, *2*(1), 16–25.

Dhrifi, A. (2020). Public health expenditure and child mortality: Does institutional quality matter? *Journal of the Knowledge Economy*, *11*(2), 692–706.

Dickey, D. A. ve Fuller, W. A. (1981). Likelihood ratio statistics for autoregressive time series with a unit root. *Econometrica*, *49*(4), 1057–1072.

Erol, H., & Özdemir, A. (2019). Türkiye'de 1980 Sonrası Sağlık Politikalarında Dönüşüm ve Sağlık Harcamalarına Etkileri. *Uluslararası yönetim iktisat ve işletme dergisi*, *15*(15), 119–146.

Gujarati, D. N. (2004) *Basic econometrics*, Fourth Edition. New York: The McGraw-Hill Companies.

Gülşen, M. A., & Yıldıran, M. (2017). Sağlıkta Dönüşüm Programı Sonrasında Uygulanan Sağlık Regülasyonlarının Üniversite Hastanelerinin Mali Yapılarına Etkisi. *Ömer Halisdemir Üniversitesi İktisadi ve İdari Bilimler Fakültesi Dergisi*, *10*(4), 159–172.

Gürsoy, K. (2015). An overview of the Turkish healthcare system after health transformation program: Main successes, performance assessment, further challenges, and policy options. *Sosyal Güvence*, *7*, 83–112.

Hao, L., Xu, X., Dupre, M. E., Guo, A., Zhang, X., Qiu, L., . . . & Gu, D. (2020). Adequate access to healthcare and added life expectancy among older adults in China. *BMC Geriatrics*, 20, 1–15.

Horton, R., & Lo, S. (2013). Turkey's democratic transition to universal health coverage. *The Lancet*, *382*(9886), 3.

İleri, H., Seçer, B., & Ertaş, H. (2016). Sağlık Politikası Kavramı ve Türkiye'de Sağlık Politikalarının İncelenmesi. *Selçuk Üniversitesi Sosyal ve Teknik Araştırmalar Dergisi*, *12*, 176–186.

İlgün, G., Konca, M., & Sönmez, S. (2023). The relationship between the health transformation program and health expenditures: Evidence from an autoregressive distributed lag testing approach. *Value in Health Regional Issues*, *38*, 101–108.

Kesbiç, C. Y., & Salman, G. (2018). Türkiye'de sağlık harcamaları ve ekonomik büyüme arasındaki ilişkinin tespiti: 1980–2014 VAR model analizi. *Finans Politik ve Ekonomik Yorumlar*, *639*, 1163–1180.

Kiross, G. T., Chojenta, C., Barker, D., & Loxton, D. (2021). Optimum maternal healthcare service utilization and infant mortality in Ethiopia. *BMC Pregnancy and Childbirth*, *21*(1), 390.

Kockaya, G., Oguzhan, G., & Çalşkan, Z. (2021). Changes in catastrophic health expenditures depend on health policies in Turkey. *Frontiers in Public Health*, *8*, 614449.

Koçyiğit, S. Ç., Bulut, Ö. U., Çinibulak, M., & Horoz, M. (2023). Sağlık Harcamaları İle Sağlık Hizmeti Kullanım Düzeyi Arasındaki İlişkinin İncelenmesi: 2002–2020 Dönemi Türkiye Örneği. *Nişantaşı Üniversitesi Sosyal Bilimler Dergisi*, *11*(2), 283–307.

Manyika, W., Gonah, L., Hanvongse, A., Shamu, S., & January, J. (2019). Health financing: Relationship between public health expenditure and maternal mortality in Zimbabwe between the years 1980 to 2010. *Medical Journal of Zambia*, *46*(1), 61–70.

The Ministry of Health of Turkey. (2004). *Sağlık istatistikleri 2003* [Healthstatistics 2003]. In: *Yayın no. 677*. Ankara: Sağlık Bakanlık [inTurkish].

Morina, F., Komoni, A., Kilaj, D., Selmonaj, D., & Grima, S. (2022). The effect of health expenditure on life expectancy. *International Journal of Sustainable Development and Planning*, *17*(5), 1389–1401.

Mucuk, M., & Alptekin, V. (2008). Türkiye'de vergi ve ekonomik büyüme ilişkisi: VAR Analiz (1975–2006). *Maliye Dergisi*, *155*, 155–174.

O.E.C.D. (2024). https://data-explorer.oecd.org/ (accessed 2024 May)

Ökem, Z. G., & Çakar, M. (2015). What have health care reforms achieved in Turkey? An appraisal of the "health transformation programme". *Health Policy*, *119*(9), 1153–1163.

Owusu, P. A., Sarkodie, S. A., & Pedersen, P. A. (2021). Relationship between mortality and health care expenditure: Sustainable assessment of health care system. *Plos One*, *16*(2), e0247413.

Özgen, F. B., & Güloğlu, B. (2004). Türkiye'de iç borçların iktisadi etkilerinin VAR tekniğiyle analizi. *ODTÜ Gelişme Dergisi*, *31*(1),93–114.

Rana, R. H., Alam, K., & Gow, J. (2018). Health expenditure, child and maternal mortality nexus: A comparative global analysis. *BMC International Health and Human Rights*, *18*, 1–15.

Samancı, M., & Noyan, E. (2023). Türkiye Yüzyılında Kamu Harcamaları ve Kamu Gelirleri İlişkisi: VAR Analizi. *Türkiye Siyaset Bilimi Dergisi*, *6*(1), 1–11.

San, S. (2020). Türkiye'de Sağlıkta Dönüşüm Programı ve hasta memnuniyeti üzerine etkileri. *Ankara Sağlık Bilimleri Dergisi*, *9*(2), 55–66.

Sarıtaş, H., Genç, A., & Avcı, T. (2018). Türkiye'de enerji ithalatı, cari açık ve büyüme ilişkisi: VAR ve Granger nedensellik analizi. *Ekonomik ve Sosyal Araştırmalar Dergisi*, *14*(2), 181–200.

Sert, S. (2019). *Türkiye'de sağlık sistemi ve sağlıkta dönüşüm programı (2003–2019)* (Master's thesis, Namık Kemal Üniversitesi).

Shi, L., Macinko, J., Starfield, B., Xu, J., Regan, J., Politzer, R., & Wulu, J. (2004). Primary care, infant mortality, and low birth weight in the states of the USA. *Journal of Epidemiology & Community Health*, *58*(5), 374–380.

Sims, C. (1980). Macroeconomics and reality, *Econometrica*, *48*(1), 1–48.

Stokes, J., Gurol–Urganci, I., Hone, T., & Atun, R. (2015). Effect of health system reforms in Turkey on user satisfaction. *Journal of Global Health*, *5*(2).

Tatar, M., Mollahaliloğlu, S., Şahin, B., Aydın, S., Maresso, A., Hernández-Quevedo, C., & World Health Organization. (2011). Turkey: Health system review. *Health System Transit, 13*(6), 1–186, xiii–xiv. PMID: 22455830.

Turkish Statistical Institute. (2024). *TurkStat, life satisfaction survey, 2003–2023.* Yaşam Memnuniyeti Araştırması. [https://data.tuik.gov.tr/Kategori/GetKategori?p=Gelir,-Yasam,-Tuketim-ve-Yoksulluk-107] [in Turkish].

Ugur, Z., & Tirgil, A. (2018). Sağlıkta Dönüşüm Programı ve Kamunun Sağlık Hizmetlerinden Memnuniyeti. *Ombudsman Akademik, 1,* 295–327.

Van den Heuvel, W. J., & Olaroiu, M. (2017). How important are healthcare expenditures for life expectancy? A comparative, European analysis. *Journal of the American Medical Directors Association, 18*(3), 276.e9-276.e12.

Wise, P. H., First, L. R., Lamb, G. A., Kotelchuck, M., Chen, D. W., Ewing, A., . . . & Rideout, J. (1988). Infant mortality increase despite high access to tertiary care: An evolving relationship among infant mortality, health care, and socioeconomic change. *Pediatrics, 81*(4), 542–548.

World Bank. (2024). *Life expectancy at birth, total (years).* https://databank.worldbank.org/reports. aspx?source=2&series=SP.DYN.LE00.IN&country. Data from the database: World Development Indicators. [accessed 2024 March]

Yardim, M. S., Cilingiroglu, N., & Yardim, N. (2014). Financial protection in health in Turkey: The effects of the health transformation programme. *Health Policy and Planning, 29*(2), 177–192.

Yasar, G. Y. (2011). Health transformation programme in Turkey: An assessment. *The International Journal of Health Planning and Management, 26*(2), 110–133.

Yılmaztürk, A. (2023). Cumhuriyetten günümüze Türkiye'nin 100 yıllık sağlık politikaları dönüşüm süreci. *Balıkesir Üniversitesi Sosyal Bilimler Enstitüsü Dergisi, 26*(49–1), 437–458.

Chapter 3

The Pharmaceutical Pricing and Reimbursement Policies with Health Transformation Programme in Turkey

Zafer Çalışkan

Contents

3.1 Introduction

A country's healthcare system is considered as a reflection of the health policies adopted. However, health policies are also in flux and are closely related to both demand-side and supply-side developments such as changes in the socioeconomic structure, changes in the demographic structure, and advances in healthcare technology. Since the fundamental transformation of health policies is achieved through health reform processes, reforms in healthcare services are considered critical turning points. Healthcare sector reform is therefore a continuous process of fundamental change in the policies and institutional arrangements of the healthcare sector, organized and managed by the government. It is seen that the reform process is carried out in areas covering the four main basic functions of the health system such as governance, supply, financing, and resource production. Although the main goal is to protect and improve the health status of the population, ensuring equality, efficiency, quality, financing, and sustainability in the provision of health services

DOI: 10.4324/9781003539896-4

is also seen as an important part of the reform. Because the dominant argument on the need for reform in health services is based on the assumed belief that the public sector cannot operate effectively as a service provider. It is argued that the public administration of health services often results in inadequate access to health services, ineffective financial management, and a decline in service quality. At this point, it should be noted that there is no consistently implemented universal measure package that constitutes health sector reform. According to World Health Organization, most countries usually focus attention on the contents of the reform, rather than on the process. This focus on content runs the risk of equating health sector reform with one set of prescriptions, for example, the introduction of market mechanisms, user charges, establishing joint management bodies with low responsibility, reducing the size of the public sector, cost-containment, and redistribution of resources. According to Collins et al. (1999), health sector reform in developed, developing, and transitional societies has been influenced by the worldwide ideological hegemony of neoliberal, market-driven, and 'New Right' approaches to social, economic, and political change. Reform has frequently expressed key elements of this ideological transition through the introduction of user choice, the promotion of the private sector, changes in the internal structure and operation of the public sector (through competition, markets, decentralization, and new incentives), the introduction of limits on the role of the public sector, and changes in the financing of healthcare (particularly in the transition from tax-based systems to more individually based ones such as user fees and insurance systems). The reform usually ignores the question of feasibility of implementing the change. What is needed is to increasingly understand the issues in reform processes to complement what has been learned about the content of reforms. Such an understanding might lead to the development of strategies for publicizing or marketing reforms or identification of ways that governments can anticipate and plan for the reactions of organized interest groups (W.H.O., 2000). Regardless of how the need for reforms arises, it is clear that the main goal for every healthcare system is to ensure the highest health status with the least resources. In other words, value for money spent becomes increasingly important, considering that the country's resources are limited. Therefore, an important concept that will shape the health systems of countries in recent years is "value-based health care".

Value-based healthcare focuses on providing value to patients, shifting service delivery in healthcare systems from volume-focused to value-focused or value-based, and value is defined as the health outcomes achieved per dollar spent (Lakdawalla et al., 2018). Value may increase by lowering healthcare costs or improving outcomes or both. Interest in change toward a value-driven healthcare system accelerated when Porter and Teisberg introduced value-based healthcare, a new strategy for how healthcare should be delivered and measured (Porter and Teisberg, 2006). The essence of value-based healthcare questions the necessity of ineffective and inefficient medical interventions that are relatively costly but have low health outcomes or outcomes. Therefore, it encourages health policymakers not to seek services with high opportunity costs. According to Porter, true reform will require both moving toward universal insurance coverage and restructuring the care delivery system (Porter, 2009). These two components are profoundly interrelated, and both are essential. Achieving universal coverage is crucial not only for fairness but also to enable a high-value delivery system. When many people lack access to primary and preventive care, and cross-subsidies among patients create major inefficiencies, high-value care is difficult to achieve.

In Turkey, as in many countries, in recent years, the general goal in healthcare services for providers as well as all other stakeholders has begun to be defined as increasing value for patients. Improving value requires improving one or more outcomes without increasing costs, reducing costs without sacrificing outcomes, or both.

Therefore, it becomes inevitable to have important regulations in the provision of health services, the form of financing, health labor, medicine, and medical supplies. The Health Transformation Programme (H.T.P) implemented in Turkey in 2003 includes regulations made for this purpose. Although this programme has many components, it includes giving the Ministry of Health (M.o.H.) a new role as planner and controller; it was aimed at reorganizing the provision of health services by establishing a general health insurance system, introducing the practice of family medicine, and making hospitals autonomous in terms of financing (Akdağ, 2009, 2015). The factors that create the need for transformation in health are the low health insurance coverage and the existence of obstacles in accessing services, which are seen as the main structural problems of the pre-transformation period, low service quality, as well as low governance and efficiency.

3.2 Background of Turkish Healthcare System

Before 2003, Turkey had a fragmented health system in terms of provision and financing, and health insurance was provided by five separate public schemes, each with its own provider network and differing benefit packages bringing huge disparities in quality and access to health services. Conversely, after 2003, Turkey enlarged the scope of financial protection to the population through expansions in the breadth and depth of health insurance coverage, combined with service delivery reforms to improve equity in access to health services. With the H.T.P., it is aimed to put an end to a fragmented and multiple structure in the provision and financing of health services and to provide health services in an effective, efficient, and equitable manner with such a restructuring (Gürsoy, 2015).

The main objectives of the Health Transformation Programme can be listed as follows:

i) Reorganizing the health sector of the M.o.H. with a structure in which vertical structuring is eliminated and integrated health service provision is emphasized, and its main duty and responsibility is to prepare policies and supervise the order.

ii) Directly proportional to citizens' ability to pay and services.
  ■ A general health service that they can use in line with their needs.
  ■ Establishment of insurance system.

iii) Providing continuous health services to people by appointing a physician to each family through strengthened primary health services
  ■ Strengthening preventive health services and increasing the satisfaction rate.

iv) Establishing a new curriculum for family medicine and family health and strengthening health management as a discipline independent of medicine to ensure the success of the program.

v) Training teams that have public health knowledge and skills, who will apply public health science using advanced techniques and from a multidisciplinary perspective, and establishing a structure that will plan these applications.

vi) Establishment of the National Quality and Accreditation Agency and authorization of this institution to standardize health services, regulate licensing, certification, and accreditation activities.

vii) Standardization, licensing, and registration of pharmaceuticals and medical devices institutional framework that will meet the international norms for rational management structuring of formations.

■ Establishing the Turkish Medicines and Medical Devices Agency (T.İ.T.C.K) and ensuring the effectiveness and transparency of licensing processes

viii) Establishing an integrated health information system that will ensure the integration of all components of the Health Transformation Programme, provide access to necessary and sufficient information to be used in analysis and decision-making mechanisms, and provide the opportunity to audit the provision of healthcare services.

One of the major arrangements launched with H.T.P. is that fragmented public financial systems have been merged under one roof. Social Insurance Institution for working class, Pension Fund for public civil servants, Social Security Organization for Artisans and Self-Employed for self-employed, and Green Card practice for poor individuals without any social security were merged under Social Security Institution. The major arrangement launched with H.T.P. is that all individuals have been covered under the General Health Insurance since 2012; namely, universal coverage has been ensured (see in Figure 3.1). In addition, all public health institutions were brought under the M.o.H. in 2005 (Atun et al., 2013; İlgün et al., 2023). One of the other important arrangements was as follows: in 2003, providing free healthcare for the emergency calls; in 2004, making payments to healthcare service providers based on their performances; in 2004, introducing reference-based pricing for the pricing of medications; in 2006, the outsourcing of the Social Security Institution from private hospitals with cost-sharing agreement; in 2006, all primary care services were made free, regardless of social security status; in 2008, all healthcare services for the population younger than 18 years were made free, regardless of the social security status of parents; in 2010, providing family practice to ensure access to primary healthcare services for whole society; in 2011, establishing specific units for the implementation of activities regarding the improvement of healthcare services and supervision; and in 2012, introducing decentralization in public hospitals to improve their managerial and financial autonomy. Since the introduction of the General Health Insurance Scheme and the H.T.P., population coverage has gradually expanded. Along with these changes, the H.T.P. strengthened information systems and unified public hospitals under the M.o.H. Almost 99% of Turkish citizens in 2019 had general health insurance coverage, compared to 91.6% in 2003 and 93.2% in 2008.

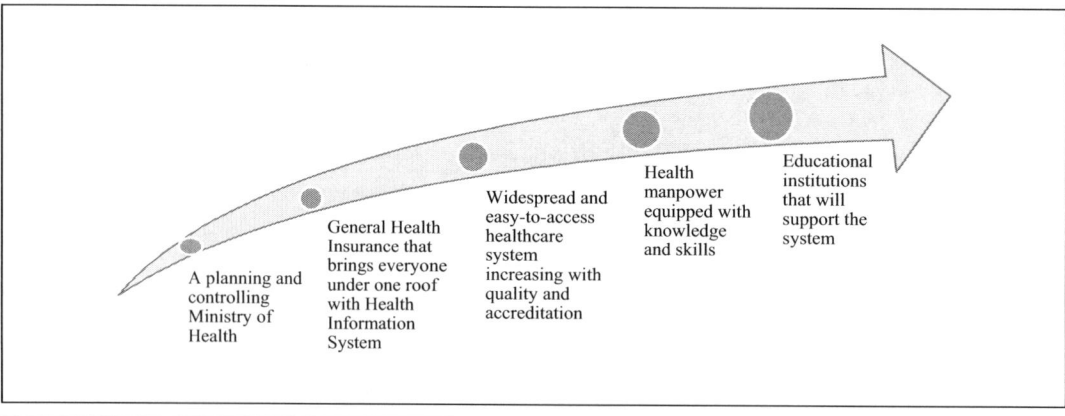

Figure 3.1 Health Transformation Programme components.

Despite the positive effects of the health transformation, Turkey, like other countries, faces some important challenges. The two most important challenges are the sustainability of health expenditures and the increasing burden of noncommunicable diseases. Health spending has been rising not only globally but also in Turkey throughout time as a result of governments' recognition of the value of the healthcare system. As a result of governments realizing the value of the healthcare system, healthcare expenditures have been increasing over time not only in the world but also in Turkey. However, the real challenge at this point is about the sustainability of these expenditures. With the transformation in health, the increase in health insurance coverage, the increasing burden of noncommunicable diseases, aging, and the need to treat chronic diseases using high-priced health technologies have started to strain the financial resources of health expenditures. As a country that allocates resources to health at approximately 4%t of G.D.P., below the O.E.C.D. average, Turkey cannot provide sufficient financing. This causes the progress made in access and quality at the beginning of the health transformation to slow down. However, given the amount of money spent on healthcare, it is always necessary to assess if these costs truly result in better health outcomes. Health indicators like mortality and morbidity, as well as changes in them, are crucial because of this. Noncommunicable diseases (NCDs) and their burden have gained recognition as measures of a health system's effectiveness in recent years.

In Turkey, as in other countries, people suffer as a result of these dangers and are more vulnerable to a number of illnesses, such as infectious diseases, NCDs, child and maternal mortality, and a shortage of healthcare services. According to estimates, NCDs account for 86% of all deaths in Turkey. In Turkey, between 2000 and 2017, there was a notable increase in the prevalence of noncommunicable diseases, including ischemic heart disease, cancer, chronic obstructive pulmonary disease, diabetes, and mental illnesses (Breda et al., 2021). After H.T.P., the Multisectoral Action Plan of Turkey for Noncommunicable Diseases 2017–2025 was implemented in 2017, marking the beginning of efforts to raise the awareness of NCDs and NCD risk factors. The primary objectives are to lower preventable early death; achieve the Sustainable Development Goal (SDG) targets related to NCDs; and lessen the harm that NCDs pose to public health, the economy, society, and the environment. However, a variety of factors, including shifting lifestyles, socioeconomic structures, low health literacy, regional differences, and cultural traits, can influence how much of the risk of NCDs is absorbed.

Since treatment services account for a significant amount of health costs in this country, as in many others, there is a need to enhance the resources allotted to NCDs treatment. As a result, the need for medicines for non-communicable diseases and patient access to these medicines are becoming increasingly important. Access to pharmaceuticals is thus significantly impacted by the nation's policies regarding pricing policies and reimbursement procedures. As was previously mentioned, the Turkish Medicines and Medical Devices Agency's (T.İ.T.C.K.) founding was a crucial stage for pharmaceuticals pricing in Turkey. However, the establishment of the Social Security Institution (S.S.I.) regulates another aspect of the pharmaceutical laws. Reimbursement for medical services and prescription pharmaceuticals was decided upon by a reimbursement panel that was founded in 2004. Therefore, in a sense, pharmaceuticals' pricing and reimbursement processes are regulated in Turkey with both T.İ.T.C.K. and Social Security Institution Reimbursement Commission.

3.3 The Overview: Pharmaceutical Pricing and Reimbursement Implementation

In particular, the launch of new pharmaceuticals and the recent macroeconomic turmoil in many countries have put pressure on pharmaceutical prices and related costs, forcing healthcare systems to develop methods for both pricing and reimbursement of pharmaceuticals. The two important challenges, namely the sustainability of health expenditures and the need to treat NCDs with new/innovative pharmaceuticals, lead to an increase in health and pharmaceutical expenditures, which leads to the regulation of the pharmaceutical industry by the public authority, especially with price and reimbursement regulation. However, the most important constraints for these regulations are the timely and quality pharmaceutical supply. In other words, pharmaceuticals' access to the patient should not affect these regulations or should be minimally affected under any circumstances. Therefore, pharmaceutical companies are increasing their research and development (R&D) expenses for drugs that can be used to treat non-communicable diseases such as diabetes, cancer, and heart disease that the aging population is prone to, as the incidence of these diseases is increasing. Additionally, as a result of this trend's acceleration of production and marketing efforts, pharmaceutical costs now account for a sizeable and rising share of all healthcare spending. This circumstance has a significant impact on the economy and healthcare systems, stimulating the pharmaceutical industry's creative problem-solving and the creation of more potent treatment approaches.

Health spending has increased globally over time as a result of governments' recognition of the healthcare system's significance. The majority of public taxes are used to fund health expenses, which are increasing faster than the global economy and making up 10% of the G.D.P. (Anwar et al., 2023). The average ratio of total health expenditures to G.D.P. in O.E.C.D. countries was 4.6% in the 1970s and climbed to 8.5% in 2022, despite the fact that health expenditures vary greatly between countries (16.9% in the United States and 4.2% in Turkey). It is anticipated that this ratio would rise further in the upcoming years. The cost of pharmaceuticals has also gone up concurrently. The United States ranks first with 1,432 dollars spent per person on pharmaceuticals, compared to an average of 614 dollars spent by O.E.C.D. nations per person. According to O.E.C.D. Health at a Glance 2023, the nations with the lowest pharmaceutical expenditures are Chile, Denmark, Estonia, and Croatia. Prescription pharmaceuticals and over the counter (O.T.C.) pharmaceuticals make up the two primary categories of spending. Prescription pharmaceuticals make up the majority in O.E.C.D. nations, making up almost three-quarters of total retail pharmaceutical spending. Concurrently, the price of pharmaceuticals has increased as well (OECD, 2023).

Pricing strategies and reimbursement regulations of a country can have a considerable impact on pharmaceutical expenditures, both overall and per capita. The one pertaining to pharmaceutical prices is the most significant of all regulations. Governments in certain nations enforce stringent laws to regulate the cost of prescription pharmaceuticals. Generally speaking, the purpose of these rules is to set ceiling prices, base them on a reference pricing system, or involve pharmaceutical companies in discussions to lower their prices. This guarantees a decrease in pharmaceutical costs. A wide range of pricing policies was implemented on the basis of product price control (the most common), reference pricing (Germany), reference pricing (the Netherlands), and profit control (UK) (Danzon et al., 2005; Dunlop et al., 2018).

However, the established reimbursement guidelines are regarded as an additional instrument for cost containment. The pharmaceuticals that are covered by public or private insurance and their prices are determined by the regulations regarding reimbursement. Nonetheless, nations with extensive insurance programs and generous payment practices might see an increase in pharmaceutical costs since patients would have easier access to a larger selection of pharmaceuticals and would consequently use them more frequently. The pharmaceutical costs are influenced by the organization of the health system as well. Pharmaceutical spending can also be influenced by the makeup of a nation's healthcare system, especially the role played by public and private insurance.

Pharmaceutical spending, for instance, may be subject to stricter regulations in single-payer systems – where the government serves as the major payer for healthcare – than in systems with a combination of public and private payers. The most significant institutional regulation in recent years has been Health Technology Assessment (H.T.A.), which allows for value-based payment to be applied to pharmaceutical expenses more efficiently. Prior to granting reimbursement approval, certain nations carry out health H.T.A. to appraise the clinical and financial efficacy of novel pharmaceuticals. The pharmaceutical spending landscape can be influenced by H.T.A. processes that determine which pharmaceuticals are covered and at what cost.

One of the intervention strategies that have been used in recent years to guarantee that pharmaceutical costs and prices are set at a reasonable and acceptable level is the reference pricing system (Herr et al., 2014). There are two types of reference pricing systems that are used in practice: internal reference pricing, which uses domestic prices to compare therapeutically equivalent pharmaceuticals, and external/international reference pricing, which bases pharmaceutical prices on a group of countries. But external reference price is more significant, particularly because it severely restricts spending on pharmaceuticals. External reference price (Festbeträge) was first used in Germany in 1989 (Çalışkan, 2008). It became widespread after it was put into practice, such as in the Netherlands (1991), Norway (1993), Sweden (1993), Denmark (1993), Hungary (1999), Spain (2000), Belgium (2001), and Italy (2001). It was adopted by other countries and quickly put into practice. External reference price (E.R.F.), which is implemented as an important expenditure control tool in almost 70% of European countries, has begun to be implemented rapidly in countries outside Europe such as Australia (1990), New Zealand (1993), and British Colombia – Canada (1995). The World Health Organization Collaborating Centre for Pharmaceutical Pricing and Reimbursement Policies defined external reference pricing, also known as international reference pricing, international price comparison, external price referencing, or cross-reference pricing, as a pricing strategy in which a government compares the cost of a medicine to one or more other nations to derive a benchmark or reference price for the purpose of setting or negotiating the price or reimbursement rate of the product in the own country or context. An instrument for controlling prices is external reference pricing, which makes sure that the cost of a pharmaceutical product in a payer organization or country does not unnecessarily surpass the cost of the same in comparator organizations or countries.

3.4 The Pharmaceutical Pricing and Reimbursement in Turkey

Access to health services and pharmaceuticals is a fundamental human right; some countries incorporate it in their national constitution. Countries currently working toward universal health coverage and where a large part of pharmaceutical spending is still out of pocket are facing many challenges to achieving equitable access to affordable, safe, efficacious, and quality medicines. In this context, pharmaceutical pricing and reimbursement policies have a substantial impact on controlling pharmaceutical costs of in-patent medicines – particularly innovative and expensive ones that also carry a significant financial burden for overall health expenditure (Dahmani et al., 2023).

Although the implementation results of H.T.P. regulations in Turkey are closely related to each other, they are separated by institutional and legislative regulations. As a matter of fact, with the H.T.P., the pharmaceutical pricing and reimbursement process in Turkey has also changed. The M.o.H and the Social Security Institution are the two critical government bodies in Turkey. The M.o.H is responsible for market approval and pricing, and Social Security Institution is responsible for reimbursement decisions. SSI has a commission that is named the Medical and Economic

Evaluation Commission. The submitted products are primarily evaluated by the Medical and Economic Evaluation Commission, and the final decision is taken by the Reimbursement Commission. Under the M.o.H., the Turkish Medicines and Medical Devices Agency is in charge of pharmaceutical regulation in Turkey. Turkish Medicines and Medical Devices Agency is the main authority for marketing authorizations/product licenses, clinical trial authorizations, post-marketing surveillance, regulation of advertising, laboratory analysis of samples, price regulation, and good manufacturing practice (G.M.P.) inspections. The Turkish Medicines and Medical Devices Agency is in charge of making sure that medications and medical equipment fulfil the required requirements for quality, safety, and efficacy. Before being sold in Turkey, pharmaceutical items must first have marketing clearance from the Turkish Medicines and Medical Devices Agency. This entails a thorough examination of the product's quality, safety, and efficacy data. Applications are assessed by the Turkish Medicines and Medical Devices Agency according to international standards compliance, manufacturing procedures, and data from clinical trials. Pre-market assessment and post-market monitoring are steps in the approval process. As can be seen, in Turkey, the availability of a pharmaceutical on the market and within the scope of reimbursement is the joint responsibility of the M.O.H. and the Social Security Institution. The process of a pharmaceutical being available on the market in Turkey and being offered within the scope of reimbursement consists of the evaluation processes of these two institutions and the stages of licensing, determining the price and evaluation for the scope of reimbursement, respectively.

After H.T.P. implementation, the external reference price system has served as the foundation for pharmaceutical prices in Turkey since 2004. Pharmaceutical prices are determined by accepting the cheapest factory sales price of the product in the five EU member countries determined by the Ministry, namely France, Italy, Spain, Portugal, and Greece, as the reference price. However, if the countries where the relevant product is manufactured or imported are other than the reference countries in question and there is a sales price to the warehouse determined below the reference country prices in these countries, the price in the country with the lower sales price to the warehouse is accepted as the reference price (Figure 3.2). The price change is linked to the TL/Euro exchange rate. A Euro value in Turkish lira to be used in pricing medicinal products for human use is determined by multiplying the annual average Euro value, which will be calculated on the basis of the daily Euro sales rate realizations of the Central Bank of the Republic of Turkey, which is indicative and declared

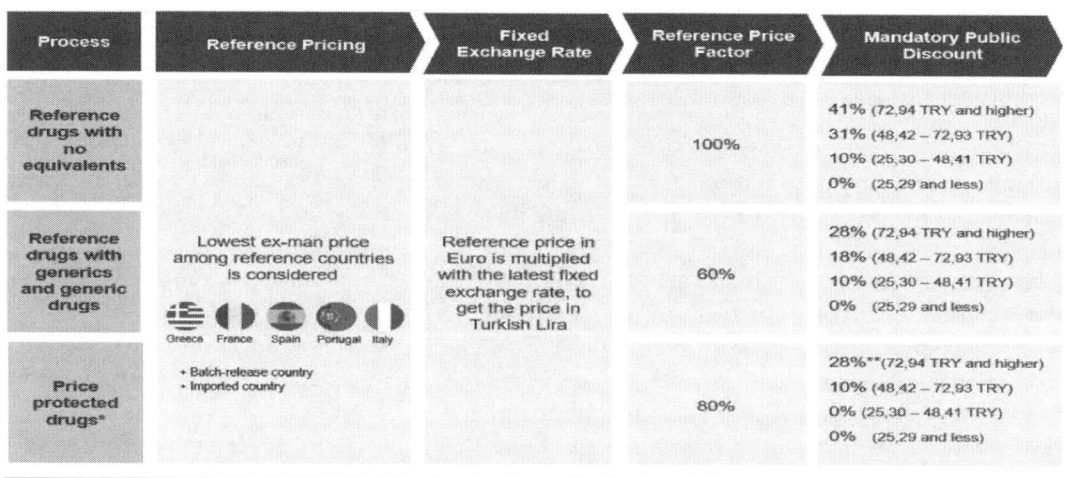

Figure 3.2   Pharmaceutical pricing system in Turkey.

in the Official Gazette of the previous year by the adjustment coefficient determined as 60%. This rate was applied as 70% between 2015 and 2019. In recent years, it has been observed that the TL/Euro exchange rate has been approved by the relevant authority at dates and rates outside of the legislation. The Price Evaluation Commission meets within the first 45 days of each year and announces the value of 1 Euro to be used in the pricing of medicinal products for human use. With the Decision No. 7954 published in the Official Gazette No. 32401 on December 16, 2023, the periodic euro rate was determined as 17.5483. Furthermore, there are various regulations on authorization, pricing, and reimbursement of pharmaceuticals, biologicals, and medical devices in Turkey. In general, these are based on the Law on Pharmaceutical and Medical Preparations numbered 1262 published in the Turkish Official Gazette dated 26 May 1928 and numbered 898 (İspençiyari ve Tıbbi Müstahzarlar Kanunu).

Another process related to access and availability of medicine in a country is the method of reimbursement. Reimbursement can be expressed as the process of deciding whether a drug will be paid for current and potential users by the reimbursement agency on behalf of these groups. In Turkey, the authorized institution for this is the S.S.I. The general reimbursement system in Turkey is based on a positive list where pharmaceutical companies can apply for reimbursement to S.S.I. Within the scope of S.S.I., a "Reimbursement Commission" was established in 2007 to determine the payment procedures and principles for human medicinal products and human pharmaceuticals. A reimbursement decision is the responsibility of the inter-ministerial Medicines Reimbursement Commission. Companies submit a dossier to the Medical and Economic Evaluation Commission to get reimbursement that contains general information, clinical data, literature review, and a pharmacoeconomic evaluation. The Medical and Economic Evaluation Commission examines the drugs to be included in the reimbursement list in terms of pharmacoeconomic, epidemiological, pharmacological, clinical, and public health organizations. When necessary, it also takes into account the opinions of the relevant organizations and submits its evaluation in a report to the Payment Commission. The Commission decides whether a pharmaceutical will be reimbursed or not by evaluating the opinions prepared by the Medical and Economic Evaluation Commission. The most important criteria in deciding whether to reimburse a pharmaceutical are clinical effectiveness, safety, quality, cost-effectiveness, and affordability. A cost-effectiveness and therapeutic benefit analysis is used to determine which medications should be on the reimbursement list. Therefore, we can say that the pharmaceutical reimbursement is largely based on pharmacoeconomic evaluation. With its reimbursement policies, S.S.I. provides medicines to people under its system and takes measures to ensure that pharmaceutical expenditures do not exceed their budgets.

3.5 The Health Economics and Pharma Sector in Turkey

It is observed that the resources allocated to health from the general budget in Turkey have been increasing in absolute terms in recent years. Although the share allocated from G.D.P. does not change much, the total health expenditure, which is approximately 607 billion TRY in 2022, is expected to increase to approximately 700 billion TRY in 2023. The ratio of general government health expenditure to total health expenditure was approximately 76% in 2023, similar to previous years. The ratio of total health expenditure to G.D.P. was 4.9% in 2021 and 4.0% in 2022. The ratio of current health expenditure to G.D.P. is calculated as 4.6% in 2021 and 3.7% in 2022 (TurkStat, 2023). As can be seen, the public has the largest share in both the provision and financing of health services in Turkey. Healthcare expenditures made through the Social Security Institution constitute approximately half of the total health expenditures (Figure 3.3). As the sole

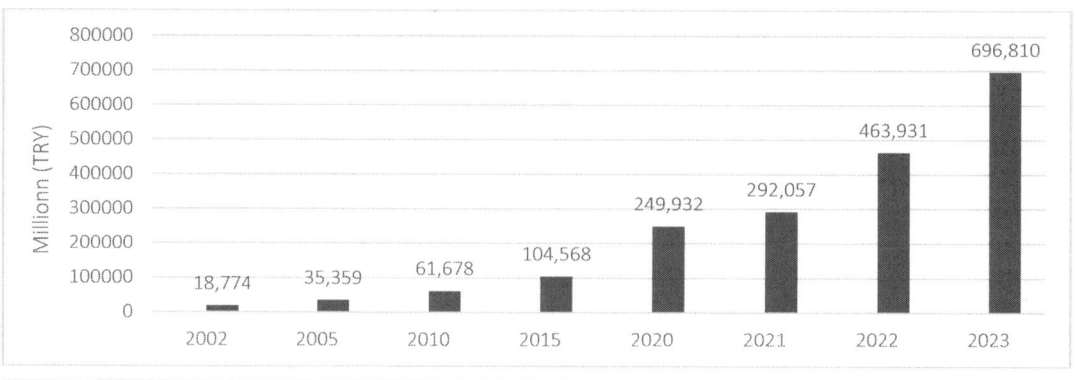

Figure 3.3   Health expenditure, 2002–2023.

payer institution of health services, S.S.I. has an important place in the health system in Turkey in this respect. The financing of the social security system is created by S.S.I.

However, the functional distribution of health expenditures is more important than the increase in expenditures. In Turkey, a large portion of the expenses are incurred in hospitals for treatment services. Considering that pharmaceuticals are an important part of your treatment, the size and sustainability of the resources allocated for pharmaceuticals are important. This also provides information about the structure and size of the pharmaceutical sector. Therefore, the structure and size of the pharmaceutical industry of countries can be depicted with two basic indicators. The first is the per-capita expenditure on pharmaceuticals, which serves as a performance measure for the nation's healthcare system. The second, which is crucial in illustrating the nation's position in the international pharmaceutical industry, is the portion of G.D.P. that the nation allots to pharmaceuticals.

According to Association of Research-Based Pharmaceutical Companies (AİFD) 2023 annual report as in health expenditures, the United States ranks first in terms of pharmaceutical expenditures. Among other leading countries in 2022, pharmaceutical sales in the United States were $1,901 per capita, while they were $834 in Switzerland, $764 in Canada, and $715 in Germany. At $91 in pharmaceutical sales per person, Turkey was the O.E.C.D. nation with the lowest sales in 2022. On the other hand, the United States held the highest G.D.P. proportion in pharmaceutical sales (2.5%), akin to health spending. Despite the 1.2% O.E.C.D. average, Greece, Spain, and Portugal had the highest pharmaceutical sales to G.D.P. ratios, at 2.3%, 2.1%, and 1.8%, respectively, after the United States. Turkey, with a 0.9% rate, comes in 29th place among O.E.C.D. nations. The same report indicated that in 2022, the size of the Turkish pharmaceutical market was 7.7 billion dollars. Accordingly, while Turkey is ahead of countries such as Greece and Portugal in terms of pharmaceutical market size, it lags behind countries such as Germany and France, to which it is more similar in terms of population. Although Turkey, whose box sales grew by 7.9% in the pharmaceutical market between 2020 and 2022, was the country with the highest growth in terms of boxes among the selected countries, it was the only country where the market narrowed in dollar terms (Figure 3.4). On a volume scale, the market reached 2.93 billion boxes in 2023, an increase of 32.4% from 2.21 billion boxes in 2015. This increase is 3.6% on a compound annual basis (CAGR). The aging and expanding population's increased demand, the availability of more options, particularly for non-pharmaceutical items like vitamins and natural supplements, and the easier access to public health services and physicians in the pharmaceutical class are the main factors driving the volume growth (A.İ.F.D., 2023; İ.E.İ.S., 2023).

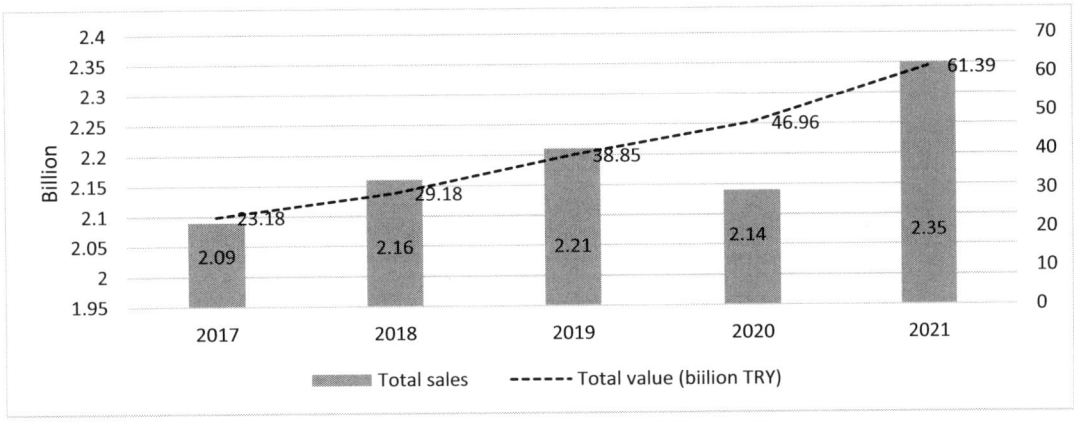

Figure 3.4   Pharmaceutical market in Turkey, 2017–2021.

When the pharmaceutical market is examined in terms of concentration, it is seen that 230 distributor companies sell pharmaceuticals in the market. While the product range of 38 companies in the Turkish pharmaceutical market consists of only imported pharmaceuticals, 121 companies are in the market with only manufactured pharmaceuticals. Seventy-one companies, which own 60% of the pharmaceuticals in the market, have both imported and manufactured pharmaceuticals and represent 68% of the market in value and volume. In 2023, the market share of the top 50 companies in the value ranking is 85% in value and 82% in volume. The market value of pharmaceuticals within the scope of reimbursement in the pharmaceutical market was 199 billion TL in 2023. In other words, 94.3% of the pharmaceuticals sold in the market in terms of value consist of pharmaceuticals used within the scope of reimbursement. The fourfold difference between the average prices of prescription pharmaceuticals that are not covered by reimbursement and those that are covered by reimbursement is striking. The reference pharmaceutical market reached 131 billion TL from 71.4 billion TL with an increase of 83.4% in 2023. On a box scale, it decreased by 1.8%, from 0.99 billion boxes to 0.97 billion boxes. The generic pharmaceutical market reached 80 billion TL from 38.4 billion TL with a growth of 108.4% in 2023. On a box scale, generic pharmaceuticals grew by 8.7% and reached a volume of 1.7 billion boxes (İ.E.İ.S., 2023).

3.6 The Issues and Options for Turkish Pharmaceutical Sector

The delivery of health services in Turkey has seen substantial changes in both form and capability as a result of the H.T.P. The organizational structure of the health system, as well as the costs and financing of healthcare, reflect these changes. Since the start of the health transformation, there has been a shift in perceptions toward health policy. It demonstrates that one of the elements and objectives of the health transformation has been substantially met in this particular situation. The primary consequence of this shift is that, in comparison to the subsistence period, access to health services is now easier and more plentiful. When the H.T.P. began in 2022, the number of visits per capita to physicians in healthcare facilities was 3.1; by the same year, that number had risen to 10. Inevitably, the demand for other elements of treatment services, including pharmaceuticals, has also been impacted by this increase. The processes pertaining to pharmaceutical supply and access in Turkey have become even more crucial when combined with the rising incidence of noncommunicable diseases. Turkey's changing population structure, rising prevalence of noncommunicable diseases, and increasing demand for healthcare services and investments in healthcare services make this a vital market for pharmaceuticals. Improving the quality of health services and increasing patients' access to health services and medicines have also inevitably led to an increase in public health and pharmaceutical expenditures. This increase leads public institutions to implement a strict pharmaceutical pricing and reimbursement policy. Although the pricing and reimbursement regulations implemented with the H.T.P. have had significant impacts on issues such as rational pharmaceutical use and access to quality and safe pharmaceuticals, in recent years, reference prices, exchange rate regulations, and reimbursement regarding access to pharmaceuticals have mostly depended on the evaluations made on the budget impact. The difficulties experienced in recent years regarding the availability and access of pharmaceuticals have brought about discussions about the revision and renewal of the new structure introduced by the H.T.P.

For this reason, although the situation is similar in some countries, the biggest problem in Turkey in recent years is the limited access to new and innovative medicines. Although medicines seemingly make up the smallest portion of healthcare spending, they can also provide additional savings by significantly reducing costs in other areas of healthcare, including early diagnosis, hospital stays, and long-term care costs. This can often be achieved with new and innovative pharmaceuticals (Cowling et al., 2023). Because the changing nature of the diseases requires treatment with these pharmaceuticals. According to Lichtenberg, the number of DALYs lost is significantly inversely related to the number of pharmaceuticals that had ever been launched 9–20 years earlier, and that the number of years of lost life (YLLs) is significantly inversely related to the number of pharmaceuticals that had ever been launched 11–20 years earlier for Canada. The launch of a pharmaceutical had the largest (most negative) impact on the number of DALYs and YLLs, 15 years after it was launched (Lichtenberg, 2019). Danzon et al. (2005) stated that countries with lower expected prices or smaller expected market size have fewer launches and longer launch delays, controlling for per capita income and other country and firm characteristics. Therefore, since the late 1980s and early 1990s, regulators and Health Technology Assessment (H.T.A.) bodies/payers around the world have been actively pursuing various approaches to making important medicines available to the patients who need them in a timely manner, recognizing that patients and providers are willing to tolerate greater risks, especially risks of the unknown about medicines, when the morbidity of the disease is significant or when the disease is potentially life-threatening. The development of new approaches to provide timely access has continued since their earliest introduction and continues today. There are currently several approaches/pathways that have been implemented by regulators and H.T.A. bodies/payers in various regions, and this has resulted in some confusion among stakeholder groups about their differences, often making it difficult to determine which approach might best be applied to a specific medicine and which might yield the greatest benefits and/or unacceptable risks (Baird et al., 2014).

Reducing the challenges encountered in the manufacture and supply of pharmaceuticals, one of the domains where the process that ensued following the disruption in health, to two fundamental elements is necessary. The first is the progressive reduction in the portion allotted to medical and healthcare as a result of the worsening economic forecast. As a result, allocating health resources at the level of the nations listed in the preceding sections has become essential. This is the first and most crucial requirement for getting prompt, appropriate, and high-quality medical care. In actuality, the price and payment system's antiquatedness poses a problem to patients' access to medicine and the pharmaceutical business. The main barriers to the entry of new pharmaceuticals are now the real exchange rate, which gradually deviates from the periodic euro exchange rate, and the increase in production and distribution costs brought on by recent exchange rate increases, despite the fact that the H.T.P. process began with institutional and practical regulations. The 2021 results of the W.A.I.T. survey, which has been conducted regularly by E.F.P.I.A. and I.Q.V.I.A. for 18 years and measures the level of patient access to innovative treatments in countries, were announced on April 6, 2022. According to the results of the report, which used data on access to new medicines in 39 countries (27 E.U. countries and 12 non-E.U. countries) and examined 160 innovative medicines licensed by the European Medicines Agency between 2017 and 2020, the access rate to new medicines in developed countries such as Germany, Denmark, Austria, Italy, and Switzerland was above 70%, while the EU average was 46%. With an access rate of 15%, Turkey lagged behind the EU average and its neighbours Greece (49%) and Bulgaria (31%) (I.Q.V.I.A., 2023). Access rates in all five European countries that Turkey uses as benchmarks for pharmaceutical pricing were above the Turkish average (Italy (79%), France (66%), Spain (53%), Portugal (51%) and Greece (49%)). The results of the W.A.I.T. Survey, which reveals the rate of access to innovative products in Turkey compared to European countries, are shared by A.I.F.D. with relevant stakeholders, particularly at congresses of medical specialty associations, and awareness is raised on this issue. Pharmaceutical prices may vary in response to increases in costs, fluctuations in exchange rates, and adjustments to reference prices (Figure 3.5). Nevertheless, there is an upper limit that applies to the differences that result from these increases. Even though ex-officio and instantaneous medicine price reductions are implemented in response to exchange rate fluctuations, practical exchange rate price rises may still be accompanied by uncertainty and delays. The timeframes outlined in the law and the methodology for determining the pace at which pharmaceutical prices would rise in the event of exchange rate fluctuations have expanded in recent years.

A growing challenge faced by public healthcare payers around the world is deciding which medicines to approve for reimbursement, and at what price. As higher-cost medicines put increasing pressure on public healthcare budgets, the need to identify 'fair' prices for medicines has never been greater (Paulden, 2024). In an effort to lessen and counteract the strain that the economic crisis was placing on Turkey's public finances, the country began implementing a global budget in

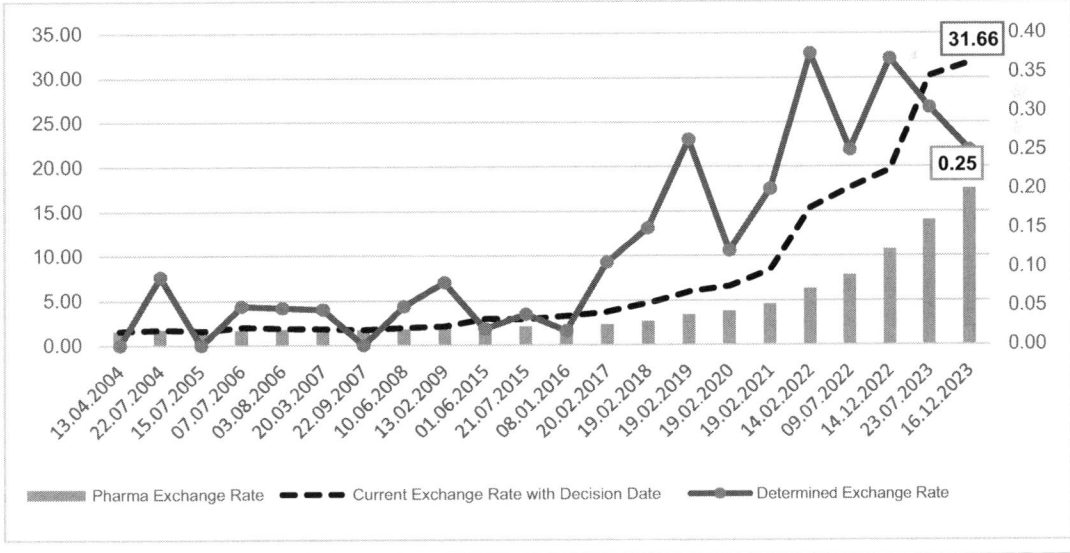

Figure 3.5 The relationship between the pharma exchange rate applied to pharmaceutical prices in Turkey and the current exchange rate.

2009. It has been noted that the goal set throughout the H.T.P. process – which was to guarantee reasonable pharmaceutical use and efficient pharmaceutical budget utilization – has lagged. Even though practically all prescription medications in Turkey are paid for, it would be wise to give priority to the resources that will guarantee localization in order to avoid becoming dependent on medications from outside the nation. Since the pharmaceutical sector is an area of economic activity, domestic production will provide an uninterrupted supply, while domestic production can reduce the current account deficit and stimulate the economy. The Turkish drug industry should be supported, and more resources should be transferred to R&D activities. R&D activities must be conducted regarding biologic medicines, biosimilar products, and biotechnology products, which are of increasing importance in the world. These can be thought of as long-term objectives. It is obvious that, in the near future, more funding must be allotted to the pharmaceutical industry and that the procedures governing pricing and reimbursement must be modernized (maybe by setting up a new, independent fund specifically for novel medications). The value-based approach of the existing price and reimbursement procedure may not be appropriate because, for example, biological therapies are now used to treat changing diseases instead of traditional pharmaceuticals, and because these are expensive pharmaceuticals.

References

A.İ.F.D. (https://www.aifd.org.tr/wpcontent/uploads/2024/05/20231213_Turkish_Pharmaceutical_Sector_Report_Summary_AIFD.pdf).

Akdağ, R. (2009). *Health transformation program in Turkey-progress report*. Ministry of Health Ankara, Turkey.

Akdağ, R. (2015). Lessons from health transformation in Turkey: Leadership and challenges. *Health Systems & Reform*, 1(1), 3–8.

Anwar, A., Hyder, S., Mohamed Nor, N., & Younis, M. (2023). Government health expenditures and health outcome nexus: A study on OECD countries. *Frontiers in Public Health*, 11, 1123759.

Atun, R., Aydın, S., Chakraborty, S., Sümer, S., Aran, M., Gürol, I., . . . & Akdağ, R. (2013). Universal health coverage in Turkey: Enhancement of equity. *The Lancet*, 382(9886), 65–99.

Baird, L. G., Banken, R., Eichler, H. G., Kristensen, F. B., Lee, D. K., Lim, J. C. W., . . . & Hirsch, G. (2014). Accelerated access to innovative medicines for patients in need. *Clinical Pharmacology & Therapeutics*, 96(5), 559–571.

Breda, J., Allen, L. N., Tibet, B., Erguder, T., Karabulut, E., Yildirim, H. H., . . . & Wickramasinghe, K. (2021). Estimating the impact of achieving Turkey's non-communicable disease policy targets: A macro-simulation modelling study. *The Lancet Regional Health–Europe*, 1.

Çalışkan, Z. (2008). Referans fiyat ve ilaç piyasası. *Hacettepe Sağlık İdaresi Dergisi*, 11(1), 49–75.

Collins, C., Green, A., & Hunter, D. (1999). Health sector reform and the interpretation of policy context. *Health Policy*, 47(1), 69–83.

Cowling, T., Nayakarathna, R., Wills, A. L., Tankala, D., Paul Roc, N., & Barakat, S. (2023). Early access for innovative oncology medicines: A different story in each nation. *Journal of Medical Economics*, 26(1), 944–953.

Dahmani, H., Fradi, I., Achour, L., Toumi, M., & Maghreb Research Group. (2023). Pharmaceutical pricing and reimbursement policies in Algeria, Morocco, and Tunisia: Comparative analysis. *Journal of Market Access & Health Policy*, 11(1), 2244304.

Danzon, P. M., Wang, Y. R., & Wang, L. (2005). The impact of price regulation on the launch delay of new drugs – evidence from twenty-five major markets in the 1990s. *Health Economics*, 14(3), 269–292.

Dunlop, W. C., Staufer, A., Levy, P., & Edwards, G. J. (2018). Innovative pharmaceutical pricing agreements in five European markets: A survey of stakeholder attitudes and experience. *Health Policy*, 122(5), 528–532.

Gürsoy, K. (2015). An overview of Turkish healthcare system after health transformation program: Main successes, performance assessment, further challenges, and policy options. *Sosyal Güvence*, 7, 83–112.

Herr, A., Stühmeier, T., & Wenzel, T. (2014). Reference pricing and cost-sharing: Theory and evidence on German off-patent drugs. In *Beiträge zur Jahrestagung des Vereins für Socialpolitik 2014*. https://www.econstor.eu/bitstream/10419/100556/1/VfS_2014_pid_411.pdf

İ.E.İ.S. (2023). *Turkish pharmaceutical report 2023*. https://www.ieis.org.tr/static/shared/publications/pdf/26624aGVi_tr_ilac_sektoru_raporu_2023.pdf

I.Q.V.I.A. (2023). https://www.efpia.eu/media/s4qf1eqo/efpia_patient_wait_indicator_final_report.pdf

İlgün, G., Konca, M., & Sönmez, S. (2023). The Relationship between the health transformation program and health expenditures: Evidence from an autoregressive distributed lag testing approach. *Value in Health Regional Issues*, 38, 101–108.

Lakdawalla, D. N., Doshi, J. A., Garrison Jr, L. P., Phelps, C. E., Basu, A., & Danzon, P. M. (2018). Defining elements of value in health care – a health economics approach: An ISPOR special task force report [3]. *Value in Health*, 21(2), 131–139.

Lichtenberg, F. R. (2019). The impact of pharmaceutical innovation on the burden of disease in Canada, 2000–2016. *SSM-Population Health*, 8, 100457.

OECD. (2023). *Health at a glance 2023: OECD indicators*. OECD Publishing, Paris. https://doi.org/10.1787/7a7afb35-en.

Paulden, M. (2024). A framework for the fair pricing of medicines. *Pharmacoeconomics*, 42(2), 145–164.

Porter, M. E. (2009). A strategy for health care reform – toward a value-based system. *New England Journal of Medicine*, 361(2), 109–112.

Porter, M. E., & Teisberg, E. O. (2006). *Redefining Health care: Creating value-based competition on results*. Harvard Business School Press.

TurkStat. (2023). https://data.tuik.gov.tr/Bulten/Index?p=Saglik-Harcamalari-Istatistikleri-2023-53561

World Health Organization. (2000). *Health sector reform issues and opportunities*. https://iris.who.int/bitstream/handle/10665/127574/WP_HlthSecRefm_Final%20Version.pdf?sequence=1&isAllowed=y

Chapter 4

Strangers in a New Land: Evaluating the Diagnostic Effectiveness of the Turkish Health System in the Context of Syrian Refugees

İlhan Can Özen and Berna Tuncay Alpanda

Contents

4.1 Introduction

The increasing population of refugees creates several challenges to the healthcare systems of the receiving host countries and populations. Nevertheless, refugees may need more healthcare services in the context of an initial reception centre concerning mental disorders as well as specific infectious diseases. Forced migrants are typically displaced from poor economic conditions, and they arrive in the host country with low health profiles as a result of poverty (Tuncay et al., 2022). Therefore, it is

DOI: 10.4324/9781003539896-5

crucially important to determine the possible medical needs of refugees through their utilization of health services resulting in the medical diagnoses given by the healthcare providers.

The forced migration in Syria in recent years is one of the most important migration events in history. The civil war started in 2011 in Syria and millions of Syrians had to leave their home country with great difficulty. Over 3.5 million of these refugees moved to Turkey until the end of 2016 (TDEMA, 2017). Syrian refugees are entitled to temporary residence permits by the Turkish government, and all refugees are given right to benefit from healthcare facilities in the same way as native residents (Tuncay et al., 2022). This large influx of Syrian refugees and the generous policies implemented by the Turkish government have put pressure on the health system in Turkey (Savas et al., 2016). Several studies report that the high level of healthcare utilization among Syrian refugees caused capacity problems in hospitals and diminished access to healthcare services in the border provinces (Center for Middle Eastern Strategic Studies, 2015; Ekmekci, 2017).

Over the past decade, Turkish authorities have implemented effective healthcare reforms through the Health Transformation Programme (H.T.P) to improve crucial health variables such as maternal mortality, infant mortality, life expectancy, and access to healthcare services. Universal Health Coverage (U.H.C.) is one of these effective health system reforms that have expanded health insurance coverage and increased patient's access to healthcare services (Tuncay et al., 2022). Moreover, Turkey's recent strides in healthcare have highlighted a pivotal shift toward equity in diagnosis and treatment across its public healthcare system. While the introduction of electronic health records (E.H.R.) is instrumental in facilitating anonymized data access for research, the fundamental improvement in diagnosis and treatment outcomes stems from the more equitable distribution of diagnostic and treatment resources. This equitable distribution includes imaging technologies, technicians, specialized clinics, doctors, and treatment machinery which have been more evenly dispersed across the country's healthcare landscape. The recent refugee influx gives us a crucial context, where the diagnosis and treatment capacities of the health system had to be put into the service of a population that was especially vulnerable in terms of health demand and health needs. Not only this, but also the health system that was providing generous services to them had very little experience with providing for this specific group (Syrians with little to no Turkish), and a sizeable refugee group coming straight from a war experience created significant human costs and maladies on this group, in general.

Turkish health system has undergone a significant "upgrading" in the 2010–2020 period, where the number of intensive care beds; the number of specialists; the number of hospitals; and the number, spread, and use of imaging technology per capita have increased by significant amounts. However, all these curative dimensions overlook the crucial position of diagnostic capabilities and achievements in the health system. Without correct diagnosis, all these upgrades on the treatment level will influence the costs, but not necessarily the effectiveness of health services. The influx of Syrian refugees into Turkey since 2011 has posed numerous challenges to the Turkish healthcare system. One critical issue has been the significantly higher rate of underdiagnoses among Syrian refugees during the initial integration period. This study aims to investigate why Syrian refugees experienced significantly higher rates of underdiagnoses at the start of their integration into the Turkish health system, and what the micro-regressors of underdiagnoses reveal about the integration process and the broader characteristics and limitations of the Turkish health system. By leveraging extensive electronic health records (E.H.R.) data and a rich set of regressors, we provide unprecedented insights into the factors driving underdiagnoses and the systemic challenges within the Turkish healthcare framework.

The rest of the chapter is organized as follows. The next section provides a literature review, Section 4.3 describes the data and empirical methodology. The results are given in Section 4.4. Discussion and conclusion are provided in Section 4.5.

4.2 Literature Review

The health integration of refugees has been widely studied, with a focus on the barriers and facilitators to accessing healthcare services (Norredam et al., 2006; Woodgate et al., 2017). These studies highlight the importance of understanding the specific needs of refugee populations and the systemic adjustments required to accommodate these needs. In the context of underdiagnosis, research has identified various contributing factors, including healthcare provider workload, diagnostic capabilities, and resource allocation.

Studies have shown that underdiagnosis can lead to poorer health outcomes and increased healthcare costs, underscoring the importance of accurate and timely diagnoses. Evans et al. (2015) state that discordance in the classification of tuberculosis (TB) disease overseas compared to classification in the United States has been observed among immigrant populations between 2005 and 2012. Their findings suggest that TB misclassification among recent immigrants evaluated at a refugee/community health centre remains widespread, and screening procedures both before and after resettlement should be better synchronized. Gubi et al. (2022) investigated the underutilization of mental health services among migrant youth and found that migrant children were exposed to underdiagnoses of several mental health conditions, and, when reaching mental health services, they were not able to receive the optimal care available.

The existing literature on refugee health integration and underdiagnosis provides essential context for this study. Research has shown that refugees often face barriers to accessing healthcare, including language barriers, cultural differences, and lack of familiarity with the healthcare system (Norredam et al., 2006; Woodgate et al., 2017). Underdiagnosis, particularly in vulnerable populations, has been linked to systemic issues such as resource allocation, healthcare provider workload, and diagnostic capabilities (Starfield et al., 2005). Kleinert et al. (2019) state that refugees' diagnoses are difficult to assess because of the short duration of treatment and serious language barriers. Some symptoms must exist for a certain period of time in order to be diagnosed. Therefore, it is possible to say that refugees can be underdiagnosed regarding their health status and medical needs. Halley et al. (2021) compare the precarious migrants' health problems managed in Médecins du Monde's health and social care centres (C.A.S.O.) with those of patients attending general practice in France and find that both chronic somatic and mental conditions of precarious migrants are presumably underdiagnosed. The authors suggest that their screening should be improved in primary care. Maier et al. (2010) investigated adult refugees' mental health status and healthcare utilization in Switzerland. Their results show that refugees face higher healthcare expenditures than comparable residents, and mentally ill refugees are underdiagnosed and insufficiently treated.

Moreover, regarding chronic diseases, several other studies show that the statistics for COPD and asthma conditions are likely to be underdiagnosed among undocumented migrant adults in primary healthcare. The main reasons might be due to the lower frequency of their visits to primary healthcare services or access barriers such as sociocultural norms or fear of deportation (Dalmau-Bueno et al., 2021; Mladovsky et al., 2012; Willen, 2012). Similarly, Jelastopulu et al. (2009), Odone et al. (2011), Rossi et al. (2017), and Watkins et al. (2005) report that the most important reason for underdiagnosis is the barriers to healthcare service access faced by refugees. They emphasized that the most obvious barrier for migrants to infectious disease reporting is the fear of being classified as irregular residents. Our study contributes to the literature by providing a detailed analysis of underdiagnosis within the Turkish health system using a unique and extensive dataset of E.H.R.

4.3 Data and Methodology

This study utilizes an unprecedented dataset of electronic health records (E.H.R.) from the Turkish health system (for services provided for Syrians Under Temporary Protection Status (S.U.T.P.S)) covering a wide range of variables including patient age, time of the day of application, hospital role group, severity score, doctor utilization levels for Syrian groups, and MR machine utilization rates of the hospitals (see Table 4.1). This panel data, with an unsurpassed size in the number of patients, institutions, and institution types that it covers in the public healthcare system of Turkey, can be used to answer many questions. However, we propose to utilize the size and richness of this dataset to provide a comprehensive view of the factors influencing underdiagnosis in Turkey, which we believe has been understudied for all populations.

While the regression setup employed in this study is not novel, the measurement of underdiagnosis, using a specific code (R_Code_Prob) consistently identified and applied across the health system combined with the extensive data available with a significant time dimension, offers unique insights into the systemic issues impacting healthcare delivery in Turkey. R_Codes that we have zeroed in on have the common characteristic of being defined by "Symptoms, Signs, and Abnormal Clinical and Laboratory Findings, Not Elsewhere Classified". After classifying this as underdiagnosis, we also note that for Turkish citizens, there is also a much longer time trend, where the R-code prevalence, which stood at 6.25% around 2005, was able to be decreased to around 2.5% by 2015 as the diagnosis capacities, standardization, and spread of skilled personnel in the treatment and diagnosis arm of the system grew exponentially in this period. 2011–2015 was a significant period, where this same-time trend held for the Turkish citizen population for the reasons listed before.

Despite the advantages, there are limitations to using E.H.R. data. Potential issues include data entry errors, variability in data quality across different healthcare providers, and the possibility of missing data. Additionally, E.H.R. data may not capture all relevant patient information, such as socioeconomic status or detailed clinical histories, which could affect the analysis.

The regression results in the chapter aim to explore the factors contributing to "underdiagnosis" events, which signify either incomplete diagnoses or compromised diagnostic capabilities. In the analysis, the effects of several variables thought to affect accurate and complete diagnosis in the literature are examined at different levels. This will be the analysis at the level of the doctor, the level of

Table 4.1 Descriptives of the Dataset

Variables	R Code Observations	Size of Dataset
Observation # (E.H.R.)	1.275.480	10.444.322
Patient #	514.578	4.749.569
Hospital #	1.762	7.912
Doctor #	15.330	42.900

the hospital, and the level of the patient and the illness. The doctors will be limited in their diagnosis capacity, as their mental capacity is overtaxed, which is checked for by looking at the times of the day and days of the year when the doctors will be expected to be overtaxed, either due to overwork and fatigue (in the later part of the day) or due to the fact that the auxiliary personnel's help will be at a minimum (vacation days, when public hospitals are at most half-staffed). At the hospital level, the predictor of diagnosis capacities was the intensity[1] of how they used their imaging machines, which is a plus if they are using it actively, with a certain number of auxiliary staff, but we also look at the right tail of the distribution, where overuse might create quality issues and congestion issues, which might be limiting their use in times of special need, when they are necessary assets of diagnosis. At the level of the patient, we look at the age and gender of the patient to see whether these predictors have a significant effect. At the level of the disease, we look at the severity of the disease to see if the more serious diseases are more or less likely to be underdiagnosed, where there is a possibility that a lower diagnosis ability makes a disease less correctly treated, which can itself increase the severity of the disease (bidirectional causality). We look at the subsequent development of the disease-application trajectory to see if there is a significant effect here.

In our regression analysis, the dependent variable is an R Code Observation which is a binary variable indicating if the diagnosis is classified as an "underdiagnosis". Independent variables are summarized as follows:

- time_category: Indicator of the time of the day; 0 reference category for the start of the day, 1 for the middle of the day, 2 for later in the day.
- day_category: Indicator for whether it is a vacation day.
- central_hospital: Indicator of whether the hospital is a central hospital (1 if central, 0 otherwise).
- severity_score: A continuous variable representing the severity of the individualized disease.
- MR_capacity_hospital: Continuous variable representing the MR diagnostic capacity that is currently used (per machine) at the hospital level.

Our regression equation (logistical distribution is assumed) is defined as given in the following format:

$$R\_Code\_Prob_i = \beta 0 + \beta 1 Patient\_Age_i + \beta 2 time\_category1_i + \beta 3 time\_category2_i + \beta 4 day\_category\ (Vacation\ Day)I + \beta 5 hospital\_role\_group\ (Other)I + \beta 6 severity\_score_i + \beta 7 doctor\_utilization\_levels1_i + \beta 8 doctor\_utilization\_levels2_i + \beta 9 MR\_utilization\_levels1_i + \beta 10 MR\_utilization\_levels2_i + u_i$$

4.4 Empirical Results

4.4.1 Main Findings

Our analysis indicates the following key findings:

In Table 4.2, the positive and statistically significant coefficient for time_category 2 indicates that the likelihood of "underdiagnosis" observation becomes significantly higher later in the day.

Table 4.2 Regression Results

Variables	Time Category2	Central Hospital	MR Capacity at Hospital	Severity Score	Patient Age	Day Category
Coefficient	0.0374939	0.0182033	−4.87e-06	0.0077136	0.0067861	0.3624409
Standard error	0.0083395	0.00562	1.17e-07	0.0000208	0.0000486	0.0027777
t-Value and z-value	4.50 (t-value)	3.24 (t-value)	−41.69 (z-value)	370.33 (z-value)	139.61 (z-value)	130.48 (z-value)
p-Value	0.000	0.001	0.000	0.000	0.000	0.000
95% confidence interval	[0.0211462, 0.0538415]	[0.0071867, 0.02922]	[−5.10e-06, −4.64e-06]	[0.0076728, 0.0077544]	[0.0066908, 0.0068814]	[0.3569967, 0.367885]

This suggests that doctors' diagnostic capabilities may be diminished due to mental fatigue after seeing many patients. The positive and statistically significant coefficient for central_hospital suggests that central hospitals are more likely to report "underdiagnosis" codes compared to noncentral hospitals. This might be due to central hospitals handling more complex cases or higher patient loads. Higher MR diagnostic capacity at hospitals is significantly associated with a lower likelihood of underdiagnosis. This indicates that better diagnostic facilities contribute to more accurate diagnoses.

In addition, the positive and statistically significant coefficient for severity_score indicates that as the severity of the disease increases, the likelihood of an "underdiagnosis event" also increases. This suggests that more severe cases are harder to diagnose accurately, leading to a higher probability of underdiagnosis. This would make a negative feedback loop, where worse cases, untreated or mistreated due to underdiagnosis, could lead to a significant burden on the healthcare system and on the patients who are unfortunate to fall into said category. The positive and statistically significant coefficient for patient age indicates that as patients age, the likelihood of an underdiagnosis increases slightly. This might be due to older patients presenting with more complex medical histories, making accurate diagnosis more challenging. Vacation days are associated with a higher likelihood of underdiagnosis, potentially due to reduced staffing and increased workload on available healthcare providers.

4.4.2 Implications for Diagnosis and Treatment in the Turkish Healthcare System

4.4.2.1 Regional and Institutional Factors

The significant impact of regional differences, particularly in Istanbul (where the more complicated cases are referred), and the role of central hospitals indicate resource overflow and complexity while ensuring equitable distribution of diagnostic resources across regions and addressing specific challenges in high-volume hospitals through targeted resource allocation and support.

4.4.2.2 Diagnostic Capacity

The negative correlation between MR diagnostic capacity and underdiagnosis events highlights the importance of investing in diagnostic technologies while ensuring equitable distribution of advanced diagnostic tools across all hospitals and providing training for healthcare professionals to effectively use these technologies.

4.4.2.3 Analysis of Syrian Refugees at the Level of the Diagnosis Code

The preliminary analysis suggests that Syrian refugees received "underdiagnosis" codes significantly more frequently than the native Turkish population during the initial period of integration (2012–2014). Specifically, the rate of "underdiagnosis" codes for refugees was 12.2% of all diagnoses during the first period, compared to 7.37% in the following period, where the health integration improved, whereas the rate for the Turkish native population remained relatively stable at around 2.4% in both periods. Syrians can be especially vulnerable at the starting period to this high severity-low diagnosis negative feedback loop. The results are consistent with an earlier study (Tuncay et al., 2022), where a significant health shock was observed in the Turkish healthcare system during the 2012–2014 period, with a relatively fast period of adaptation and integration, occurring largely due to the efforts of the Turkish health workforce in 2015 and 2016. Our initial results from 2012 to 2014 also point to an adaptation process, where Turkish doctors with significant interaction with the Syrian patient group (as measured by doctor utilization levels) do much better in terms of avoiding underdiagnosis for this S.U.T.P.S. group. Whether this is due to patient selection effects, where the Syrians select the doctors who will give them a more complete diagnosis, must be investigated in a different study.

4.4.2.4 Time of the Day and Mental Fatigue

The significant increase in the likelihood of underdiagnosis toward the end of the day highlights the critical impact of mental fatigue on diagnostic accuracy. This finding suggests the need for interventions to manage doctors' workloads more effectively while implementing rotational schedules to balance patient load throughout the day and providing additional support and breaks for doctors during peak hours.

4.4.2.5 Disease Severity

The positive relationship between disease severity and the likelihood of an underdiagnosis underscores the challenges faced in diagnosing more complex cases. This finding calls for:

- Enhanced training programs focused on diagnosing complex and severe conditions.
- Investment in advanced diagnostic tools and technologies to support doctors in making accurate diagnoses for severe cases.

When we divided and focused on the observations where the first visit to the Turkish health system for a Syrian refugee led to an underdiagnosis, we were able to show how this was operational in leading to higher disease severities down the road.

The provided Table 4.3 shows the results of a two-sample *t*-test comparing the subsequent severity score based on whether the first visit resulted in an underdiagnosis (first_visit_R_code = 1) or not (first_visit_R_code = 0).

Summary of results is given as follows:

Table 4.3 Two-Sample *t*-Test Results

Group	Observations	Mean Severity Score	Std. Error	Std. Dev.	95% Confidence Interval
0	9,851,827	−1.413611	0.0128406	40.30368	[−1.438778, −1.388444]
1	500,290	11.63645	0.0045247	3.200402	[11.62759, 11.64532]
Combined	10,352,117	−0.7829366	0.0122529	39.42349	[−0.8069519, −0.7589212]
Difference		−13.05006	0.0569906		[−13.16176, −12.93837]

1. Mean Severity Score:
   ■ For patients whose first visit did not lead to an underdiagnosis (first_visit_R_code = 0), the mean subsequent severity score is −1.413611.
   ■ For patients whose first visit resulted in an underdiagnosis (first_visit_R_code = 1), the mean subsequent severity score is 11.63645.
2. Difference in Means:
   ■ The difference in mean severity scores between the two groups is −13.05006.
   ■ This difference is statistically significant with a p-value of 0.0000, indicating that the observed difference is not due to random chance.
3. Standard Errors and Confidence Intervals:
   ■ The standard errors are 0.0128406 for group 0 and 0.0045247 for group 1.
   ■ The 95% confidence intervals for the mean severity scores do not overlap, further supporting the conclusion that there is a significant difference between the two groups.

These results indicate that patients who experienced an underdiagnosis during their first visit (indicated by first_visit_R_code = 1) have a significantly higher subsequent severity score compared to those who did not experience an underdiagnosis during their first visit. The mean subsequent severity score for the underdiagnosed patient group is significantly higher (11.63645) than the non-underdiagnosed patient group (−1.413611), with a large and statistically significant difference in means (−13.05006). This suggests that initial underdiagnosis is associated with more severe health outcomes in subsequent visits, highlighting the importance of accurate and timely diagnosis, especially for vulnerable populations such as Syrian refugees. The findings underscore the need for interventions to improve diagnostic accuracy and reduce the occurrence of underdiagnosis to prevent worsening health conditions over time. The demand conditions (and their impact) faced by doctors are crucial in determining the probability of more consistent, complete, and actionable disease diagnoses. The time of the day, as indicated by the significant coefficient for time_category 2, plays a critical role.[2] Doctors seeing patients later in the day may experience mental fatigue, leading to an increased likelihood of incomplete or compromised diagnoses.

4.5 Discussion and Conclusion

The primary objective of this study is to uncover the reasons and challenges associated with correct diagnosis in the Turkish healthcare system, particularly, though not exclusively, for vulnerable populations such as Syrian refugees.[3] The research has allowed us to conclude that the following healthcare factors should be examined more thoroughly for a sustainable healthcare path with a better average diagnostic ability:

- Resource Allocation: Ensuring equitable distribution of diagnostic resources, including imaging technologies and skilled personnel, across different regions and hospitals is crucial.
- Healthcare Accessibility: Assessing the accessibility of healthcare services for refugees and other marginalized groups matters. Research has already shown that in general accessibility for refugees, the healthcare system of Turkey grades especially high for the significant number it is giving service to. However, giving access to the resources must be followed by giving access to correct and effective treatment, which has to follow scaling correct and complicated diagnosis challenges.
- Diagnostic Protocols: Evaluating the consistency and thoroughness of diagnostic protocols across different healthcare settings forms the basis of a well-functioning health system. Although our regression results are signalling the problem in central hospitals, the truth is that this could be a "composition effect" bias, which is generated when the smaller hospitals just look after the simplest cases, leaving the bulk of the health burden and the more complicated part of the health burden to the centralized and already heavily burdened general hospitals in the public healthcare system.
- Impact of Central Hospitals: Understanding why central hospitals are more likely to report "unknown disease" diagnoses and identifying areas for improvement are important to create a more advanced healthcare system.

The final regression results underscore significant temporal, age-related, regional, and disease-severity-related differences in the likelihood of underdiagnosis within the Turkish healthcare system. Addressing these disparities in underdiagnosis requires a comprehensive analysis of the factors influencing diagnostic accuracy and completeness, with a particular focus on vulnerable populations such as Syrian refugees. By leveraging E.H.R. data and conducting thorough comparative analyses, researchers can provide actionable insights to policymakers and healthcare providers, ultimately aiming to improve diagnostic outcomes and healthcare equity across the nation. This endeavour underscores the importance of addressing demand conditions and systemic challenges to ensure equitable healthcare access and quality for all Turkish citizens, as well as the refugees who have been afforded full access to the public healthcare institutions of Turkey.

4.6 Acknowledgment

This work is supported by TÜBİTAK, the Scientific and Technological Research Council of Turkey under grant number 22AG008.

Notes

1 Intensity was measured as monthly use of these machines, per every machine the hospital owned.
2 The difference between the start and the middle of the day being insignificant in generating underdiagnosis suggests that the effect is far from linear, having a much more cumulative effect issue, where the significant problem becomes significantly worse in the later time of the day.
3 In the reference period of this study (2012—2014), the underdiagnosis rates for the Syrian population were five times the Turkish citizen average (12.2% to 2.4%). In the secondary part of the dataset (2015–2016) with only a cursory examination, the rate of underdiagnosis for the Syrian population nearly halved though still representing a significantly higher proportion compared to the Turkish citizen number.

References

Center for Middle Eastern Strategic Studies (ORSAM). 2015. *Effects of the Syrian refugees on Turkey*, ORSAM Report No: 195.

Dalmau-Bueno, A., García-Altés, A., Vela, E., Clèries, M., Pérez, C.V., and Argimon, J.M. 2021. Frequency of health-care service use and severity of illness in undocumented migrants in Catalonia, Spain: A population based, cross-sectional study. *Lancet Planet Health*. 5: e286–96.

Ekmekci, P.E. 2017. Syrian refugees, health and migration legislation in Turkey. *J Immigr Minor Health*. 19(6): 1434–1441.

Evans, T.B., Mador, M.J., Glick, M., and Ahmad, I. 2015. Tuberculosis misclassification among resettled refugees in Buffalo, New York, USA. *Int J Tuberc Lung Dis*. 19(2): 231–236.

Gubi, E., Sjöqvist, H., Viksten-Assel, K., Bäärnhielm, S., Dalman, C., and Hollander, AC. 2022. Mental health service use among migrant and Swedish-born children and youth: A register-based cohort study of 472,129 individuals in Stockholm. *Soc Psychiatry Psychiatr Epidemiol*. 57(1): 161–171.

Halley, E., Giai, J., Chappuis, M., Tomasino, A., Henaine, R., and Letrilliart, L. 2021. Health profile of precarious migrants attending the Médecins du Monde's health and social care centres in France: A cross-sectional study. *Int J Public Health*. 66: 602394.

Jelastopulu, E., Alexopoulos, E.C., Venieri, D., Tsiros, G., Komninou, G., Constantinidis, T.C., and Chrysanthopoulos, K. 2009. Substantial underreporting of tuberculosis in West Greece: Implications for local and national surveillance. *Euro Surveill*. 14.

Kleinert, E., Müller, F., Furaijat, G., Hillermann, N., Jablonka, A., Happle, C., and Simmenroth, A. 2019. Does refugee status matter? Medical needs of newly arrived asylum seekers and resettlement refugees – a retrospective observational study of diagnoses in a primary care setting. *Conflict and Health*. 13: 39.

Maier, T., Schmidt, M., and Mueller, J. 2010. Mental health and healthcare utilisation in adult asylum seekers. *Swiss Med Wkly*. 140: w13110.

Mladovsky, P., Ingleby, D., McKee, M., and Rechel, B. 2012. Good practices in migrant health: The European experience. *Clin Med*. 12: 248–252.

Norredam, M., Mygind, A., and Krasnik, A. 2006. Access to health care for asylum seekers in the European Union – a comparative study of country policies. *Eur J Public Health*. 16(3): 286–290.

Odone, A., Riccò, M., Morandi, M., Borrini, B.M., Pasquarella, C., and Signorelli, C. 2011. Epidemiology of tuberculosis in a low-incidence Italian region with high immigration rates: Differences between not Italy-born and Italy-born TB cases. *BMC Public Health*. 11: 376.

Rossi, P.G., Riccardo, F., Pezzarossi, A., Ballotari, P., Dente, M.G., Napoli, C., Chiarenza, A., Munoz, C.V., Noori, T., and Declich, S. 2017. Factors influencing the accuracy of infectious disease reporting in migrants: A scoping review. *Int J Environ Res Public Health*. 14: 720.

Savas, N., Arslan, E., Inandi, T., Yeniceri, A., Erdem, M., Kabacagoglu, M., Peker, E., and Aliskin, O. 2016. Syrian refugees in Hatay/Turkey and their influence on health care at the university hospital. *Int J Clin Exp Med*. 9(9): 18281–18290.

Starfield, B., Shi, L., and Macinko, J. 2005. Contribution of primary care to health systems and health. *Milbank Q*. 83(3): 457–502.

TDEMA, Turkish Disaster and Emergency Management Authority (AFAD). 2017. *Population influx from Syria to Turkey, Life in Turkey as a Syrian guest*. AFAD.

Tuncay, B., Özen, İ.C., and Bump, J.B. 2022. Shelter from the storm: health service access and utilization among Syrian refugees in Turkey. *J Public Health*. 30(11): 2627–2640.

Watkins, R.E., Plant, A.J., Sang, D., O'Rourke, T.F., Eltom, A.A., Streeton, J., and Gushulak, B. 2005. The association between subjective and clinical indicators of health in prospective Vietnamese migrants. *Asia Pac J Public Health*. 17: 46–50.

Willen, S.S. 2012. Migration, "illegality," and health: Mapping embodied vulnerability and debating health-related deservingness. *Soc Sci Med*. 74: 805–811.

Woodgate, R.L., Busolo, D.S., Crockett, M., Dean, R.A., Amaladas, M.R., and Plourde, P.J. 2017. A qualitative study on African immigrant and refugee families' experiences of accessing primary health care services in Manitoba, Canada: It's not easy!. *Int J Equity Health*. 16: 5.

Chapter 5

Efficiency of Private Hospitals under the Health Transformation Programme

Seher Nur Sülkü, Yağmur Tokatlıoğlu,
Aziz Küçük, and Alper Mortaş

Contents

5.1 Introduction

The private healthcare sector has become a crucial player in health-care provision in many low- and middle-income countries in recent decades (Sriram et al., 2024). According to the literature, people prefer private hospitals due to the perceived higher quality of care, better hygienic conditions, accountability, and various services at the household level (Prasad, 2013; Lakshmi et al., 2020). In addition, the ratio of health workers and health facilities to the population, differences between the development levels of a country's regions, and rural/urban characteristics are seen as facilitating factors at the public level (Andersen and Newman, 2005). Moreover, the availability of affordable health insurance and the convenience of public hospitals also influence hospital choice

DOI: 10.4324/9781003539896-6

(Kassean and Juwaheer, 2010). Since the performance of the private healthcare sector is inherently linked to the organization and performance of the public sector, to ensure that population benefit from the private sector, health system regulators should take a holistic approach to the entire health-care sector (Morgan et al., 2016).

In Turkey, since the launch of the "Health Transformation Programme" (H.T.P.) in 2003, private healthcare sector has flourished. The policies implemented within the scope of the H.T.P. aimed to improve the quality of healthcare services, expand access to healthcare, strengthen the healthcare infrastructure, and make the healthcare system more effective, efficient, and sustainable. The introduction of Universal Health Insurance (U.H.I.) in 2008 ended the private–public distinction in treatment services, as the costs of treatments in private hospitals were covered by the Social Security Institution (S.S.I.) through a protocol signed between them.

During the first phase of the H.T.P., the largest growth in the number of hospitals and beds was seen in the private sector: The number of private hospitals increased by 47.60% to 400, while the number of beds rose by 69% to almost 21,000 from 2002 to 2008. The upward trend continued during the second phase of the reforms. By 2022, the private sector accounted for almost 37% of all hospitals with 572 hospitals and had 21% of all hospital beds (M.o.H., 2024). According to Griffin (1989), increasing the number of privately owned hospitals is an alternative and complement to the privatization of public hospitals. Incentives to the private sector, such as allowing them to bill extra, public hospitals outsourcing diagnostic/diagnostic services to the private sector, and increased access to private sector health services, have led to a greater than expected increase in the number of private hospitals and payments to these facilities. In parallel, the number of admissions to private hospitals has increased more than 12-fold in the last 20 years (M.o.H., 2024). This growth has been driven by the increase in private health insurance as well as the fact that all citizens under the S.S.I. agreement can benefit from private hospitals.

In Turkey, the shortage of health workers is one of the most significant problems in the health-care system. In 2021, the total numbers of physicians and nurses and midwives per 100,000 population were, respectively, 203.6 and 340 (World Bank, 2024), well below the W.H.O. Strategic Development Goal index threshold of 445 (W.H.O., 2016). Since 2004, a performance-based payment system has been introduced to public hospitals to promote the performance of healthcare personnel and compensate for the increased demand since the improved access was brought about by the H.T.P. reforms (Sulku, 2012). Indeed, the increase in the number of private healthcare facilities was intended to alleviate the workload of public hospitals. However, as the private health sector expanded due to the incentives of the H.T.P., the private sector's high wage policy for doctors due to the competition has worsened the problem of insufficient health workers in the public sector. This situation further exacerbates barriers to access such as long waiting times and late appointments in public facilities (Tokatlioglu and Sulku, 2023; Sulku et al., 2023). In order to encourage doctors to work in public hospitals, the Ministry of Health (M.o.H.) has introduced a full-time work parameter in performance payments. A draft law on the transition to full-time practice in public hospitals was drafted in June 2009. However, after a challenge in the Constitutional Court, the new rearrangements required only the staff at the M.o.H. facilities to choose between full-time public or private practice, while staff based in public university facilities could still practice in both sectors, provided that their daily full-time public duties were met first. In 2011, the full-time law for healthcare staff came into force.

In order to ensure financial sustainability, private hospitals that have a contract with the S.S.I. were allowed to charge a maximum price difference of 30% to the price of the Health Implementation Communiqué (H.I.C.) in July 2008. Currently, private hospitals with an S.S.I. contract can charge up to 200% differential fees. The S.S.I. covers all or part of the costs for private hospitals, so the remaining costs must be paid as private expenses. Since 2013, amounts exceeding the statutory health insurance prices can be covered by supplementary or complementary insurance (S.S.I. circular 2012/25).

Due to the scarcity of resources in health systems, improving efficiency is one of the key issues of the H.T.P. in both the provision and financing of healthcare. In this chapter, we will look at the efficiency of the Turkish hospital sector from the perspective of private hospitals. The literature on hospital efficiency in Turkey is dominated by studies focusing on public hospitals (Sülkü et al., 2023; Bağcı and Çil Koçyiğit, 2023; Manavgat and Demirci, 2020; İlgün and Konca, 2019; Şahin and İlgün, 2019). Although Özgen Narcı et al. (2015) and Yildiz et al. (2018) have analysed the hospital sector in both the public and private sectors, their studies are based on data from 2010 and 2012, respectively. We aim to contribute to the literature by analysing the efficiency of private hospitals using the most recent data from the Turkish Ministry of Health for the period [2019–2023] through stochastic frontier analysis (S.F.A.).

Data Envelopment Analysis (D.E.A.) and S.F.A. are the most commonly used methods for measuring efficiency in any sector, including healthcare (Yeşilyurt et al., 2021; Hollingsworth and Wildman, 2003). D.E.A. is a nonparametric method that enables us to analyse multiple outputs and inputs simultaneously. On the other hand, S.F.A. is a parametric method that allows us to examine one output at a time using multiple inputs. However, S.F.A. introduces an error term that is beyond the control of decision units. Given that our study period encompasses the COVID-19 pandemic and the 2023 earthquake, utilizing S.F.A. instead of D.E.A. will help us understand how external factors, outside of management's control, may affect hospitals' production function. We expect that our findings will offer valuable insights for private sector healthcare providers seeking to enhance their performance. Since the private sector is a major source of healthcare delivery, measuring its efficiency is crucial for developing intelligent strategies for regulators to create a comprehensive approach to shaping the entire healthcare system.

The rest of this chapter is organized as follows. First, the evolution of the dynamics of the private hospital sector under the Turkish health reforms is discussed. Second, the S.F.A. methodology is explained, and the dataset is introduced through a basic descriptive analysis. Third, the findings of S.F.A. and private hospitals' production functions' returns to scale analysis are presented in the empirical findings section. Finally, our results are discussed, and the study is concluded.

5.2 The Development of Private Hospitals in Turkey via Health Transformation Programme

Private hospitals are healthcare institutions owned by natural or private legal entities that provide outpatient and inpatient examination, diagnosis, and treatment services to patients in one or more specialties on a continuous and regular basis, 24 hours a day, provided they meet the minimum building, service, and personnel standards stipulated by the legislation (Official Gazette, 2002).

The development of private hospitals in Turkey is based on Law No. 2219 on Private Hospitals, published in 1933. During these years, most hospitals were located in big cities such as Istanbul and were mostly owned by minorities and foreigners. For this reason, after the 1950s, the government tended to remove obstacles for private entrepreneurs. For example, during the planned development period, draft laws were prepared with privileges such as financial support and tax exemptions to encourage the private sector and develop private hospitalization (Tunca, 1965). However, although this picture started to change with the neoliberal policies implemented after 1980, private hospitalization did not achieve the desired development until the second half of the 1990s. As a result of the incentives transferred from public resources to the private health sector during this period, "the share of private sector investments in total health investments, which was 9% in 1980, reached 35% in 1992. The most important feature of these investments is that they were made in technology-intensive areas and 50% of them were based on imports" (Gökçay, 1995). Despite all these incentive measures, it was observed that real investments in the field of "private hospitalization" have not been realized; in other words, contrary to expectations, the private sector, whose tax burden has been eased, has not directed its efforts toward investments. In 1982, the number of private hospitals (including associations, private individuals, foreigners, and minorities for comparison) was 101, whereas this figure rose to only 115 in 1990. During the same period, the ratio of private hospitals to total hospitals declined from 16% to 13%. Similarly, the proportion of private hospital beds remained at 4.3%, and the number of polyclinics remained at 6 per 1,000 (Küçük, 2018). Therefore, there has been no qualitative or quantitative positive change in favour of the private sector regarding the development toward the liberalization of the private sector based on a market economy in the field of private hospitalization.

Between 1994 and 2000, public health services did not experience a significant growth due to crises and financial constraints. However, there was a notable increase in the number of private hospitals during this time, which reflects a shift in the role and function of the state. In 1994, there were 144 private hospitals, but by 2000, this number had grown to 261. The share of private hospitals in the total number of hospitals also increased from 14% in 1994 to 19% in 2000. One of the main reasons for this growth was the introduction of investment incentive measures after 1994. In the health sector, there were 773 investment incentive certificates issued between 1992 and 1999, totalling over 500 billion TL. This led to the private sector expanding significantly, as they were able to benefit from the state supports provided through these certificates. As a result, the health sector became one of the most encouraged areas for investment. Furthermore, it is important to consider that Turkey signed the 1994 G.A.T.S. agreement in 1995 as a founding member of the World Trade Organization. One of the sectors to which Turkey committed was health-related social services, specifically hospital services. This commitment also played a role in the development of the private hospital sector during this time.

The "Health Transformation Programme" has been the driving force behind the growth of private hospitals. The private healthcare sector has expanded rapidly over the last two decades due to the demographic structure, the demand for quality healthcare services, and the investments made. The impact of private health institutions and organizations providing services to citizens covered by public insurance can be seen in the increase in the number of private hospitals during this period. As shown in Figure 5.1, while the number of M.o.H. hospitals increased by a modest 18% between 2002 and 2022, the number of private hospitals rose by 110%, from 271 in 2002 to 572 in 2022 (M.o.H., 2024).

As seen in Table 5.1, the total number of visits to physicians and surgical operations in private hospitals increased enormously from 2002 to 2022. In Turkey, currently, all S.S.I.-covered citizens can access services from private hospitals that have contracts with the institution. A portion of the private healthcare services provided are covered by the S.S.I., while private hospitals may also charge an additional fee, as long as it does not exceed the rate set by the S.S.I., which is paid by the patient. One of the major obstacles to the growth of the private sector is that health planners often limit the private sector on the grounds that it serves only wealthy individuals. However, in Turkey, in 2003, with the "Regulation on the Addition of an Additional Article to the Regulation on Treatment Assistance and Funeral Expenses of Civil Servants", civil servants were allowed to be referred to private health institutions for treatment from official health institutions and organizations. To establish procedures and principles in line with this regulation, the "Protocol Determining the Procedures and Principles of Patient Referral to Private Health Institutions" was signed between the M.o.H. and the

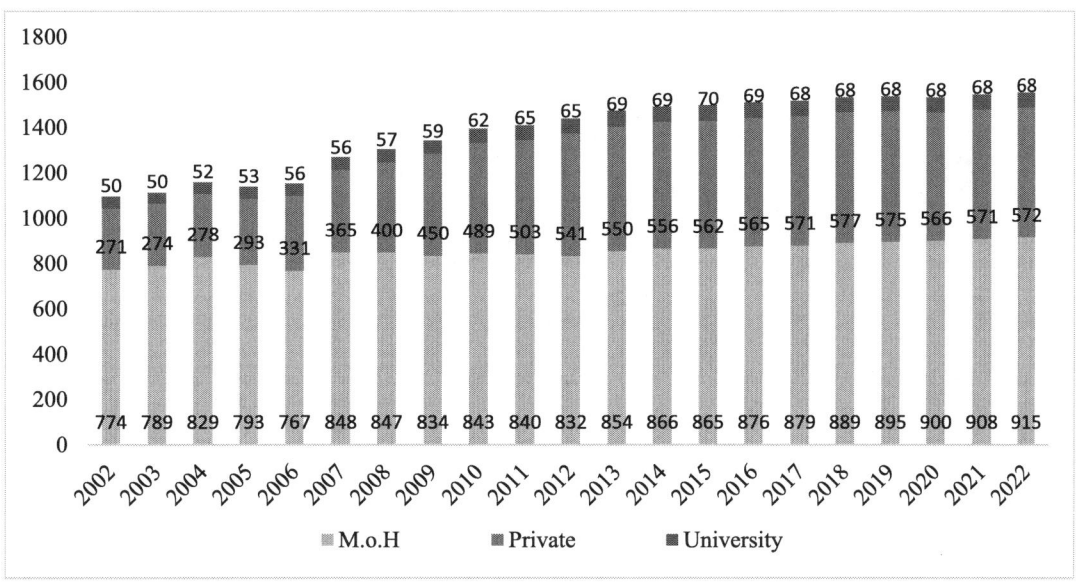

Figure 5.1 Number of hospitals by years and sectors (2002–2022).

Ministry of Finance. Since June 1, 2003, civil servants have been able to benefit from private healthcare institutions. In 2006, an amendment allowed them to also benefit from private healthcare organizations. This protocol enabled public employees to receive services from all hospitals licensed by the M.o.H. and contracted with the state. They could also seek care from private hospitals and outpatient diagnosis and treatment centres with a referral from primary healthcare institutions (Küçük, 2018). To address access issues, the Social Security Institution (S.S.I.) implemented an insurance system. Private hospitals began offering services in rural areas by partnering with the S.S.I., improving access to healthcare services. In 2010, physicians working in M.o.H.-affiliated hospitals in Turkey were required to work full-time in public service, ending private practice arrangements. Professors and associate professors in university hospitals were allowed to work in private hospitals or foundation university hospitals outside of office hours under specific conditions. Private clinics continued operating outside of office hours, and faculty members in public university hospitals charged an additional fee for examinations and treatments during those times.

In 2019, two significant amendments were made to the Regulation Amending the Regulation on Private Hospitals. The first amendment, on May 31, 2019, allowed private hospitals to transfer necessary staff between themselves within the same region without requiring ministry permission. The second amendment, published in the Official Gazette on September 28, 2019 (numbered 30902), mandated that newly opened private hospitals must have a minimum of 100 beds to enhance the efficient use of healthcare personnel and medical equipment. Private hospitals with fewer than 100 beds were permitted to increase their bed count to 100 by either expanding within their current premises or relocating, provided they have at least 33 specialized physicians. Consequently, multiple small hospital operations were encouraged to consolidate and expand, while larger hospitals underwent consolidation.

Health Minister Fahrettin Koca stated that thanks to the regulations implemented under the White Reform, which made health institutions affiliated with the Ministry more attractive, 8,855 physicians returned to public service through direct appointments (Koca, 2023).

Table 5.1 Number of Hospital Beds, Visits, and Surgical Operations by Years (2002–2022)

Indicators	M.o.H.			University			Private		
	2002	2022	Increase (%)	2002	2022	Increase (%)	2002	2022	Increase (%)
Number of hospital beds	107,394	163,207	52.0	26,341	43,914	66.7	12,387	55,069	344.6
Total number of physicians	57,291	116,991	104.2	19,568	42,083	115.1	11,766	35,614	202.7
Number of surgical operations	1,072,417	2,997,651	179.5	307,108	1,077,013	250.7	218,837	1,698,385	676.1
Total number of visits to a physician	109,793,128	375,842,435	242.3	8,823,361	45,746,680	418.5	5,697,170	74,777,721	1212.5

Source: M.o.H. (2024), Turkey Health Statistics Yearbook 2002

5.3 Methodology: Stochastic Frontier Analysis

In our study, we use the stochastic frontier production model with a translog generation function that generalizes the Cobb–Douglas form specification of Aigner et al. (1977) and Meeusen and Broeck (1977). This model offers a flexible functional form, specifically a quadratic approximation as shown in Equation (5.1):

$$\ln y_{it} = \beta_0 + \sum_{j=1}^{h} \beta_j \ln x_{jit} + \frac{1}{2} \sum_{j=1}^{h} \sum_{k=1}^{h} \beta_{jk} \ln x_{jit} \ln x_{kit} + \left(v_{it} - u_{it} \right) \qquad (5.1)$$

here y_{it} is ith hospital's output production in time period t, x_{jit} is jth-type input amount of the ith hospital in time period t, u_{it} is an inefficiency component, $u_{it} \sim N^+\left(0, \sigma_u^2\right)$, that shows the quantity that is less than the maximum feasible production frontier, and finally v_{it} is an idiosyncratic error term, $v_{it} \sim N\left(0, \sigma_v^2\right)$. The original half-normal model of Aigner et al. (1977) assumes that the error components (u_{it}, v_{it}) are homoscedastic, but there have been studies showing that these random variables are heteroscedastic, resulting in inconsistency over estimators (Caudill and Ford, 1993; Caudill et al., 1995; Hadri, 1999; Wang and Schmidt, 2002). In order to account for this heteroscedasticity, they propose a vector of observable variables and related parameters that address exogenous factors contributing to inefficiency as shown in Equation (5.2):

$$\sigma_{u,i}^2 = \exp\left(z'_{u,it} \delta_u\right) \qquad (5.2)$$

here, $z_{u,it}$ is a *mxt* vector of explanatory variables related to inefficiency, and δ_u is the *mx*1 corresponding parameter vector. $z_{u,it}$ variables are also known as inefficiency factors (or external factors) such as when their δ_u coefficients are positively (or negatively) associated with the variance of inefficiency component ($\sigma_{u,i}^2$) in Equation (5.2), they have the opposite effect on the efficiency of the hospitals in Equation (5.1). The hospital management has no control over these external factors such as M.o.H. intervention and the age distribution of the workforce (Coelli et al., 2005: 281).

In our study, we combined the panel data and treated it as cross-sectional data for our investigation. The random error and inefficiency components can be independently and identically distributed or they can be heteroscedastic when using the pooled data technique. This allows for time-varying inefficiency (Zhang, 2012). Time trend variables or time dummies can be used to capture temporal fluctuation in inefficiency, which is not achievable with panel data (Kumbhakar et al., 2015).

In S.F.A., the production frontier is determined by applying the maximum likelihood estimation methodology for the regression analysis. Thereafter, deviations from this frontier are projected. Technical efficiency assesses the ratio of the actual output amount of the ith hospital to its potential output relative to the relevant input amount. Output-oriented technical efficiency is calculated as $TE_{it} = \exp\left(-u_{it}\right)$. This measure of technical efficiency ranges from 0 to 1, with efficiency improving as TE_{it} approaches 1.

5.4 Dataset

Our study includes 541 private hospitals in Turkey from 2019 to 2023, 23 of which belong to private universities, and 518 are general private hospitals. The data is obtained from the Basic Health Statistics Module (T. S. I. M.) with the permission of the M.o.H. The data is categorized into production outputs, labour and capital inputs for hospital production, and inefficiency variables. To minimize data heterogeneity, we only included hospitals with at least 20 beds and 10 staff, excluding branch hospitals. Table 5.2 introduces the variables and provides the descriptive statistics of our unbalanced[1] pooled dataset.

In our study, we selected input, output, and external efficiency variables based on the literature (Mbau et al., 2023; Asbu et al., 2020) and data availability. As shown in Table 5.2, the outputs consist of total outpatient services, which are the sum of emergency department and policlinic visits and the total number of inpatients adjusted by the case-mix index (C.M.I.). The inputs include the total number of physicians, nurses, other medical staff, nonmedical staff employed,

Table 5.2 Variables and Descriptive Statistics, Unbalanced Pooled Data, 2018–2023

Variable	Definition	Mean	Std. Dev.	Min	Max
Output					
outpatient	The number of outpatient visits within a year	7853.6	5420.6	128	38004
inpatient	The annual number of hospitalized cases (including both discharges and deaths) adjusted by C.M.I.	26801.9	24889.4	4.1	192853.6
Case Mix Index (C.M.I.)					
C.M.I.	Romer's C.M.I.	3.2	2.2	0.04	22.7
A.L.S.	Average length of stay	3.1	1.7	1	24.9
O.R.	Occupancy rate (%)	56.9	21.5	1.3	100
Input					
bed	All type of hospital beds	106.1	68.6	20	810
physician	Physicians including specialists and general practitioners	49.4	33.6	10	365
nurse	Nurse	65.2	61.9	10	546
other medical	Other medical staff such as health officers, health technicians, and pharmacists	80.2	66.2	10	1385
nonmedical	Nonmedical staff working outside health services	154.5	151.6	10	1553
Inefficiency Variables					
income	Per capita income ($1,000)	10.5	4.0	2.9	17.1
65age	Population rate over 65 years (%)	12.7	3.8	5.5	29.2
d2020	Dummy variable of 2020	0.2	0.4	0	1
d2021	Dummy variable of 2021	0.2	0.4	0	1
d2022	Dummy variable of 2022	0.2	0.4	0	1
d2023	Dummy variable of 2023	0.2	0.4	0	1
dearthquake	Dummy variable for earthquake	0.02	0.12	0	1

Note: Total number of observations: 2,226

Total number of hospital: 541 (23 university hospitals, 548 general hospitals)

and the total number of beds ready for use in the hospital. In recent research, patient activities are often measured by discharge outputs. However, due to significant resource consumption variations among patient classifications, adjusting for hospital service complexity through an index has become common in hospital efficiency analyses (Sulku, 2012). In our study, we used the C.M.I. proposed by Roemer et al. (1968) to adjust hospital inpatient cases. The Roemer case-mix index is calculated by multiplying the average length of stay (A.L.S.) of a hospital by its occupancy rate (O.R.) and then dividing by the average O.R. of the related year's sample.

Since health services are typically considered normal goods, it is suggested that an increase in income leads to a higher demand for health services and improves the efficiency of healthcare facilities (Santerre and Neun, 2010). Therefore, we introduced the *income* variable, which is the annual per capita income of the province where the hospital is located, as an inefficiency variable. The data was obtained from the Gross Domestic Product by Provinces Report of the Turkish Statistical Institute (TURKSTAT, 2023). We also included the *65age* variable, representing the proportion of the population over the age of 65, due to its impact on increasing the overall demand for health services (Folland et al., 2007). The data was obtained from the Turkish Statistical Institute, which has sensitivity in terms of years and age groups through the address-based registration system (TURKSTAT, 2024). We had initially planned to assess the population density of the region as an inefficiency factor, but the high correlation between population density and income hindered this analysis, as provinces with higher incomes in Turkey also tend to have larger populations.

Moreover, to account for year effects, dummy variables *d2020, d2021, d2022,* and *d2023* were defined for each year, with 2019 serving as the reference year. The years 2020 and 2021 allow us to observe changes in efficiency during the COVID-19 period. Additionally, a dummy variable, *dearthquake*, was defined to represent the six provinces most affected by the earthquake in 2023 (Gaziantep, Hatay, Malatya, Osmaniye, Adıyaman, Kahramanmaraş).

Furthermore, we examined trends in the production of in/outpatient services in the private hospital sector from 2019 to 2023, as depicted in Figure 5.2.

As seen in Figure 5.2, the total number of outpatient and inpatient services declined in 2020 due to the impact of COVID-19, followed by a recovery in 2021. Compared to the realizations in 2019, there was a 16% decrease in the number of outpatient services and a 12% decrease in total inpatient services in 2020. By 2022, the total outputs had reached the levels of 2019, the year before the pandemic (nearly 65,000,000 total outpatient and 3,700,000 total inpatient services). However, from 2022 to 2023, there was a decline of 10% in the number of both outpatient and inpatient

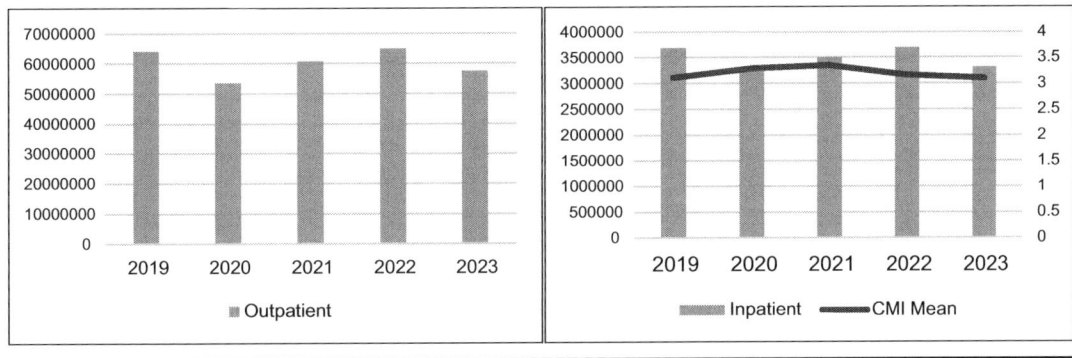

Figure 5.2 The outputs over years.

services. On the other hand, the mean of the C.M.I., which measures the severity of inpatient treatment, showed a small increase during the pandemic years and then decreased to a score of 3.1.

5.5 Empirical Findings

5.5.1 Stochastic Frontier Estimation Results

First, in order to select the appropriate model that best fits our pooled data, we utilized the Likelihood Ratio (L.R.) test. As shown in Table 5.3, the L.R. test indicated that the stochastic frontier estimation procedure is preferred to ordinary least square method. Subsequently, we applied the stochastic generation model outlined in methodology to each of the output variables, namely the outpatient and inpatient care services (Y_{it}'s in Equation (5.1)). The estimated parameters of the stochastic frontier production functions with inefficiency effects were obtained by STATA 17.0, and the specific source codes for S.F.A., which is provided by Kumbhakar et al. (2015), are presented in Table 5.3. Robust standard error estimators were employed to produce more reliable results by mitigating the impact of outliers.

Table 5.3 S.F.A.: Estimated Parameters

	Outpatient	*Inpatient*
Constant	7.08 (0.00***)	−4.48 (0.009***)
Inputs ($\hat{\beta}_j$): Direct effect		
bed		2.79 (0.00***)
physician	0.57 (0.02**)	0.95 (0.03**)
nurse	0.18 (0.27)	0.86 (0.04**)
othermedical	0.79 (0.00***)	1.55 (0.00***)
nonmedical	0.23 (0.07*)	−0.20 (0.27)
Quadratic terms ($\hat{\beta}_{jk}$ when $k \neq j$)		
bed × bed		−0.17 (0.56)
physician × physician	−0.36 (0.00***)	−0.34 (0.028**)
nurse × nurse	0.00 (0.94)	−0.15 (0.33)
othermedical × othermedical	−0.09 (0.048**)	−0.16 (0.00***)
nonmedical × nonmedical	0.05 (0.09*)	0.08 (0.011**)
Cross products ($\hat{\beta}_{jk}$ when $k \neq j$)		
bed × physician		−0.20 (0.14)
bed × nurse		0.12 (0.462)
bed × othermedical		−0.25 (0.000**)

Table 5.3 (*Continued*) S.F.A.: Estimated Parameters

	Outpatient	*Inpatient*
bed × nonmedical		0.00 (0.176)
physician × nurse	0.23 (0.00***)	0.14 (0.15)
physician × othermedical	0.02 (0.7)	0.05 (0.40)
physician × nonmedical	0.005 (0.882)	0.09 (0.057*)
nurse × othermedical	−0.08 (0.049**)	−0.04 (0.48)
nurse × nonmedical	−0.11 (0.00**)	−0.19 (0.00***)
othermedical × nonmedical	0.00 (0.956)	0.08 (0.03**)
Inefficiency effects $\left(\hat{\delta}_m\right)$		
Constant	−1.65 (0.00***)	−1.27 (0.00***)
Income	0.09 (0.00***)	0.03 (0.00***)
65age	−0.004 (0.78)	0.02 (0.04**)
d2020	0.47 (0.00***)	0.22 (0.11)
d2021	0.16 (0.23)	0.04 (0.80)
d2022	−0.001 (0.99)	−0.007 (0.95)
d2023	0.30 (0.02***)	0.24 (0.09*)
dearthquake	1.42 (0.00***)	0.25 (0.00***)
Log Likelihood	−1,511	−2,586
L.R. Test	613***	768***
n+	2,226	2,226

*** *significant at the 0.01 level,* ** *significant at the 0.05 level,* * *significant at the 0.10 level,* +*unbalanced pooled data for the total number of 541 private hospitals over the [2019, 2023] period.*

First, the estimated β_j coefficient $(\hat{\beta}_j)$ of x_j input variable signifies the input's direct influence on the examined output. According to our findings on the production of outpatient services, all labour force including physicians and other medical and nonmedical staff have positive and statistically significant direct effects except for nurses ($\hat{\beta}_{nurse} = 0.18, p-val = 0.27$). In the production of inpatient services, all health personnel (except non-medical staff) have positive and significant direct effects, and the contribution of hospital bed capacity notably stands out ($\hat{\beta}_{Bed} = 2.79, p-val = 0.00$).

The responses of the input to the scale information are displayed by the coefficients of quadratic terms. As seen in Table 5.3, *physician × physician* and *othermedical × othermedical* quadratic terms have negative coefficients for both outpatient and inpatient services production, which implies decreasing marginal productivity. Accordingly, huge increases in the number of health personnel may have a negative impact on the quantity of services provided in hospitals, even though their direct effects were positive. On the other hand, the coefficient of the squared nonmedical staff size is significant and positive, demonstrating the increasing productivity of nonmedical employees.

The cross-products in Table 5.3 represent the complementarity or substitutability between the input variables. For example, in the outpatient services production, a 1% increase in the number of physicians rises the need for nurses by 0.23% ($p-val=0.00$). This finding indicates that in the production of outpatient services in private hospitals, physicians and nurses are complement of each other. However, nurses and other medical staff and nonmedical staff are substitutes for each other. Since a 1% increase in the number of nurses reduces the requirement for other medical staff and nonmedical staff by 0.08% ($p-val=0.049$) and 0.11% ($p-val=0.00$) respectively. When we consider the production of inpatient services, a 1% increase in the number of nurses may cause a 0.19% ($p-val=0.00$) decrease in nonmedical staff. In addition, a 1% raise in the number of beds can result in a fall in the number of other medical staff by 0.25%.

When we consider inpatient services production in private hospitals, it is seen that physicians and nonmedical staff complement each other, while nurses are substitutes for nonmedical staff as a 1% increase in the number of nurses may require a 0.19% reduction in the number of nonmedical staff.

Finally, we interpret the impact of inefficiency factors on private hospitals' service production; if an inefficiency factor is positively associated with inefficiency component (u_{it}) in Equation (5.2) then it actually decreases the efficiency of the hospitals in Equation (5.1). Thus, as the income level of the province is a positive significant factor of inefficiency on both outpatient and inpatient services' production ($\hat{\delta}_{income}^{outpatient}=0.09$ and $\hat{\delta}_{income}^{inpatient}=0.03$, $p-val<0.01$), it reduces the hospitals' efficiencies. Furthermore, the rate of population over 65 years is significantly positively correlated only with the inefficiencies in inpatient services, so it decreases the efficiency of the production of inpatient services.

Lastly, significant effects of year dummies on inefficiency are observed. The pandemic effect on hospital inefficiencies is captured by the dummy variables *d2020* and *d2021*. It was found that the efficiency of outpatient services significantly tends to reduce by the 2020 year as the inefficiency significantly increases ($\hat{\delta}_{d2020}^{outpatient}=0.47, -val<0.01$). However, the pandemic effect on outpatient services production mitigates and becomes insignificant in 2021 ($\hat{\delta}_{d2021}^{outpatient}=0.16$, $p-val=0.23$). Moreover, it is seen that the efficiency of private hospitals' inpatient care services is not impacted by the COVID-19 pandemic as both *d2020* and *d2021*'s coefficients are small and insignificant.

In addition, the dummies associated with the year 2023 and this year's earthquake zones (*dearthquake*) affect the efficiency scores of both outpatient and inpatient services significantly and negatively. The loss in efficiency is more severe for outpatient services compared to inpatient services. In parallel to our findings, we observe a decrease in the average efficiency scores of private hospitals' outpatient services in 2023 in Table 5.3.

After obtaining the S.F.A. model estimation, we calculated the technical efficiency scores for each private hospital in our pooled sample. The average technical efficiency of private hospitals was 60% for outpatient services and 46% for inpatient services as shown in Figure 5.3. This also indicates a 40% potential for improvement for outpatient services and a 54% potential for improvement for inpatient services through more effective use of the input bundle, given the present state of technology.

Furthermore, we observed that efficiency score averages did not vary significantly based on years, types, regions, or sizes. Please refer to Appendix Table 5.1 for the distribution of the efficiency scores. The year averages were mostly consistent with the overall averages mentioned before. The average efficiency scores of general private hospitals were slightly higher than those

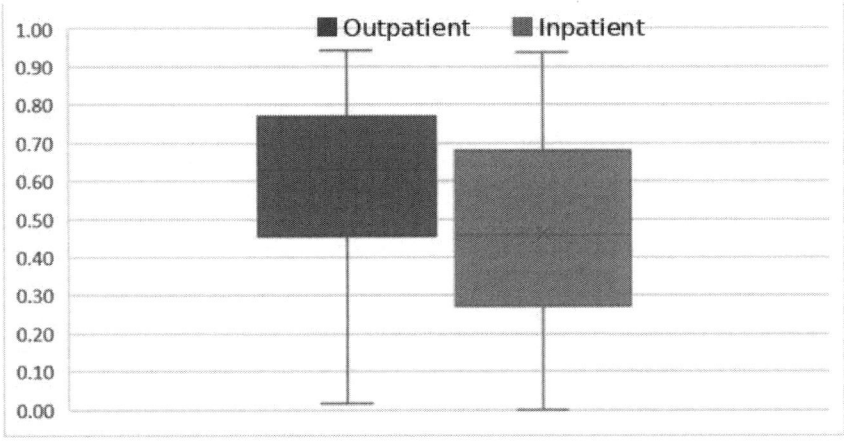

Figure 5.3 Average technical efficiency.

of private university hospitals with less deviation. When considering regions, private hospitals located in South-eastern Anatolia had the highest average efficiency scores in both in/outpatient services, while those in Central Anatolia had the lowest averages. Additionally, when categorizing hospitals based on size, specifically the number of beds, although small-sized hospitals were somewhat above the averages of others, there was no significant difference in efficiencies.

5.5.2 Private Hospitals' Production Function: Returns to Scale Analysis

Returns to scale (*R.T.S.*) is a long-run concept that defines, under constant technology and perfect competition, how hospitals' production responds to changes in inputs. When considering the Turkish hospital sector, competition has improved and increased over time, although restrictions still exist (Torun et al., 2013; Özbilen, 2019). In our study, after we derived the estimation for Equation (5.1) via S.F.A., the output elasticities of each of the input variables, x_j, at their mean are calculated as in Equation (5.3) below:

$$e_j = \frac{\partial \ln y}{\partial \ln x_j} = \hat{\beta}_j + \sum_j \hat{\beta}_{jk} \ln x_j \tag{5.3}$$

Here e_j measures the estimated percentage change in the outputs against a 1% change in the inputs. In Equation (5.3), $\hat{\beta}_j$ represents the estimated direct effect of 1% change in input x_j on the percentage change in production, and $\sum \hat{\beta}_{jk} \ln x_j$ represents the estimated total indirect effect resulting from the interaction of input x_j with itself, that is, quadratic terms, and with other input variables, that is, cross product terms.

In Table 5.4, we measured the returns to scales for both inpatient and outpatient production by summing up the input elasticities, $\text{RTS} = \sum e_j$, as given in Equation (5.3). Depending on whether this estimate is greater than, equal to, or less than 1, the R.T.S. will be increasing, constant, or decreasing, respectively. According to the output elasticities, the most important factor in outpatient services is physicians, with an elasticity of 0.24, whereas the most important factor

Table 5.4 Output Elasticities of Input Variables

	bed	*physician*	*nurse*	*other medical*	*nonmedical*	*Summation: R.T.S.*
Outpatient		0.24	0.22	0.20	0.09	0.75
Inpatient × C.M.I.	0.74	0	0.27	0.16	−0.26	0.91

in inpatient services is bed size, with an elasticity of 0.74. The sum of the outpatient elasticity coefficients is 0.75, and the sum of the inpatient elasticity coefficients is 0.91, indicating that the production process exhibits decreasing returns to scale for both services. If all inputs are increased by 1%, the number of outpatient services only increases by 0.74%, and the number of inpatient services only increases by 0.91%. Decreasing R.T.S. occurs when a private hospital grows beyond its capacity to be effectively managed, resulting in less efficient production as its size increases.

5.6 Discussion and Conclusion

In this chapter, we have assessed the technical efficiency of private hospitals in the production of inpatient and outpatient services for the period [2019, 2023] by the S.F.A., which covers both the pandemic period and the earthquake time zone. Looking first at the descriptive statistics, at the beginning of the COVID-19 pandemic, the number of outpatient services and inpatient services provided by private hospitals decreased by 16% and 12% respectively. In fact, public hospitals were found to have a higher decrease in patient numbers during this period (Sulku et al., 2023). We conclude that private hospitals did not lose a significant number of patients during the pandemic. Indeed, M.o.H. shared the burden of the pandemic by including private hospitals in its anti-pandemic program. Diagnosis and treatment services for COVID-19 were included in the scope of emergency health services. Coronavirus treatment expenditures and drugs used in the treatment were covered by the S.S.I. The S.S.I. has taken steps to address the financial challenges faced by private hospitals by introducing supplementary reimbursement support. Following the modification to the Health Implementation Communiqué, the payments for intensive care services have been augmented. Furthermore, a new fee known as "pandemic care service" has been introduced alongside the existing reimbursement fee for inpatients. Notably, the government has initiated the provision of additional daily allowances to individuals hospitalized due to COVID-19. The costs associated with immune plasma supply, testing, and pharmaceuticals utilized in the diagnosis and treatment of COVID-19 are now being covered by the S.S.I. (Küçük, 2022; Kayaalp and Isik, 2020).

In addition, the descriptive statistics point to a 10% decrease in both outpatient and inpatient services in 2023. The main reason for this situation can be shown as the increase in inflation and input costs, leading to a decrease in people's purchasing power and consequently making private hospitals expensive (O.H.S.A.D., 2023). It is expected that the transition of doctors from the private sector to the public sector following the implementation of the "White Reform" in 2022 will lead to a partial decrease in the utilization of services at private hospitals. Health Minister Fahrettin Koca confirmed that, due to the measures implemented as part of the White Reform initiative, 8,855 doctors opted to return to the public sector through open appointments. This decision was motivated by the increased attractiveness of healthcare institutions under the Ministry's supervision (Koca, 2023). Furthermore, the hospitals in the earthquake region could not maintain their services in 2023. However, despite the decrease in total output amounts shown in Figure 5.2 and also the negative effect of the year-based dummy variables on efficiency, there was no drastic fall in average efficiencies of 2023 showed in Table 5.3. It can therefore be concluded that private hospitals do not suffer a loss of efficiency as a result of a well-planned reduction in outputs and inputs together.

According to our S.F.A. results for the production of inpatient services, doctors, nurses, and other medical staff improve production, similar to the literature (Goudarzi et al., 2014; Sülkü et al., 2023). In the production of outpatient services, nurses have a positive but insignificant effect, while nonmedical staff is a significant factor. In addition, marginal productivity decreases in the short term when the number of physicians and other medical staff increases so much. Furthermore, it has been observed that an increase in the number of doctors leads to a corresponding increase in the demand for nursing staff in the production of both inpatient and outpatient services. Besides, an increase in the number of nurses leads to a decrease in the need for additional healthcare personnel. Indeed, an increase in the number of nurses correlates with a reduction in the need for non-medical staff for both inpatient and outpatient services. Also, a growth in the number of beds may consequentially bring about a decline in the requisite number of other medical personnel but increase in the number of nurses. Thus, our findings imply that nurses and other medical and non-medical personnel can be considered as potential substitutes, which is indeed valid in the production context (Butler et al., 2020). Private hospitals exhibit a preference for increasing the number of nurses within their healthcare staff, owing to their versatile utilization across various domains ranging from patient registration to medical treatment. Consequently, the percentage of nurses relative to the overall healthcare staff in private hospitals stands notably elevated. This accentuates the significance and contributions of nurses in the landscape of healthcare provision compared to other personnel.

Beyond the input–output mechanism, the (in)/efficiencies of healthcare facilities may depend on their surrounding environment. According to the literature, factors such as more developed cities, better socioeconomic conditions, and higher G.D.P. per capita income levels can increase the demand for hospitals (Andersen and Newman, 2005). Therefore, when considering the influence of external factors on the production of private hospitals, it is evident that the income level of the province significantly affects the production efficiency of both types of services. In our findings, surprisingly, contrary to existing literature, an increase in income distribution in regions leads to a positive effect on inefficiency, resulting in a relatively lower efficiency score. In fact, in Turkey, private hospitals are generally concentrated in three major cities, with almost two-thirds of the private hospital capacity located in Ankara, Istanbul, and Izmir. Nearly half of the private hospitals are in Istanbul alone. Despite this, Istanbul lags behind the Turkish average in the number of hospital beds per capita (Yıldırım and Konca, 2018; İ.P.A., 2023). Additionally, Istanbul is known for longer waiting times compared to the rest of Turkey (Tokatlioglu and Sulku, 2023). This unbalanced distribution of health facilities may lead to conflicting results in the efficiencies of private sector hospitals. Furthermore, private hospitals in Turkey exhibit varying standards and patient demographics. In major urban centres, private hospitals predominantly serve patients with private insurance coverage, whereas those in Anatolian cities cater almost exclusively to S.S.I. beneficiaries (Akman Dömbekçi et al., 2018). This also highlights the inefficiency in the relationship between income level and productivity.

Moreover, the proportion of the population aged 65 and above significantly influences the production of inpatient services. The negative relationship between the elderly population factor and inefficiency in inpatient services indicates an improvement in the efficiency of inpatient services production. Individuals with universal health insurance also seek treatment at private medical facilities, leading to a high demand for services covered by universal health insurance in economically disadvantaged regions (Anarwat, 2022). Private hospitals in such areas do not impose exorbitant additional service charges.

It was found that private-general hospitals exhibited slightly higher and more consistent average efficiency scores compared to university hospitals in terms of institution type. Private foundation university hospitals, primarily located in major metropolitan areas like Istanbul, Ankara, and Izmir, operate with a profit motive while also emphasizing the delivery of high-quality services. Consequently, their efficiency perception, which emphasizes quality over quantity, tends to be lower than that of private-general hospitals. These hospitals typically cater to the middle- to upper-income demographics and place a strong emphasis on providing superior quality services rather than focusing on sheer quantity. Essentially, their objective is to enhance revenue by delivering exceptional service to a smaller number of patients.

Private hospitals in the South-eastern Anatolia region demonstrated the highest average efficiency score, while their counterparts in Central Anatolia showed the lowest average efficiency. According to the 2022 Health Statistics Yearbook, the South-eastern Anatolia region boasts the highest 0–14 age population rate at 33% (M.o.H., 2024). This demographic composition leads to a notable influx in hospital admissions, particularly in the fields of gynaecology and paediatric care. The region with the lowest number of doctors per 100 thousand people, standing at 109 doctors, experiences a high volume of applications to physicians. In the Central Anatolia region, due to the region's elevated rural population density, there is a notable volume of visits to doctors per capita in primary healthcare facilities, standing at 4.9 applications. According to data sourced from the M.o.H. (M.o.H., 2024: 156), the Central Anatolia Region exhibits the highest number of such visits in comparison to other regions. Moreover, the utilization of hospital services within this region, as depicted by metrics such as bed occupancy rate, the number of surgeries conducted, and the count of inpatients, registers levels notably lower than the national average in Turkey.

Finally, our findings suggest that an increase in the quantity of physicians does not lead to a proportional rise in the number of patients. This observation points toward diminishing returns to scale in the correlation between physician numbers and patient numbers. The study results indicate the existence of diminishing returns to scale in the production technology of private hospitals, which may result in inefficiencies at a specific scale. In larger private hospitals, there seems to be a greater emphasis on patients requiring specialized care rather than on a high volume of patients.

In our study, we examine the private hospital sector's technical efficiencies, but it should not be forgotten that the private sector is working for profit. Thus, the limitation of the study is that we cannot do a cost-effectiveness or profitability analysis because of the lack of data. Since the private sector is a crucial source of healthcare provision, studying its efficiency from all aspects is valuable for providing insight to policymakers, enabling them to implement wise strategies to shape the entire healthcare system.

Note

1 For some years, there is a lack of specific hospitals' data because of closing or union with others, but we still prefer to keep most of the data by constructing the unbalanced pooled data set.

References

Aigner, D., Lovell, C. K., & Schmidt, P. (1977). Formulation and estimation of stochastic frontier production function models. *Journal of Econometrics*, 6(1), 21–37. https://doi.org/10.1016/0304-4076(77)90052-5

Akman Dömbekçi, H., Yılmaz, F. Ö., & Özata, M. (2018). Özel hastane işletmeciliğinin mevcut durumu ve geleceği: Konya örneği. *Hacettepe Sağlık İdaresi Dergisi*, 21(4), 675–697.

Anarwat, S. G. (2022). Health insurance for economically disadvantaged people in LMICs: What are the best options?. In A. I. Tavares (ed.), *Health insurance*. IntechOpen. https://doi.org/10.5772/intechopen.105679

Andersen, R., & Newman, J. F. (2005). Societal and individual determinants of medical care utilization in the United States. *Milbank Quarterly*, 83(4), 1–28. https://doi.org/10.1111/j.1468-0009.2005.00428.x

Asbu, E. Z., Masri, M. D., & Al Naboulsi, M. (2020). Determinants of hospital efficiency: A literature review. *International Journal of Healthcare*, 6(2). https://doi.org/10.5430/ijh.v6n2p44

Bağcı, H., & Çil Koçyiğit, S. (2023). Evaluating the decentralization of public hospitals in Turkey in terms of technical efficiency: Data envelopment analysis and Malmquist index. *Benchmarking: An International Journal*, 30(10), 4425–4460. https://doi.org/10.1108/BIJ-03-2021-0140

Butler, M., Schultz, T. J., & Drennan, J. (2020). Substitution of nurses for physicians in the hospital setting for patient, process of care, and economic outcomes. *Cochrane Database of Systematic Reviews*, 2020(5), CD013616. https://doi.org/10.1002/14651858.CD013616

Caudill, S. B., & Ford, J. M. (1993). Biases in frontier estimation due to heteroscedasticity. *Economics Letters*, 41(1), 17–20. https://doi.org/10.1016/0165-1765(93)90104-K

Caudill, S. B., Ford, J. M., & Gropper, D. M. (1995). Frontier estimation and firm-specific inefficiency measures in the presence of heteroscedasticity. *Journal of Business & Economic Statistics*, 13(1), 105–111. https://doi.org/10.2307/1392525

Coelli, T. J., Rao, D. S. P., O'Donnell, C. J., & Battese, G. E. (2005). *An introduction to efficiency and productivity analysis* (2nd ed.). New York: Springer.

Folland, S., Goodman, A. C., & Stano, M. (2007). *The economics of health and health care* (5th ed.). Taylor & Francis.

Gökçay, İ. (1995). *Özelleştirme Değil Kamulaştırma*. Sağlık Hizmetleri. İstanbul: Kaynak Yayınları.

Goudarzi, R., Pourreza, A., Shokoohi, M., Askari, R., Mahdavi, M., & Moghri, J. (2014). Technical efficiency of teaching hospitals in Iran: The use of stochastic frontier analysis, 1999–2011. *International Journal of Health Policy and Management*, 3, 91–97. https://doi.org/10.15171/ijhpm.2014.66

Griffin, C. C. (1989). *Strengthening health services in developing countries through the private sector*. Discussion Paper No. 4. Washington, D.C.: The World Bank and International Finance Corporation.

Hadri, K. (1999). Estimation of a doubly heteroscedastic stochastic frontier cost function. *Journal of Business & Economic Statistics*, 17(3), 359–363. https://doi.org/10.2307/1392293

Hollingsworth, B., & Wildman, J. (2003). The efficiency of health production: Re-estimating the WHO panel data using parametric and nonparametric approaches to provide additional information. *Health Economics*, 12(6), 493–504. https://doi.org/10.1002/hec.751

İ.P.A. (2023). *Bir İnsan Hakkı Olarak Sağlığa Erişim: İstanbul'da Sağlık Altyapısının Sektörel Bazda İncelenmesi*. İstanbul Planlama Ajansı. İstanbul: İstanbul Büyükşehir Belediye iştiraki Kültür A.Ş.

İlgün, G., & Konca, M. (2019). Assessment of efficiency levels of training and research hospitals in Turkey and the factors affecting their efficiencies. *Health Policy and Technology*, 8(4), 343–348. https://doi.org/10.1016/j.hlpt.2019.08.008

Kassean, H., & Juwaheer, T. D. (2010). Comparing healthcare in private clinics vs. public hospital services sector. *International Research Symposium in Service Management*. Retrieved June 25, 2024, from https://www.academia.edu/76230776/Comparing_Healthcare_in_Private_Clinics_v_s_Public_Hospital_Services_Sector

Kayaalp, E., & Isik, İ. B. (2020). COVID-19 and healthcare infrastructure in Turkey. *Medical Anthropology Quarterly Rapid Response Blog Series*. Retrieved July 3, 2024, from http://medanthroquarterly.org/?p=542

Koca, F. (2023). Sağlık Bakanı Koca: 8855 hekimimiz açıktan atamayla kamuya döndü. Retrieved February 23, 2024, from https://www.aa.com.tr/tr/saglik/saglik-bakani-koca-8855-hekimimiz-aciktan-atamayla-kamuya-dondu/3048315

Küçük, A. (2018). *Kapitalizm, Devlet, Sağlık ve Türkiye*. Ankara: Akademisyen Yayınevi.

Küçük, A. (2022). Financial impacts of COVID-19 pandemic for Turkish public hospitals. *Süleyman Demirel Üniversitesi Vizyoner Dergisi*, *13*(34), 354–363. https://doi.org/10.21076/vizyoner.993956

Kumbhakar, S. C., Wang, H., & Horncastle, A. P. (2015). *A practitioner's guide to stochastic frontier analysis using stata*. United States of America: Cambridge University Press.

Lakshmi, B., Parthasarathi, B. N. V., Jain, S., Bhalerao, M., Saini, D., Mishra, V., Tiwari, G., Rathee, P., Kareem, A., Nemuri, S., Varma, J., & Kuchana, P. (2020). Patient preference between private and government hospital in Hyderabad region. *International Journal of Innovative Science and Research Technology (IJISRT)*, *5*(8), 1400–1406. https://doi.org/10.38124/IJISRT20AUG728

M.o.H. (2024). *The ministry of health of Türkiye health statistics yearbook-2022*. Ankara: Republic of Türkiye Ministry of Health.

Manavgat, G., & Demirci, A. (2020). Decentralization matter of healthcare and effect on regional healthcare efficiency: Evidence from Turkey. *Sosyoekonomi*, *28*(44), 261–281. https://doi.org/10.17233/sosyoekonomi.2020.02.12

Mbau, R., Musiega, A., Nyawira, L., Tsofa, B., Mulwa, A., Molyneux, S., Maina, I., Jemutai, J., Normand, C., Hanson, K., & Barasa, E. (2023). Analysing the efficiency of health systems: A systematic review of the literature. *Applied Health Economics and Health Policy*, *21*(2), 205–224. https://doi.org/10.1007/s40258-022-00785-2

Meeusen, W., & Van den Broeck, J. (1977). Efficiency estimation from Cobb-Douglas production functions with composed error. *International Economic Review*, *18*(2), 435–444. https://doi.org/10.2307/2525757

Morgan, R., Ensor, T., & Waters, H. (2016). Performance of private sector health care: Implications for universal health coverage. *The Lancet*, *388*(10044), 606–612. https://doi.org/10.1016/S0140-6736(16)00343-3

O.H.S.A.D. (2023). Artan maliyetler nedeniyle birçok özel hastanenin yoğun bakım ünitesinin kapısına kilit vuruluyor. *Özel Hastaneler ve Sağlık kuruluşları Derneği*. Retrieved July 29, 2024, from https://ohsad.org/independent-turkce-artan-maliyetler-nedeniyle-bircok-ozel-hastanenin-yogun-bakim-unitesinin-kapisina-kilit-vuruluyor-9-mart-2023/

Official Gazette. (2002). 27 Mart 2002 tarihli ve 24708 sayılı Özel Hastaneler Yönetmeliği. Retrieved June 2, 2024, from https://www.mevzuat.gov.tr/mevzuat?MevzuatNo=4854&MevzuatTur=7&MevzuatTertip=5

Özbilen, P. (2019). A structural analysis of the Turkish hospital industry using Porter's Diamond framework: A case from an emerging market. *Ege Academic Review*, *19*(1), 103–118. https://doi.org/10.21121/eab.2019148778

Özgen Narcı, H., Ozcan, Y., Şahin, İ., Tarcan, M., & Narcı, M. (2015). An examination of competition and efficiency for hospital industry in Turkey. *Health Care Management Science*, *18*, 407–418. https://doi.org/10.1007/s10729-014-9315-x

Prasad, S. (2013). Preference of hospital usage in India. *Annals of Tropical Medicine and Public Health*, *6*(4), 472. https://doi.org/10.4103/1755-6783.127804

Roemer, M. I., Moustafa, A. T., & Hopkins, C. E. (1968). A proposed hospital quality index: Hospital death rates adjusted for case severity. *Health Services Research*, *3*(2), 96–118.

Şahin, B., & İlgün, G. (2019). Assessment of the impact of public hospital associations (PHAs) on the efficiency of hospitals under the ministry of health in Turkey with data envelopment analysis. *Health Care Management Science*, *22*, 437–446. https://doi.org/10.1007/s10729-018-9463-5

Santerre, R. E., & Neun, S. P. (2010). *Health economics: Theory, insights, and industry studies* (5th ed.). United States of America: South-Western Cengage Learning.

Sriram, V., Yilmaz, V., Kaur, S., Andres, C., Cheng, M., & Meessen, B. (2024). The role of private healthcare sector actors in health service delivery and financing policy processes in low-and middle-income countries: A scoping review. *BMJ Global Health*, *8*(Suppl 5), e013408. https://doi.org/10.1136/bmjgh-2023-013408

Sulku, S. N. (2012). The health sector reforms and the efficiency of public hospitals in Turkey: Provincial markets. *European Journal of Public Health*, *22*(5), 634–638. https://doi.org/10.1093/eurpub/ckr163

Sülkü, S. N., Mortaş, A., & Küçük, A. (2023). Measuring efficiency of public hospitals under the impact of COVID-19: The case of Türkiye. *Cost Effectiveness and Resource Allocation*, *21*, 70. https://doi.org/10.1186/s12962-023-00480-6

Sulku, S. N., Tokatlioglu, Y., & Cosar, K. (2023). Receiving or not deemed necessary healthcare services. *BMC Public Health*, *23*, 208. https://doi.org/10.1186/s12889-023-15135-7

Tokatlioglu, Y., & Sulku, S. N. (2023). The impact of the covid-19 outbreak on unmet health care needs in istanbul. *Preventive Medicine Reports*, *36*, 102400. https://doi.org/10.1186/s12889-023-15135-7

Torun, N., Celik, Y., & Younis, M. Z. (2013). Competition among Turkish hospitals and its effect on hospital efficiency and service quality. *Journal of Health Care Finance*, *40*, 42–58.

Tunca, Y. (1965). *Sağlık ve Sosyal Yardım Bakanlığı Çalışmaları ve Tıbbi İstatistik Yıllığı 1960–1963*. Sağlık ve Sosyal Yardım Bakanlığı Yayınları No: 317, Ankara: Balkanoğlu Matbaacılık.

TURKSTAT. (2023). İl Bazında Gayrisafi Yurt İçi Hasıla, 2022. *Turkish Statistical Institute*. Retrieved June 19, 2024, from https://data.tuik.gov.tr/Bulten/Index?p=Il-Bazinda-Gayrisafi-Yurt-Ici-Hasila-2022-45867

TURKSTAT. (2024). The statistic tables of address based population registration system. *Turkish Statistical Institute*. Retrieved June 19, 2024, from https://data.tuik.gov.tr/Kategori/GetKategori?p=nufus-ve-demografi-109&dil=1

W.H.O. (2016). *Health workforce requirements for universal health coverage and the Sustainable Development Goals*. Human Resources for Health Observer, 17. Switzerland, Geneva: World Health Organization.

Wang, Hj., & Schmidt, P. (2002). One-step and two-step estimation of the effects of exogenous variables on technical efficiency levels. *Journal of Productivity Analysis*, *18*, 129–144. https://doi.org/10.1023/A:1016565719882

World Bank. (2024). World Bank Group Data. Retrieved April 5, 2016, from https://data.worldbank.org/indicator/SH.MED.PHYS.ZS?locations=OE.

Yeşilyurt, M. E., Şahin, E., Elbi, M. D., Kızılkaya, A., Koyuncuoğlu, M. U., & Akbaş-Yeşilyurt, F. (2021). A novel method for computing single output for DEA with application in hospital efficiency. *Socio-Economic Planning Sciences*, *76*, 100995. https://doi.org/10.1016/j.seps.2020.100995

Yıldırım, H. H., & Konca, M. (2018). *Türkiye'de özel sağlık kurumları sektörü: Mevcut durum, sorunlar ve çözüm önerileri*. TÜSPE Analiz: 2018/5. Ankara: TÜSPE Yayınları.

Yildiz, M. S., Heboyan, V., & Khan, M. M. (2018). Estimating technical efficiency of Turkish hospitals: implications for hospital reform initiatives. *BMC Health Services Research*, *18*, 401. https://doi.org/10.1186/s12913-018-3239-y

Zhang, M. (2012). *The comparison of stochastic frontier analysis with panel data models* (Master's thesis). Loughborough University School of Business and Economics.

Appendix

Appendix Table 5.1 Efficiency Scores' Distribution

	Outpatient		Inpatient × C.M.I.	
	Mean	S.D.	Mean	S.D.
All sample	0.60	0.21	0.46	0.24
Year				
2019	0.60	0.20	0.46	0.24
2020	0.60	0.21	0.47	0.25
2021	0.60	0.21	0.45	0.24
2022	0.61	0.21	0.46	0.24
2023	0.59	0.21	0.46	0.25
Hospital type				
General	0.60	0.21	0.46	0.24
Private university	0.58	0.22	0.45	0.26
Region				
Southeast Anatolia	0.63	0.20	0.52	0.24
Mediterranean	0.61	0.21	0.47	0.24
East Anatolia	0.61	0.20	0.46	0.24
Marmara	0.60	0.21	0.46	0.24
Aegean	0.60	0.20	0.45	0.23
Black Sea	0.60	0.21	0.44	0.23
Central Anatolia	0.57	0.22	0.43	0.26
Hospital size: Bed capacity				
Less than 50	0.63	0.20	0.47	0.23
50–100	0.59	0.21	0.46	0.24
100–150	0.61	0.21	0.46	0.24
More than 150	0.60	0.21	0.45	0.24

Chapter 6

Examining Trends and Predictors of Satisfaction with Healthcare Providers in Turkey: Exploring the Impact of the Health Transformation Programme (2006–2022)

Abdullah Tirgil and Fatih Cemil Özbuğday

Contents

6.1 Introduction

Quality is considered more crucial in the healthcare sector than in any other industry (Özbuğday, 2017). First, the direct link between healthcare quality and care recipient's well-being is clear, as higher quality often correlates with better recovery or survival rates (e.g. Kruk et al., 2018). The effectiveness of the overall healthcare industry is significantly affected by this quality, as improved patient outcomes contribute to a healthier population and reduce the long-term burden on healthcare systems. Second, quality is seen as the primary competitive factor among healthcare providers, especially in regions where government regulation controls pricing and health insurance shields

DOI: 10.4324/9781003539896-7

consumers from the full cost (Gaynor, 2006; Gaynor & Town, 2011). Overall, the effectiveness of the healthcare industry as a whole depends on maintaining high standards of quality, ensuring that healthcare providers can deliver the best possible care and improve overall public health.

Quality in healthcare services is measured through various methods and indicators to assess the effectiveness, safety, efficiency, patient-centredness, timeliness, and equity of care. *Clinical outcomes* such as mortality rates are fundamental measures, focusing on the results of healthcare interventions on patients' health status. *Adherence to clinical guidelines* is an important process measure of quality in healthcare services. *Efficiency and cost-effectiveness measures* such as length of hospital stay, readmission rates, and cost per patient treated assess how resources are utilized in delivering healthcare services. *Patient safety indicators*, including medication errors, hospital-acquired infections, falls, and other adverse events, are crucial for preventing harm to patients during their care. *Access to care indicators* evaluate how easily patients can obtain healthcare services when needed. These include wait times for appointments, availability of services, and geographic accessibility. Ensuring timely access to care is critical for preventing delays in treatment and improving health outcomes. *Health equity measures* evaluate fairness and equality in healthcare delivery across different population groups. These measures assess disparities in access to care, health outcomes, and quality of care based on race, ethnicity, socio-economic status, and geographic location. Promoting health equity ensures that all patients receive high-quality care, regardless of their background.

Patient satisfaction is highly relevant to healthcare quality regarding the effectiveness of healthcare services and the overall patient experience (Uğurluoğlu et al., 2019). Patient satisfaction is a vital measure for assessing the quality of healthcare services, reflecting how well the healthcare system meets patients' needs and expectations and indicating the level of care and service quality delivered. When patients report high satisfaction levels, it generally suggests that the healthcare services are high quality.

Regularly administered *satisfaction surveys* representative of the population are the primary means of gauging satisfaction levels with healthcare services. These surveys also play a crucial role in assessing the impact of healthcare programmes by capturing the perspectives and experiences of patients. They provide valuable insights into patient experience before and after programme implementation, allowing healthcare organizations to compare changes in satisfaction levels over time and identify areas for improvement. These surveys also serve as tools for monitoring the quality of care to evaluate whether transformation programmes have positively impacted patient outcomes. Regularly administering satisfaction surveys tracks the progress and long-term effects of transformation programmes.

One such transformation programme is the Health Transformation Programme (H.T.P) of Turkey, initiated in 2003 to enhance the healthcare system's accessibility, efficiency, and quality of care. Various scientific studies have analysed the impact of the H.T.P from different perspectives (see Ökem & Çakar, 2015) for a review of studies up to 2015). The evolution of patient satisfaction since the initiation of the H.T.P has also been the subject of several studies over the past two decades. Bostan (2013) compared patient satisfaction levels before and after the H.T.P, showing an increase from 39% in 2003 to 76% in 2012. The study found that reforms reduced complaints about basic healthcare services and improved overall satisfaction, particularly among men, married individuals, and older people. The reforms also diminished the disparity in satisfaction between public and private healthcare providers. Ali Jadoo et al. (2014) conducted a cross-sectional survey to gauge public opinion on healthcare reforms. The study revealed that most respondents believed that the reforms under the H.T.P had positive effects, including increased accessibility, availability of health resources, and improved quality of care. Most respondents seem to have preferred the current healthcare system over the previous one, with significant positive opinions observed among the elderly, married females, and those who perceived themselves as healthy.

A study by Stokes et al. (2015) analysed data from 2004 to 2012 and found an approximately 20% rise in reported health service use, coinciding with increased insurance coverage and access to services within the context of H.T.P. The study revealed a significant increase in user satisfaction with health services, with the odds of being satisfied in 2012 being 2.56 times higher than in 2004. This improvement was particularly notable in public primary care services, which saw increased patient preference and satisfaction due to enhanced quality indicators. Hazama (2015) analysed the impact of the H.T.P on satisfaction among the poor from 2003 to 2011. The study found that satisfaction among the lowest income group increased significantly post-reform, indicating an improved access to quality services at reasonable costs. The gap in satisfaction between lower and higher income groups narrowed, suggesting that the reforms were particularly beneficial for the poorer segments of the population.

Hone et al. (2017) examined the impact of primary healthcare reforms, specifically the introduction of family medicine, on health service utilization and user satisfaction from 2002 to 2013. The study found that the average number of primary healthcare (P.H.C.) consultations per person increased significantly, with a 9.5% rise in P.H.C. as the preferred provider. The reforms also led to improvements in service satisfaction, reduced reports of poor facility hygiene, difficulty in getting appointments, poor physician behaviour, and high costs, particularly in urban, low-income, and working-age populations. Aydin (2018) explored overall patient satisfaction from 2008 to 2012, showing a progressive increase in satisfaction over the years. The study noted that certain groups, such as those with private health insurance or specific allowances, experienced lower satisfaction levels. Additionally, barriers such as long travel distances, fear of treatment, and late appointments affected hospital admission rates.

Uğurluoğlu et al. (2019) used data from the 2015 Life Satisfaction Statistics survey to identify factors impacting satisfaction with public healthcare services. The study highlighted the importance of securing appointments, costs of examinations and medications, cleanliness, and the attitudes of medical personnel as key determinants of satisfaction. The implementation of the H.T.P in Turkey significantly increased satisfaction rates from 39.5% in 2003 to 71.4% in 2017. Caner and Cilasun (2019) focused on healthcare services for the elderly, using data from the Survey on Income and Living Conditions and the Life Satisfaction Survey. They found that overall satisfaction increased until 2012 but then declined due to increased costs and a shortage of doctors. The study emphasized the need for investment in health human capital to maintain service quality, especially for the elderly.

In summary, these studies collectively demonstrate that healthcare reforms in Turkey under the scope of the H.T.P have significantly improved patient satisfaction by enhancing access to services, quality of care, and equity in healthcare delivery. Despite some challenges, such as shortages of medical personnel and increased costs, the overall trend indicates that the reforms have been largely successful in meeting the needs and expectations of the population.

Considering the significant changes since the most recent studies in 2019, including the COVID-19 pandemic, shifts in economic conditions, and demographic transformations, a new research effort into patient satisfaction in Turkey is warranted. The pandemic has undoubtedly reshaped healthcare delivery, patient expectations, and the healthcare system. Economic challenges and demographic shifts have likely influenced access to care, resource allocation, and the quality of services. Additionally, the strain on healthcare systems during the pandemic and subsequent recovery phases may have altered patient satisfaction dynamics. Therefore, a contemporary study is essential to capture the current state of patient satisfaction, identify new challenges, and assess the effectiveness of recent healthcare policies and reforms in this changed environment. We attempt to fulfil this need in the current chapter.

6.2 Data

In this study, we use the Life Satisfaction Surveys (L.S.S) conducted by the Turkish Statistical Institute (TurkStat) every year since 2003. L.S.S covers non-institutionalized individuals aged 18 and above living in the boundaries of the Republic of Turkey. Furthermore, L.S.S is a repeated cross-sectional survey administered through face-to-face interviews. The sampling method of the surveys is a two-stage stratified cluster sampling.

The main purpose of the L.S.S is to measure satisfaction with public services over time, such as health, education, transportation, and public security. Between 2003 and 2012, the survey sample size was calculated to produce representative estimates for Turkey's rural and urban locations. In 2013, the sample size was designed to give estimates based on the N.U.T.S-3 level. Starting in 2014, the sample size of the survey has only been representative of Turkey.

In this study, we use the Life Satisfaction Surveys for the years 2006–2022. In 2006, the survey was administered to 6,432 individuals, 196,203 in 2013, and 9,841 in 2022. In total, for 2006–2022, we have 330,625 observations for our analysis.

These datasets cover a wide range of topics, including demographic and socio-economic characteristics of interviewees, healthcare utilization, and satisfaction with the healthcare services by the type of provider.

First, since our dependent variable is related to respondents' health service satisfaction, we only include individuals in our analysis who responded with a "yes" to the question in the L.S.S framed as "Did you apply to any health institution and receive health care in the survey year?"

Second, Life Satisfaction Surveys ask, "Where do you usually go first when you get sick?" which is a categorical variable for which responses are family health centres, state hospitals, university hospitals, and private hospitals. We condition our analysis based on these healthcare providers.

Then, we construct our dependent variable based on the question: "Are you satisfied with health services?", which includes responses from 1 (very satisfied) to 5 (not satisfied at all) to 6 (no idea). Our dependent variable is discrete, taking the values of 1 (very satisfied and satisfied) and 0 (not satisfied at all, not satisfied, neither satisfied nor unsatisfied), and we exclude those who responded "no idea" from the analysis. Besides, we cannot include the pre-2006 period in the analysis because there has been a change in the healthcare providers.

L.S.S individual-level microdata also provides information regarding respondents' demographic and socio-economic indicators such as age, gender (zero: male, one: female), employment status (zero: unemployed, one: employed), marital status (i.e. never married, married, divorced, widowed), educational level (i.e. primary school or below, secondary education or equivalent, high school or equivalent, college or above).

We also include two important variables from household-level datasets in our analysis regarding households' economic situation. First, we construct our household income variable, dividing into five categories: Low income, mid-low income, mid-income, mid-high income, and high income. In addition, another significant variable is "Difficulty meeting the needs with current income level," categorized as very easily, easily, hardly, nor easily, hardly, and very hardly.

Furthermore, the survey asks about identifying individuals with serious health problems. The question is framed as follows: "In the last year, I have had a serious health problem", which is a dummy variable taking the value of zero if there was no serious health problem in the last year and one if there was a serious health problem in the last year.

Another question asks about individuals' satisfaction with their health. The question is categorized into three options: Not satisfied, neither satisfied nor unsatisfied, and satisfied. Finally, we have a variable indicating respondents' insurance status. This variable has five categories: Own pay, Green Card, social security institution (S.G.K.), private insurance, and other.

6.3 Methodology

To study the determinants of satisfaction with the services of healthcare providers, we estimate the following regression model via Ordinary Least Squares (O.L.S):

$$y_i = \alpha + \beta X_i + \gamma_t + u_i \tag{6.1}$$

where y_i denotes satisfaction with the services of healthcare providers such as family physicians, public hospitals, university hospitals, and private hospitals. X_i includes respondents' demographic and socio-economic characteristics such as age, gender, employment status, marital status, educational level, income level, satisfaction with own health, insurance status (or channel of healthcare service payment), and serious health condition. γ_t captures time-fixed effects. Finally, α is the constant term, and u_i the error term.

The next part of the chapter will provide estimates on the predictors of satisfaction with the services of healthcare providers, specifically focusing on family health centres, state hospitals, private hospitals, university hospitals, and city hospitals since these have the greatest utilization rates compared to other healthcare providers. In other words, we will explore respondents' socio-economic and demographic variables that might be associated with healthcare service satisfaction. We will also explore trends over time regarding satisfaction with healthcare services by the type of providers.

6.4 Results

Figures 6.1–6.4 report year-fixed effects' estimates (or coefficients) obtained from implementing the O.L.S regression method to Equation (6.1). Our dataset has information regarding satisfaction with family physicians since 2009. Figure 6.1 reveals that there has been a gradual increase in the satisfaction of family physicians from 2011 until 2012, which is statistically significant. What is striking in Figure 6.1 is that although all coefficients, except for 2022, produce positive estimates, about half of them provide statistically significant outcomes, such as the 2011, 2012, 2013, 2016, and

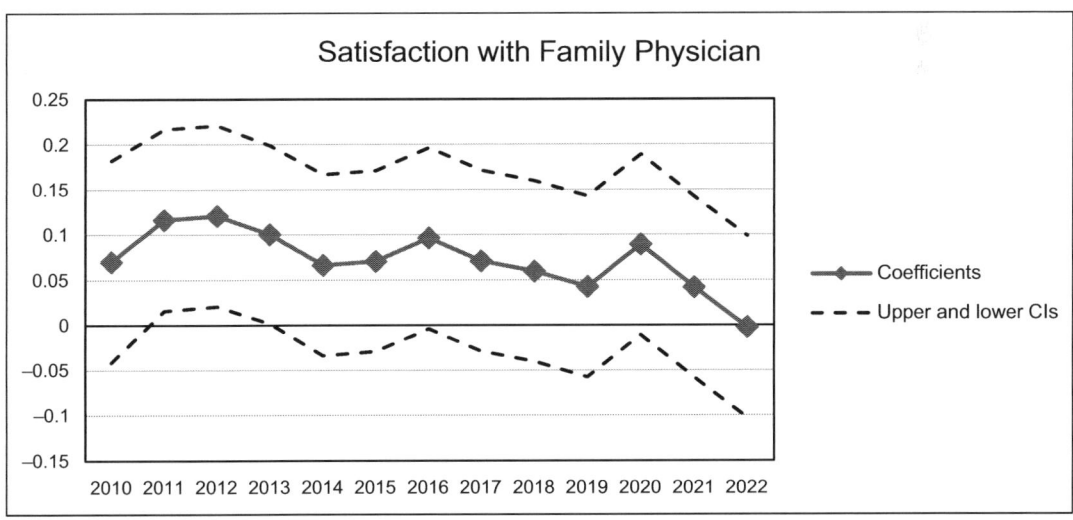

Figure 6.1   Year- fixed effects estimates of satisfaction with family physicians.

2020 estimates. What can be seen in Figure 6.1 is the variability of the coefficients over the years. Regression results produce a slightly significant coefficient for 2020. A possible explanation for this might be that during the COVID-19 pandemic, people were satisfied with the healthcare services that family physicians offer. Furthermore, the coefficients fell to a low point of –0.002 in 2022, which is statistically insignificant. Overall, satisfaction with family physicians declines, although coefficients are positive and even statistically significant in some years relative to 2009 data.

The year-fixed effects results obtained from executing O.L.S in Equation (6.1) for satisfaction with public hospitals are presented in Figure 6.2. Confidence intervals are much smaller than that of family physicians in Figure 6.1. This table is quite revealing in several ways. First, from the data in Figure 6.2, it is apparent that public hospital healthcare service satisfaction has stayed positive and statistically significant over the years. Second, Figure 6.2 shows the ups and downs over the studied period. For instance, up to 2011, compared to 2006, coefficients have been increasing, then started declining until 2014, and continued to increase again, and so on. Third, the magnitude of the coefficient in 2022 is lower than the 2007 level overall. In addition, satisfaction reached two high points of 0.237 and 0.234 in 2011 and 2016, respectively, and a low point of 0.110 in 2022. In summary, these results show that respondents who utilized healthcare services during the survey year are satisfied with public hospital health services.

The next question asked the respondents whether they were satisfied with university hospitals' healthcare services. Figure 6.3 presents the results obtained from the preliminary analysis of satisfaction with healthcare services in university hospitals, for which we have data between 2006 and 2022. As shown in Figure 6.3, confidence intervals are much bigger than in Figure 6.2. What is striking about the results in Figure 6.3 is that none of the coefficients produce statistically significant outcomes. In other words, coefficients on year dummies in Equation (6.1) are not statistically significantly different from zero, indicating no evidence that people are satisfied with healthcare services provided by university hospitals between 2006 and 2022. Furthermore, from this analysis, we can see that year dummies resulted in the lowest value of –0.090, which is statistically insignificant.

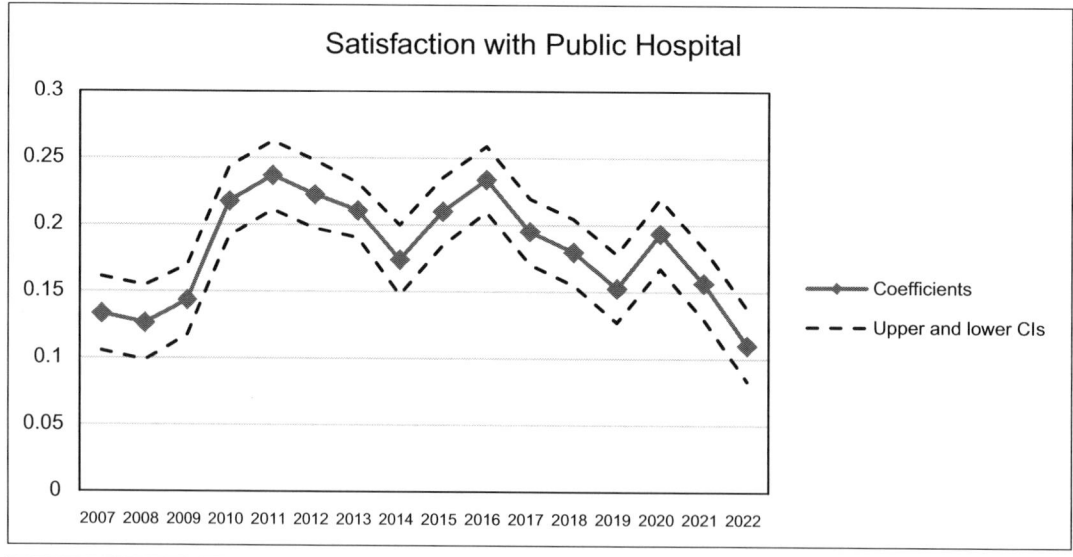

Figure 6.2   Year-fixed effects estimates of satisfaction with public hospitals.

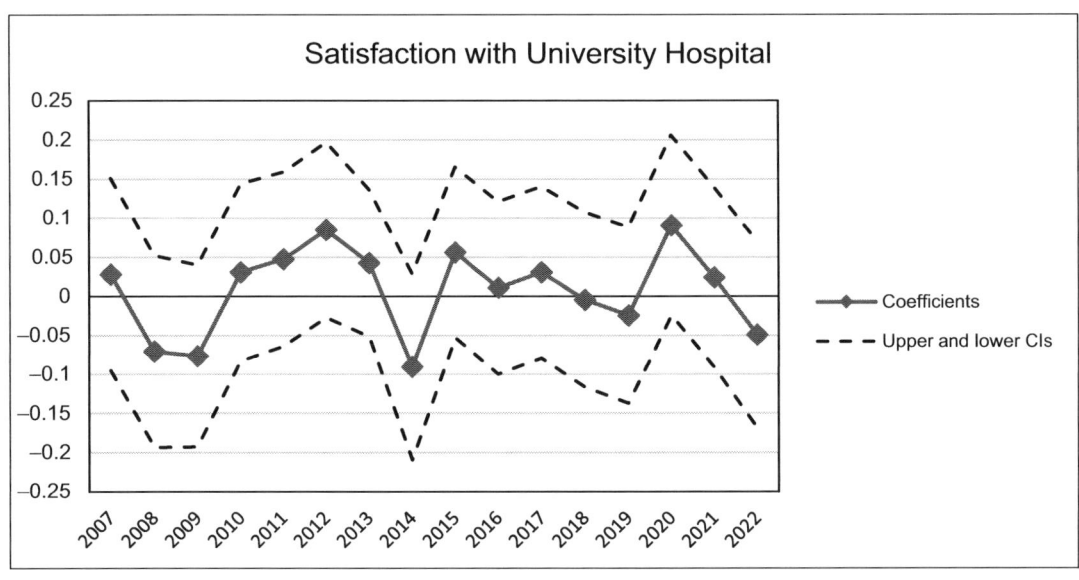

Figure 6.3 Year-fixed effects estimates of satisfaction with university hospitals.

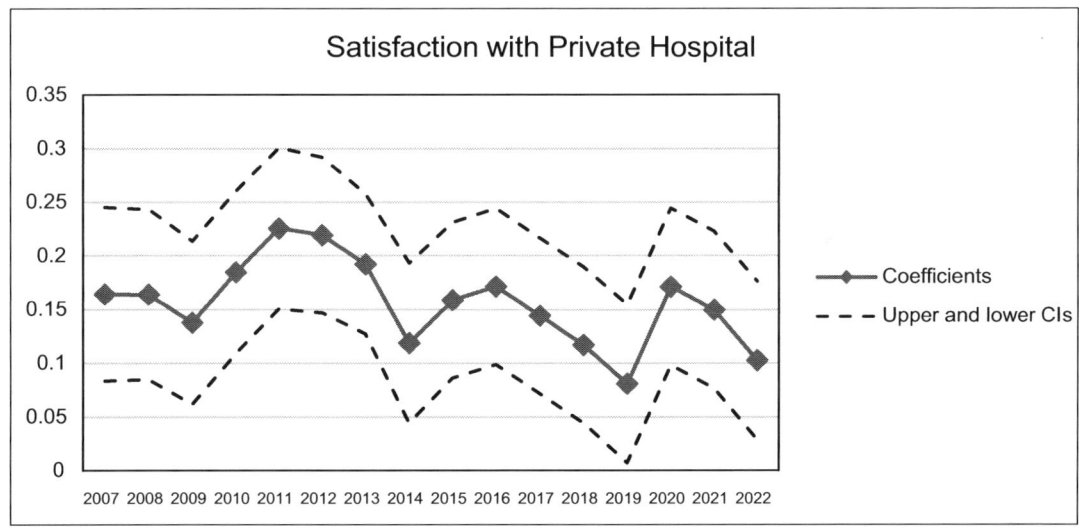

Figure 6.4 Year-fixed effects' estimates of satisfaction with private hospitals.

Turning now to the evidence on satisfaction with private healthcare providers in Figure 6.4, we see that all the coefficients are positive and statistically significantly different from zero, meaning that there is evidence that healthcare consumers are satisfied with the healthcare services offered by private hospitals. Our data includes the period from 2006 to 2022, which coincides with the H.T.P. The most interesting aspect of Figure 6.4 is the variability of the coefficients. In addition,

Figure 6.4 reveals that there has been a decline in the magnitude of the coefficients between 2007 and 2022. In other words, in 2007, respondents were more likely to be satisfied with private healthcare providers by 16.4 percentage points than in 2006. In 2022, they will likely be satisfied with private hospitals by 10.3 percentage points. Furthermore, it is apparent from this graph that satisfaction rose to a high point of 0.226 and peaked in 2011.

To assess the predictors of satisfaction with healthcare providers such as family physicians, public hospitals, university hospitals, and private hospitals, we utilize some demographic and socio-economic variables obtained from the respondents' life satisfaction surveys. Table 6.1 presents summary statistics of these variables used in this study.

Approximately 73% of those surveyed agreed that they are satisfied with healthcare services provided by healthcare providers. The mean age of individuals in the sample is about 45 years, ranging from 18 to 101. More than 50% of the respondents are female, and just under 40% of those who responded are employed. Almost a third of those surveyed reported that they had a serious health condition in the last year.

Regarding marital status, well over half of those interviewed (76%) indicated they are married, 15% never married, 3% divorced, and 7% widowed. On the question of education, over half of those surveyed (55%) indicated that they had educational attainments of primary school or below, 12% secondary education or equivalent, 18% high school or equivalent, and 15% college or above. Regarding income levels of individuals, we divided them into five main categories: Low income, mid-low income, mid-income, mid-high income, and high income. Approximately 40% of the respondents indicated low income, 19% mid-low income, 18% mid-income, 14% mid-high income, and 12% indicated high income.

In terms of satisfaction with their health, well over half of those surveyed (66%) indicated that they are satisfied with their overall health, 17% neither satisfied nor unsatisfied, and 16% unsatisfied. As regards the first choice of healthcare provider when getting sick, public hospitals have the highest proportion (51%), family physicians are the second (32%), private hospitals are the third (10%), and then come the university hospitals (3%). With respect to insurance status, just over 80% of those who responded agreed that their healthcare expenses are covered by social security institutions, about 10% agreed that their healthcare expenses are covered by Green Card insurance scheme for low-income individuals, 6% by own pay, 2% by other, and 1% by private insurance.

We have a variable in life satisfaction surveys, classified on the basis of the difficulty of meeting the needs with the current income level into five categories. Just above one-third of the respondents (37%) agreed that they are neither hardly nor easily meeting their needs with their current income level, with 33% hardly meeting their needs, 16% very hardly meeting their needs, 12% easily making their needs, and 2% very easily meeting their needs.

Having defined descriptive statistics for the variables used in the study, we will now discuss the results of the regression analysis. The results obtained from the preliminary analysis of determinants of satisfaction with healthcare services by the type of provider are presented across columns 1–4 in Table 6.2. In column 1, our dependent variable is the satisfaction with family physicians, satisfaction with public hospitals in column 2, satisfaction with university hospitals in column 3, and satisfaction with private hospitals in column 4. As noted earlier, we only keep those in our sample who utilized healthcare services during the survey year. We control demographic and socio-economic variables through all columns. We also account for year-fixed effects by including year dummies in our estimations. We include year dummies in the analysis because some unobserved changes in different years might exist.

Table 6.1 Descriptive Statistics

Variables	Description	Mean	SD	Min	Max	Observation
Satisfaction with health-care services	Categorical variable: 0 = not satisfied at all, not satisfied, neither satisfied nor unsatisfied; 1 = satisfied, very satisfied	0.729	0.444	0	1	237529
Age	Age of the individual	44.620	16.481	18	101	237821
Female	Dummy variable: 0 = male and 1 = female	0.570	0.494	0	1	237821
Employment status	Dummy variable: 0 = not employed and 1 = employed	0.366	0.481	0	1	237821
Serious health condition	Dummy variable: 0 = there was no serious health problem in last year, 1 = there was serious health problem in last year	0.297	0.456			237395
Marital Status						
Never married		0.145	0.352	0	1	237819
Married		0.756	0.429	0	1	237819
Divorced		0.026	0.159	0	1	237819
Widowed		0.071	0.258	0	1	237819
Educational Level						
Primary school or below		0.549	0.497	0	1	237821
Secondary education or equivalent		0.124	0.330	0	1	237821
High school or equivalent		0.178	0.382	0	1	237821
College or above		0.148	0.355	0	1	237821

(Continued)

Table 6.1 *(Continued)*   Descriptive Statistics

Variables	Description	Mean	SD	Min	Max	Observation
Income Level						
Low income		0.375	0.484	0	1	237821
Mid-low income		0.187	0.390	0	1	237821
Mid-income		0.176	0.380	0	1	237821
Mid-high income		0.144	0.352	0	1	237821
High income		0.115	0.319	0	1	237821
Satisfaction with own health						
Not satisfied		0.164	0.371	0	1	237821
Neither satisfied nor unsatisfied		0.170	0.376	0	1	237821
Satisfied		0.664	0.472	0	1	237821
First choice of healthcare provider when get sick						
Family physician/family health centre		0.318	0.465	0	1	237192
Public hospital		0.513	0.499	0	1	237192
University hospital		0.026	0.159	0	1	237192
Private hospital		0.104	0.305	0	1	237192
Private polyclinic/medical centre		0.006	0.081	0	1	237192
Private surgery		0.002	0.047	0	1	237192
Institutional physician		0.006	0.078	0	1	237192
Health centre		0.022	0.148	0	1	237192

Table 6.1 (Continued) Descriptive Statistics

Variables	Description	Mean	SD	Min	Max	Observation
Insurance status						
Own pay		0.061	0.240	0	1	237821
Green Card		0.095	0.294	0	1	237821
Social Security Institution		0.813	0.389	0	1	237821
Private insurance		0.012	0.111	0	1	237821
Other		0.016	0.128	0	1	237821
Difficulty of meeting the needs with the current income level						
Very easily		0.016	0.128	0	1	237821
Easily		0.123	0.328	0	1	237821
Neither hardly, nor easily		0.367	0.482	0	1	237821
Hardly		0.334	0.471	0	1	237821
Very hardly		0.158	0.364	0	1	237821

Table 6.2 Socio-economic and Demographic Predictors of Healthcare Services Satisfaction

	(1)	*(2)*	*(3)*	*(4)*
	Family Physician	*Public Hospital*	*University Hospital*	*Private Hospital*
Age	0.003*** (0.000)	0.003*** (0.000)	0.003*** (0.000)	0.003*** (0.000)
Female	−0.000 (0.004)	0.010*** (0.003)	−0.002 (0.013)	−0.000 (0.007)
Employed	−0.015*** (0.004)	−0.014*** (0.003)	−0.007 (0.015)	−0.055*** (0.008)
Serious health condition	−0.023*** (0.004)	−0.016*** (0.003)	−0.029** (0.015)	−0.012 (0.008)
Marital Status				
Never married	*Ref.*	*Ref.*	*Ref.*	*Ref.*
Married	−0.021*** (0.006)	−0.022*** (0.004)	0.001 (0.020)	−0.021** (0.009)
Divorced	−0.070*** (0.011)	−0.055*** (0.009)	−0.030 (0.039)	−0.076*** (0.020)
Widowed	−0.014 (0.009)	−0.005 (0.007)	−0.008 (0.032)	0.002 (0.017)
Educational Level				
Primary school or below	*Ref.*	*Ref.*	*Ref.*	*Ref.*
Secondary education or equivalent	−0.056*** (0.005)	−0.059*** (0.004)	−0.079*** (0.021)	−0.070*** (0.011)
High school or equivalent	−0.129*** (0.005)	−0.111*** (0.004)	−0.133*** (0.018)	−0.142*** (0.009)
College or above	−0.189*** (0.006)	−0.163*** (0.005)	−0.206*** (0.020)	−0.185*** (0.010)
Income Level				
Low income	*Ref.*	*Ref.*	*Ref.*	*Ref.*
Mid-low income	−0.018*** (0.004)	−0.009** (0.004)	−0.033* (0.018)	−0.029*** (0.011)
Mid income	−0.032*** (0.005)	−0.021*** (0.004)	−0.054*** (0.018)	−0.032*** (0.010)

Table 6.2 *(Continued)* **Socio-economic and Demographic Predictors of Healthcare Services Satisfaction**

	(1)	*(2)*	*(3)*	*(4)*
	Family Physician	*Public Hospital*	*University Hospital*	*Private Hospital*
Mid-high income	−0.045*** (0.005)	−0.028*** (0.005)	−0.036* (0.020)	−0.041*** (0.011)
High income	−0.051*** (0.007)	−0.039*** (0.006)	−0.064*** (0.022)	−0.033*** (0.011)
Satisfaction With Own Health				
Not satisfied	*Ref.*	*Ref.*	*Ref.*	*Ref.*
Neither satisfied nor unsatisfied	0.035*** (0.006)	0.025*** (0.004)	0.027 (0.019)	0.019* (0.012)
Satisfied	0.167*** (0.005)	0.171*** (0.004)	0.176*** (0.016)	0.176*** (0.010)
Channel of Healthcare Service Payment				
Own pay	*Ref.*	*Ref.*	*Ref.*	*Ref.*
Green Card	0.083*** (0.009)	0.052*** (0.007)	0.143*** (0.048)	0.027 (0.037)
Social Security Institution	0.061*** (0.008)	0.074*** (0.006)	0.145*** (0.036)	0.089*** (0.013)
Private insurance	0.057** (0.022)	0.070*** (0.017)	0.182*** (0.067)	0.136*** (0.018)
Other	0.051*** (0.013)	0.053*** (0.011)	0.102* (0.061)	0.017 (0.035)
Year-fixed effects	+	+	+	+
R-squared	0.077	0.074	0.085	0.074
N	75,331	121,620	6,215	24,746

Notes: In our regression analysis, we keep only those who used healthcare services in the survey year. We cluster standard errors at the household level and in parentheses. * $p < .1$, ** $p < .05$, *** $p < .01$. Regression analysis covers the period 2006–2022 in columns 2–4 and 2009–2022 in column 1.

A closer inspection of Table 6.2 shows that satisfaction increases with age for all healthcare providers, such as family physicians, public hospitals, university hospitals, and private hospitals, and the magnitudes of coefficients are highly similar. From column 2 of Table 6.2, we can see that females are more likely to be satisfied with health services in public hospitals, which is statistically significant ($p < 0.01$). Although the rest of the columns indicate a negative relationship for females, the coefficients are not statistically significant.

With respect to respondents' employment status, employed individuals are less likely than unemployed individuals to be satisfied with healthcare services in all types of healthcare providers except university hospitals. Quantitatively, for instance, satisfaction with private hospitals declines by 5.5 percentage points for employed individuals compared to unemployed ones. As far as the serious health conditions of respondents are concerned, there was a significant difference between the two conditions such that those with serious health conditions tend to be less satisfied than those without serious health conditions. The coefficients are precisely estimated at the $p = 0.01$ and $p = 0.05$ levels for all columns except the fourth column for private hospitals. The inconsistency with private providers may be because those with serious health problems avoid being treated in private hospitals due to potentially high treatment costs.

A negative correlation was found between marital status and satisfaction with healthcare services provided by family physicians in column 1, public hospitals in column 2, and private hospitals in column 4. For instance married individuals are less likely to be satisfied with health services by family physicians than never-married individuals by 2.1 percentage points, which is significant at $p = 0.01$ level. In the same way, divorced people are less likely than never-married people to be satisfied with health services by 7.0 percentage points. Furthermore, we find no significant evidence that widowed individuals are less satisfied with health services than never-married individuals.

Regarding educational level, there was a significant ($p < 0.01$) negative correlation between more education and satisfaction with health services across columns. In other words, as the education level increases, satisfaction with health services declines for each type of provider. For example while those with secondary education are less satisfied than primary schoolers with public hospitals' health services by 6.00 percentage points, college graduates are less satisfied than primary schoolers by 16.00 percentage points. This pattern is also valid for other types of healthcare organizations, as seen across columns in Table 6.2.

Income is also an important factor determining satisfaction with healthcare services. According to the results in Table 6.2, we found a negative correlation between income and satisfaction with healthcare services. For example the difference between the high- and low-income groups was significant at $p = 0.01$. Quantitatively, those in the high-income group are less likely than those in the low-income group to be satisfied with family physicians' healthcare services by 5.00 percentage points. Similarly, those in the high-income group are four times less likely to be satisfied than those in the mid-low-income group with public hospitals' healthcare services.

Satisfaction with one's own health is seen as a major predictor of satisfaction with healthcare services. Further analysis showed that there is strong evidence of the relationship between one's satisfaction with one's own health and satisfaction with healthcare services. For example those satisfied with their health are more likely to be satisfied with healthcare services that different organizations provide. Quantitatively, those satisfied with their health are more likely to be satisfied with healthcare services that family physicians offer than those unsatisfied with their health by about 16.70 percentage points. Likewise, those satisfied with their health are more likely to be satisfied with healthcare services that public hospitals offer than those unsatisfied with their health by 17.1 percentage points.

In addition, it is important to ask how the channel of healthcare service payment (i.e. health insurance status) is correlated with the satisfaction with healthcare services that different providers offer. Our reference category here is the status of "own pay". We have different channels to make service payments, such as "Green Card" health insurance for low-income individuals, "social security institutions" including formal sector employees, "private" insurance, and "other" channels. A positive correlation was found between health insurance and satisfaction with healthcare services. For example for each type of provider except for private hospitals, those with Green Card health insurance schemes tend to be more satisfied with healthcare services than those who make their payment when getting treatment from healthcare providers. Quantitatively, for instance, Green Card holders are more likely to be satisfied with university hospitals' services than those with the "own pay" option by 14.00 percentage points. Likewise, those who fall into the "social security scheme" option are more likely to be satisfied with public hospitals' healthcare services than those with the "own pay" option by 7.4 percentage points.

Table 6.3 Socio-Economic and Demographic Predictors of Healthcare Services Satisfaction for Years between 2018 and 2022

	(1)	*(2)*	*(3)*	*(4)*
	Family Physician	*Public Hospital*	*University Hospital*	*Private Hospital*
Age	0.002***	0.003***	0.006***	0.002***
	(0.000)	(0.000)	(0.001)	(0.001)
Female	−0.023***	0.004	0.038	−0.010
	(0.008)	(0.007)	(0.034)	(0.016)
Employed	−0.019**	−0.022***	−0.002	−0.071***
	(0.009)	(0.008)	(0.038)	(0.018)
Serious health condition	−0.011	−0.019**	0.023	−0.013
	(0.012)	(0.010)	(0.039)	(0.022)
Marital Status				
Never married	*Ref.*	*Ref.*	*Ref.*	*Ref.*
Married	−0.028**	−0.028**	−0.092*	−0.008
	(0.014)	(0.011)	(0.048)	(0.021)
Divorced	−0.105***	−0.043**	−0.212**	−0.076*
	(0.025)	(0.021)	(0.082)	(0.042)
Widowed	0.010	−0.016	−0.210**	0.071
	(0.021)	(0.019)	(0.089)	(0.044)
Educational Level				
Primary school or below	*Ref.*	*Ref.*	*Ref.*	*Ref.*
Secondary education or equivalent	−0.080***	−0.070***	−0.042	−0.066**
	(0.013)	(0.011)	(0.051)	(0.031)

Table 6.3 *(Continued)* **Socio-Economic and Demographic Predictors of Healthcare Services Satisfaction for Years between 2018 and 2022**

	(1)	*(2)*	*(3)*	*(4)*
	Family Physician	*Public Hospital*	*University Hospital*	*Private Hospital*
High school or equivalent	−0.154*** (0.012)	−0.100*** (0.011)	−0.080* (0.046)	−0.128*** (0.025)
College or above	−0.222*** (0.014)	−0.163*** (0.013)	−0.180*** (0.049)	−0.160*** (0.025)
Income Level				
Low income	*Ref.*	*Ref.*	*Ref.*	*Ref.*
Mid-low income	−0.042*** (0.013)	−0.025** (0.011)	−0.102* (0.053)	−0.090** (0.037)
Mid income	−0.041*** (0.013)	−0.034*** (0.012)	−0.041 (0.055)	−0.085** (0.035)
Mid-high income	−0.047*** (0.014)	−0.039*** (0.012)	−0.037 (0.058)	−0.067** (0.034)
High income	−0.051*** (0.015)	−0.036** (0.014)	−0.111* (0.058)	−0.066** (0.034)
Satisfaction with Own Health				
Not satisfied	*Ref.*	*Ref.*	*Ref.*	*Ref.*
Neither satisfied nor unsatisfied	0.056*** (0.015)	0.011 (0.013)	0.081 (0.051)	0.063** (0.030)
Satisfied	0.216*** (0.014)	0.200*** (0.011)	0.243*** (0.045)	0.252*** (0.028)
Channel of Healthcare Service Payment				
Own pay	*Ref.*	*Ref.*	*Ref.*	*Ref.*
SGK 4-a	0.047*** (0.017)	0.026* (0.015)	0.223** (0.092)	0.080*** (0.026)
SGK 4-b	0.068*** (0.020)	0.065*** (0.018)	0.274*** (0.099)	0.100*** (0.032)
SGK 4-c	0.075*** (0.021)	0.053*** (0.019)	0.269*** (0.097)	0.050 (0.033)
Green Card	0.061*** (0.022)	0.034* (0.018)	0.180 (0.112)	0.027 (0.065)

Table 6.3 *(Continued)* **Socio-Economic and Demographic Predictors of Healthcare Services Satisfaction for Years between 2018 and 2022**

	(1)	*(2)*	*(3)*	*(4)*
	Family Physician	*Public Hospital*	*University Hospital*	*Private Hospital*
Private Insurance	−0.085 (0.063)	0.163*** (0.051)	0.540*** (0.119)	0.153*** (0.034)
Year-fixed effects	+	+	+	+
R-squared	0.087	0.070	0.106	0.068
N	13,711	18,038	966	4,463

Notes: In our regression analysis, we keep only those who used healthcare services in the survey year. We cluster standard errors at the household level and in parentheses. * $p < .1$, ** $p < .05$, *** $p < .01$. Regression analysis covers the period 2018–2022.

In this part of the analysis, we wanted to keep our sample between 2018 and 2022 because life satisfaction surveys provide detailed channels of healthcare service payment options such as S.G.K 4-a for members of the private sector, S.G.K 4-b for self-employed, and S.G.K 4-c for civil servants. Table 6.3 compares the results obtained from the preliminary analysis of various insurance schemes. In this analysis, our reference group is that whose channel of healthcare service payment is the "own pay" option.

Table 6.3 shows that members of the private sector (insured through S.G.K. 4-a) are more likely than those with the "own pay" option to be satisfied with the healthcare services that four different organizations offer. For example S.G.K. 4-a members tend to be more satisfied than those in the reference group for family physician services by 4.7 percentage points. The most striking result to emerge from Table 6.3 is that S.G.K. 4-a members are more likely to be satisfied with university hospitals' healthcare services than the reference group by a large magnitude of about 22.00 percentage points.

Regarding self-employed respondents (insured through S.G.K 4-b), our findings indicate statistically significant and positive differences from the reference group for each type of healthcare provider. Quantitatively, S.G.K 4-b members are more likely to be satisfied with the health services of public and private hospitals than the reference group by 6.5 and 10.00 percentage points, respectively. The more surprising correlation is with the services of university hospitals such that S.G.K 4-b insurance members appear to be more satisfied by about 27 percentage points.

The experience of the civil servants (insured through S.G.K 4-c) in terms of satisfaction with the healthcare services of different providers is similar to that of S.G.K 4-a and S.G.K 4-b insurance members. There is one exception: No significant increase in satisfaction was found compared with the reference group in terms of the health services of private hospitals.

There was no evidence that being insured via the Green Card scheme has an influence on satisfaction with the healthcare services of university and private hospitals compared with the reference group. Nonetheless, there is a statistically significant difference between these two groups with respect to satisfaction with family physician services ($p < 0.01$) and public hospitals ($p < 0.10$), indicating that Green Card holders are more likely to be satisfied with these services. Concerning the private insurance scheme, except for the services of family physicians, they are highly satisfied with health services, especially university hospitals, by 54.00 percentage points compared to the reference group. Overall, these results suggest that S.G.K 4-a, S.G.K 4-b, S.G.K 4-c, Green Card, and private insurance members are more satisfied with the health services of different providers than with the "own pay" plan.

We move on now to consider some heterogenous analysis. As pointed out in the data section, we categorized the income variable into five main sub-groups: low income, mid-low income, mid-income, mid-high income, and high income. We separately execute Equation (6.1) for each income classification for satisfaction with the health services that family physicians offer and report the results in Table 6.4. What is striking about the findings in Table 6.4 is that females in the low-income category tend to be satisfied with family physicians' services. However, the outcomes suggest the opposite for females in mid-high and high-income groups.

Table 6.4 Socio-Economic and Demographic Predictors of Healthcare Services' Satisfaction from Family Physicians for Different Income Groups

	(1)	*(2)*	*(3)*	*(4)*	*(5)*
	Low Income	*Mid-Low Income*	*Mid-Income*	*Mid-High Income*	*High Income*
Age	0.003***	0.003***	0.001***	0.001***	0.001***
	(0.000)	(0.000)	(0.000)	(0.000)	(0.001)
Female	0.025***	0.008	−0.009	−0.041***	−0.036***
	(0.006)	(0.008)	(0.009)	(0.010)	(0.011)
Employed	0.004	−0.021**	−0.034***	−0.015	−0.007
	(0.007)	(0.009)	(0.009)	(0.010)	(0.013)
Serious health condition	−0.013**	−0.022**	−0.034***	−0.009	−0.026
	(0.006)	(0.010)	(0.012)	(0.013)	(0.018)
Marital Status					
Never married	*Ref.*	*Ref.*	*Ref.*	*Ref.*	*Ref.*
Married	−0.037***	−0.027**	−0.000	0.002	−0.005
	(0.011)	(0.014)	(0.014)	(0.015)	(0.018)
Divorced	−0.073***	−0.086***	−0.055*	−0.014	−0.075*
	(0.017)	(0.027)	(0.028)	(0.032)	(0.041)
Widowed	−0.052***	−0.020	0.039*	−0.008	0.014
	(0.013)	(0.020)	(0.022)	(0.028)	(0.036)
Educational Level					
Primary school or below	*Ref.*	*Ref.*	*Ref.*	*Ref.*	*Ref.*
Secondary education or equivalent	−0.046***	−0.058***	−0.054***	−0.062***	−0.090***
	(0.008)	(0.010)	(0.011)	(0.014)	(0.021)

Table 6.4 *(Continued)* **Socio-Economic and Demographic Predictors of Healthcare Services' Satisfaction from Family Physicians for Different Income Groups**

	(1)	*(2)*	*(3)*	*(4)*	*(5)*
	Low Income	*Mid-Low Income*	*Mid-Income*	*Mid-High Income*	*High Income*
High school or equivalent	−0.132*** (0.010)	−0.124*** (0.011)	−0.132*** (0.011)	−0.137*** (0.012)	−0.151*** (0.017)
College or above	−0.173*** (0.019)	−0.183*** (0.016)	−0.203*** (0.014)	−0.212*** (0.012)	−0.233*** (0.015)
Satisfaction with Own Health					
Not satisfied	*Ref.*	*Ref.*	*Ref.*	*Ref.*	*Ref.*
Neither satisfied nor unsatisfied	0.029*** (0.009)	0.025* (0.013)	0.033** (0.016)	0.046** (0.019)	0.026 (0.024)
Satisfied	0.140*** (0.007)	0.145*** (0.012)	0.166*** (0.014)	0.170*** (0.017)	0.174*** (0.022)
Channel of Healthcare Service Payment					
Own pay	*Ref.*	*Ref.*	*Ref.*	*Ref.*	*Ref.*
Green Card	0.098*** (0.011)	0.045* (0.024)	0.094*** (0.033)	0.086* (0.047)	0.006 (0.086)
Social Security Institution	0.056*** (0.010)	0.021 (0.017)	0.066*** (0.021)	0.050* (0.028)	0.052 (0.035)
Private insurance	0.052 (0.035)	0.091** (0.046)	−0.009 (0.062)	0.032 (0.060)	0.028 (0.061)
Other	0.064*** (0.016)	−0.004 (0.035)	0.044 (0.041)	0.059 (0.057)	0.126 (0.083)
Difficulty of Meeting the Needs with Earned Income					
Very easily	*Ref.*	*Ref.*	*Ref.*	*Ref.*	*Ref.*
Easily	0.040 (0.031)	−0.041 (0.028)	0.030 (0.033)	−0.045* (0.023)	−0.044** (0.021)
Neither hardly nor easily	0.009 (0.031)	−0.088*** (0.027)	−0.028 (0.032)	−0.125*** (0.023)	−0.139*** (0.020)
Hardly	−0.034 (0.031)	−0.158*** (0.028)	−0.093*** (0.033)	−0.208*** (0.024)	−0.224*** (0.024)
Very hardly	−0.075** (0.031)	−0.206*** (0.029)	−0.137*** (0.035)	−0.255*** (0.030)	−0.273*** (0.042)
R-squared	0.071	0.085	0.082	0.082	0.087

Table 6.4 *(Continued)* Socio-Economic and Demographic Predictors of Healthcare Services' Satisfaction from Family Physicians for Different Income Groups

	(1)	*(2)*	*(3)*	*(4)*	*(5)*
	Low Income	*Mid-Low Income*	*Mid-Income*	*Mid-High Income*	*High Income*
N	26,973	14,989	13,608	11,527	8,234

Notes: In our regression analysis, we keep only those who used healthcare services in the survey year. We cluster standard errors at the household level and in parentheses. * $p < .1$, ** $p < .05$, *** $p < .01$. Regression analysis covers the period 2009–2022.

Another significant finding in Table 6.4 is that although those with serious health conditions in three income categories, such as low income, mid-low income, and mid-income, produce statistically significant and negative results in terms of satisfaction with family physicians' services, those in higher income groups (i.e. mid-high income and high income) do not yield significant outcomes, albeit negative coefficients.

The correlation between "the difficulty of meeting the needs with earned income" and satisfaction with healthcare services by family physicians is interesting because as income increases, satisfaction declines substantially. However, in the low-income group, only those who respond "very hardly" to the earlier question indicate dissatisfaction with the health services.

Table 6.5 presents socio-economic and demographic determinants of healthcare service satisfaction from public hospitals for various income groups. It is worth noting that there were significant differences between females in low-income and high-income groups. Females in the

Table 6.5 Socio-Economic and Demographic Predictors of Healthcare Services' Satisfaction from Public Hospitals for Different Income Groups

	(1)	*(2)*	*(3)*	*(4)*	*(5)*
	Low Income	*Mid-Low Income*	*Mid-Income*	*Mid-High Income*	*High Income*
Age	0.003***	0.003***	0.003***	0.002***	0.002***
	(0.000)	(0.000)	(0.000)	(0.000)	(0.000)
Female	0.028***	0.011*	−0.006	−0.010	−0.035***
	(0.004)	(0.007)	(0.007)	(0.008)	(0.010)
Employed	−0.007	−0.014**	−0.014*	−0.021**	−0.021*
	(0.005)	(0.007)	(0.007)	(0.009)	(0.012)
Serious health condition	−0.009**	−0.014*	−0.020**	−0.032***	−0.002
	(0.005)	(0.008)	(0.008)	(0.011)	(0.014)
Marital Status					
Never married	*Ref.*	*Ref.*	*Ref.*	*Ref.*	*Ref.*
Married	−0.007	−0.028***	−0.011	−0.031***	−0.015
	(0.007)	(0.010)	(0.010)	(0.012)	(0.016)

Table 6.5 *(Continued)* **Socio-Economic and Demographic Predictors of Healthcare Services' Satisfaction from Public Hospitals for Different Income Groups**

	(1)	*(2)*	*(3)*	*(4)*	*(5)*
	Low Income	*Mid-Low Income*	*Mid-Income*	*Mid-High Income*	*High Income*
Divorced	−0.019 (0.013)	−0.052** (0.022)	−0.089*** (0.023)	−0.079*** (0.027)	−0.029 (0.035)
Widowed	−0.005 (0.010)	−0.020 (0.016)	0.012 (0.017)	0.031 (0.022)	0.027 (0.032)
Educational Level					
Primary school or below	*Ref.*	*Ref.*	*Ref.*	*Ref.*	*Ref.*
Secondary education or equivalent	−0.042*** (0.007)	−0.059*** (0.009)	−0.059*** (0.010)	−0.092*** (0.012)	−0.095*** (0.018)
High school or equivalent	−0.111*** (0.008)	−0.115*** (0.009)	−0.105*** (0.009)	−0.132*** (0.010)	−0.139*** (0.015)
College or above	−0.161*** (0.015)	−0.153*** (0.014)	−0.164*** (0.012)	−0.191*** (0.011)	−0.212*** (0.014)
Satisfaction with Own Health					
Not satisfied	*Ref.*	*Ref.*	*Ref.*	*Ref.*	*Ref.*
Neither satisfied nor unsatisfied	0.024*** (0.006)	0.013 (0.011)	0.014 (0.012)	0.053*** (0.015)	0.012 (0.021)
Satisfied	0.149*** (0.005)	0.160*** (0.009)	0.163*** (0.010)	0.194*** (0.013)	0.190*** (0.019)
Channel of Healthcare Service Payment					
Own pay	*Ref.*	*Ref.*	*Ref.*	*Ref.*	*Ref.*
Green Card	0.060*** (0.008)	0.044** (0.017)	0.042* (0.023)	0.077** (0.032)	0.054 (0.056)
Social Security Institution	0.069*** (0.008)	0.050*** (0.014)	0.047*** (0.016)	0.087*** (0.021)	0.059* (0.033)
Private insurance	0.062*** (0.022)	0.004 (0.047)	0.056 (0.043)	0.042 (0.054)	0.114* (0.062)
Other	0.054*** (0.013)	0.059** (0.027)	0.036 (0.034)	0.019 (0.049)	0.096 (0.070)

Table 6.5 *(Continued)* **Socio-Economic and Demographic Predictors of Healthcare Services' Satisfaction from Public Hospitals for Different Income Groups**

	(1)	*(2)*	*(3)*	*(4)*	*(5)*
	Low Income	*Mid-Low Income*	*Mid-Income*	*Mid-High Income*	*High Income*
Difficulty of Meeting the Needs with Earned Income					
Very easily	*Ref.*	*Ref.*	*Ref.*	*Ref.*	*Ref.*
Easily	0.034 (0.025)	0.010 (0.034)	0.022 (0.030)	0.015 (0.024)	−0.013 (0.020)
Neither hardly, nor easily	0.012 (0.025)	−0.038 (0.033)	−0.032 (0.029)	−0.046* (0.024)	−0.103*** (0.019)
Hardly	−0.031 (0.025)	−0.084** (0.034)	−0.087*** (0.029)	−0.100*** (0.024)	−0.143*** (0.023)
Very hardly	−0.067*** (0.025)	−0.124*** (0.034)	−0.117*** (0.031)	−0.151*** (0.029)	−0.149*** (0.037)
R-squared	0.076	0.080	0.080	0.080	0.082
N	52,748	23,175	20,937	15,444	9,316

Notes: In our regression analysis, we keep only those who used healthcare services in the survey year. We cluster standard errors at the household level and in parentheses. * $p < .1$, ** $p < .05$, *** $p < .01$. Regression analysis covers the period 2006–2022.

low-income group show statistically significant outcomes in terms of satisfaction with health services from public hospitals. Quantitatively, females are more likely to be satisfied than men in the low-income group. On the other hand, females in the high-income groups are less likely to be satisfied than men with public hospitals' services.

Another significant finding in Table 6.5 is that no matter what income group respondents fall into, satisfaction with health services decreases if one has a serious health condition. However, this case is not valid for the high-income group, which produces an insignificant coefficient, albeit a negative one.

In addition, from our analysis, we see that one's satisfaction with one's own health is of great importance for satisfaction with health services from various providers. Our findings in Table 6.5 indicate a correlation between satisfaction with own health and satisfaction with healthcare services. In other words, across all columns in Table 6.5, we find statistically significant and positive coefficients, indicating that satisfaction with own health increases the satisfaction with health services compared to those unsatisfied with their health.

To conclude this section, we identified some socio-economic and demographic variables, such as age, employment status, serious health condition, marital status, education and income levels, satisfaction with own health, and insurance status, which are correlated with the healthcare service satisfaction that various healthcare organizations offer.

The following section discusses our findings by comparing them with the current literature.

6.5 Discussion and Conclusion

The Health Transformation Programme of Turkey, initiated in 2003, aimed to enhance accessibility, efficiency, and quality of care. The evolution of patient satisfaction since the initiation of the H.T.P has been the subject of several studies over the past two decades. This study aims to capture the current state of patient satisfaction, identify new challenges, and assess the effectiveness of recent policies and reforms across various healthcare providers, including family physicians, public hospitals, university hospitals, and private hospitals. It also aims to determine the demographic and socio-economic predictors of healthcare service satisfaction that different healthcare providers offer.

The results indicate that respondents are generally satisfied with public hospital services, though there is no significant change in satisfaction with university hospitals from 2006 to 2022. Satisfaction with private healthcare providers is consistently positive, though it declined slightly from 2007 to 2022, peaking in 2011. Approximately 73% of respondents are satisfied with various healthcare services. This increase in overall satisfaction with healthcare services in Turkey is consistent with the findings of related studies (e.g. Stokes et al., 2015; Hone et al., 2017; Uğurluoğlu et al., 2019; Caner & Cilasun, 2019). Nevertheless, despite significantly differing from zero and staying mostly positive, year-fixed effects' coefficients decline over the years even though we have addressed time trends, time-varying confounders, and seasonal variation. Thus, while the positive coefficients indicate an overall satisfaction or improvement, the diminishing magnitude of these coefficients suggests that the rate of improvement or satisfaction is decreasing over time. This finding could imply that initial gains or enhancements in the healthcare services' quality, efficiency, or other measured outcomes due to the implementation of the H.T.P were stronger in the earlier years; however, the impact has lessened in more recent years.

An intriguing finding of the study is the statistically insignificant results regarding health service satisfaction in university hospitals' healthcare services for almost two decades. There could be a couple of explanations for this finding. First, university hospitals might have exhibited a consistent level of service quality over the years, neither significantly improving nor declining. This stability likely contributes to the absence of significant changes in satisfaction levels. Second, patients often have higher expectations from university hospitals due to their association with research and advanced medical training. When these expectations are not consistently met, satisfaction levels tend to remain stagnant. Third, university hospitals frequently handle more complex and severe medical cases (Frick et al., 1985). The challenges associated with treating such cases can impact overall satisfaction, as patient outcomes are less predictable and more complicated than those at general or private hospitals. Finally, university hospitals might have faced challenges related to resource allocation. Balancing the needs of patient care, research, and education requires careful management. These competing demands can negatively affect patient satisfaction if they are not effectively addressed. Regardless of the root cause of the stagnant satisfaction with university hospitals' healthcare services, policymakers and authorities should investigate this finding further.

A finding of the analysis consistent with the related literature (e.g. Atkinson & Haran, 2005; Calnan et al., 1994; Hekkert et al., 2009) is that age increases satisfaction across all provider types. The results also indicate that females show higher satisfaction with public hospitals, as shown by Calnan et al. (1994). Employed individuals are less satisfied with healthcare services than the unemployed, except in university hospitals. Married individuals report lower satisfaction with healthcare services. This finding aligns with some studies, such as Quintana et al. (2006), while it is inconsistent with others (e.g. Hall & Dornan, 1990). Similarly, as in many studies (e.g. Kersnik, 2001), those with lower education levels report higher satisfaction with healthcare services.

Higher income correlates negatively with satisfaction as opposed to the findings of Yuan (2021) using an international sample. A possible explanation could be that wealthier Turkish nationals might have higher expectations for the quality and efficiency of healthcare services, making them more critical when these expectations are unmet. Additionally, higher-income Turkish individuals might be more aware of and sensitive to any deficiencies in the healthcare system, thus influencing their overall satisfaction negatively.

Furthermore, satisfaction with one's health positively influences overall healthcare satisfaction, which is consistent with the findings of the related literature (e.g. Zhang et al., 2007). Finally, insured individuals, particularly those with S.G.K and Green Card plans, report higher satisfaction than those paying out-of-pocket. Several factors contribute to this higher satisfaction among insured individuals. For instance insurance coverage reduces the financial burden of healthcare costs, making medical services more affordable and accessible. This financial relief can lead to a more positive overall experience, as patients are less likely to feel stressed or anxious about the cost of their care. Alternatively, insurance plans often provide access to a broader network of healthcare providers and services, ensuring that insured individuals receive timely and appropriate care. This can enhance the quality of care and increase patient satisfaction.

In conclusion, the H.T.P initiated in 2003 has significantly influenced patient satisfaction with healthcare services in Turkey, with notable increases in overall satisfaction, especially in public and private hospitals. Various predictors of patient satisfaction, including demographic and socio-economic factors such as age, gender, employment status, marital status, education level, income, personal health satisfaction, and insurance coverage, play crucial roles in shaping these satisfaction levels. Nevertheless, although the initial impact of the H.T.P on healthcare quality and efficiency was substantial, its effects have diminished over time, necessitating renewed focus and strategies to sustain improvements.

References

Ali Jadoo, S. A., Aljunid, S. M., Sulku, S. N., & Nur, A. M. (2014). Turkish health system reform from the people's perspective: A cross sectional study. *BMC Health Services Research, 14*, 1–9. https://doi.org/10.1186/1472-6963-14-30

Atkinson, S., & Haran, D. (2005). Individual and district scale determinants of users' satisfaction with primary health care in developing countries. *Social Science & Medicine, 60*(3), 501–513. https://doi.org/10.1016/j.socscimed.2004.05.019

Aydin, S. (2018). *Factors affecting patient satisfaction with healthcare system of Turkey* (Doctoral dissertation, University of South Carolina).

Bostan, S. (2013). What has the health transformation program in Turkey changed for patients?. *Hacettepe Sağlık İdaresi Dergisi, 16*(2), 91–103.

Calnan, M., Katsouyiannopoulos, V., Ovcharov, V. K., Prokhorskas, R., Ramic, H., & Willims, S. (1994). Major determinants of consumer satisfaction with primary care in different health systems. *Family Practice, 11*(4), 468–478. https://doi.org/10.1093/fampra/11.4.468

Caner, A., & Cilasun, S. M. (2019). Health care services and the elderly: Utilization and satisfaction in the aftermath of the Turkish health transformation program. *Gerontology and Geriatric Medicine, 5*, 2333721418822868. https://doi.org/10.1177/2333721418822868

Frick, A. P., Martin, S. G., & Shwartz, M. (1985). Case-mix and cost differences between teaching and nonteaching hospitals. *Medical Care, 23*(4), 283–295.

Gaynor, M. (2006). *What do we know about competition and quality in health care markets?*, NBER Working Paper 12301. NBER. https://doi.org/10.3386/w12301

Gaynor, M., & Town, R. J. (2011). Competition in Health Care Markets, in M. V. Pauly, T. G. Mcguire & P. P. Barros (eds.), *Handbook of health economics*, Vol. 2, Chapter 10, 639–690. Chapter 9, 499–637. Elsevier.

Hall, J. A., & Dornan, M. C. (1990). Patient sociodemographic characteristics as predictors of satisfaction with medical care: A meta-analysis. *Social Science & Medicine, 30*(7), 811–818. https://doi.org/10.1016/0277-9536(90)90205-7

Hazama, Y. (2015). Health reform and service satisfaction in the poor: Turkey 2003–11. *Turkish Studies, 16*(1), 36–53. https://doi.org/10.1080/14683849.2015.1023193

Hekkert, K. D., Cihangir, S., Kleefstra, S. M., Van Den Berg, B., & Kool, R. B. (2009). Patient satisfaction revisited: A multilevel approach. *Social Science & Medicine, 69*(1), 68–75. https://doi.org/10.1016/j.socscimed.2009.04.016

Hone, T., Gurol-Urganci, I., Millett, C., Başara, B., Akdağ, R., & Atun, R. (2017). Effect of primary health care reforms in Turkey on health service utilization and user satisfaction. *Health Policy and Planning, 32*(1), 57–67. https://doi.org/10.1093/heapol/czw098

Kersnik, J. (2001). Determinants of customer satisfaction with the health care system, with the possibility to choose a personal physician and with a family doctor in a transition country. *Health Policy, 57*(2), 155–164. https://doi.org/10.1016/S0168-8510(01)00118-X

Kruk, M. E., Gage, A. D., Joseph, N. T., Danaei, G., García-Saisó, S., & Salomon, J. A. (2018). Mortality due to low-quality health systems in the universal health coverage era: A systematic analysis of amenable deaths in 137 countries. *The Lancet, 392*(10160), 2203–2212.

Ökem, Z. G., & Çakar, M. (2015). What have health care reforms achieved in Turkey? An appraisal of the "Health Transformation Programme". *Health Policy, 119*(9), 1153–1163. https://doi.org/10.1016/j.healthpol.2015.06.003

Özbuğday, F. C. (2017). Hospital quality and demand: An analysis of German hospitals using distance-metric approach. *Ege Academic Review, 17*(4), 493–504.

Quintana, J. M., González, N., Bilbao, A., Aizpuru, F., Escobar, A., Esteban, C., . . . & Thompson, A. (2006). Predictors of patient satisfaction with hospital health care. *BMC Health Services Research, 6*, 1–9. https://doi.org/10.1186/1472-6963-6-102

Stokes, J., Gurol–Urganci, I., Hone, T., & Atun, R. (2015). Effect of health system reforms in Turkey on user satisfaction. *Journal of Global Health, 5*(2). https://doi.org/10.7189/jogh.05.020403

Uğurluoğlu, Ö., Ürek, D., & Demir, İ. B. (2019). Evaluation of individuals' satisfaction with health care services in Turkey. *Health Policy and Technology, 8*(1), 24–29. https://doi.org/10.1016/j.hlpt.2019.02.003

Yuan, Y. (2021). Public satisfaction with health care system in 30 countries: The effects of individual characteristics and social contexts. *Health Policy, 125*(10), 1359–1366. https://doi.org/10.1016/j.healthpol.2021.08.0053

Zhang, Y., Rohrer, J., Borders, T., & Farrell, T. (2007). Patient satisfaction, self-rated health status, and health confidence: An assessment of the utility of single-item questions. *American Journal of Medical Quality, 22*(1), 42–49. https://doi.org/10.1177/1062860606296329

Chapter 7

Determinants of Household Health Expenditures in the Era of the Health Transformation Programme in Turkey

Işın Kortan Saraçoğlu

Contents

7.1 Introduction

The good health status of individuals is the primary goal for countries, and also it is a major factor in ensuring economic development and reducing poverty. Therefore, increasing investments in healthcare increases income substantially annually, especially in low-income countries. The economic costs of avoidable illnesses are extremely high for countries. The diseases lower annual societal incomes, economic growth prospects, and individual lifetime earnings. Especially for poor households, diseases can lead to severe poverty, when they must sell assets to cover healthcare expenditures. Thus, investing in health is important in poverty reduction strategies, specifically in low-income countries. Health is essential for job productivity, learning capacity, and personal development, and health and education form the foundation of human capital. The good health status of individuals is crucial for their economic well-being and poverty reduction, long-term

DOI: 10.4324/9781003539896-8

economic development, and economic growth on a societal level (W.H.O., 2001: 16–23). Health systems aim to improve people's health and protect them from financial burdens caused by illnesses. The challenge for governments, especially in low-income countries, is to reduce the burden of paying out-of-pocket (O.O.P.) health expenditures for health by expanding prepayment plans (W.H.O., 2000: ix). The O.O.P. health expenditures are considered an inherently regressive form of financing. This implies that households with lower incomes bear a higher relative burden of O.O.P. health expenditures compared to households with higher incomes (Wagstaff et al., 2020).

O.O.P. health expenditures are one of the indicators of unequal healthcare costs and reflect the degree of effectiveness of a healthcare financing system (Villanueva & Aranas, 2023). Direct household O.O.P. health expenditures constitute the largest share of health financing in many countries. Recent data shows that 2 billion people experience financial hardships due to impoverished O.O.P. healthcare expenditures, catastrophic healthcare expenses, or both (W.H.O. & W.B., 2023). O.O.P. health spending corresponds to health spending made by individuals, funded by their income, savings, and loans. O.O.P. healthcare expenses contain payments made by individuals when using any health service or good. In other words, O.O.P. healthcare expenses consist of payments made by individuals to any healthcare provider for the care they receive in all settings for all types of diseases, sicknesses, and health conditions. This type of spending encompasses both formal and informal payments but does not cover upfront costs such as taxes, social security contributions, or insurance premiums from third parties. It also excludes reimbursements made by the government, health insurance funds, or private insurance companies. Additionally, indirect costs unrelated to healthcare, such as non-emergency transportation expenses and opportunity costs like income lost due to time spent receiving healthcare, are not considered part of O.O.P. health spending (W.H.O. &W.B., 2023). O.O.P. health expenditures include payments for health services such as outpatient and inpatient treatment services, diagnostic and laboratory services, emergency transportation and rescue services, as well as payments for medicines and health products. Among medicines, over-the-counter medicines and medicines prescribed in outpatient treatment are also included in O.O.P. expenses. In addition to that, payments for healthcare products like masks and other preventive and protective devices, medical diagnostic products, and ancillary products are included in O.O.P. expenses (W.H.O. & W.B., 2023). Briefly, the O.O.P. healthcare payments contain medical fees, buys of medicines whether prescribed or not, user fees for public care, payments for appliances, insurance copayments, diagnostic tests, etc. (Van Doorslaer et al., 2006). Individuals with identical health conditions might incur varying expenses due to a multitude of factors. For instance individuals might have varying insurance policies, and some could have additional health conditions that influence the kind of treatment they need. Additionally, individuals differ in their ability to pay O.O.P. for healthcare, which means that some individuals might not acquire all the healthcare they require, while others may receive unnecessary treatments without recognizing it (Wagstaff et al., 2020).

Table 7.1 indicates the O.O.P. health expenditures in Turkey between 2000 and 2020. According to Table 7.1, O.O.P. expenditures as a percentage of current health expenditures increased from 18.93% in 2003 to 24.18% in 2005. Subsequently, this proportion started to decrease and fell to 14.51% in 2009. After 2009, it started to increase again and rose to 17.73% in 2014. In 2016, it decreased to 16.47% and increased to 17.05% in 2019. It fell to 16.43% in 2020. In summary, if we evaluate, O.O.P. health expenditures' allocation in current health expenditures was 18.93% in 2003, while it was observed that it decreased to 16.43% in 2020. This indicates a decrease in the share of total health expenditures that are directly paid by individuals over the specified period. While O.O.P. health expenditures per capita were $45 in 2003, they increased to $121 in 2007. It decreased after 2007 and dropped to $65 in 2020. Moreover, the O.O.P.

Table 7.1 O.O.P. Health Expenditures of Turkey

Years	O.O.P. Expenditure (% of Current Health Expenditure)	O.O.P. Expenditure Per Capita (Current US$)	O.O.P. Expenditure Per Capita, PPP (Current International $)
2003	18.93	45	91
2004	20.18	60	108
2005	24.18	87	140
2006	23.65	97	165
2007	23.88	121	185
2008	19.18	108	160
2009	14.51	72	123
2010	16.87	90	147
2011	15.9	84	145
2012	15.93	83	146
2013	16.93	93	165
2014	17.73	92	183
2015	16.95	76	177
2016	16.47	76	184
2017	17.38	76	200
2018	17.49	68	201
2019	17.05	68	206
2020	16.43	65	210

Source: (W.B., 2024).

expenditures per capita, according to purchasing power parity, increased from $91 in 2003 to $210 in 2020. Adjusting the data for purchasing power parity means that these data will more accurately reflect economic indicators.

Significant reforms have been implemented in the healthcare system of Turkey with the H.T.P. in 2003. The H.T.P. aims to organize, finance, and deliver healthcare services effectively, efficiently, and equitably (The Ministry of Health of Turkey (M.O.H.), 2012). The main innovations implemented for this purpose include the restructuring of healthcare provision, the restructuring of the financial system, and the introduction of a general health coverage system.

One of the most important aspects of the H.T.P. was its emphasis on increasing general health coverage, including measures to reduce the financial burden on individuals and households in accessing health services. When healthcare in Turkey is considered, it is seen that the financing system and the provision of public healthcare services were fragmented structures before the H.T.P. Before 2003, different public institutions in the Turkish healthcare system financed and provided healthcare services. Even individuals with insurance encounter difficulties in accessing health services within this system, because of the fragmented structure of the healthcare financing system and the public healthcare provision (O.E.C.D., 2008: 11; Atun et al., 2013). The fragmented structure of the financial system and the lack of health insurance that covers all individuals also lead to O.O.P. spending (M.O.H., 2012).

Since 2003, the H.T.P. has led to important changes in the health system. The primary healthcare services have been made free of charge within the scope of preventive and basic health services with the H.T.P. In this context, primary healthcare services have been strengthened with the family medicine practice introduced. The vast majority of public hospitals in Turkey, including hospitals previously managed by the social security institution, are gathered under a single umbrella, within the Ministry of Health. As a result of the reforms, different social security institutions have converged into a single institution and have shared databases and claims and utilization managing systems. "The Social Security and General Health Insurance Law" came into force in October 2008, and with this, a single-payer system was installed for public patients in Turkey (O.E.C.D., 2008). H.T.P. aims to include citizens under the social security umbrella, to decrease the ratio of O.O.P. expenditures of households to total health expenditures, and to eliminate the impoverishing effects of O.O.P. expenditures on households (M.O.H., 2012).

This chapter aims to determine the factors impacting O.O.P. health expenditures in Turkey and to evaluate how these factors change with the H.T.P. In this context, first, the relationship between the H.T.P. and O.O.P. expenditures in Turkey is discussed. Then, the literature on the factors determining O.O.P. expenditures is reviewed. In the chapter, the factors impacting O.O.P. health expenditures in Turkey during the H.T.P. process are comparatively analysed using the L.I.T.S. I, L.I.T.S. II, and L.I.T.S. III data sets, and the differences and similarities are evaluated in the context of the existing literature.

7.2 Literature Review

Household O.O.P. expenditures are the direct means of financing healthcare services in many developing countries. In addition, O.O.P. health expenditures affect the capacity of individuals to benefit from health services and provide information about the status of the implemented health system. Therefore, data on household health expenditures are crucial for formulating an effective financing policy for a country's healthcare system. In this context, it would be useful for policymakers to know the factors determining O.O.P. health expenditures to improve the health system. Many studies have been conducted in the literature for many countries to identify the factors determining O.O.P. health expenditures, and it is seen that the most important factors determining O.O.P. health expenditures are the differences in demographic and socio-economic household features and geographic factors in the literature (Demir et al., 2022; Aregbeshola & Khan, 2021).

In this context, many studies conducted in different countries have explored whether gender is the determinant of O.O.P. health expenditures (Bora Başara & Şahin, 2008; You & Kobayashi, 2011; Bock et al., 2014). Researches conducted in Turkey show that being a female increases the probability of incurring O.O.P. health expenditures (Bora Başara & Şahin, 2008). Similarly, research conducted in several cities in Pakistan demonstrated that being a male head of household has a reducing effect on O.O.P. health expenditures (Muhammad Malik & Azam Syed, 2012). Bock et al. (2014) reveal that females incur notably higher O.O.P. health expenditures in the outpatient sector than males in Germany. Aregbeshola and Khan (2021) also found similar results in their study for Nigeria, showing that male-headed households reduce the likelihood of O.O.P.

health expenditures. The study for Bangladesh identified the relationship between gender and O.O.P. and displayed that being a woman has an increasing effect on O.O.P. health expenditure (Mahumud et al., 2017).

Age has been identified as an important determinant of O.O.P. health expenditures in many studies (Bora Başara & Şahin, 2008; You & Kobayashi, 2011; Masiye & Kaonga, 2016). According to Bora Başara & Şahin (2008), there is a significant and negative relationship between O.O.P. health expenditures and the 5–14 age group in Turkey. When the 0–4 age group is taken as a reference group, O.O.P. health expenditure is lower in the 5–14 age group. A study conducted in China found that being over 65 years of age has a significant impact on O.O.P. health expenditures. According to this study, when individuals age, especially over 65 years, they are prone to do higher O.O.P. health expenditures in China (You & Kobayashi, 2011). Likewise, according to Mahumud et al. (2017), the O.O.P. healthcare expenditures are significantly associated with age level, with the greatest effect observed among the elderly in Bangladesh. In addition, Aregbeshola and Khan (2021) show that the presence of a household member aged 65 years or older decreases the probability of O.O.P. health expenditures in Nigeria. According to Molla et al. (2017), the presence of children under five and the elderly in a household increases the O.O.P. health expenditures in Bangladesh. Łyszczarz and Abdi (2021) found a positive correlation between the proportions of children (aged 0–9) and elderly (70+ years) in the population and O.O.P. health expenditures in their study of Poland from 1999 to 2019.

Many studies indicate that O.O.P. health expenditures are affected by household size. Aregbeshola and Khan (2021) indicated that having more than five people in the household is more likely to increase O.O.P. health expenditure in Nigeria. Mohanty et al. (2013) support these results in their research for India and indicated that larger household sizes had higher O.O.P. health expenditures. In research conducted in Turkey, a significant but negative relationship was found between household size and O.O.P. health expenditures. Accordingly, as household size increases, O.O.P. health expenditures in Turkey decrease. This situation can be explained by the fact that large families in Turkey generally have low socio-economic levels, and they are incapable of accessing healthcare services due to financial restrictions (Bora Başara & Şahin, 2008; Demir et al., 2022).

Many studies have indicated that as the education level of a household increases, O.O.P. health expenditures increase. Chu et al. (2005) underline that an individual who is better educated is likely to have greater household O.O.P. health expenditures in Taiwan. According to Muhammad Malik and Azam Syed (2012), households where both the head and the spouse are literate reported more increased O.O.P. health expenditures than other households in Pakistan. According to one of the studies conducted in Bangladesh, having a higher level of education increases O.O.P. health expenditure (Mahumud et al., 2017). Similarly, Aregbeshola and Khan (2021) supported the other research in the literature, and they indicated that having household heads with secondary or primary education levels is more likely to increase O.O.P. health expenditure in Nigeria.

The region where individuals live, such as, whether they live in an urban or a rural area, is a factor that determines O.O.P. expenditures. The research in Zambia states that residing in rural areas correlates with a decreased likelihood of seeking formal medical care. The level of O.O.P. health expenditure incurred during a visit to health institutions is notably associated with household economic well-being, distance to a health facility, and various other contributing factors. According to this research, individuals living in remote and rural areas tend to have greater distances to access health facilities, leading to increased O.O.P. payments associated with travel costs. The O.O.P. health expenditures tend to rise in tandem with increasing remoteness (Masiye & Kaonga, 2016). A study in Bangladesh has shown that living urban is significantly associated with higher O.O.P. health expenditures (Mahumud et al., 2017). Molla et al. (2017) support this finding in their results for Bangladesh. The study for Pakistan also supports other studies and shows that households who live in urban incurred more O.O.P. health expenditures (Muhammad Malik & Azam Syed, 2012). Differently from the status of residences where individuals live in urban or rural areas, Bora Başara and Şahin (2008) evaluated the effect of the region where individuals live in Turkey on O.O.P. health expenditures and emphasized that living in the Eastern region increases O.O.P. health expenditures.

The income level of the household is one of the significant determinants of O.O.P. health expenditures. Research reveals that as the income level of the household increases or the household becomes wealthier, the O.O.P. health expenditures also rise (Bora Başara & Şahin, 2008; You & Kobayashi, 2011; Bock et al., 2014; Mahumud et al., 2017). Bock et al. (2014) indicated that increasing income is associated with higher O.O.P. health expenditures in Germany. Particularly in the outpatient sector, higher income is a cause of higher O.O.P. health expenditures. On the other hand, Aregbeshola and Khan (2021) stated that wealthier households are less likely to incur O.O.P. health expenditure in Nigeria. Kočiš Krůtilová et al. (2021) conducted research in Belgium, the Czech Republic, and Germany. According to this research, compared to the first income quartile, older adults who have chronic diseases in all other quartiles spend a lower share on O.O.P. health expenditures. The lowest spending share is observed in the highest income quartile.

The other determinant of O.O.P. health expenditures is employment status (Chu et al., 2005; Bora Başara & Şahin, 2008). Chu et al. (2005) indicate that an unemployed individual is likely to have greater household O.O.P. health expenditures in Taiwan. Similarly, Bora Başara and Şahin (2008) underline that not working in a job that generates income also increases O.O.P. health expenditures in Turkey. On the other hand, according to Aregbeshola and Khan (2021), being employed raises the likelihood of incurring O.O.P. healthcare expenditures compared to those being unemployed in Nigeria.

Having a chronic disease in the household is also one of the factors impacting O.O.P. health expenditures (Bora Başara & Şahin, 2008; You & Kobayashi, 2011; Molla et al., 2017). Molla et al. (2017) showed that the presence of chronic disease is one of the predictors of health expenditures in Bangladesh. Aregbeshola and Khan (2021) also stated in their study that household heads who have chronic diseases and visit public health institutions are more likely to increase their O.O.P. health expenditures.

A literature review of studies conducted in Turkey and other countries revealed that there are correlations between socio-economic and demographic factors and O.O.P. health expenditures. Unlike other studies, this study also provides a comparative assessment of the factors determining O.O.P. health expenditures within the context of the H.T.P. in Turkey.

7.3 Data and Methods

7.3.1 Data

The data set used in this chapter stems from the L.I.T.S. which was developed jointly by the E.B.R.D. and W.B. The L.I.T.S. was conducted in 2006, 2010, and 2016. The L.I.T.S. I was conducted in 2006, covering 29 countries. Each country contains data for 1,000 households. Then, L.I.T.S. II was applied to 35 countries in 2010. The target number of interviews was determined as 1,500 for six countries and 1,000 for other countries, which are including Turkey. In 2016, L.I.T.S. III was conducted in 34 countries by interviewing 1,500 households from each country.

The coverage of L.I.T.S. III is larger than the other two surveys. While the number of observations was 1,000 households in L.I.T.S. I and L.I.T.S. II, 1,500 households were interviewed in L.I.T.S. III (E.B.R.D., 2024).

This chapter uses the Turkish sample obtained from L.I.T.S. I, L.I.T.S. II, and L.I.T.S. III, completed in 2006, 2010, and 2016. The data from Turkey are analysed, and the findings are examined comparatively for the years 2006, 2010, and 2016. Independent and dependent variables, which have been selected by considering the studies in the literature, have been revised categorically to be suitable for logistic analysis. While O.O.P. health expenditures are used as dependent variables in the chapter, gender, age, education level, residence, wealth status, household size, and employment status are used as independent variables. The dependent variable in the chapter is the O.O.P. health expenditures of households. In all three data sets, individuals were asked approximately how much their household spent on the stated options in the last 12 months. Among these stated options, the answers given to health expenditures were used as the dependent variable in the chapter. The datasets include the gender variable categorized as male and female. Age is counted in the analysis, categorized in six groups which are 18–24, 25–34, 35–44, 45–54, 55–64, and ≥65 years. For education level, each individual is asked the highest level of education to have currently completed. Answer options are classified into five categories which are no degree, primary, secondary higher than secondary education, and bachelor's, or post-graduate degree, from the answers obtained in each three data sets. Another independent variable is residence, which provides information about whether individuals live in the rural or the urban area. The employment variable provides data about whether individuals have been employed in a job in the last 12 months. Individuals are asked whether they have worked to earn income in the last 12 months to define their employment status for this variable. The answer choices are "yes" and "no".

Household income level is among the important determinants of O.O.P. health expenditures (Chu et al., 2005; Bock et al., 2014). In this chapter, instead of the income variable, a wealth index was created on the basis of the assets of individuals as an indicator of their wealth status. This wealth index was classified into three categories: low wealth, medium wealth, and high wealth and was included in the analysis as an independent variable. The low wealth represented the poorest, and the high wealth represented the richest. The high wealth served as the reference group. Another variable that is most used in determining O.O.P. health expenditures is household size. In the chapter, five categories were created for household size. These categories are Household size = 1, Household size = 2, Household size = 3, Household size = 4, and Household size = 5. Each group reflects the number of individuals living in the household. The final category (Household size = 5 includes five or more individuals living in the same household). Household size = 1 represents one-member household as the reference group. The descriptive statistics are provided in Table 7.2.

7.3.2 Methods

The factors determining the O.O.P. health expenditures are analysed by using logit regression analysis in this chapter. The most typically utilized model for binary consequences in applied statistics is the logit model. Two standard parametric models for binary outcome data are the probit model and the logit model. These define different functional forms for a regressors' function, and the models are fit by using maximum likelihood (M.L.). Because of the nonlinearity of these models, the parameters' direct interpretation is more complicated. The resultant predicted probabilities and marginal effects (M.E.s) are similar to the two models (Cameron & Trivedi, 2022b).

Binary outcomes represent the simplest form of categorical data, with only two possible consequences. The dependent variable y accepts one of two values, coded as 0 or 1, for simplicity in binary

Table 7.2 Descriptive Statistics

Continuous Variables						
Variable Name	*Years*	*Observation*	*Mean*	*Std. Dev.*	*Min*	*Max*
O.O.P. health expenditure	2006	1,000	318.268	492.9928	0	3344
	2010	985	453.1503	1098.08	0	25000
	2016	939	414.7274	681.2397	0	4000

Categorical Variables (%)	2006		2010		2016	
	Frequencies	*Percent*	*Frequencies*	*Percent*	*Frequencies*	*Percent*
Gender (Reference: Female)						
Female	114	11.4	256	25.5	731	48.73
Male	886	88.6	748	74.5	769	51.27
Age (Reference: ≥65 years)						
18–24 years	22	2.2	31	3.09	179	11.93
25–34 years	216	21.6	214	21.31	540	36
35–44 years	254	25.4	257	25.6	384	25.6
45–54 years	220	22	199	19.82	241	16.07
55–64 years	152	15.2	183	18.23	116	7.73
≥65 years	136	13.6	120	11.95	40	2.67
Education Level (Reference: No degree)						
No degree	516	51.6	94	9.36	31	2.07
Primary	378	37.8	413	41.14	344	22.93
Secondary	68	6.8	372	37.05	713	47.53

(Continued)

Table 7.2 (Continued) Descriptive Statistics

Categorical Variables (%)	2006		2010		2016	
	Frequencies	*Percent*	*Frequencies*	*Percent*	*Frequencies*	*Percent*
Higher than secondary education	9	0.9	46	4.58	272	18.13
Bachelor's or post-graduate degree	11	1.1	79	7.87	140	9.33
Residence (Reference: Rural)						
Urban	660	66	769	76.59	1436	95.73
Rural	340	34	235	23.41	64	4.27
Employment (Reference: Unemployment)						
Yes	410	41	316	31.47	599	39.93
No	590	59	688	68.53	901	60.07
Wealth status (Reference: High wealth)						
Low Wealth	481	48.1	344	34.26	575	38.33
Medium Wealth	223	22.3	331	32.97	445	29.67
High wealth	296	22.6	329	32.77	480	32
Household Size (Reference: Household Size= 1)						
Household size = 1	76	7.6	61	6.08	24	1.6
Household size = 2	180	18	238	23.71	640	42.67
Household size = 3	184	18.4	223	22.21	466	31.07
Household size = 4	230	23	233	23.21	256	17.07
Household size = 5	330	33	249	24.8	114	7.6

Source: Author's calculations.

outcome models. Then, the distribution of y is the Bernoulli. If the probability that $y = 1$ is p, then the probability that $y = 0$ is necessarily $1 - p$ (Cameron, 2010: 1; Cameron & Trivedi, 2022a).

Binary outcome regression models allow p to vary with the regressors x. The linear model $p = x'\beta$ does not confine the likelihood to lie between "0" and "1". More suitable models set $p = F(x'\beta)$, in which $F(.)$ is a known function with the property that $0 \langle F(.) \rangle 1$. Any cumulative distribution function (c,d,f) $F(z)$ for variable z continuous on $(-\infty, \infty)$ has this preferred property. The logit model and the probit logit model differ in this specified function $F(.)$.

The logit model defines:

$$\Pr\left(y_i = 1 | x_i\right) = \Lambda\left(x_i'\beta\right) \tag{7.1}$$

Where $\Lambda(.)$ is the logistic cumulative distribution function, and $\Lambda(z) = e^z / \left(1 + e^z\right)$.

The logit and probit models are non-linear functions of the regressors, so the M.E. on $\Pr(y = 1 | x)$ of a change in the jth regressor is no longer simply β_j; it also counts on the value of the regressors x (Cameron & Trivedi, 2022a).

The M.E. in the logit model is:

$$M.E._j = \left[\Lambda\left(x'\beta\right) \times \left\{1 - \Lambda\left(x'\beta\right)\right\}\right]\beta_j \tag{7.2}$$

Because $0 \leq \Lambda(.) \times \left\{1 - \Lambda(.)\right\} \leq 0.25$ always, it follows that the sign of the M.E. equals the sign of β_j and that $M.E._j \leq 0.25 \times \beta_j$ (Cameron & Trivedi, 2022a).

7.4 Results

The multicollinearity of independent variables is examined by estimating the Variance Inflation Factor (V.I.F.) (Kumara & Samaratunge, 2016). The V.I.F. test results are 2.15, 2.43, and 6.91 for 2006, 2010, and 2016, respectively. They showed no evidence of multicollinearity in the models.

The estimation results of the logit model (the coefficients and the odds ratios) for 2006, 2010, and 2016 are represented in Table 7.3. According to coefficients for 2006, the age group of 25–34 has a significant effect on the household's health expenditures. The reference category is aged 65 years and older for age groups. Individuals 25–34 years have a higher probability of O.O.P. health expenditure compared to aged 65 years and older. People aged 25–34 years are 1.86 times more likely to make O.O.P. expenditures compared to those aged 65 years and older years.

The reference category selected for the education level is "having no degree". Completing a primary education level creates a decreasing effect on the probability of O.O.P. health expenditure. Therefore, individuals who completed primary education have a lower probability of O.O.P. health expenditure compared to those who do not have any education degree. According to the odds ratio in Table 7.3, individuals with completed primary education levels are 0.65 times less likely to incur O.O.P. health expenditures compared to those with no education.

Living in a rural area is the reference category for the residence variable. Living in an urban area increases the likelihood of incurring O.O.P. health expenditures compared to living in a rural area. According to the odds ratio in Table 7.3, individuals living in an urban area are 1.52 times more likely to increase incurring O.O.P. health expenditures compared to those living in rural areas.

Table 7.3 Estimation Results for the Logit Model

Independent Variables	2006		2010		2016	
	Coefficients	Odds Ratio	Coefficients	Odds Ratio	Coefficients	Odds Ratio
Male	−.0596912 (.2868025)	.9420554 (.2701838)	−.6331455** (.2506957)	.5309191** (.1330991)	5.906862 (2.195509)	.989192 (.1581469)
18–24 years	.1185431 (.5828108)	1.125855 (.6561606)	.1597228 (.5436963)	1.173186 (.6378567)	1.2281*** (.4542001)	3.414735*** (1.550973)
25–34 years	.6216407* (.3285338)	1.86198* (.6117235)	.3098941 (.3399407)	1.363281 (.4634347)	1.207882*** (.4018775)	3.346388*** (1.344838)
35–44 years	.1837751 (.3121833)	1.201746 (.3751649)	.5906617* (.3416838)	1.805182* (.6168015)	.8010856** (.4022197)	2.227958** (.8961287)
45–54 years	.0208168 (.2988469)	1.021035 (.3051332)	.2888187 (.3474131)	1.33485 (.4637442)	1.256683*** (.4263118)	3.513747*** (1.497952)
55–64 years	−.0235242 (.3062563)	.9767504 (.2991359)	.8180331** (.3628477)	2.266038** (.8222267)	.8233751* (.4361545)	2.278176* (.9936366)
Primary education	−.4269249** (.1804497)	.6525125** (.1177457)	−.6849227* (.4001922)	.5041292* (.2017486)	.0757115 (.5213973)	1.078651 (.5624059)
Secondary education	.2358201 (.3864246)	1.265946 (.4891929)	−.4970097 (.4174836)	.6083471 (.253975)	.4073873 (.5296289)	1.502886 (.795972)
Higher than secondary education	−.2179217 (.8359052)	.8041884 (.6722253)	−.9413179* (.5301838)	.3901134* (.2066318)	−.0605273 (.5506072)	.9412681 (.518269)
Bachelor's or post-graduate degree	−.0386905 (.8162184)	.9620484 (.7852416)	−.0088925 (.5316849)	.9911469 (.5269779)	−.3400937 (.582669)	.717036 (.4146877)
Urban	.4234875** (.1884803)	1.527279** (.287862)	−1.015715*** (.2824438)	.3621433*** (.1022851)	1.217459*** (.2907186)	3.378592*** (.9822196)

Table 7.3 (Continued) Estimation Results for the Logit Model

Independent Variables	2006		2010		2016	
	Coefficients	Odds Ratio	Coefficients	Odds Ratio	Coefficients	Odds Ratio
Employment	-.1731666 (.173074)	.8409975 (.1455548)	-.1978543 (.2165609)	.8204894 (.1776859)	.0833846 (.1750728)	1.08696 (.1902971)
Low wealth	.337178 (.2094429)	1.400988 (.2934271)	.3120604 (.2470936)	1.366237 (.3375884)	.0844933 (.1973863)	1.088166 (.214789)
Medium wealth	.3721958 (.231869)	1.450917 (.3364227)	.5485839** (.2414576)	1.7308** (.4179149)	-.0732684 (.2005585)	.9293513 (.1863893)
Household size = 2	1.09791*** (.3409404)	2.997893** (1.022103)	1.154671*** (.3475222)	3.172978*** (1.10268)	-.7096882 (.7580727)	.4917975 (.3728183)
Household size = 3	.8305215** (.3481696)	2.294515** (.7988805)	1.52231*** (.3593856)	4.582801*** (1.646993)	-.687798 (.7610628)	.5026817 (.3825723)
Household size = 4	.9009458** (.3484841)	2.461931** (.8579436)	1.642557*** (.3701554)	5.168367*** (1.913099)	-.5475784 (.7762212)	.5783487 (.4489265)
Household size ≥ 5	1.229954*** (.3421114)	3.421074*** (1.170388)	1.776115*** (.3716879)	5.906862*** (2.195509)	-.2758399 (.8176746)	.7589344 (.6205614)

Notes: (1) Standard errors are indicated in parentheses. (2) *** $p < 0.01$, ** $p < 0.05$, * $p < 0.1$. (3) The reference categories for the independent variables are being female, being aged ≥ 65 years, having no degree, rural residence, unemployment, being in the low wealth index category, and household size equal to 1, respectively.

The household-size variable has five categories, and a one-member household is the reference category. According to coefficients for 2006, a two-member household is highly statistically significant. Individuals living in a two-member household are 2.99 times more probably to increase incurring O.O.P. health expenditures compared to those in a one-member household. Additionally, individuals living in a three-member household and living in a four-member household increase the likelihood of incurring O.O.P. health expenditures. According to the odds ratios in Table 7.3, individuals living in a three-member household are 2.29 times more likely and those living in a four-member household are 2.46 times more likely to increase O.O.P. health expenditures. Lastly, individuals living in a five-member household and over a five-member household are probably to have increased O.O.P. health expenditures. Individuals living in a five-member and over five-member household are 3.42 times more likely to increase O.O.P. health expenditures compared to those living in a one-member household. To sum up, the coefficients for 2006 reveal that an increase in household size leads to O.O.P. health expenditures to increase.

The estimation results of the logit model 2010 are illustrated in Table 7.3. According to the coefficient in Table 7.3, being male decreases the O.O.P. health expenditures compared to being female. Being a male is approximately 47% less likely to incur O.O.P. health expenditures compared to being female.

Being in the 35–44 age group has a positive coefficient, and it is statistically significant. People 35–44 years old have a higher likelihood of incurring O.O.P. health expenditures compared to those aged 65 years and older. Individuals who are aged 35–44 years are approximately 1.81 times more likely to incur O.O.P. expenditures than 65 years and older. Being aged 55–64 years has also a positive coefficient, and it is statistically significant. According to the odds ratio, being aged 55–64 years is approximately 2.26 times more likely to make O.O.P. expenditures compared to those 65 years and older.

Completing primary education and higher than secondary education has a significant and negative coefficient. It means that completing primary education and higher than secondary education creates a decreasing effect on the probability of incurring O.O.P. health expenditure. According to these, individuals who completed primary education and higher than secondary education have a lower probability of O.O.P. health expenditure compared to those who do not have any education degree. Additionally, individuals with completed primary education levels are 0.50 times less likely to incur O.O.P. health expenditures compared to those with no education. Also, those who completed higher secondary education levels are 0.39 times less likely to incur O.O.P. health expenditures compared to those with no education.

According to the results of 2010, living in an urban area decreases the O.O.P. health expenditures compared to living in a rural area. For individuals living in an urban area, the likelihood of incurring O.O.P. health expenditures is about 0.36 times less than those living in rural areas.

The results of 2010 demonstrated that individuals who are in the medium category of the wealth index have a positive coefficient, and it is statistically significant. According to the odds ratio, those having medium wealth are approximately 1.73 times more likely to incur O.O.P. health expenditures compared to those having high wealth.

According to coefficients for 2010, a two-member household is highly statistically significant. Individuals living in a two-member household are 3.17 times more likely to increase incurring O.O.P. health expenditures compared to those in a one-member household. Additionally, according to the odds ratios in Table 7.3, individuals living in a three-member household are 4.58 times more likely, and those living in a four-member household are 5.16 times more likely to increase their O.O.P. health expenditures. Lastly, individuals living in a five-member household and over a five-member household are likely to incur O.O.P. health expenditures. Individuals living in a five-member and over five-member household are 5.90 times more likely to increase O.O.P. health expenditures compared to those living in a one-member household. To sum up, the coefficients for 2010 reveal that an increase in household size leads to O.O.P. health expenditures to increase.

The results, in Table 7.3, suggest that all the age groups are significant determinants of O.O.P. health expenditures in 2016. The age groups of 18–24 years, 25–34 years, 35–44 years, 45–54 years, and 55–64 years have a higher probability of incurring O.O.P. health expenditures compared to those 65 years and older. The positive coefficient indicates that people aged 18–24 years are more likely to incur O.O.P. health expenditures compared to those 65 years and older. The probability of incurring O.O.P. health expenditures is more than 3.41 times higher for being aged 18–24 years compared to those 65 years and older. The positive coefficient suggests that people aged 25–34 years are more likely to incur O.O.P. health expenditures compared to those 65 years and older. The probability of incurring O.O.P. health expenditures is more than 3.44 times higher for people aged 25–34 years compared to those 65 years and older. Also, individuals existing in the 35–44 age group, 45–54 age group, and 55–64 age group have positive coefficients, and it implies that people of 35–44 age group, 45–54 age group, and of 55–64 age group have a higher probability of incurring O.O.P. health expenditures compared to those 65 years and older. The likelihood of incurring O.O.P. health expenditures is more than 2.22 times higher for people aged 34–44 years compared to those 65 years and older. Similarly, people aged 45–54 years are 3.51 times more likely to make O.O.P. expenditures compared to those over 65 years and older. Lastly, the probability of incurring O.O.P. health expenditures is more than 2.27 times higher for people aged 55–64 years compared to those 65 years and older.

Living in an urban area increases the likelihood of incurring O.O.P. health expenditures compared to living in a rural area in 2016. According to the odds ratio in Table 7.3, individuals living in an urban area are 3.37 times more likely to increase incurring O.O.P. health expenditures compared to those living in rural areas.

7.5 Conclusion and Discussion

This chapter examines the factors determining O.O.P. health expenditures during the H.T.P. in Turkey and how these factors evolved throughout the process. In this context, logit analysis was applied for the years 2006, 2010, and 2016 by using the L.I.T.S. I, L.I.T.S. II, and L.I.T.S. III data sets.

The results of this chapter reveal that gender is a determining factor in O.O.P. health expenditures for only 2010. In other words, being male creates a reducing effect on the likelihood of incurring O.O.P. health expenditures compared to being female for this year. This result is consistent with findings from previous studies, such as those by Bora Başara and Şahin (2008), Muhammad Malik and Azam Syed (2012), and Bock et al. (2014).

The other determinant used in this chapter, age, indicates that individuals younger than 65 years of age have a higher probability of incurring O.O.P. health expenditures in general. This means that individuals will spend less on healthcare as they age, and it is consistent with Aregbeshola and Khan (2021). As a consequence of the initiation of the family medicine model as a part of H.T.P., the elderly have the option of using healthcare free of charge. Hence, the access of the elderly to free-of-charge healthcare services has increased, and this may result in a decrease in the probability of incurring O.O.P. health expenditures.

The results for education level reflect that having a higher education level than no education level decreases the probability of incurring O.O.P. health expenditure for 2006 and 2010.

However, there is no significant relationship between the education level and the likelihood of incurring O.O.P. health expenditure in 2016. As the level of education increases, individuals become more aware of their health, resulting in reduced O.O.P. health expenditures. H.T.P. aims to increase children's health awareness by implementing programmes and projects to raise awareness about the health of school-age children. Increasing access to education and healthcare services reduces O.O.P. health expenditures, especially for individuals with high health awareness and higher levels of education. The results obtained in 2006 and 2010 align with the aim of the H.T.P.

The urban–rural difference is another important determinant for O.O.P. health expenditures but with reversing effects for the years analysed. Specifically, compared to living in a rural area, living in an urban area increases the likelihood of incurring O.O.P. health expenditures in 2006 and 2016, while it decreases this likelihood in 2010. These results from 2006 and 2016 are consistent with findings from Muhammad Malik and Azam Syed (2012), Mahumud et al. (2017), and Molla et al. (2017). According to the results obtained in 2010, it can be concluded that the implementation of family medicine and free mobile health services in rural areas through the H.T.P. has contributed to a reduction in O.O.P. health expenditures in these areas. Additionally, as part of the H.T.P., the emergency telephone line has become operational in rural areas. In this context, the H.T.P. likely alleviated the financial burden of seeking medical care by enhancing healthcare access and offering essential services closer to rural populations, thereby reducing the necessity for long-distance travel and associated costs. On the other hand, according to the 2016 results, it is thought that O.O.P. health expenditures in urban areas may have increased due to higher private healthcare costs, increased demand, and diverse service fees. A broader range of healthcare services may contain options with diverse fee structures, some of which may not be eligible for insurance coverage, thus resulting in elevated O.O.P. health expenditures.

Wealth status is another important determinant. The related results represent having medium wealth increases the possibility of incurring O.O.P. health expenditures compared to those having high wealth in 2010. It is consistent with Aregbeshola and Khan (2021). On the other hand, there is no significant relationship between wealth status and the probability of incurring O.O.P. health expenditure for either 2006 or 2016.

The results for household size significantly affect the possibility of incurring O.O.P. health expenditures for 2006 and 2010 but not for 2016. All household sizes of more than one member create an increasing effect on the possibility of incurring O.O.P. health expenditures compared to one member household for 2006 and 2010. The probability of O.O.P. health expenditures increases in households with more than one member compared to those with only one member, and it is consistent with Chu et al. (2005).

According to the results obtained, gender, age, education level, wealth status, residence, and household size are among the determinants of O.O.P. health expenditures in Turkey.

Among the determinants mentioned here, household size and being younger are the most important factors of O.O.P. health expenditures in Turkey according to odds ratios. This implies that despite the improvements achieved by H.T.P. in terms of increasing general health coverage, decreasing household O.O.P. expenditures on health, etc., demographic factors may increase the probability of incurring the probability of O.O.P. health expenditures in Turkey. Contrarily, the other demographic factor, level of education, has a reducing effect on the probability of incurring the probability of O.O.P. health expenditures in Turkey, in general. This condition should be maintained to reduce the financial burden on individuals and households, which is one of the aims of H.T.P.

Policymakers should consider the demographic factors during the design and implementation of policies about O.O.P. health expenditures in Turkey. For instance these policies may focus on eradicating the increasing effects of household size and younger age on O.O.P. health expenditures. Policies aiming to increase the health awareness of each member of the household may lead them to protect themselves from illnesses that result in a decrease in O.O.P. health expenditures. Further studies analysing regional differences in the probability of incurring O.O.P. health expenditures in the era of H.T.P. in Turkey will contribute to the related literature.

References

Aregbeshola, B. S., & Khan, S. M. (2021). Out-of-pocket health-care spending and its determinants among households in Nigeria: A national study. *Journal of Public Health*, 29, 931–942. https://doi.org/10.1007/s10389-020-01199-x.

Atun, R., Aydın, S., Chakraborty, S., Sümer, S., Aran, M., Gürol, I., Nazlıoğlu, S., Ozgülcü, S., Aydoğan, U., Ayar, B., Dilmen, U., & Akdağ, R. (2013). Universal health coverage in Turkey: enhancement of equity. *Lancet (London, England)*, 382(9886), 65–99. https://doi.org/10.1016/S0140-6736(13)61051-X.

Bock, J. O., Matschinger, H., Brenner, H., Wild, B., Haefeli, W. E., Quinzler, R., Saum, K. U., Heider, D., & König, H. H. (2014). Inequalities in out-of-pocket payments for health care services among elderly Germans – results of a population-based cross-sectional study. *International Journal for Equity in Health*, 13, 3. https://doi.org/10.1186/1475-9276-13-3.

Bora Başara, B., & Şahin, İ. (2008). Türkiye'de Cepten Yapılan Sağlık Harcamalarını Etkileyen Etmenler. *H.Ü. İktisadi ve İdari Bilimler Fakültesi Dergisi*, 26(2), 319–340.

Cameron, A. C. (2010). Categorical data. In S. N. Durlauf & E. Blume (eds.), *Microeconometrics* (2nd ed. pp. 1–5). Macmillan Publishers Ltd.

Cameron, A. C., & Trivedi, P. K. (2022a). *Microeconometrics using stata volume I: Cross-sectional and panel regression methods* (2nd ed.). Published by Stata Press.

Cameron, A. C., & Trivedi, P. K. (2022b). *Microeconometrics using stata volume II: Volume II: nonlinear models and causal inference methods* (2nd ed.). Published by Stata Press.

Chu, T.-B., Liu, T.-C., Chen, C.-S., Tsai, Y.-W., & Chiu, W.-T. (2005). Household out-of-pocket medical expenditures and national health insurance in Taiwan: Income and regional inequality. *BMC Health Services Research*, 5(1). https://doi.org/10.1186/1472-6963-5-60.

Demir, A., Alkan, Ö., Bilgiç, A., Florkowski, W. J., & Karaaslan, A. (2022). Determinants of Turkish households' out-of-pocket expenditures on three categories of health care services: A multivariate probit approach. *The International Journal of Health Planning and Management*, 37(4), 2303–2327. https://doi.org/10.1002/hpm.3470.

European Bank for Reconstruction and Development [E.B.R.D.]. (2024). *Life in Transition Survey (LITS)*. https://www.ebrd.com/what-we-do/economic-research-and-data/data/lits.html.

Kočiš Krůtilová, V., Bahnsen, L., & De Graeve, D. (2021). The out-of-pocket burden of chronic diseases: The cases of Belgian, Czech and German older adults. *BMC Health Services Research*, 21(1), 239. https://doi.org/10.1186/s12913-021-06259-w.

Kumara, A. S., & Samaratunge, R. (2016). Patterns and determinants of out-of-pocket health care expenditure in Sri Lanka: Evidence from household surveys. *Health Policy and Planning*, 31(8), 970–983. https://doi.org/10.1093/heapol/czw021.

Łyszczarz, B., & Abdi, Z. (2021). Factors associated with Out-of-pocket health expenditure in polish regions. *Healthcare (Basel, Switzerland)*, 9(12), 1750. https://doi.org/10.3390/healthcare9121750.

Mahumud, R. A., Sarker, A. R., Sultana, M., Islam, Z., Khan, J., & Morton, A. (2017). Distribution and determinants of out-of-pocket healthcare expenditures in Bangladesh. *Journal of Preventive Medicine and Public Health*, 50(2), 91–99. https://doi.org/10.3961/jpmph.16.089.

Masiye, F., & Kaonga, O. (2016). Determinants of healthcare utilisation and out-of-pocket payments in the context of free public primary healthcare in Zambia. *International Journal of Health Policy and Management*, 5(12), 693–703. https://doi.org/10.15171/ijhpm.2016.65.

The Ministry of Health of Turkey [M.O.H.]. (2012). *Türkiye'de Sağlıkta Dönüşüm Programı, Değerlendirme Raporu (2003–2011)*.

Mohanty, S. K., Chauhan, R. K., Mazumdar, S., & Srivastava, A. (2013). Out-of-pocket expenditure on health care among elderly and non-elderly households in India. *Social Indicators Research*, 115(3), 1137–1157. https://doi.org/10.1007/s11205-013-0261-7.

Molla, A. A., Chi, C., & Mondaca, A. L. (2017). Predictors of high out-of-pocket healthcare expenditure: An analysis using Bangladesh household income and expenditure survey, 2010. *BMC Health Services Research*, 17(1), 94. https://doi.org/10.1186/s12913-017-2047-0.

Muhammad Malik, A., & Azam Syed, S. (2012). Socio-economic determinants of household out-of-pocket payments on healthcare in Pakistan. *International Journal for Equity in Health*, 11(1), 51. https://doi.org/10.1186/1475-9276-11-51.

Organisation for Economic Co-operation and Development (O.E.C.D.). (2008). *O.E.C.D. Sağlık Sistemi İncelemeleri Türkiye*. O.E.C.D. ve Dünya Bankası.

Van Doorslaer, E., O'Donnell, O., Rannan-Eliya, R. P., Somanathan, A., Adhikari, S. R., Garg, C. C., . . . & Zhao, Y. (2006). Effect of payments for health care on poverty estimates in 11 countries in Asia: An analysis of household survey data. *The Lancet*, 368(9544), 1357–1364. https://doi.org/10.1016/s0140-6736(06)69560-3.

Villanueva, W. M. D. J., & Aranas, J. B. (2023). Catastrophic out-of-pocket expenditure on health: Evidence from the regions in the Philippines. *Journal Healthcare Treatment Development (JHTD)*, 3(06), 18–28, ISSN: 2799–1148. https://doi.org/10.55529/jhtd.36.18.28.

Wagstaff, A., Eozenou, P., & Smitz, M. (2020). Out-of-pocket expenditures on health: A global stocktake. *The World Bank Research Observer*, 35(2), 123–157, https://doi.org/10.1093/wbro/lkz009.

WHO Commission on Macroeconomics and Health. (2001). *Macroeconomics and health: Investing in health for economic development / report of the commission on macroeconomics and health*. World Health Organization. https://iris.who.int/handle/10665/42435.

World Bank [W.B.]. (2024). *World development indicators*. https://databank.worldbank.org/source/world-development-indicators.

World Health Organization [W.H.O.]. (2000). *The World health report: 2000: health systems: improving performance*. World Health Organization. https://iris.who.int/handle/10665/42281.

World Health Organization (W.H.O.) & World Bank (W.B.). (2023). *Tracking universal health coverage: 2023 global monitoring report*. Washington, DC: World Bank. http://hdl.handle.net/10986/40348. License: CC BY-NC-SA 3.0 IGO.

You, X., & Kobayashi, Y. (2011). Determinants of out-of-pocket health expenditure in China. *Applied Health Economics and Health Policy*, 9(1), 39–49. https://doi.org/10.2165/11530730-000000000-00000.

Chapter 8

Healthcare Users' Experience with E-Health: Benefits, Drawbacks, and the Future

Zeynep Güldem Ökem and Didem Pekkurnaz

Contents

8.1 Introduction

The demand for health services rises constantly due to technological advances that cause the increase in the possibilities of diagnosis and treatment, increased life expectancy, and the related rise in the incidence of chronic diseases and aging. With the aging population, the need for long-term healthcare services increases. On the other hand, the expectation for quality and innovative healthcare services rises with higher income levels. These factors create a higher burden on the government budget. Thus, patients' right to choose is gaining prominence alongside patients' expectations of access to the safest, latest, and highest possible quality treatment. Instead of using services determined by health personnel and decision-makers, patients prefer to involve themselves in decisions concerning their health. Due to these changes, a greater need for novel approaches to improve performance and efficiency in the health sector has emerged, and new service delivery models have been developed. E-health applications that provide better quality, patient-centred, and accessible health services; increase efficiency; and reduce costs have come to feature heavily in the health policies of most countries.

DOI: 10.4324/9781003539896-9

Turkey and most European Union countries have committed to promoting equity in health services through universal health coverage (U.H.C.) to meet the healthcare needs of their population. The e-health applications, particularly telemedicine and electronic health records, contribute to expanding health service coverage. E-health is mostly beneficial for countries where access problems and health disparities exist, the poor and disadvantaged people are deprived of health services, or the healthcare infrastructure and health personnel are not evenly distributed. This also applies to Turkey even with structural reforms (known as the Health Transformation Programme – H.T.P.) in health services to improve health service accessibility and efficiency (Ökem & Çakar, 2015).

E-health or the use of information and communications technologies in health system constituted one of the key components of "transformation" in health services. E-health project has been overseen by the Ministry of Health. Important investments have been made for e-health applications in hospital management (hospital and clinical information systems), health service delivery (e-Nabız, the Family Physicians System, e-prescription, e-referral, telemedicine, etc.), and reimbursement decisions in health financing (Medula) (Dogac et al., 2014). Considerable progress has been made in time for the usability and interoperability of these systems. All healthcare providers with contracts with the Social Security Institution have been connected to the Medula system. Public hospitals (63.1%) have the capacity to perform basic functions, and 36% of them have comprehensive electronic health record functions (Kose et al., 2020). e-Nabız has reached more than 80% of the population (Birinci, 2023). Despite these achievements, users should also be informed about e-health applications and be able to use them effectively. Regional and socio-demographic differences in access to and use of e-health should also be considered. Thus, the purpose of this study is to evaluate users' awareness, knowledge, and the use of these applications through assessing the existing literature on e-health in Turkey. This allows for realizing the benefits of e-health and hence its contribution to U.H.C.

8.2 The Importance and Benefits of E-health

Technological advances are most widely used in health services. E-health applications, defined as the use of information and communication technologies, make critical contributions to the delivery and financing of health services. The e-health systems allow doctors, patients, healthcare policymakers, and managers to communicate, store, transmit, and share all data related to health services and health and disease-related information and data within and beyond the healthcare system (Moen et al., 2013).

The use of information and communication technologies has been continuously evolving in health services. As the use of the internet becomes more widespread, clinical and hospital information systems, telemedicine, and electronic medical and health records have been implemented in healthcare. Radical changes in the digital era have influenced individuals' awareness and knowledge about their health behaviours and physician–patient relationships. New mobile applications for individual health purposes, known as m-health have been introduced. Among these, the mobile health apps for chronic disease management, online health information sources and platforms, smart wearable devices, and personal health records are incorporating the growing role of patients who want to take responsibility for their health. Recently, virtual reality, artificial intelligence, big data analytics, and block chain have been used to contribute to e-health systems (World Health Organization, 2021).

E-health, including various digital tools, platforms, and systems, offers several benefits. All health-related information exchanged within and beyond the boundaries of the health sector facilitates the overall management of the health system while supporting all stakeholders. The most beneficial effect of e-health is improved access to health services, especially for people living in rural areas, the poor, and the elderly. Telemedicine, teleconsultation, tele-diagnostics, and other remote service delivery systems enable one to contact doctors remotely and receive diagnosis, treatment, and advice about individuals' health and diseases. Continuous advances in medicine and technology create the need for specialization. However, it is not possible and feasible to have specialists in every health facility. In cases where the number of doctors and the required expertise are not sufficient, telemedicine services are used to provide expertise to a wider range of patients and thus contribute to U.H.C. For example, Picture Archiving and Communication Systems (P.A.C.S.) enable imaging results to be shared so that they can be evaluated by specialists. This means that medical imaging tests and results can be performed rapidly, reducing the waiting time for diagnosis and allowing treatment to be started earlier. According to a study conducted in British Columbia, Canada, the use of P.A.C.S. reduced the time to start treatment by 41% (Organisation for Economic Co-operation and Development, 2010). In addition, the capacity to meet the increasing demand for health services due to aging, contagious diseases, technology, and financial hardship will improve. As an example of meeting more health needs by improving the accessibility to primary health services and chronic care, in the Netherlands, doctors' electronic access to patient summaries enables them to provide primary healthcare services outside the working hours (Organisation for Economic Co-operation and Development, 2010).

Using mobile devices for health tracking, reminders for medication compliance and diet, appointment scheduling, and other mobile applications empowers patients to manage their health and chronic conditions. The health portals improve patient–doctor interaction, better monitoring of own health status, and improved quality of care (Carini et al., 2021).

E-health supports health professionals and policymakers for planning in the prevention, diagnosis, and treatment of diseases. Timely and accurate collection and sharing of personal health information through national and regional health information systems will enable the monitoring of the course of disease and effectiveness of treatment. Personal health records are particularly effective in monitoring chronic diseases, where clinical protocols are used effectively, patient adherence to recommended treatment is ensured, and the disease can be prevented from reaching a more advanced stage (Organisation for Economic Co-operation and Development, 2010). Hospital information systems allow health professionals an easy access to clinical guidelines and clinical protocols. Health and administrative personnel do not need to deal with paperwork; without dealing with documents and forms, operating costs can be reduced by saving time in clinical services. A study evaluating the benefits of e-Nabız in Turkey reported that a considerable amount of paper saving was obtained due to e-prescriptions (Birinci, 2023). Moreover, the registration of radiological images in the system led to a 27.5% reduction in radiological image prints (Birinci, 2023). Other potential savings for health systems were associated with improved health outcomes with more accessible healthcare and shorter waiting times and reduced hospital visits and tests. In addition, avoiding travel costs and reduced labour and productivity losses through e-health applications that replace traveling to see a doctor constitute societal savings (Liddy et al., 2016).

Tracking of diseases and financial information ensures better quality and more efficient service delivery and healthcare resource use. In addition, the analysis of a large volume of stored and shared data serves as the basis for the formulation of an evidenced-based health policy and planning. Analysis of health-sector-related data also provides information about health and demographic trends, disease patterns, effects of health interventions, and health service utilization including pharmaceuticals and medical devices to decision- makers at all levels. E-health also accelerates research and supports medical education (World Health Organization, 2021).

8.3 E-health Implementations in Turkey after the H.T.P.

E-health applications in Turkey have gained pace since 2003, and the e-health strategy was developed in 2004 (Mandil, 2004). Initially, the Health-Net (*Sağlık-Net*), which is an information sharing and communication platform, was set up for the realization of national e-health system. The main objective of the Health-NET project is to establish a National Health Information System that enables the sharing of health data among authorized health professionals and the access of individuals to their health data. The scope of Health-NET includes the electronic health record database, which collects individual health data, and the Decision Support System for analysing data collected through the electronic health record. To ensure smooth information flow through the national health information infrastructure, the National Health Data Dictionary (*Ulusal Sağlık Veri Sözlüğü*) and Health Coding Reference Server (*Sağlık Kodlama Referans Sunucusu*) were formed (Dogac et al., 2014). Common standards allow health data and information to be collected at international standards and to be more easily transformed into information for decision-makers. Since 2015, e-Nabız which allows individuals to manage their health has been introduced. The system has several components including the retrieval of relevant data at the point of care, information, and knowledge for treatment, prevention, health promotion, and health-related services about the individual. An individual can authorize the family physician as well as other physicians to see personal health data. The information in the personal health record can be shared with health institutions when needed. In addition, personal health records can be used anonymously by authorized decision-makers. As of 2022, 39 public institutions and more than 28,000 health facilities have been integrated with the e-Nabız system. Throughout the country, e-Nabız users have reached almost 80% in 2022 (Birinci, 2023).

The system enables patients to view their hospital visits, prescriptions, reports, diagnostics, images, and medication. e-Nabız also involves providing supportive services to improve the quality of life of individuals including advice on diet and physical activities and to assess individual health risks such as heart attack, obesity, etc. Patients can add their specific conditions that may create health risks such as having allergies, and emergency physicians can see this information. The component "e-diagnosis" (*NeyimVar*) permits individuals to make possible diagnoses about their conditions and receives recommendations for referral to a family physician or a specialist accordingly. The central physician appointment system (*Merkezi Hekim Randevu Sistemi* – M.H.R.S.) provides individuals to schedule an appointment from public and university hospitals.

Other important e-health applications are the Family Physician Information System (*Aile Hekimliği Bilgi Sistemi*), electronic referral system, e-prescription, drug tracking system, and telemedicine, particularly teleradiology. The terms and scope of telemedicine services have been defined by the Regulation on the Provision of Remote Healthcare Services enacted in February 2022, and the Guidelines on Remote Healthcare Information System (*Uzaktan Sağlık Bilgi Sistemi* – U.S.B.S.) were published in May 2022. As of August 2022, more than 20 private healthcare institutions have registered to the U.S.B.S. system to provide remote healthcare service.[1] The Ministry of Health established the Turkish Institute for Health Data Research and Artificial Intelligence Applications (*Türkiye Sağlık Veri Araştırmaları ve Yapay Zekâ Uygulamaları Enstitüsü*) in 2019 to promote and disseminate developments in the field of health data research and artificial intelligence applications.

8.4 Awareness, Use of, and Preferences for E-health Technologies in Turkey

Although the research on the factors impacting the awareness, use, and preferences of e-health technologies from the perspectives of healthcare users in Turkey is limited, the studies mentioned next focus on understanding and improving the implementation and usage of e-health applications, with a particular emphasis on user satisfaction, usability issues, and socio-demographic influences.

Basoglu et al. (2012) were interested in evaluating the preferences of patients for remote monitoring technologies. A survey was implemented to collect data from diabetes and obesity patients in Istanbul, Turkey. The study aimed to figure out the essential features of remote monitoring technologies for patients using them. Conjoint analysis showed that users preferred input effort as the most important feature. That means people want to make less effort when they use such technologies. Other important characteristics of the e-health services revealed by the analysis were opportunity to have face-to-face interaction with physician, getting technical support when the user faces a problem, short response time, and a lower cost.

A study carried out in Turkey evaluated the effects of some important socio-demographic factors on online application usage behaviour of internet users (Kutlu & Ozturan, 2012). An online survey was employed to interview 350 internet users from which 324 valid responses were obtained. The first set of regression analysis showed that the behaviour of using online app was significantly affected by the socio-demographic variables. These variables include age, income, education, internet use, and life attitudes. The direction of the effect of each of these variables was consistent with the expectations. The second set of analysis revealed that online app usage behaviour, attitudes towards personal health data privacy, and beliefs about health services had significantly affected e-health readiness of internet users.

Taşkın et al. (2018) conducted a survey for 16 people, half of whom were female and were aged between 18 and 55 years, to analyse the usefulness of the M.H.R.S. mobile application, which has been used to make hospital appointments. Study participants who had no experience of using this app were asked to do some tasks such as downloading the app, logging into the system, and making/cancelling appointments. Task performances differed with respect to the socio-demographic characteristics of the individuals. Younger participants were good at downloading and installing the app and changing their e-mail and passwords. In addition, participants with higher education levels performed better in logging into the system and arranging appointments. Gender differences were also observed in performing the tasks. Males scored better than females. In addition, having an experience of the usage of touchscreen devices made participants more successful in downloading the app and logging into the system. Finally, the participants expressed their ideas about positive and negative features of the app when they were performing the tasks. Results indicated that participants were getting confused due to the lack of enough guidance in the app, and there were some issues in the interface. Participants also stated their recommendations for the app such as more information about physicians, larger buttons, and bright colours.

Another survey conducted by Yorulmaz et al. (2018) asked 288 individuals from different age groups living in Konya, a province in Turkey, about their awareness of digital health services and also the utilization of e-Nabız system. Analysis of the data revealed that almost half of the participants (49.7%) heard about the e-Nabız system. However, the rate of registration to e-Nabız was very low (17%). Moreover, 85.1% of the participants could not state their satisfaction of the e-Nabız system since they had not used the system before. Majority of the participants listed M.H.R.S. and Alo182 as their preferred services instead of e-Nabız to make hospital appointments. Participants also stated their purposes of using the e-Nabız system. Almost 13% used e-Nabız to check their medical history; 4% used it to make/cancel hospital appointments, and around 2% of participants used e-Nabız to record their illnesses into the system and share their health information with the healthcare providers.

Kose and Oymak (2019) focused on the e-health usage of individuals by exploring a data set covering a large number of people (13,510) aged from 16 to 74 years. The data set was obtained from the Information and Communication Technology Usage Survey of 2016. Two e-health-related activities were included in the study: Online search to get information on health, and making an online doctor appointment. Probit models were constructed to estimate the probability of these two activities as a function of socio-economic variables. Being female, having higher education level, and frequently using internet increased the probability of doing both e-health-related activities. On the other hand, higher level of household income was positively associated with the online health information search. Results also showed that middle-aged individuals were more likely to engage in e-health activities.

Kuh and Erdem (2021) investigated the existence of digital divide by conducting a survey among 450 individuals from three provinces in Turkey, namely Antalya, Isparta, and Burdur. The survey asked individuals about their level of knowledge and utilization of digital health applications. These applications include M.H.R.S., e-Nabız, and some other apps such as medicine reminder, heart rate monitoring, wearable medical tools, and healthy living. Age was found to be positively associated with the knowledge and utilization. Specifically, younger people had higher awareness and used digital health tools more than older ones. In addition, higher education level and being unmarried were correlated with higher knowledge and utilization of digital health applications. Results also revealed that preferences of application usage changed by gender. Therefore, a digital divide exists based on the study findings.

Erkek and Gündoğdu (2022) evaluated e-health services from the perspective of users by measuring awareness, usage, and satisfaction levels and examining the relationship between satisfaction levels and socio-economic and demographic factors. They gathered data through online and face-to-face surveys involving 394 participants residing in Konya, Turkey, aged 18 years and above. The surveys included 37 questions divided into five sections: Demographic information, e-Devlet (i.e. government services in digital format) usage, e-health services usage, awareness of e-health services, and satisfaction with e-health services. The most commonly used application was the M.H.R.S. application for doctor appointments, and most of the participants used e-health services like e-Nabız to learn test results. All participants had an e-Devlet password, indicating high awareness and access to e-Devlet services. Participants expressed high satisfaction with the speed and efficiency of e-health services, particularly in meeting service demands without waiting for appointments. Awareness of and satisfaction from specific e-health services varied with the socio-demographic characteristics of individuals. Analysis revealed that participants' education levels were found to be correlated with the satisfaction with e-health services, and the occupation was found to be related to awareness through the level of knowledge and adaptation to e-health services.

Ülke and Atilla (2020) investigated the role of information systems in healthcare and the usage of internet health information sources according to different socio-demographic factors. A survey was conducted among a total of 1,140 patients from a state hospital, a university hospital, and a private hospital in Ankara, Turkey. Analysis showed significant differences in the usage of internet health information sources based on demographic factors, hospital type, and frequency of internet use. Women use internet health information sources more than men. People from age groups of 20–29 and 30–39 years use internet health information sources more frequently. Students and public employees use internet health information sources more than other occupational groups for various reasons. Higher education levels correlate with an increased use of internet health information sources. Participants who use the internet for more than four hours daily were more likely to use internet health information sources.

Aydin and Kumru (2023) focused on the adoption of personal e-health records by Generation Z (Gen-Z) to understand the determinants of Gen-Z's intention to use e-health records and explore the barriers to the adoption of these systems among Gen-Z. A survey was conducted with 1,000 Gen-Z university students in Turkey. Analysis showed that social influence significantly impacted Gen-Z's intention to adopt e-health records. The perceived benefits and usefulness of e-health records positively influenced adoption intentions. Gen-Z values the accessibility and the features such as navigation and ambulance request provided by these systems. Higher levels of e-health literacy correlate with increased intentions to use e-health records. Privacy issues are a major barrier, deterring Gen-Z from using e-health records.

Kaya and Eke (2023) examined the mobile health application use frequency and investigated the factors behind the users' application preferences and concerns regarding them. The study also aimed to establish the relationship between application usage and e-health literacy among users. Data for the study was collected through online survey from 539 participants. The study employed the Turkish-adapted version of the "e-Health Literacy Scale" introduced by Norman and Skinner (2006). Almost all study participants used mobile health applications, and the most frequently used application was online hospital appointment booking. The participants' e-health literacy levels were generally high, and there were significant differences across education levels and employment status. Although the high level of e-health literacy among users indicated a positive trend towards the adoption of digital health technologies, 14% of participants stated privacy and security concerns.

Ozan and Kiliç (2023) measured the impact of the level of health literacy on the e-health application usage among 476 public employees in Yozgat, Turkey. Data were collected using online surveys. The top three most used e-health applications were e-Nabız, Hayat Eve Sığar (i.e. developed for tracking COVID-19 cases, vaccination, etc.), and M.H.R.S., respectively, while no significant differences in e-health application usage based on health literacy levels were found. The regression analysis showed that factors like having a chronic disease, using social media, and obtaining health information from reliable sources significantly influenced the use of multiple e-Nabız menus.

8.5 Discussion

Despite the benefits offered by e-health services to their users, the implementation of e-health technologies faces several challenges. One of the major challenges is equitable access to e-health services due to demographic and socio-economic differences. The aforementioned studies for Turkey typically have found that age, education, income, internet use, and gender significantly affect the level of knowledge, usage, and preferences for e-health applications. Demographic and socio-economic differences in terms of utilization, awareness, and usage of e-health services have also been highlighted in studies for other countries. A review of literature by Reiners et al. (2019) emphasized that older adults, less educated people, and lower-income groups face significant barriers to e-health adoption due to limited digital literacy and access to technology.

As in the studies for Turkish samples, age was among the significant factors impacting e-health service use in other countries as well (Alam et al., 2019; Ali et al., 2021; Kontos et al., 2014; Paccoud et al., 2021; Płaciszewski et al., 2023). Young and middle-aged individuals were particularly noted for their higher engagement with e-health services. It was reported that the highest usage rate of e-Nabız (87%) was observed among 25- to 29-year-old persons (Birinci, 2023). Middle-aged individuals might require more comprehensive health information because adults may be more likely to develop non-communicable diseases than people from other age groups (Alam et al., 2019). The adaptation to new technologies and internet makes it necessary to learn new skills making it uncomfortable and difficult for older people due to decline in their physical, visual, and cognitive functions (Hussain et al., 2018). In addition, a lack of desire in using e-health tools, being afraid of making mistakes, and feeling insecure while using digital technologies and internet are among the other barriers reported for older adults (Andrews et al., 2019; Gordon & Hornbrook, 2016; Hussain et al., 2018). Hence, they are at risk of being digitally excluded (Heponiemi et al., 2022).

Individuals from higher socio-economic backgrounds, including those with higher levels of education and income, used e-health technologies more than others. This observation for Turkey was in line with the literature from different countries (Alam et al., 2019; Ali et al., 2021; Kontos et al., 2014; Paccoud et al., 2021; Płaciszewski et al., 2023; Reiners et al., 2019; Sun et al., 2020). Individuals with lower levels of education exhibit significantly less tendency to use e-health services, likely due to their limited proficiency with e-health services, insufficient literacy, and lower access to technologies necessary for such services (Kanter, 2009; Newman et al., 2012). Use of internet and the necessary computer and hardware requirements are generally positively associated with the level of income (DiMaggio et al., 2001).

Gender appears to be another factor associated with e-health usage and preferences in studies for Turkey. Females' preferences for particular e-health applications differ from that for males. Notably, the healthy lifestyle apps available on mobile devices, such as those for quitting smoking, water intake reminders, and menstrual cycle tracking, were more frequently used by females than men (Kuh & Erdem, 2021). Gender differences in the utilization of e-health technologies have also been evident in other studies. Women, compared to men, more frequently utilized teleconsultation services with doctors (Płaciszewski et al., 2023). This is partly because they are more actively involved in health-related online activities (Fox & Duggan, 2013). More importantly, the adoption of e-health within households stems from the healthcare duties typically assigned to women by their families (Torrent-Sellens et al., 2016).

Another major challenge is that e-health services bring forth significant concerns regarding security, privacy, and the overall integrity of health information systems. Data security and privacy issues were highlighted in studies mentioned in the previous section for Turkey (Aydın & Kumru, 2023; Basoglu et al., 2012; Kaya & Eke, 2023; Kutlu & Ozturan, 2012). E-health systems should ensure privacy and security (Michalas et al., 2014; Özkar & Sandıkkaya, 2020). Patients' trust in e-health systems relies on the assurance that their personal health information is safeguarded. Privacy in e-health includes not only storing and safeguarding data on personal medical and genetic records but also preventing unauthorized individuals from accessing the system. Having the patient consent is required before allowing the third-party access to maintain an adequate privacy (Çoban & Tüysüz, 2019). Unauthorized access to health records can lead to violations to privacy and misuse of information. As discussed by Çoban and Tüysüz (2019), there are possible opportunities and associated risks related to e-health systems, and solutions must be developed to ensure privacy and security including: (i) The use of cryptographic systems as an opportunity to ensure data confidentiality; (ii) an appropriate access control mechanism to ensure the patient's privacy; (iii) enhancing the user authorization in access control to avoid data violations; (iv) the use of digital signatures to prevent unauthorized individuals from changing data; and (v) evaluating the existing e-health systems for legal compliance and the implementation of a national standardized framework for electronic health records.

While the existing studies in Turkey offer valuable insights into the demographic and socio-economic variations in the knowledge, usage, and preferences for e-health technologies, many are limited by their sampling methods, often focusing on individuals from a specific province and thus not representing the entire population. Additionally, available studies have not addressed potential urban/rural or regional disparities in e-health knowledge and usage. To gain a better understanding of the e-health-related needs of healthcare users in Turkey, more comprehensive data collection is required. Furthermore, qualitative studies should be conducted, particularly with disadvantaged groups, to uncover their preferences and challenges related to e-health services that may not be evident in the survey data.

8.6 Conclusion and Policy Suggestions

The H.T.P. in Turkey has laid a solid foundation for the implementation of various e-health practices. Demographic and socio-economic differences impacting preferences and the usage of e-health services must be considered when designing, implementing new e-health technologies, and updating the current ones. As access to knowledge, adaptation, and relevant infrastructure differ among healthcare users, a transition to e-health use should be facilitated through establishing an ongoing support to use these systems. While significant progress has been made, addressing challenges related to data security and regulatory frameworks is essential for the sustainable development of e-health. By leveraging the benefits of e-health and overcoming these challenges, the U.H.C. in Turkey will be enhanced, ultimately leading to better health outcomes for its population. The focus should be on creating an inclusive and secure digital health environment that benefits all citizens. This will require ongoing collaboration between healthcare providers, policymakers, technology developers, and the users to ensure that e-health solutions are effective, equitable, and sustainable.

Note

1 https://kayittescil.saglik.gov.tr/TR-90715/aktif-usbs-listesi.html

References

Alam, K., Mahumud, R.A., Alam, F., Keramat, S.A., Erdiaw-Kwasie, M.O., & Sarker, A.R. (2019). Determinants of access to eHealth services in regional Australia. *International Journal of Medical Informatics*, *131*, 103960. https://doi.org/10.1016/j.ijmedinf.2019.103960
Ali, M.A., Alam, K., Taylor, B., & Ashraf, M. (2021). Examining the determinants of eHealth usage among elderly people with disability: The moderating role of behavioural aspects. *International Journal of Medical Informatics*, *149*, 104411. https://doi.org/10.1016/j.ijmedinf.2021.104411

Andrews, J.A., Brown, L.J., Hawley, M.S., & Astell, A.J. (2019). Older adults' perspectives on using digital technology to maintain good mental health: Interactive group study. *Journal of Medical Internet Research, 21*(2), e11694. https://doi.org/10.2196/11694

Aydin, G., & Kumru, S. (2023). Paving the way for increased e- health record use: Elaborating intentions of Gen-Z. *Health Systems, 12*(3), 281–298. https://10.1080/20476965.2022.2129471

Basoglu, N., Daim, T.U., & Topacan, U. (2012). Determining patient preferences for remote monitoring. *Journal of Medical Systems, 36*, 1389–1401. https://doi.org/10.1007/s10916-010-9601-1

Birinci, Ş. (2023). A digital opportunity for patients to manage their health: Turkey national personal health record system (the e-Nabız). *Balkan Medical Journal, 40*(3), 215–21. https://doi.org/10.4274/balkanmedj.galenos.2023.2023-2-77

Carini, E., Villani, L., Pezzullo, A.M., Gentili, A., Barbara, A., Ricciardi, W., & Boccia, S. (2021). The impact of digital patient portals on health outcomes, system efficiency, and patient attitudes: Updated systematic literature review. *Journal of Medical Internet Research, 23*(9), e26189. https://doi.org/10.2196/26189

Çoban, Ç., & Tüysüz, M.F. (2019). E-health and privacy: Risks, opportunities and solutions. In *2019 4th international conference on computer science and engineering (UBMK)* (pp. 554–559). Samsun, Turkey. https://doi.org/10.1109/UBMK.2019.8907079

DiMaggio, P., Hargittai, E., Celeste, C., & Shafer, S. (2001). *Digital inequality: From unequal access to differentiated use: A literature review and agenda for research on digital inequality.* Russell Sage Foundation. https://www.russellsage.org/sites/all/files/u4/DiMaggio%20et%20al.pdf

Dogac, A., Yuksel, M., Ertürkmen, G.L., Kabak, Y., Namli, T., Yıldız, M.H., Ay, Y., Ceyhan, B., Hülür, Ü., Öztürk, H., & Atbakan, E. (2014). Healthcare information technology infrastructures in Turkey. *Yearbook of Medical Informatics, 9*(1), 228–234. https://doi.org/10.15265/IY-2014-0001

Erkek, S., & Gündoğdu, S. (2022). Vatandaş gözünden e-sağlık hizmetlerinin değerlendirilmesi: farkındalık, kullanım ve memnuniyet düzeyleri. *Selçuk Üniversitesi Sosyal Bilimler Meslek Yüksekokulu Dergisi, 25*(2), 646–667. https://doi.org/10.29249/selcuksbmyd.1166357

Fox, S., & Duggan, M. (2013). *Health online 2013.* Pew Internet & American Life Project. https://www.pewinternet.org/wp-content/uploads/sites/9/media/Files/Reports/PIP_HealthOnline.pdf

Gordon, N.P., & Hornbrook, M.C. (2016). Differences in access to and preferences for using patient portals and other eHealth technologies based on race, ethnicity, and age: A database and survey study of seniors in a large health plan. *Journal of Medical Internet Research, 18*(3), e50. https://doi.org/10.2196/jmir.5105

Heponiemi, T., Kaihlanen, A-M., Kouvonen, A., Leemann, L., Taipale, S., & Gluschkoff, K. (2022). The role of age and digital competence on the use of online health and social care services: A cross-sectional population-based survey. *Digital Health, 8*. https://doi.org/10.1177/20552076221074485

Hussain, D., Ross, P., & Bednar, P. (2018). The perception of the benefits and drawbacks of internet usage by the elderly people. In C. Rossignoli, F. Virili, S. Za (eds.), *Digital technology and organizational change. Lecture notes in information systems and organisation* (vol. 23). Springer International Publishing. https://doi.org/10.1007/978-3-319-62051-0_17

Kanter, M. (2009). *Realizing the equity potential of e-health: Improving health promotion and self-management in Ontario.* Wellesley Institute. https://www.wellesleyinstitute.com/wp-content/uploads/2011/11/E-Health_Through_and_Equity_Lens_FINAL_FORMATTED.pdf

Kaya, E., & Eke, E. (2023). Bireylerin mobil sağlık uygulaması kullanım durumu ve e-sağlık okuryazarlığı ilişkisi. *İşletme Bilimi Dergisi, 11*(1), 1–15. https://10.22139/jobs.1159206

Kontos, E., Blake, K.D., Chou, W.-Y.S., & Prestin, A. (2014). Predictors of eHealth usage: Insights on the digital divide from the Health Information National Trends Survey 2012. *Journal of Medical Internet Research, 16*(7), e172. https://doi.org/10.2196/jmir.3117

Kose, I., Rayner, J., Birinci, S., Ulgu, M.M., Yilmaz, I., Guner, S., HIMSS Analytics Team & MoH Team. (2020). Adoption rates of electronic health records in Turkish hospitals and the relation with hospital sizes. *BMC Health Services Research, 20*, 967. https://doi.org/10.1186/s12913-020-05767-5

Kose, T., & Oymak, C. (2019). E-health in Turkey: an analysis of consumer activities. *Health and Technology, 9*, 113–121. https://doi.org/10.1007/s12553-018-0256-0

Kuh, Z., & Erdem, R. (2021). Dijital sağlık uygulamalarının bilinirliğinin ve kullanımının dijital bölünme çerçevesinde incelenmesi. *Hacettepe Sağlık İdaresi Dergisi, 24*(2), 255–274.

Kutlu, B., & Ozturan, M. (2012). Determinants of E-health readiness of end-users. *International Medical Journal, 19*(4),287–291.

Liddy, C., Drosinis, P., Armstrong C.D., McKellips, F., Afkham, A., & Keely, E. (2016) What are the cost savings associated with providing access to specialist care through the champlain BASE eConsult service? A costing evaluation. *BMJ Open, 6*(6), e010920. https://doi.org/10.1136/bmjopen-2015-010920

Mandil, S. (2004). *Review of and recommended improvements to Turkey eHealth strategy*. https://joinup. ec.europa.eu/sites/default/files/document/2014-12/Review%20of%20and%20recommended%20 improvements%20to%20Turkey%20eHealth%20Strategy.pdf

Michalas, A., Paladi, N., & Gehrmann, C. (2014). Security aspects of e-Health systems migration to the cloud. In *2014 IEEE 16th international conference on e-Health networking, applications and services (Healthcom)* (pp. 212–218). Natal, Brazil. https://doi.org/10.1109/HealthCom.2014.7001843

Moen, A., Hackl, W.O., Hofdijk, J., Van Gemert-Pijnen, L., Ammenwerth, E., Nykänen, P., & Hoerbst, A. (2013). eHealth in Europe – status and challenges. *Yearbook of Medical Informatics, 8*, 59–63.

Newman, L., Patel, K., & Barton, E. (2012). *The role and impact of digital and traditional information and communication pathways in health service access and equity*. South Australian Community Health Research Unit, Flinders University, Adelaide, Australia. https://apo.org.au/sites/default/files/resource-files/2012-08/apo-nid64561.pdf

Norman, C.D., & Skinner, H.A. (2006). eHealth literacy: Essential skills for consumer health in a networked world. *Journal of Medical Internet Research, 8*(2), e9. https://doi.org/10.2196/jmir.8.2.e9

Ökem, Z.G., & Çakar, M. (2015). What have health care reforms achieved in Turkey? An appraisal of the "Health Transformation Programme". *Health Policy, 119*(9), 1153–1163. http://doi.org/10.1016/j.healthpol.2015.06.003

Organisation for Economic Co-operation and Development. (2010). *Improving health sector efficiency: The role of information and communication Technologies*. OECD Health Policy Studies, OECD Publishing, Paris, https://doi.org/10.1787/9789264084612-en

Ozan, D., & Kiliç, M. (2023). The effect of health literacy level on the use of e-health applications. *International Journal of Statistics in Medical Research, 12*, 1–11. https://10.6000/1929-6029.2023.12.01

Özkar, M., & Sandıkkaya, M.T. (2020). A survey on security & privacy design in e-health. In *2020 5th international conference on computer science and engineering (UBMK'20)* (pp. 208–213), Diyarbakır, Turkey. https://doi.org/10.1109/UBMK50275.2020.9219372

Paccoud, I., Baumann, M., Bihan, E.L., Pétré, B., Breinbauer, M., Böhme, P., Chauvel, L., & Leist, A.K. (2021). Socioeconomic and behavioural factors associated with access to and use of personal health records. *BMC Medical Informatics and Decision Making, 21*, 18. https://doi.org/10.1186/s12911-020-01383-9

Płaciszewski, K., Wierzba, W., Ostrowski, J., Pinkas, J., & Jankowski, M. (2023). Factors associated with the use of public eHealth services in Poland – a 2022 nationwide cross-sectional survey. *Annals of Agricultural and Environmental Medicine, 30*(1), 127–134. https://doi.org/10.26444/aaem/158027

Reiners, F., Sturm, J., Bouw, L.J.W., & Wouters, E.J.M. (2019). Sociodemographic factors influencing the Use of eHealth in people with chronic diseases. *International Journal of Environmental Research and Public Health, 16*(4), 645. https://doi.org/10.3390/ijerph16040645

Sun, X., Yan, W., Zhou, H., Wang, Z., Zhang, X., Huang, S., & Li, L. (2020). Internet use and need for digital health technology among the elderly: A cross-sectional survey in China. *BMC Public Health, 20*, 1386. https://doi.org/10.1186/s12889-020-09448-0

Taşkın, B., Coşkun, H.R., & Tüzün, H. (2018). Usability evaluation of the mobile application of Centralized Hospital Appointment System (CHAS). In S. Saeed, T. Ramayah & Z. Mahmood (eds.), *User centric e-government: Challenges and opportunities* (pp. 231–248). Springer International Publishing. https://doi.org/10.1007/978-3-319-59442-2_13

Torrent-Sellens, J., Díaz-Chao, Á., Soler-Ramos, I., & Saigí-Rubió, F. (2016). Modelling and predicting eHealth usage in Europe: A multidimensional approach from an online survey of 13,000 European union internet users. *Journal of Medical Internet Research, 18*(7), e188. https://doi.org/10.2196/jmir.5605

Ülke, R., & Atilla, E.A. (2020). Sağlık hizmetlerinde bilişim sistemleri ve e-Sağlık: Ankara ili örneği. *Gazi İktisat ve İşletme Dergisi, 6*(1), 86–100. https://doi.org/10.30855/gjeb.2020.6.1.006

World Health Organization. (2021). *Global strategy on digital health 2020–2025.* https://www.who.int/docs/default-source/documents/gs4dhdaa2a9f352b0445bafbc79ca799dce4d.pdf

Yorulmaz, M., Odacı, Ş., & Akkan, M. (2018). Dijital sağlık ve e-nabız farkındalık düzeyi belirleme çalışması. *Selçuk Üniversitesi Sosyal ve Teknik Araştırmalar Dergisi, 16*, 1–11.

Chapter 9

Evaluation of the Health Transformation Programme from the Perspectives of Effectiveness and Satisfaction

İsmail Çakmak

Contents

9.1 Introduction

Turkish health system has experienced many changes over the years. Changes are necessary for two main reasons. First, as in every country, healthcare services and systems must be adapted to new technology in parallel with technological developments, and second, it is necessary to keep up with the changing needs of society over the years. These changes, of course, have been actualized around limited labour force and resources. Health Transformation Programme (H.T.P.), which has been introduced in 2003, is one of the most comprehensive of these changes. The main purpose of the programme has been determined by the authorities as to organize, to finance, and to deliver the health system in an effective, efficient, and equitable manner (Ministry of Health, 2003). H.T.P. presented particularly within the framework of transformation rather than any concept, and many new practices have been introduced in health policy in Turkey. Public expectations were naturally high from the program, which is presented as a transformation rather than a reform. After the programme was announced, considerable amount of literature has been published on H.T.P. These studies tried to discuss the programme from every aspect. Two decades have passed since the programme was launched. It may be considered, there is now enough data to control the harmony between the initial goals and actual realizations. In this context, this chapter analysed the compatibility between actual realizations and targets by considering many dimensions. First, the current study focuses on child and infant mortality rates in Turkey which are considered a preferential basis on the program. The main purpose was trying to observe whether there was a significant change in infant and child mortality rates before and after the program. Additionally, life expectancy in Turkey is also examined in this section. Following this, individuals' perceived satisfaction levels with healthcare services have been assessed by focusing on key elements of the healthcare system, including healthcare staff, appointments, and examination queues. The programme not only focuses and prioritizes patient satisfaction, but it also aims to purchase better quality healthcare services at more affordable cost. These targets are clearly defined at the programme framework (Ministry of Health, 2003). For this reason, in addition to parameters of individuals' satisfaction with healthcare services, the pricing satisfaction of both drugs and examination is also analysed in the study.

9.2 Primary Outcomes and Indicators

The issue of infant and child mortality has been prioritized within the relevant sections of the H.T.P. and assessed as "deal with immediately" (Ministry of Health, 2003). In this context, the study discusses the infant and child mortality rates by considering the pre- and post-H.T.P. period together. Thus, it might be seen whether there was a significant change in infant and child mortality rates post-H.T.P. In addition, life expectancy rates in Turkey are included in this section. Because almost two decades passed since the H.T.P. started, and the effects of the H.T.P. on life expectations are also aimed to be observed.

Figure 9.1 shows the rapid downtrend about infant and child mortality in Turkey over the 50 years. In 2003, when the H.T.P. started, infant and child deaths were measured as approximately 25 and 30 per 1,000 births, respectively. These rates were periodically high, especially when compared to the average of the European countries. Infant and child mortality rates, which continued to decrease over the years, dropped to 9 per 1,000 births by the 2020s. Based on UNICEF (2024) reports, it is noticeable that the current situation is still high compared to Europe but low compared to Asia.

Figure 9.2 shows the life expectancy in Turkey over the years. It is seen that life expectancy of women is higher than that of men; however, this is valid in almost all developed and developing countries. When compared to other countries, life expectancy in Turkey is below most O.E.C.D. countries (OECD, 2024). Figure 9.2 illustrates that the improvement in life expectancy started long before the programme, and the momentum is maintained after the H.T.P.

9.3 Targets and Perceived Realizations: Examination of the Post-Programme Period Based on Selected Indicators

This chapter seeks to examine the link between the targets of the H.T.P. and realizations. The current study particularly focuses on whether the primary goals set in H.T.P. are achieved and

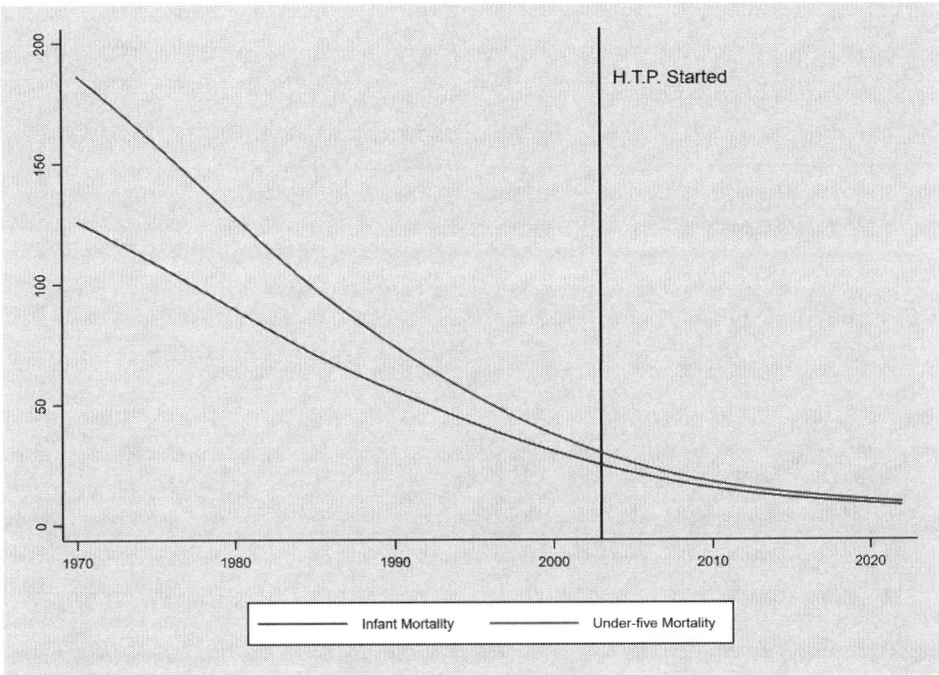

Figure 9.1   Infant and under-five mortality rates (deaths per 1,000 live births).

Source: Prepared by the author based on UNICEF (2024)

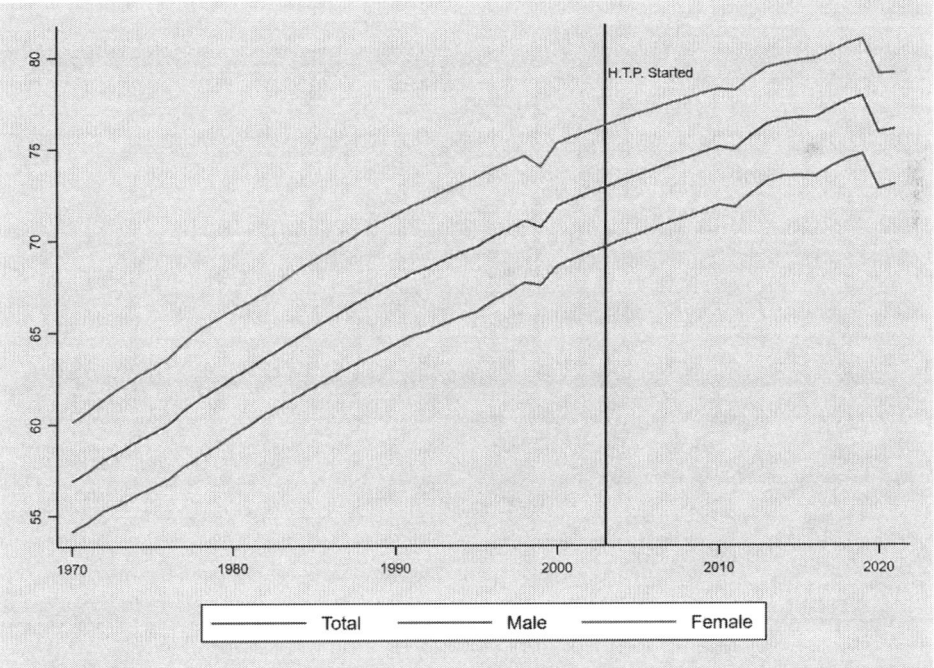

Figure 9.2   Life expectancy at birth.

Source: World Bank (2024)

whether there is a significant change in individuals' satisfaction with health services post- H.T.P. In this context, this part of the study consists of two subsections. First, it focuses on perceived satisfaction with the healthcare system and, then, satisfaction with the health-related pricing.

9.3.1 Satisfaction Indicators Regarding the Healthcare System

One of the main goals of the H.T.P. was to increase the satisfaction of healthcare services. The healthcare services may be seen as adequate or even perfect by the service provider, but the perceived satisfaction of the patients who receive the service is a kind of invisible measurement of agreement between the patients and the providers. TURKSTAT Life Satisfaction Survey (L.S.S.) includes various questions that can also indicate individuals' satisfaction with health services. In this context, this study used 2004–2022 LSS micro data to check whether there is a good match between H.T.P. targets and perceived satisfaction of the individuals. Figure 9.3 gives information about satisfaction level of individuals with health services between 2004 and 2022.

Figure 9.3 clearly points that the perceived satisfaction level with health services is quite high. However, in the first years of the H.T.P, the percentage of people who declared they are dissatisfied with health services was very high, but in the following years, the percentage of dissatisfaction decreased, despite fluctuations. For example 26% of participants in 2004 declared that they are dissatisfied with health services. This percentage entered a dramatic downward trend and dropped to single digits in 2012 (9.90%). In the following years, even if the rising trend is observed in the number of those who said they are not satisfied, this never gets close to the years when the H.T.P.

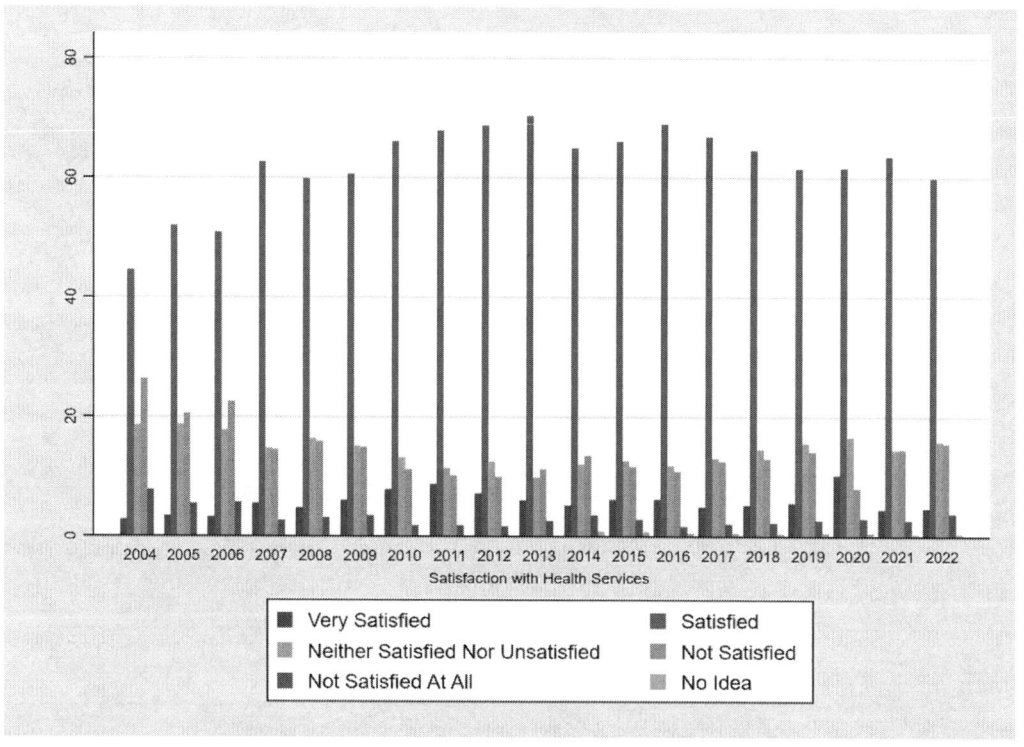

Figure 9.3   Health services' satisfaction of individuals.

Source: Prepared by the author based on TURKSTAT L.L.S. 2004–2022

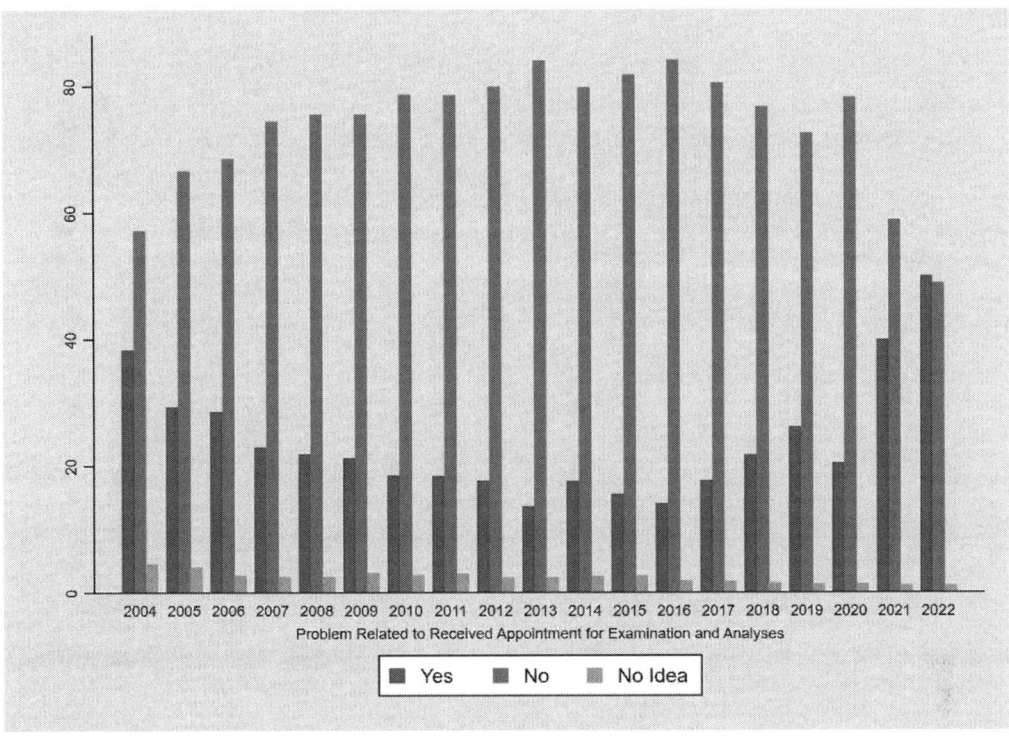

Figure 9.4   Problems when making an appointment for examination and analysis.

Source: Prepared by the author based on TURKSTAT L.S.S. 2004–2022

was first implemented during the examined period. By 2022, the percentage of those who said they are satisfied is approximately 60, while 15% declared that they are not satisfied. In this context, a significant improvement can be noted in individuals' satisfaction with health services after the H.T.P. However, the factors that have caused the decrease in satisfaction in recent years should be followed, and the reasons should not be ignored.

The medical examination appointment has always been the subject of intense debate within the community, and this has become one of the most controversial health-related issues in Turkey. The H.T.P. aimed to provide a solution to this particular problematic by increasing the effectiveness and efficiency in the healthcare system. To achieve this goal, the central physician appointment system (MHRS-CPAS) has been introduced in 2010 (Kördeve et al., 2017). It is provided as an option with MHRS to individuals to be able to make appointment with physicians of their choice, either via the internet or call centres. The system, which has been tested initially in a few cities in Turkey in 2010, was made applicable in all hospitals affiliated with the Ministry of Health throughout the country in 2012. Figure 9.4 shows individuals' statements about whether they perceived problems with examination and analysis appointments. Figure 9.4 indicates that more individuals are satisfied with the appointment during the examined period. More precisely, downward trend is observed in the proportion of individuals who declared problems with appointments after 2004, especially until 2013. However, after 2013, a significant increase is observed in the proportion of individuals who declared problems with their appointments. Another striking detail in Figure 9.4 is that there was a rapid increase after 2020 in the percentage of those who declared problems with their appointments. In fact, in 2022, this exceeded the percentage of those who declared no problem with their

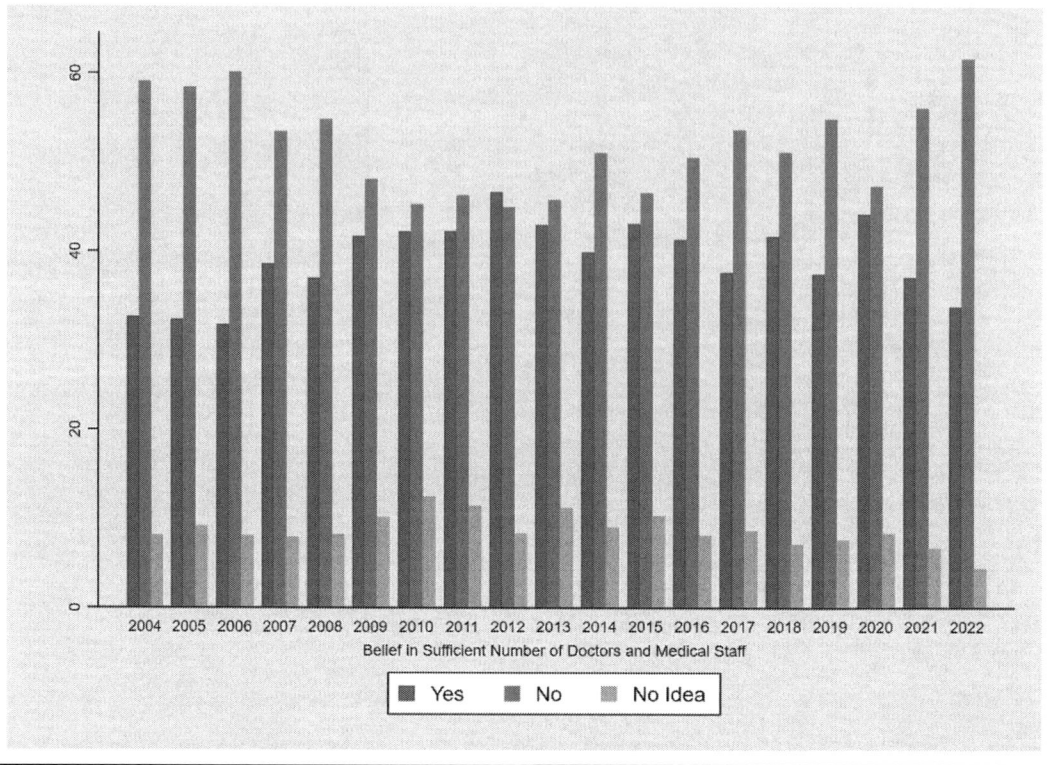

Figure 9.5   Statements of individuals regarding sufficient doctors and medical personnel.

Source: Prepared by the author based on TURKSTAT L.S.S. 2004–2022

appointments. This situation can be discussed in two aspects: First, the dramatic intensity in the healthcare system after the pandemic and the problems that come with it and, second, the economic deteriorations that were felt more in Turkey, especially as of 2021.

The problematics of whether there are sufficient numbers of healthcare personnel is another important issue in the Turkish healthcare system. This debatable issue is valid not only for developing economies such as Turkey but also even in countries with a developed ecosystem (e.g. Harvey & Trudgill, 2021 for England; Dumesnil et al., 2024 for France). In fact, the real picture on this issue has emerged dramatically, especially during the pandemic (Unruh et al., 2022). Figure 9.5 sheds light on individuals' perceptions in this issue. According to Figure 9.5, individuals think that there are an insufficient number of healthcare staff in terms of both physician and other medical staff in Turkey within the examined period (except 2012). For instance L.S.S. has declared that the number of healthcare personnel was insufficient in 2004 and 2005 which coincided with the first years of the H.T.P. In the following periods, individuals' belief in the sufficient number of healthcare personnel increased, although a fluctuating trend has been observed. However, the dramatic decline in individuals' belief in the adequate number of healthcare staff in healthcare institutions during the years 2021–2022 can also be observed from the Figure 9.5. Along with this decline, the belief in the adequacy of healthcare staff has almost reverted to the levels of 2004. This decline can be attributed to factors such as the pandemic and the economic volatility in 2021–2022.

Waiting queues for examination and analysis in the hospitals are another debatable issue in Turkey, just like getting an examination appointment. Images showing queues in front of doctors' doors in hospitals or patients waiting for their turn for tests frequently occupy the country's

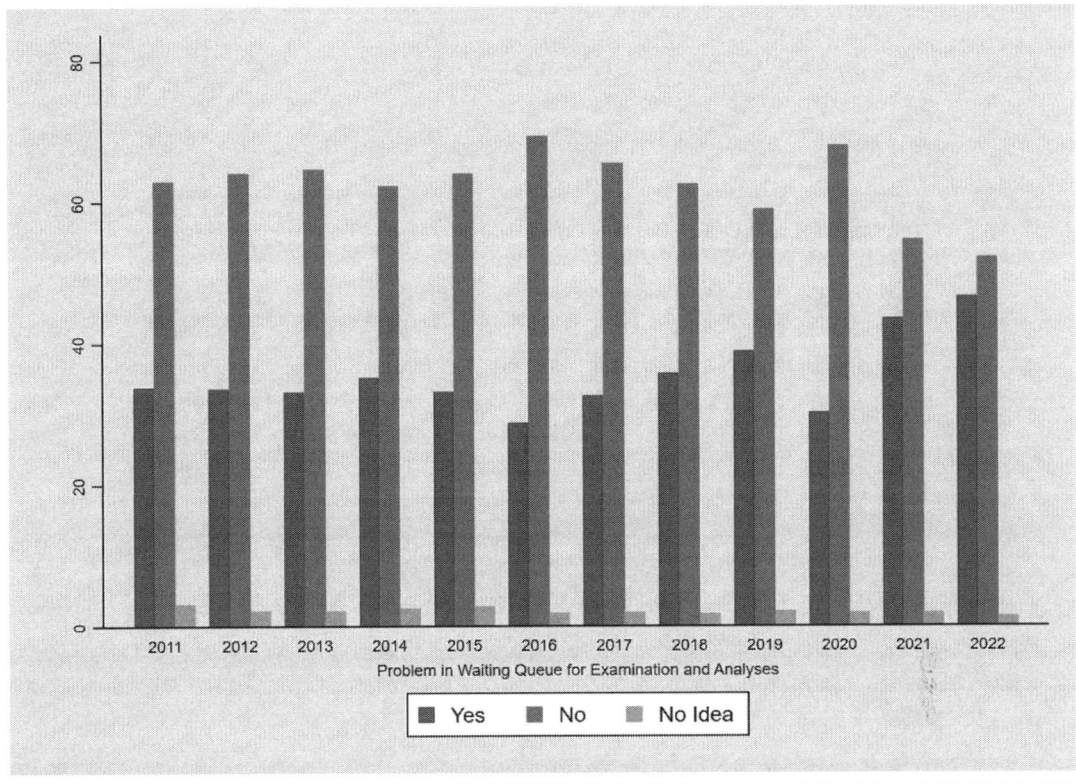

Figure 9.6   Statement of problems about waiting queue for examination and analyses.

Source: Prepared by the author based on TURKSTAT L.S.S. 2011–2022

agenda. In this context, since the H.T.P. aims to increase the effectiveness and efficiency in the healthcare system, it can be expected that the related queues will decrease after the H.T.P., and/or there will be a significant decrease in the percentage of individuals complaining about it. In this regard, Figure 9.6 shows individuals' statements regarding the examination and analysis queues. Unfortunately, no question could be related to the subject is asked to individuals in the L.S.S. data sets until 2011. For this reason, it will not be possible to directly connect individuals' positive and negative statements on this subject to the effectiveness or ineffectiveness of the H.T.P. However, it is clear from Figure 9.6 that there is a serious increase in the percentage of individuals experiencing problems for examination and analysis in hospitals in 2021 and 2022. For example from 2011 to 2022, the percentage of participants who declared they had problems waiting in queues increased by approximately 38% and reached 47%.

9.3.2 Pricing Perceptions Regarding Health System

It is emphasized by the H.T.P. that pharmaceutical pricing sometimes deviates from scientific facts (Ministry of Health, 2003). Accordingly, programme aims to reach a solution in a compromise structure by making pharmaceutical pricing on a scientific basis. Thus, individuals' perception of drug prices can be stabilized. Figure 9.7 shows individuals' opinions on drug prices between 2004 and 2022.

Figure 9.7 clearly shows that individuals' opinion about drug prices to be largely problematic at beginning of the H.T.P. For example 65% of L.S.S. participants declared a problem about drug

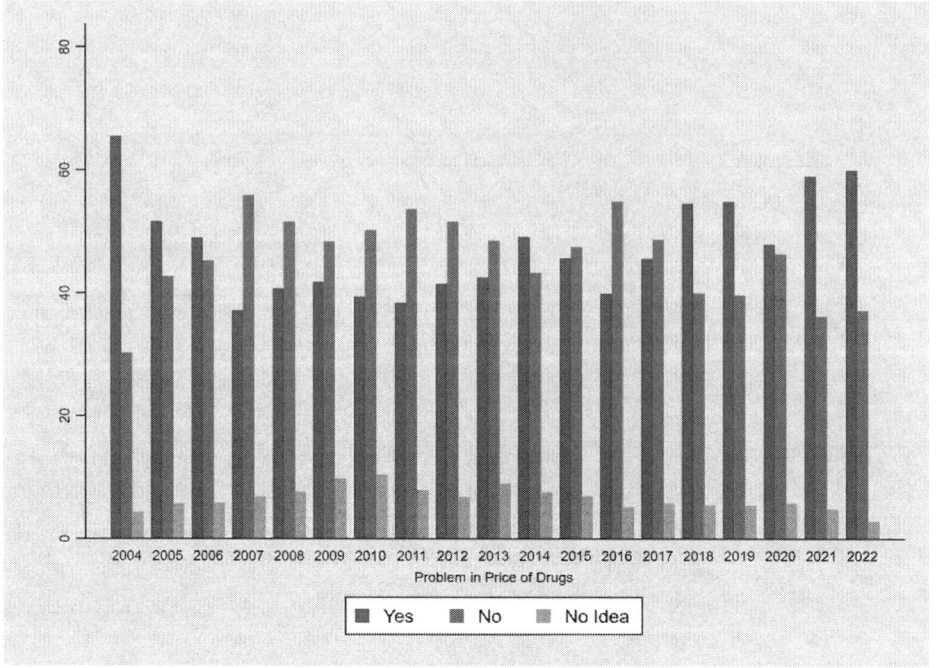

Figure 9.7   Statements of individuals regarding problem in price of drugs.

Source: Prepared by the author based on TURKSTAT L.S.S. 2004–2022

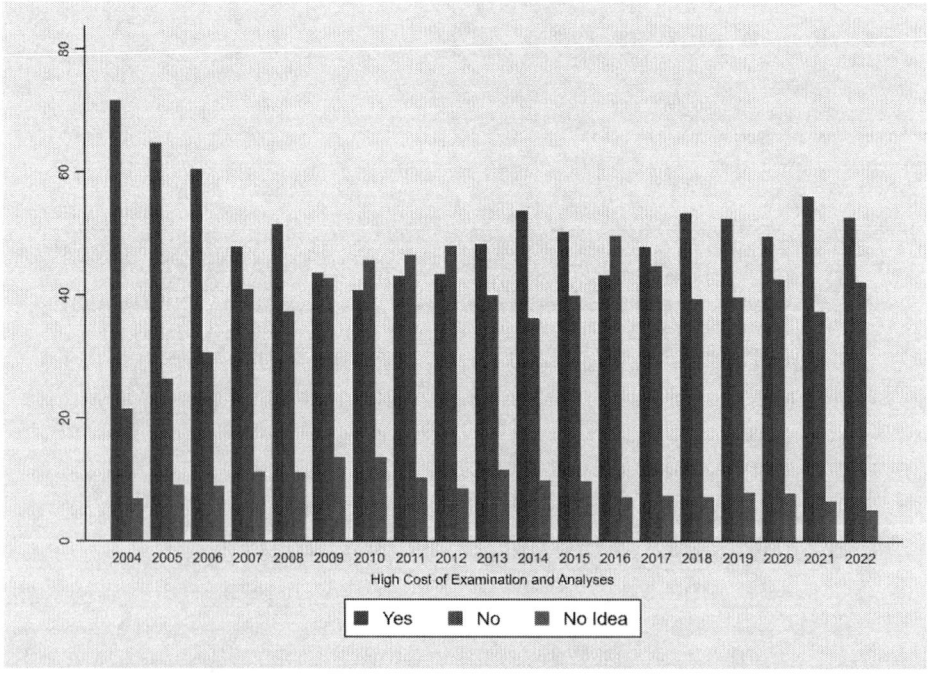

Figure 9.8   Statements of individuals regarding cost of examination and analyses.

Source: Prepared by the author based on TURKSTAT L.S.S. 2004–2022

prices in 2004. In the following years, this rate decreased, and positive opinions about the pricing increased. However, after 2018, the momentum turned negative again and even approached the values of 2004 in 2022. L.S.S. data of 2022 indicate that approximately 60% of people see drug prices as problematic.

Discussions about examination and analysis prices have always been forefront in Turkey. The purchasing power of individuals and the general conjuncture in the economy significantly affect the perception of examination and analysis prices. Especially, unmet healthcare needs of individuals increase during the periods of economic crisis, high inflation, and austerity. This occurred, for example, in Greece during the European debt crisis. As a result of the economic measures and the austerity policies, there has been a significant increase in the unmet healthcare needs in the country (Zavras et al., 2016; Pierrakos et al., 2023). A similar scenario occurred in countries such as Ireland (Thomas et al., 2014), Portugal (Doetsch et al., 2017), and Spain (Lopez-Valcarcel & Barber, 2017), which are dramatically affected by the European debt crisis. During the 2008 crisis, as in many countries, unmet needs increased in Turkey (Detollenaere et al., 2017). Related literature emphasizes that there is a significant increase in unmet needs during the pandemic (see e.g. Geranios et al., 2022; Schmidt et al., 2022; Irmak & Eyimaya, 2023; Guo et al., 2024). Although the pandemic is not a direct economic crisis, its impact on individuals and the economy in general has been devastating. Rising unemployment and difficulties in financial and living conditions have increased unmet needs. Due to the deteriorating economic situation, complaints about examination and analysis prices may increase. Here, it is emphasized that individuals' perceptions on examination pricing may not be directly associated with the H.T.P. but may be more related to the economic outlook. However, it would be useful to monitor the appearance after the H.T.P. In this context, Figure 9.8 shows individuals' perceptions of examination and analysis prices in the post-H.T.P. period. Accordingly, individuals' perceptions of examinations and analyses prices in Turkey coincide with the earlier explanations. In the early years of the H.T.P., individuals' perspectives on prices were highly negative. For example, according to the L.S.S., approximately 72% of individuals were dissatisfied with prices in 2004. Although there has been an improvement in the perception of pricing over the years, perception of prices has turned negative again especially with the effect of the deteriorating economic outlook and the pandemic.

9.4 Discussion

The current study focuses on the consistency between the targets set by the H.T.P. at the beginning and the realizations so far. Accordingly, the study analyses the aforementioned consistency in three separate phases within the context of immediate actions, individual satisfaction from healthcare services, and satisfaction from the health services pricing. The initial part of the study is focused on the realizations regarding infant and child mortality rates, which are stated in the H.T.P. to "deal with immediately". In addition, the life expectancy at birth is also included in the current study in order to control the long-term effects of both the programme and the health system. This study is pointed out a significant improvement in infant mortality and life expectancy rates in Turkey over the years. However, as can be seen from Figures 9.1 and 9.2, these improvements started before the H.T.P., and the positive trend continued in a similar pattern after the programme. In other words, it would not be correct to directly associate improvements in infant mortality and life expectancy with the H.T.P.

Following part of the study analysed the individuals' satisfaction from the healthcare services. L.S.S. micro data sets of 2004–2022 have been used to understand to satisfaction of individuals from the health services. One of the main goals of the H.T.P. is to improve the quality of the healthcare services, to provide individuals with easier access to quality health services, and ensure patient satisfaction. L.S.S. is one of the proper data sets that could be used to check the consistency of these goals of the programme. First, L.S.S. is not having a regional restriction, and, second, it is suitable for making inferences about Turkey in general due to the sample and cluster structure. Individuals' general satisfaction level with the healthcare system, ease/difficulty in accessing examination, perceived adequacy of the number of healthcare staff, and examination of queue problems are discussed in this section. The examined indicators in this phase pointed out the following inferences regarding the H.T.P. First, individual satisfaction in almost all indicators increased dramatically, and perceived problems decreased significantly shortly after the implementation of the programme. These improvements indicate that the H.T.P. has made significant improvements in the healthcare system in the first years. Second, however, these perceived improvements began to decrease significantly, particularly as of mid-2010.

Section 9.3.2 focuses on individuals' perceived problems and satisfaction with pricing in the healthcare system. TURKSTAT L.S.S. micro data sets are used in this part. The main purpose was to observe whether there was a significant improvement in individuals' price perceptions in the healthcare system after the H.T.P. Since pricing is one of the most important issues in the Turkish Healthcare system from past to present, and in order to observe whether the H.T.P.'s targets are achieved, especially with drug prices, individuals' pricing perception is particularly addressed in the study. Figures 9.7 and 9.8, showing individuals' perceptions of examination and drug prices, reveal a picture similar to the previous part. Following the first years of the H.T.P, perceived problems related to examination and drug prices decreased significantly. However, after the mid-2010s, a rising trend has been observed in perceived problems. In this context, it can be concluded that the H.T.P. had a significant positive impact on the pricing perception in the healthcare system at the beginning.

Since the mid-2010s, the dramatic downward trends in both individuals' satisfaction with the health system and their pricing perceptions should particularly be evaluated. Individuals' self-reported satisfactions regarding the healthcare system and its pricing may not depend on systemic changes and transformations alone such as the H.T.P. Such satisfaction indicators might be influenced by many socio-economic factors. Financial conditions are one of the most important of these. When individuals' financial conditions become difficult, a decrease can be observed in their satisfaction with the healthcare system, as in every field of life. Similarly, the pandemic has significantly increased the problems related to the healthcare system and seriously reduced the satisfaction. Related studies also point to similar results. Turkey has been experiencing economic turbulence especially since 2018. During this period, high inflation triggered by the currency crisis and the devalued local currency reduced the purchasing power of individuals. This has begun to place a serious burden directly on the healthcare system. Individuals, whose purchasing power decreased and they have chosen austerity precautions, have begun to prefer public hospitals instead of private healthcare institutions, and the burden on the system increased. As a result, satisfaction with the health system began to decrease, and perceived problems began to increase. On the other hand, the increase in examination and drug prices and complaints of individuals whose purchasing power has decreased may be due to this.

9.5 Conclusion

This chapter analysed the consistency between the H.T.P. goals and the perceived realizations by individuals. It is observed that achievements in critically important topics such as infant and child mortality rates, which are stated in the programme to require acute and urgent intervention, are quite positive. However, since the child and infant mortality rates already began to decrease before the program, it would not be correct to associate this momentum only with the H.T.P. This study also focused on individuals' perceived satisfaction with health services after the H.T.P. in the context of selected indicators. The current study has revealed that there is an increase in individuals' satisfaction with health services and a decrease in perceived problems, particularly after the first years of the H.T.P. In this context, it can be stated that the health-system-related satisfaction level of individuals increased by the provided healthcare services. Despite these improvements, momentum reversed especially after the mid-2010s. This might be caused by both effect of the pandemic and the deteriorating economic conditions in Turkey. Moreover, it is observed that some improvements diminished in particular indicators and even back to the initial level. Finally, the study also examined individuals' satisfaction with pricing in the healthcare system. A similar scenario has been observed in pricing satisfaction as well. While individuals' satisfaction with examination and drug prices gradually increased in the first period of the programme, their satisfaction gradually decreased in the following periods. The study revealed that, in the context of the examined indicators, the H.T.P. targets and satisfaction perceived by individuals quite match, especially in the first years, but in the following years, individuals' satisfaction with the health system decreased due to the various internal and external factors.

References

Detollenaere, J., Hanssens, L., Vyncke, V., De Maeseneer, J., & Willems, S. (2017). Do we reap what we sow? Exploring the association between the strength of European primary healthcare systems and inequity in unmet need. *PloS One*, 12(1), e0169274. https://doi.org/10.1371/journal.pone.0169274

Doetsch, J., Pilot, E., Santana, P., & Krafft, T. (2017). Potential barriers in healthcare access of the elderly population influenced by the economic crisis and the troika agreement: A qualitative case study in Lisbon, Portugal. *International Journal for Equity in Health*, 16, 1–17. https://doi.org/10.1186/s12939-017-0679-7

Dumesnil, H., Lutaud, R., Bellon-Curutchet, J., Deffontaines, A., & Verger, P. (2024). Dealing with the doctor shortage: A qualitative study exploring French general practitioners' lived experiences, difficulties, and adaptive behaviours. *Family Practice*, cmae017. https://doi.org/10.1093/fampra/cmae017

Geranios, K., Kagabo, R., & Kim, J. (2022). Impact of COVID-19 and socioeconomic status on delayed care and unemployment. *Health Equity*, 6(1), 91–97. https://doi.org/10.1089/heq.2021.0115

Guo, C., Yuan, D., Tang, H., Hu, X., & Lei, Y. (2024). Impact of a pandemic shock on unmet medical needs of middle-aged and older adults in 10 countries. *BMJ Health & Care Informatics*, 31(1). https://doi.org/10.1136/bmjhci-2023-100865

Harvey, P. R., & Trudgill, N. J. (2021). The association between physician staff numbers and mortality in English hospitals. *EClinicalMedicine*, 32. https://doi.org/10.1016/j.eclinm.2020.100709

Irmak, A. Y., & Eyimaya, A. O. (2023). Unmet health needs during the COVID-19 pandemic. *Clinical and Experimental Health Sciences*, 13(1), 67–74. https://doi.org/10.33808/clinexphealthsci.1032287

Kördeve, M. K., Uzun, B., & Ünal, E. (2017). Merkezi hastane randevu sisteminin İşleyişi Üzerine Bir Alan Araştırması. *Uluslararası Sağlık Yönetimi ve Stratejileri Araştırma Dergisi*, 3(2), 52–61.

Lopez-Valcarcel, B. G., & Barber, P. (2017). Economic crisis, austerity policies, health and fairness: Lessons learned in Spain. *Applied Health Economics and Health Policy*, 15, 13–21. https://doi.org/10.1007/s40258-016-0263-0

Ministry of Health. (2003). *Transformations in health.* Ministry of Health of the Republic of Turkey. December 2003.

OECD. (2024). *OECD data. Life expectancy at birth.* https://data.oecd.org/pinboard-editor/

Pierrakos, G., Goula, A., & Latsou, D. (2023). Predictors of unmet healthcare needs during economic and health crisis in Greece. *International Journal of Environmental Research and Public Health*, 20(19), 6840. https://doi.org/10.3390/ijerph20196840

Schmidt, A. E., Rodrigues, R., Simmons, C., & Steiber, N. (2022). A crisis like no other? Unmet needs in healthcare during the first wave of the COVID-19 crisis in Austria. *European Journal of Public Health*, 32(6), 969–975. https://doi.org/10.1093/eurpub/ckac136

Thomas, S., Burke, S., & Barry, S. (2014). The Irish health-care system and austerity: Sharing the pain. *The Lancet*, 383(9928), 1545–1546. https://doi.org/10.1016/s0140-6736(14)60744-3

UNICEF. (2024). *Levels and trends in child mortality*. https://data.unicef.org/resources/levels-and-trends-in-child-mortality-2024/

Unruh, L., Allin, S., Marchildon, G., Burke, S., Barry, S., Siersbaek, R., . . . & Williams, G. A. (2022). A comparison of 2020 health policy responses to the COVID-19 pandemic in Canada, Ireland, the United Kingdom and the United States of America. *Health Policy*, 126(5), 427–437. https://doi.org/10.1016/j.healthpol.2021.06.012

World Bank. (2024). *World development indicators, United Nations World Population Prospects*. https://databank.worldbank.org/reports.aspx?source=2&series=SP.DYN.LE00.IN&country=

Zavras, D., Zavras, A. I., Kyriopoulos, I. I., & Kyriopoulos, J. (2016). Economic crisis, austerity and unmet healthcare needs: The case of Greece. *BMC Health Services Research*, 16, 1–7. https://doi.org/10.1186/s12913-016-1557-5

Chapter 10

Does Health Reform Reduce Inequalities?: Primary Healthcare Utilization of Young Children in Turkey

Asena Caner, Deniz Karaoğlan,[1] and
Gülbiye Yenimahalleli Yaşar

Contents

10.1 Introduction

Early childhood development is considered to be the most important developmental phase throughout the life span, as it strongly influences basic learning, school success, economic participation, social citizenry, and health (Irwin et al., 2007; Almond and Janet, 2011). Therefore, healthy early childhood development strongly influences well-being and economic participation in later life (Rarani et al., 2018; Currie et al., 2010). Early childhood development has strong links to social determinants of health, including health systems. Case et al. (2002) demonstrated that the relationship between socioeconomic status (S.E.S.) and health has its origins in early childhood and expands as children age. They report a strong relationship between parental income and several salient measures of child health, including common childhood chronic health conditions, a relationship that accumulated as children age. This relationship persisted even after controlling for other measured background characteristics, including parental education. Subramaniam et al. (2018) demonstrate that although the determinants of infant mortality vary between countries, there is evidence of long-run relationships among infant mortality, education, female fertility, income, and access to healthcare. Early childhood development can be improved by providing access to and utilization of early childhood care (W.H.O., 2019).

Inequalities and inequities in health are the most important issues in international health agenda nowadays as all the partners of United Nations are committed to meeting Sustainable Development Goals (S.D.Gs) aimed to ensure the health and well-being of the entire population (W.H.O., 2018; W.H.O., 2020; U.N., 2019). Utilization of child health services has been reported to play a significant role toward reducing inequalities and achieving the S.D.Gs of the reduction of child mortality and achieving universal health coverage (W.H.O., UNICEF, 2018). Infant and under-five mortality rates are strongly related with and reflect the effect of socioeconomic conditions on the health of mothers and new-borns (Wang, 2014; Rashad and Sharaf, 2018; Shehzad, 2006) and weaknesses of health system such as poor access, low level of utilization, and inefficiency (Ibrahim et al., 2019; Obrizan, 2019). Despite excellent progress on global public health since the Alma-Ata Declaration, the unfinished agenda of preventable child and maternal mortality remains (W.H.O., 2018).

Primary care is considered to be the major tool to overcome these problems. As the first level of contact with the healthcare system, it is supposed to address the main health problems of the population, providing preventive, curative, and rehabilitative services. However, in the past three decades, primary care systems have gone through significant reforms such as decentralization, provider deregulation, purchaser–provider split, contractual relationships, performance-based payment methods, introduction of commercial enterprises, and a focus on consumer choice. Turkey is one of the countries that have undergone significant reforms in primary care. With the introduction of the market-oriented Health Transformation Programme (H.T.P.) in 2003, a family medicine model (F.M.M.) within a performance-based contracting framework was introduced in 2005 and then extended to the whole country at the end of 2010, altering the "Socialization of Health Services" (Yenimahalleli Yasar, 2011). F.M.M. separated the functions of health centres into two different parts: Family health centres and community health centres. Family health centres provide patient-specific preventive care services (immunization and monitoring of pregnant women and infants) and diagnostic, curative, rehabilitative, and counselling services on their lists at the primary care level. On the other hand, community health centres are responsible for the collection of statistics, control of communicable diseases, environmental health services, occupational health services, health promotion and education services, and school health services at the community level (Öcek et al., 2014).

Reducing child mortality rate has been a top priority in Turkey for more than a half century (Atıcı and Erer, 2009). There have been significant improvements in the reduction of infant mortality rates in the past 30 years. Under-five mortality rate fell sharply from 61 per 1,000 live births in 1993 to 11.1 in 2022 (infant mortality from 60 to 9.1 per 1,000 live births) (Dilli, 2016; M.O.H., 2022). Turkey is among the few successful middle-income countries that have significantly reduced the under-five mortality rate below the Millennium Development Goals 2015 target levels (Aran et al., 2015). Yet, Turkey still lags behind O.E.C.D and E.U countries. In 2021, infant mortality on average was 4 per 1,000 live births in O.E.C.D countries (O.E.C.D., 2023). Therefore, the Turkish H.T.P especially focuses on improving primary care and child health. Protecting and improving child health and establishing the family medicine system are listed as the main goals of H.T.P (M.o.H., 2014, 2019). However, Şen (2019) argues that the family medicine practice is not functioning well in Turkey due to the neoliberal elements brought by the H.T.P. Turkish F.M.M includes performance evaluations, penalties, and competition among family physicians, instead of its primary objectives such as prevention of the accumulation of the patients in the secondary and tertiary healthcare institutions (gatekeeping) and the introduction of chain of referral mechanism. The author also shows that Turkish F.M.M has provided patients with equal and easier access to the primary healthcare services and also detailed patient monitoring or examination. Akman (2014) claims that the process and structure of primary care in Turkey are not as strong as in most of the European countries due to lack of manpower in primary care, high number of patients per family physician, and lack of procedures supporting team and multidisciplinary work. Moreover, the socioeconomic status of the parent still matters for the utilization of child care services in Turkey (Caner et al., 2018).

The General Health Insurance (G.H.I) system in Turkey (introduced with the H.T.P) provides near universal coverage (99% in 2021) of healthcare costs for a core set of services (O.E.C.D., 2023), in many cases with cost sharing, which usually includes consultations with doctors and specialists, tests and examinations, and surgical and therapeutic procedures. Erus et al. (2015) and a report by Turkish Court of Accounts (2018) show that a large proportion of population still lacks G.H.I despite the overarching aim of universal coverage. In response, the government announced in 2017 a new regulation, which covered all the people who were out of G.H.I in return for a premium payment of 3% of gross minimum wage, allowing for the application to Green Card (a programme that caters to low-income households who do not have other health insurance) if needed. Despite this development, O.E.C.D reports that socioeconomic disparities are still significant in most countries such as Greece, Latvia, and Turkey, where income gradient is the largest among the O.E.C.D countries. In addition, the percentage of individuals who were satisfied with the quality of healthcare in the geographical area where they reside was 53% in Turkey in 2022 (O.E.C.D., 2023). Nevertheless, Moses et al. (2019) show that Turkey is one of the countries with a substantial increase in health service utilization rates, along with China and Indonesia. The number of doctor consultations per person per year has increased substantially after the H.T.P, from 3.1 consultations per year in 2002 to 10 in 2022 (which is on average only 5.8 in O.E.C.D countries), of which only 4 are with family physicians (F.P.s) for primary healthcare (M.o.H., 2022; O.E.C.D., 2023). The low level of F.P.s' consultation mostly resulted from the non-gate-keeping policy in place in primary care, and competition among public and private hospitals to attract patients, as public hospitals also have some financial autonomy.

In this chapter, we examine whether the Turkish H.T.P immediately equalized utilization of health services between children from low-resource households and those from high-resource households. We use the data collected by the 2008, 2010, and 2012 waves of Turkish Health Research Surveys (T.H.R.S.) prepared by Turkish Statistical Institute (T.U.R.K.S.T.A.T.). We apply differences-in-differences (D.I.D.) methodology to show the causal impact of introducing F.M.M on the utilization of healthcare services by young children in Turkey. Our findings suggest that the impact of health reforms on immediate equalization of utilization has been limited.

The rest of this chapter is organized as follows. Section 10.2 introduces the dataset and presents the descriptive statistics results. Section 10.3 introduces the empirical methodology. Section 10.4 presents the D.I.D estimation results. Finally, Section 10.5 presents concluding remarks and discussion.

10.2 Data and Descriptive Statistics

In this chapter, we will utilize 2008, 2010, and 2012 rounds of Turkish Health Research Survey (T.H.R.S) dataset, prepared by the Turkish Statistical Institute (T.U.R.K.S.T.A.T). These years are chosen to compare utilization before 2010 to after 2010 so that we can examine the immediate impact of family medicine programme on utilization of healthcare services by young children, since the programme became accessible in all the provinces of Turkey in 2010.[2]

We give the definitions of the variables that we use in this research in the Appendix. We first control whether the definitions of variables are consistent or not across the survey years that we examine. We also compare descriptive statistics with administrative sources. For instance, we compare insurance ownership rates with national statistics. Samples include 2,025 children within the age range 0–5 in 2008, 1,955 in 2010, and 3,408 in 2012.

Descriptive statistics are presented in Tables 10.1 and 10.2. Table 10.1 shows that the samples before and after 2010 are comparable in children's and parents' characteristics. Parents who have primary school degree or less are the majority, despite an improvement over time in the average educational attainment. We observe that average household income has increased over time. Regarding the average number of children per household, we observe a significant decline between 2008 and 2012. In contrast, we do not observe significant change in children's average age and the occurrence of chronic illnesses. The effect of the reform is visible in statistics: The prevalence of having financial access has decreased over time. Similarly, we observe a significant rise in public insurance ownership, as well as private insurance ownership. Last, as a result of the reform, descriptive statistics show that there is a significant decline in both Green Card ownership and having no insurance.

Table 10.1 Descriptive Statistics on the Characteristics of Young Children and Parents

	2008	*2012*	*Change**
Household Resources per Child			
% *Children by the Parent's Education level*			
Elementary education or less	72.1	58.1	Decrease
Secondary education (middle school)	7.3	13.1	Increase
Secondary education (high school)	14.1	17.4	Increase
Tertiary education+	6.5	11.3	Increase
% *Children in Income Groups*			
Not revealed	60.5	60.2	
Lower income brackets	38.3	35.6	Decrease
Highest income bracket	1.2	4.2	Increase
Average Number of Children (Less Than 14 Years Old)	2.4	2.2	Decrease
Other variables			
Average Age in the Young Children Sample	2.7	2.8	
% Children with a Chronic Illness	5.1	6.0	
% Female Children	48.4	49.3	Increase
Parent's Age (Mean)	34.0	35.6	Increase
Parent's Insurance Type			
Public	66.5	78.2	Increase
Private	0.4	0.9	Increase

Table 10.1 *(Continued)* **Descriptive Statistics on the Characteristics of Young Children and Parents**

	2008	*2012*	*Change**
Green Card	21.7	16.1	Decrease
No coverage	11.4	5.0	Decrease
% of Children Based on the Parent's Access Problems			
Access problems related to financial issues	14.9	5.3	Decrease
Access problems related to physical issues	1.7	1.5	

Notes: We present weighted statistics in Table 10.1. It is important to note that in numerous questions of the survey, the respondent can choose all that fits (such as the questions regarding insurance ownership).

* Based on a test of null hypothesis of no change between 2008 and 2012 (or no change between 2010 and 2012 if 2008 data are not available). The p-values are calculated and the direction of change is shown if p-value is less than 0.05.

Source: Authors' calculations using dataset that comes from the T.H.R.S.

Health service utilization rates are presented in Table 10.2. Descriptive statistics show that there is a significant increase in the proportion of children who were taken to a health institution (T.H.I.). However, in contrast to our expectations, we did not observe a considerable change in the proportion of children who are taken to a health institution when not sick (T.H.I.N.S.) (see the Appendix for variable definitions). The participation rate for the new-born screening programme increased substantially. The utilization rate of Family health centres (F.H.C.s) also increased. Utilization rates are on average higher for children living in households where the parent is a university graduate (compared to those with lower education), has high income (compared to lower income), or where there are two or fewer children (compared to three or more children). The exception is the utilization of F.H.Cs, as the descriptive statistics show that the prevalence of being taken to an F.H.C increases with low parental education and income. The statistics also suggest that as the number of children increases in the household, and then the likelihood of being taken to an F.H.C also rises.

Table 10.2 Descriptive Statistics on the Usage of Healthcare Services by Young Children (%)

	T.H.I.		*T.H.I.N.S.*		*New-born screening programme*		*Family Health Center (F.H.C)*	
	2008	*2012*	*2008*	*2012*	*2008*	*2012*	*2010*	*2012*
All Children	59.7	71.6	33.3	33.7	17.8	74.8	64.5	73.7
Household Resources per Child								
Parental education								
Elementary education or less	56.7	66.6	32.6	28.7	15.8	70.8	75.3	78.3
Secondary education (middle school)	63.1	76.1	40.0	40.2	17.1	76.1	65.9	78.1

Table 10.2*(Continued)* **Descriptive Statistics on the Usage of Healthcare Services by Young Children (%)**

	T.H.I.		T.H.I.N.S.		New-born screening programme		Family Health Center (F.H.C)	
	2008	*2012*	*2008*	*2012*	*2008*	*2012*	*2010*	*2012*
Secondary education (high school)	69.0	78.0	41.8	48.4	24.3	78.9	56.2	71.2
Tertiary education+	68.6	82.5	44.8	57.2	27.0	87.4	45.8	61.5
Household Income								
Not revealed	61.1	74.3	36.2	39.8	18.9	77.1	65.5	73.4
Lower income brackets	56.9	65.7	33.4	29.6	15.9	69.5	69.5	75.6
Highest income bracket	82.2	83.5	45.7	57.1	23.6	87.2	24.7	68.3
Number of children (less than 14 years old)								
<= Median	63.9	75.7	39.7	42.6	22.3	78.1	63.5	72.5
> Median	50.8	61.8	25.9	22.8	8.2	66.9	68.1	79.3
Observations	2,025	3,408	2,025	3,408	2,025	3,408	627	1,265

Notes: We present weighted statistics in Table 10.2. In the table, T.H.I. refers to "Taken to a Health Institution" and T.H.I.N.S. refers to "Taken to a Health Institution when Not Sick". If the respondent answers "yes" to T.H.I.N.S., then the respondent is asked the type of health institution that the child was taken to. The answers of this question are listed can be as follows: Family health centre (F.H.C.), hospital, physician's private office. The respondent can choose all that fits.

Source: Authors' calculations using dataset that comes from the T.H.R.S.

10.3 Method

In this chapter, the theoretical framework relies on Goddard and Smith (2001), such that we collect the concepts of need, access, and utilization in our empirical model. Health reforms aim to reach "equal access for equal need", which is the basis of equity in healthcare. Hence, we expect that young children's utilization of healthcare services should be independent of the parent's socioeconomic status (S.E.S) (or to be more specific, the amount of resources that the household can allocate each child), owing to health reforms. Defining S.E.S is a challenging task. Household income is a commonly used indicator in the literature (see, for instance, Wolfe (2015); Green et al. (2014)), but there are several concerns about it: It is difficult to measure precisely in surveys; it is difficult to know how income is shared within a household; and current income may be a weak indicator of lifetime income and thereby a weak indicator of access to resources in the longer term. Parental education may be a better indicator, since the level of educational attainment usually stays constant during adulthood (unlike income that varies), and it shapes the parent's labour market experience as well as social network and access to information. Education is also much easier to measure in surveys than income. As another indicator of S.E.S, we consider the number of children (who are 14 years old or less) in the household, since it is directly related to the amount of time and financial resources that can be allocated to a child. We have chosen not to consider the parent's insurance status as an indicator of

S.E.S, because the very purpose of the introduction of the G.H.I in 2008 was to achieve universal health coverage, regardless of the financial resources of households. Coverage indeed expanded as the share of those with no insurance declined to 5% in 2012 (Table 10.1). Private insurance ownership would indicate household resources; however, it is rare in Turkey (less than 1%).)

Descriptive statistics in the previous section indicated an increase in utilization of healthcare services by young children. However, the important question here is whether the expansionary policy had a greater impact on children living in households with lower resources compared to those living in households with higher resources. In other words, we aim to assess the differential effect of the expansion of the family medicine system on children with different resources. We implement a difference-in-differences (D.I.D) analysis separately for each healthcare services, namely T.H.I., T.H.I.N.S., new-born screening programme, and F.H.C. The time dimension in the D.I.D setting is determined by the gradual expansion of the family medicine system across the provinces of Turkey. Since the system became accessible in all provinces of the country by the end of 2010, we call 2008 (2010 in the analysis of F.H.C. use) as the pre-treatment period and 2012 as the post-treatment period. Hence, we compare data in the years that are closest to 2010 (i.e., right before and right after full access). We estimate the following equation:

$$U_{iek} = \alpha + \gamma T_i + \psi \, Low_i + \beta \left(Low_i * T_i \right) + \epsilon_{iek} \qquad (10.1)$$

where U_{iek} is the binary variable that indicates whether child i in a household with resources e (where e is either high or low) uses the healthcare services in year k (before or after the reform), Low_i is a dummy variable which is 1 if the child is from a low-resource household and 0 otherwise. Depending on the resource indicator used, Low_i is 1 for children in household whose income is lower than the top-income bracket, in households at or below minimum-wage income (used as a robustness check against income brackets), with parents who have at most a primary school degree, or in a household with more than the median number of children (>2). T_i equals 1 if the child is observed in 2012 (post-reform) and 0 if observed in 2008 or 2010 (pre-reform). The interaction term $Low_i * T_i$ helps us measure the effect of the treatment on children from low-resource households relative to high-resource households. We are mainly interested in the estimate of β, which shows the treatment effect on the treated.

One major assumption behind D.I.D analysis is the common trends assumption (i.e., that treatment and control groups have the same trend in utilization rates before the reform). This assumption was tested (using the "didq" command in Stata). The null hypothesis of the test states that common dynamics existed in the low- and high-resource children before the F.M.C.s became nationally available. The test was performed on T.H.I., T.H.I.N.S., and new-born screening regressions (but not on F.H.C., since it includes only two time periods). The D.I.D analysis relies on a short time period. Therefore, to be cautious and conservative, we run D.I.D regressions both with common trends and with heterogenous (separate) trends. In the latter, we follow Green et al. (2014) and control for the time trend (survey year) and its interaction with the treatment dummy, as shown in Equation (10.2).

$$U_{iek} = \alpha + \gamma T_i + \psi \, Low_i + \beta \left(Low_i * T_i \right) + \phi \, Time \, Trend + \delta \, Time \, Trend * Low_i + \epsilon_{iek} \qquad (10.2)$$

10.4 Results

As the reform eased access to health services, children from low-resource families should be the ones to benefit the most from the reform. The reform is expected to affect children from high-resource households less, since they most probably receive proper healthcare both before and after the reform.

Table 10.3 provides the p-values for the common trends test. In the regressions with T.H.I. as the dependent variable, the null hypothesis of common trends cannot be rejected. In the regressions with T.H.I.N.S., the null hypothesis is rejected. In the regressions with new-born screening, we reject the null hypothesis (at 5% significance) for household income or education as the resource indicator, but not for the number of children.

Table 10.3 Testing Common Trends Assumption (p-Values)

Resource Indicator: Healthcare Service (U_i)	Household Income	Education	Number of Children in the Household
T.H.I.	0.394	0.617	0.686
T.H.I.N.S.	0.025	0.000	0.040
New-born screening programme	0.043	0.000	0.121

Source: Authors' calculations using dataset that comes from the T.H.R.S.

Table 10.4 presents D.I.D. estimation results for different household resource indicators. Depending on the results of the test in Table 10.3, either the specification in Equation (10.1) (common trends) or the specification in Equation (10.2) (separate trends) is presented. The results that are not presented confirm those in the table and are available upon request. When household income is used as the resource indicator, households that do not report income are excluded. (In the pooled dataset, their share is 59.35%.)

In Panel A, the estimates from T.H.I. regressions show that utilization was lower in the lower-resource group; moreover, the reform did not close the gap between children from lower-resource and higher-resource households, regardless of the resource indicator used. In contrast, the estimates from T.H.I.N.S. regressions show that the reform benefited children in the low-resource group more, and utilization in this group is higher after the reform, compared to the high-resource group (except in column (8)).

In Panel B, the estimates from the new-born screening regressions show that utilization in the low-resource group is not different from the high-resource group after the reform, except when parental education is used as the resource indicator (i.e., children whose parents have low education increased participation more than the children of better educated parents). The coefficient estimates of the interaction term $Low_i * T_i$ are positive, but they have low statistical significance. The estimates from the F.H.C. regressions, where we cannot test the common trends assumption, show that utilization in the low-resource group is lower than that in the high-resource group after the reform. (The only exception is a small positive coefficient estimate when the number of children is the resource indicator.) Surprisingly, we find no evidence for a positive differential effect of the reform on children from lower-resource households in using F.H.C.s.

10.5 Discussion and Conclusion

This chapter examines whether the H.T.P, a supply-side reform that emphasized expanding the family medicine system, had a greater impact on children from lower-resource households compared to those from higher-resource households. Because the reform aimed to facilitate access to

Table 10.4 D.I.D. Estimation Results
Panel A

	T.H.I. (Common Trends)				T.H.I.N.S. (Separate Trends)			
	(1)	(2)	(3)	(4)	(5)	(6)	(7)	(8)
	Income brackets	Minimum wage	Parental education	Number of children	Income brackets	Minimum wage	Parental education	Number of children
T_i	-0.0414 (0.398)	0.203 (0.151)	0.267*** (0.100)	0.321*** (0.0695)	-0.362 (0.716)	0.457 (0.311)	-0.423** (0.207)	0.165 (0.148)
Low_i	-1.146*** (0.327)	-0.572*** (0.126)	-0.577*** (0.0852)	-0.550*** (0.0776)	0.500 (0.879)	-0.112 (0.398)	0.360 (0.252)	-0.321 (0.257)
$Low_i{}^*T_i$	0.168 (0.408)	-0.136 (0.185)	-0.0385 (0.121)	-0.105 (0.118)	1.425* (0.748)	0.782* (0.422)	1.090*** (0.266)	0.339 (0.294)
Time trend					0.411 (0.493)	-0.240 (0.193)	0.337*** (0.129)	-0.0215 (0.0892)
Time trend* Low_i					-1.027** (0.509)	-0.473* (0.253)	-0.763*** (0.160)	-0.314* (0.170)

(Continued)

Table 7.2 (*Continued*) DID Estimation Results

Panel B

	New-born Screening				Family Health Center			
	(1) Income brackets (separate trends)	(2) Minimum wage (separate trends)	(3) Parental education (separate trends)	(4) Number of children (common trends)	(5) Income brackets	(6) Minimum wage	(7) Parental education	(8) Number of children
T_i	−1.611* (0.849)	−1.042*** (0.336)	−1.326*** (0.227)	1.645*** (0.0692)	1.886*** (0.450)	0.912*** (0.255)	0.686*** (0.151)	0.414*** (0.126)
Low_i	0.244 (1.042)	−0.987** (0.472)	−0.0365 (0.290)	−0.735*** (0.0821)	1.903*** (0.419)	0.906*** (0.326)	0.957*** (0.190)	0.203 (0.236)
Low_i*T_i	0.883 (0.874)	0.257 (0.420)	0.803*** (0.276)	0.168 (0.122)	−1.521*** (0.503)	−0.692* (0.407)	−0.513** (0.236)	0.173 (0.297)
Time trend	2.352*** (0.582)	1.686*** (0.214)	1.971*** (0.142)					
Time trend* Low_i	−0.744 (0.597)	0.0644 (0.275)	−0.429** (0.175)					

Source: Authors' calculations using dataset that comes from the T.H.R.S.

Notes: Robust standard errors in parentheses. *** $p < 0.01$, ** $p < 0.05$, * $p < 0.1$

health services, children from low-resource families should be the ones to benefit the most from improved access. Utilization rates before and after the family medicine system are compared using a difference-in-differences (D.I.D) approach. Four definitions of healthcare service utilization are considered: "T.H.I.N.S.", referred as taken to health institution when not sick; "T.H.I.", referred as taken to health institution for any reason (defined more comprehensively to include all types of health service use, to seek treatment for any health problem or for check-up); participating in new-born screening; and being taken to the family health centre (F.H.C.).

Results depend on the definition of service utilization. The reform increased the likelihood of being T.H.I.N.S. (for check-ups) in the low-resource households more than in the high-resource group, in most regressions. However, using T.H.I.N.S., utilization in the low-resource group did not increase more than the high-resource group. Such a result is somewhat to be expected, since most treatments are costly (payments may be required for tests and medications) even for general health insurance owners; hence, children from low-resource households are still at a disadvantage. Another reason might be being unregistered with a family physician. Öcek et al. (2014) show that many people are not registered with any family physician. In addition, the majority of those individuals belong to the most disadvantaged groups in society.

The reform has had no differential effect on the participation of low-resource households in the new-born screening programme. In addition, and surprisingly, the likelihood of being taken to an F.H.C. is lower in the low-resource group than in the high-resource group after the reform. The reasons may be the lack of information about the family medicine system or about the importance of the new-born screening programme. In addition to being not registered with any family physician, Öcek et al. (2014) state that family physicians reported that 40–60% of patients on their lists have never received a service from them, and the majority of those who use their services do not use family physicians as the first contact. The lack of family physicians and nurses in some cities or regions may provide another explanation (Menon et al., 2014). For example, population per family medicine unit was higher in İstanbul, Western Anatolia, Eastern Marmara, and Aegean regions than the average of Turkey in 2022. Moreover, despite improvements in access and utilization, and near universal health coverage with the introduction of G.H.I system, there still exists (at least to some extent) inadequate and unequal distribution of health services, health personnel, and infrastructure in Turkey (M.o.H., 2022).

In the 21st century, noncommunicable diseases are the top causes of mortality and morbidity. Primary level prevention is four times more effective than secondary or tertiary level prevention of noncommunicable diseases. The basis of primary prevention is periodic health examinations. Yangı et al. (2018) show that, on average, the general knowledge of family physicians in Turkey on "Periodic Health and/or Physical Examinations and Healthcare Screening Guidelines Proposed in the Family Medicine Practice" was calculated as 3.28, attitude average as 3.47, and behaviour average as 2.65. It was evaluated that family physicians' knowledge is at about medium-level at best, and even though their attitude score was higher than their knowledge score, attitudes did not necessarily translate into behaviour.

International evidence and experience indicate that well-trained family physicians are much more effective in providing primary healthcare than other physicians. Family practice was accepted as a field of specialization in Turkey, and three-year residency training programme began in 1985. As the number of family physicians was insufficient, general practitioners were allowed to obtain certification and become family physicians upon completing the M.o.H.'s training programme. Kardeş et al. (2022) found that family physicians who participated in the study did not have an adequate level of knowledge about early childhood care but were willing to know more about it.

Another important factor that should be considered is the economic crisis in 2008. Despite intentions to maintain the health budget, the slowdown in health spending experienced in many O.E.C.D countries, including Turkey, affected all parts of the health sector (O.E.C.D., 2023). The share of total health expenditures in G.D.P. decreased from 5.8% (in 2008 and 2009) to 5.3%, 4.9%, and 4.3% during 2010–2012 respectively in Turkey (M.o.H., 2018).

In the overall, the results indicate less benefit of the reform to children from low-resource households. Policy recommendations include regular examination of the possible negative impacts of user fees and other cost-sharing arrangements in the G.H.I system, and, where necessary, introduction of exemptions. Measures should be taken to ensure sufficient and equally distributed manpower in primary care, especially in the family medicine system.

10.6 Acknowledgment

This reseach is granted by Ankara University, Scientific Research Project with grant number 18B0241001, coordinated by Prof. Dr. Gulbiye Yenimahalleli Yasar. The reseach is previously published as working paper in Economic Research Forum (ERF) working paper series with number 1399.

Notes

1 Corresponding Author. Gebze Technical University, Department of Economics. E-mail: hdyurtseven@gtu.edu.tr
2 More recent waves are T.H.R.S. are available. However, the design of the questionnaire significantly differs from the previous years starting from 2014. In addition, in this study our objective is to show the immediate impact of F.M.M on utilization of healthcare services by young children. Therefore, in this chapter we use the earlier waves of T.H.R.S.

References

Akman M. Strength of Primary Care in Turkey. *Turkish Journal of Family Practice*. 2014;18(2):70–78.

Almond D., Janet C. Human Capital Development before Age Five. In Ashenfelter O., Layard R., Card D., editors. *Handbook of Labor Economics*. Vol. 4B. North-Holland; 2011. pp. 1315–1486.

Aran M.A., Aktakke N., Gurol-Urganci P., Atun R. Maternal and Child Health in Turkey Through the Health Transformation Program (2003–2008). *Development Analytics Research Paper Series*. 2015:1501.

Atıcı E., Erer S. Maternity Child Welfare and Family Planning Services in Turkish Regulations. *Turkiye Klinikleri Journal of Medical Ethics Law and History*. 2009;17(2):107.

Caner A., Karaoğlan D., Yaşar G. Utilization of Health-Care Services by Young Children: The Aftermath of the Turkish Health Transformation Program. *The International Journal of Health Planning and Management*. 2018;33(3):596–613.

Case A., Lubotsky D., Paxson C. Economic Status and Health in Childhood: The Origins of the Gradient. *American Economic Review*. 2002;92(5):1308–1334.

Currie J., Stabile M., Manivong P., Roos L.L. Child Health and Young Adult Outcomes. *The Journal of Human Resources*. 2010;45(3):517–548.

Dilli D. Recent Declines in Infant and Neonatal Mortality in Turkey from 2007 to 2012: Impact of Improvements in Health Policies. *Central European Journal of Public Health*. 2016;24(1):52–57.

Erus B., Yakut-Cakar B., Cali S., Adaman F. Health Policy for the Poor: An Exploration on the Take-up of Means-Tested Health Benefits in Turkey. *Social Science & Medicine*. 2015;130:99–106.

Goddard M., Smith P. Equity of Access to Health Care Services: Theory and Evidence from the UK. *Social Science & Medicine*. 2001;53(9):1149–1162.

Green C.P., Heywood J.S., Navarro M. Did Liberalising Bar Hours Decrease Traffic Accidents? *Journal of Health Economics*. 2014;35:189–198.

Ibrahim M.D., Daneshvar S., Hocaoğlu M.B., Olasehinde-Williams G.O. An Estimation of the Efficiency and Productivity of Healthcare Systems in Sub-Saharan Africa: Health-Centred Millennium Development Goal-Based Evidence. *Social Indicators Research*. 2019;143:371–389.

Irwin L.G., Siddiqi A., Hertzman C. *Early Child Development: A Powerful Equalizer: Final Report for the WHO's Commission on the Social Determinants of Health*. 2007. https://apps.who.int/iris/bitstream/handle/10665/69729/a91213.pdf?sequence=1. Accessed 15 Jan 2020.

Kardeş E., Saraç F., Çelikel P., Şimşek Derelioğlu S., Demir Cinisli Ö. Evaluation of a Group of Turkish Family Physicians' Attitudes and Approaches about Early Childhood Caries. *Current Research in Dental Sciences*. 2022;32(1):17–22. https://doi.org/10.17567/ataunidfd.1011984

Menon R., Nguyen S.N., Arur A., Yener A.L., Postolovska I. Turkey: Family Medicine Performance Based Contracting Scheme. In Cashin C., Chi Y.-L., Smith P.C., Borowitz M., Thomson S., editors. *Paying for Performance in Health Care: Implications for Health System Performance and Accountability*. Open University Press; 2014. pp. 189–204.

The Ministry of Health of Turkey. *Health Statistics Yearbook 2018*; 2018. https://dosyasb.saglik.gov.tr/Eklenti/36164,siy2018en2pdf.pdf?0. Accessed 20 Feb 2020.

The Ministry of Health of Turkey. *Health Statistics Yearbook 2022, General Directorate of Health Information Systems*; 2022. https://www.saglik.gov.tr/TR-103184/saglik-istatistikleri-yilligi-2022-yayinlanmistir.html. Accessed 6 May 2024.

The Ministry of Health of Turkey. *Public Health Institution Strategic Plan 2014–2017*; 2014. https://hsgm.saglik.gov.tr/depo/kurumsal/plan-ve-faaliyetler/2014-2017-stratejik-plan.pdf. Accessed 25 Feb 2020.

The Ministry of Health of Turkey. *Strategic Plan 2019–2023*; 2019. https://dosyamerkez.saglik.gov.tr/Eklenti/35748,stratejikplan2019-2023pdf.pdf?0. Accessed 25 Feb 2020.

Moses M.W., Pedroza P., Baral R., Bloom S., Brown J., Chapin A., et al. Funding and Services Needed to Achieve Universal Health Coverage: Applications of Global, Regional, and National Estimates of Utilisation of Outpatient Visits and Inpatient Admissions from 1990 to 2016, and Unit Costs from 1995 to 2016. *The Lancet: Public Health*. 2019;4(1):e49–e73.

Obrizan M. Diverging Trends in Health Care Use between 2010 and 2016: Evidence from Three Groups of Transition Countries. *Economic Systems*. 2019;43(1):19–29.

Öcek Z.A., Çiçeklioğlu M., Yücel U., et al. Family Medicine Model in Turkey: A Qualitative Assessment from the Perspectives of Primary Care Workers. *BMC Family Practice*. 2014;15:38. https://doi.org/10.1186/1471-2296-15-38

O.E.C.D. *Health at a Glance 2023: OECD Indicators*. Paris: OECD Publishing; 2023. https://www.oecd-ilibrary.org/citeas/10.1787/7a7afb35-en. Accessed 6 May 2024.

Rarani M.A., Nosratabadi M., Moeeni M. Early Childhood Development in Iran and Its Provinces: Inequality Versus Average. *The International Journal of Health Planning and Management*. 2018;33(4):1136–1145.

Rashad A.S., Sharaf M.F. Economic Growth and Child Malnutrition in Egypt: New Evidence from National Demographic and Health Survey. *Social Indicators Research*. 2018;135:769–795.

Şen, A.D. *The Family Medicine Practice in Turkey from Perspectives of the Physicians within the Framework of Neo-liberalizm*. Unpublished Master Thesis in the Department of Political Science and Public Administration in Middle East Technical University in Türkiye; 2019. chrome-extension://efaidnbmnnnibpcajpcglclefindmkaj/https://etd.lib.metu.edu.tr/upload/12624084/index.pdf. Accessed 6 May 2024.

Shehzad S. The Determinants of Child Health in Pakistan: An Economic Analysis. *Social Indicators Research*. 2006;78:531–556.

Subramaniam T., Loganathan N., Yerushalmi E., Devadason E., Bin Majid M. Determinants of Infant Mortality in Older ASEAN Economies. *Social Indicators Research*. 2018;136(1):397–415.

Turkish Court of Accounts. *The Ministry of Health: Turkish Court of Accounts Inspection Report 2017*; 2018. https://www.sayistay.gov.tr/tr/Upload/62643830/files/raporlar/kid/2017/Genel_Bütçe_Kapsamındaki_%20Kamu_İdareleri/SAĞLIK%20BAKANLIĞI.pdf. Accessed 25 Feb 2020.

Turkish Statistical Institute. *Health Survey 2012*. Ankara; 2012.https://data.tuik.gov.tr/Bulten/Index?p=Turkiye-Saglik-Arastirmasi-2012-13490. Accessed 11 Dec 2024.

United Nations. *The Sustainable Development Goals Report 2019*. https://unstats.un.org/sdgs/report/2019/The-Sustainable-Development-Goals-Report-2019.pdf. Accessed 20 Feb 2020.

Wang G. The Impact of Social and Economic Indicators on Maternal and Child Health. *Social Indicators Research*. 2014;116:935–957.

W.H.O. *10 Facts on Health Inequities and Their Causes*; 2020. https://www.who.int/features/factfiles/health_inequities/en/. Accessed 20 Jan 2020.

W.H.O. *Social Determinants of Health: Early Child Development*; 2019. https://www.who.int/social_determinants/themes/earlychilddevelopment/en/. Accessed 10 Jan 2020.

W.H.O. *World Health Statistics 2018: Monitoring Health for the SDGs, Sustainable Development Goals*; 2018. https://apps.who.int/iris/bitstream/handle/10665/272596/9789241565585-eng.pdf?ua=1. Accessed 10 Jan 2020.

W.H.O., UNICEF. *A Vision for Primary Health Care in the 21st Century: Towards Universal Health Coverage and the Sustainable Development Goals*; 2018. https://www.who.int/docs/default-source/primary-health/vision.pdf. Accessed 10 Jan 2020.

Wolfe J.D. The Effects of Socioeconomic Status on Child and Adolescent Physical Health: An Organization and Systematic Comparison of Measures. *Social Indicators Research*. 2015;123:39–58.

Yangı D.T., Görpelioğlu S., Top M. The Evaluation of Family Physicians' Knowledge Attitude and Behaviours Towards Periodic Examination Guidelines. *Türkiye Aile Hekimliği Dergisi*. 2018;22(3):104–117.

Yasar G.Y. 'Health Transformation Programme' in Turkey: An Assessment. *International Journal of Health Planning and Management*. 2011;26(2):110–133. https://doi.org/10.1002/hpm.1065

Appendix

We obtain the data for young children's utilization of health services from the 0–6 ages module of the survey. The following questions that were asked in that module are as follows:

- Whether the child participates in the new-born screening programme, which includes certain tests such as heel stick collection, hearing test, hip dysplasia detection.
- Whether the child has any chronic health problems such as loss of hearing or vision, mental retardation, etc.
- Whether the child is Taken to a Health Institution when Not Sick (T.H.I.N.S.) in the last 12 months.
- If the respondent's answer is "yes" to the previous question, then the respondent is asked about the type of health institution where the child was taken. The answers to this question are as follows: Family health centre (F.H.C.), hospital, or physician's private office. The respondent can mark all that fit.
- Within the last six months, did the child seek treatment for any of the following? A contagious disease (such as mumps or measles), an upper or lower respiratory tract infection, diarrhoea, cardiac problems, urinary tract infection, cancer, diabetes, dermatological problems, oral or dental problems, anaemia, or treatment for an injury (such as a fracture, cut, burn, insect bite, poisoning, and so on)? The binary variable Taken to a Health Institution (T.H.I.) is equal to 1 if any of the above or T.H.I.N.S. is equal to 1; otherwise, T.H.I. is zero.

The survey collects information about age and gender of each person in the household; his/her relationship to the household head (namely, the reference person); education level (elementary education or less (5 years or less); secondary education (middle school and high school) and tertiary education); and type of insurance (public, private, Green Card, no coverage). Other questions include household income (some households did not declare income; for the rest of the households, net monthly income is given in different ranges (<350, 351–500, 501–620, 621–750, 751–900, 910–1100, 1101–1300, 1301–1700, 1701–2300, >2301, all in TL) and whether the parent has financial or physical access problems in reaching the healthcare services (T.U.R.K.S.T.A.T. Health Survey, 2012).

Chapter 11

Socio-Economic Determinants of Public Healthcare Utilization in the Aftermath of the Health Transformation Programme in Turkey

Sıtkıcan Saraçoğlu

Contents

11.1 Introduction

Turkey's Health Transformation Programme (H.T.P.), which contains a breadth of reforms in financing, delivering, organizing, and managing healthcare, one of which is diminishing the inequalities in access to and utilization of healthcare countrywide, came into force in 2003 (Menon et al., 2013). Before the H.T.P., some health insurance schemes or ministries offered or purchased different benefits from other healthcare providers and owned their health facilities. The health facilities of the Social Insurance Organization (S.I.O.) which had been the second-biggest service provider behind the Ministry of Health of Turkey (M.o.H.), were transferred to M.o.H. in 2005. Thus, the fragmentation in public healthcare provision was eradicated, and the purchaser–provider split was

DOI: 10.4324/9781003539896-12

achieved in healthcare (Ökem & Çakar, 2015). In H.T.P., public healthcare was designed to prioritise improving the efficiency, effectiveness, and quality of primary healthcare (P.H.) (Caner & Cilasun, 2019). Before the H.T.P., P.H. was organised into three different categories, namely health houses, health centres, and additional primary centres, depending on the population. Health houses represented the first contact point and constituted primary providers for maternal and child healthcare, whereas health centres provided both preventive and curative healthcare. Additional primary centres at the provincial level focused on family planning, maternal and child healthcare healthcare, and tuberculosis control (Venkateswaran & Singh, 2022). As an implementation of the H.T.P., the new family medicine (F.M.) model was introduced in 2005. F.M. model, which replaced the previous P.H. system, offered a free and increased range of healthcare, including family planning, monitoring of pregnant and children, immunizations, regular health checks, and home visits. Turkey's entire population was covered by the F.M. model by 2011 (Hone et al., 2017). The developments of H.T.P. mentioned before were associated with public healthcare utilization (P.H.C.U.).

The notion of healthcare utilization refers to the use of healthcare to prevent and cure health problems, obtain information on health status, and promote the maintenance of health and well-being (Carrasquillo, 2013). To explain the determinants of healthcare utilization, the behavioural model developed by Andersen (1968) provides a useful framework constructed upon three components, namely predisposing factors, enabling factors, and need factors. Predisposing factors include individuals' socio-demographic characteristics (such as gender, age, education level, occupation status, and attitudes and knowledge about healthcare) that increase the probability of healthcare utilization. However, enabling factors encompass wealth, income, health insurance, and cost-sharing requirements which can facilitate or inhibit healthcare utilization. On the other hand, need factors comprise both the perceived and the evaluated needs for healthcare which refers to the condition or need that requires healthcare (Andersen & Davidson, 2001).

Existing studies have investigated the determinants of healthcare utilization for various countries such as Iran by Hosseinpoor et al. (2007), nine European Union countries by Economou et al. (2008), Canada and the United States by Blackwell et al. (2009), Ecuador by López-Cevallos and Chi (2010), Greece by Tountas et al. (2011), Mongolia by Gan-Yadam et al. (2013), Korea by Kim and Lee (2016), and India by Mojumdar (2018). However, for Turkey in which many reforms have been made within the scope of H.T.P., there have been limited studies directly focusing on the determinants of healthcare utilization. Şenol et al. (2023), using cross-sectional data obtained in Kayseri for 2004 and 2017, revealed that being male, higher income levels, aged ≥65 years, and negative health perception are the main determinants of healthcare utilization. On the contrary, studies using cross-sectional and nationally representative data from the surveys carried out by TURKSTAT (Turkish Statistical Institute) in the relevant literature for Turkey exist. For instance Hone et al. (2017), using data derived from Life Satisfaction Surveys (L.S.S.) for 2005–2012, demonstrated that the introduction of an F.M. model resulted in changes in healthcare utilization and user preferences over a relatively short period. Similarly, Caner and Cilasun (2019) declared that among the elderly, healthcare utilization increased, and the percentage of patients preferring primary healthcare increased coinciding with the introduction of the F.M. model by using data from the Survey of Income and Living Conditions (S.I.L.C.) for the period 2006–2015 and L.S.S. over the years 2004 to 2015. On the other hand, Sözmen and Ünal (2016), Başar et al. (2021), and Cinaroglu and Çalışkan (2022) analysed healthcare utilization in the aftermath of H.T.P. with an emphasis on equity. Sözmen and Ünal (2016) unveiled that being female, having poor self-assessed health, being in the lowest income quintile, having a lower education level, and living in a rural area increase the probability of the utilization of General Practitioner care by using data from Health Survey (H.S.) for 2008. Using H.S. for 2010, 2012, and 2014, Başar et al. (2021) concluded that the need variable is the most important determinant of healthcare utilization for all types of healthcare examined. Nevertheless, Cinaroglu and Çalışkan (2022) demonstrated that healthcare utilization for inpatient, outpatient, family medicine, and general practitioner services follows a regressive trend from 2008 to 2014 by employing data from H.S. 2008, 2010, 2012, and 2014. Consequently, the previous studies examining the healthcare utilization in Turkey have used data from S.I.L.C., L.S.S., or H.S. carried out by TURKSTAT. Hence, it is crucial to compare the results of the previous ones with those found by different data for Turkey.

This study aims to examine the socio-economic determinants of public healthcare utilization in the aftermath of H.T.P. in Turkey in the framework of the behavioural model. Using data derived from three rounds of the Life in Transition Survey (L.I.T.S.) for 2006, 2010, and 2016, which is different from previous ones, this study fills this void and contributes to the existing literature. Due to the binary nature of the dependent variable indicating whether healthcare is utilized, this study employs the probit model as an estimation method.

The rest of this chapter is organized as follows. The section "Data and Methodology" describes the data and the estimation methodology used. The section "Results" comprises the results of the analysis. The last section, "Conclusion", includes a discussion of the results as well as policy implications, limitations of this study, and suggestions for further studies.

11.2 Data and Methodology

This section first explains the data used in this study, the creation process of the variables, and descriptive statistics about variables followed by the information on the method applied for the estimation.

11.2.1 Data

This study uses data obtained from the Life in Transition Survey L.I.T.S. aims to determine the impacts of the transition to the market-oriented economic system on people's lives across a region including countries of Central and Eastern Europe and the former Soviet Union. L.I.T.S., which uses a multistage stratified random probability cluster sample design, is a nationally representative survey. L.I.T.S. provides data on demographic characteristics, education level, dwelling and living standards, asset ownership, consumption patterns, attitudes and values, work history and employment status, governance, and public services utilization (including P.H.C.U.) of individuals. L.I.T.S. was carried out three times, namely in 2006, 2010, and 2016, by a collaboration of the European Bank for Reconstruction and Development (E.B.R.D.) and the World Bank. The first round of the L.I.T.S. (L.I.T.S. I) was implemented in 29 countries, while the second round of the L.I.T.S. (L.I.T.S. II) and the third of the L.I.T.S. (L.I.T.S. III) were conducted in 35 countries and 34 countries, respectively. L.I.T.S. I includes microdata obtained from 29,002 individuals, whereas L.I.T.S. II and L.I.T.S. III contain microdata from 38,864 individuals and 51,206 individuals, respectively. Turkey, taking part in each round of the survey, has 1,000 individuals in L.I.T.S. I, 1,004 individuals in L.I.T.S. II, and 1,500 individuals in L.I.T.S. III (E.B.R.D., 2024). They yield the data used in this study.

In each round of the L.I.T.S., the P.H.C.U., which is the dependent variable of this study, is measured in the following way. Individuals are asked whether they or any member of their household have used public services during the past 12 months. Individuals are asked whether they or any household member have used public services including interaction with road police, requesting official documents such as passports and marriage or birth certificates, going to court due to a civil matter, receiving medical treatment in the public health system and public education, and requesting unemployment benefits and other social security benefits during the past 12 months. Possible answers are "yes" or "no"; hence, individuals receiving medical treatment in the public health system are classified as the P.H.C.U., and the others not receiving medical treatment in the public health system are categorized as representing the non-P.H.C.U. Hence, the dependent variable is a binary variable equal to 0 or 1, indicating the non-P.H.C.U. and the P.H.C.U., respectively.

Following the existing literature, the individuals' characteristics are defined as the independent variables of this study and structured as categorical variables.

Gender is also a binary variable and categorized as male or female, while age is classified into six age groups 18–24, 25–34, 35–44, 45–54, 55–64, and ≥65.

Self-assessed health status is measured through individuals' assessment among five categories, namely "very good" "good", "medium", "bad", and "very bad" in each round of L.I.T.S. However, due to the scarcity of observations on this variable, the categories "very good" and "good" are combined and classified as "good", and the categories "bad" and "very bad" self-assessed health status are defined as "bad". Adding the "medium" category to the other two yields a three-category variable for self-assessed health status in this study.

The individuals' education level is another independent variable for this study. Education level is measured by individuals' highest educational attainment for each round of L.I.T.S., but the number of education categories is six in L.I.T.S. I, seven for L.I.T.S. II, and eight for L.I.T.S. III. The six responses for the education level are "no degree/no education", "compulsory school education", "secondary education", "professional, vocational school/training", "higher professional degree (university, college)", and "post-graduate degree" in L.I.T.S. I. The seven responses for the education level are "no degree/no education", "primary education", "lower secondary education", "(upper) secondary education", "post-secondary non-tertiary education", "bachelor's degree or more", and "master's degree or PhD" regarding L.I.T.S. II. These seven education categories also exist in L.I.T.S. III, with an additional category namely "tertiary education (not a university diploma)" which is placed between "post-secondary non-tertiary education" and "bachelor's degree or more". Hence, a common education-level variable is created to minimize differences and enable comparison across all rounds of L.I.T.S. The category "no degree/no education" appears in each round of L.I.T.S. and constitutes the first category of the education level variable as "no degree" in this study. The category "compulsory school education" in L.I.T.S. I and the category "primary education" in both L.I.T.S. II and L.I.T.S. III correspond to the second category of the education level variable and is called "primary education" in this study. The category "secondary education" in L.I.T.S. I and the categories "lower secondary education" and "(upper) secondary education" in both L.I.T.S. II and L.I.T.S. III generate the third category of the education level variable and is described as "secondary education". The categories "professional, vocational school/training" in L.I.T.S. I, "post-secondary non-tertiary education" in L.I.T.S. II, and "post-secondary non-tertiary education" and "tertiary education (not a university diploma)" in L.I.T.S. III constitute the fourth category of the education level variable and is named as "higher than secondary education". The categories "higher professional degree (university, college)", "post-graduate degree" in L.I.T.S. I, "bachelor's degree or more", and "master's degree or PhD" in both L.I.T.S. II and L.I.T.S. III are aggregated to constitute the category "bachelor's or post-graduate degree", which is the fifth category of the education level variable. As a consequence, a five-category variable is obtained which represents the individuals' education level from lowest to highest.

The information on individuals' income only exists in L.I.T.S. III; however, the previous rounds of the survey lack information about the income. Therefore, a wealth index is constructed upon the asset ownership of individuals as a proxy of economic status. The asset ownership for each round of L.I.T.S. can be measured by the question about whether the respondent or any member of the respondent's household owns any of the listed assets. These assets comprise a car, a secondary residence, a bank account, a credit/debit card, a mobile phone, a computer, and access to the internet at home for L.I.T.S. I and L.I.T.S. II. On the contrary, asset ownership can be measured for L.I.T.S. III by the question if the respondent or any member of the respondent's household owns a mobile phone, colour TV set, computer, washing machine, car, bicycle, or motorcycle. To construct a wealth index from the variables of the asset ownership, Principal Component Analysis (P.C.A.) is applied for each round of L.I.T.S. P.C.A. is a statistical method designed to diminish the number of corre-lated variables while retaining the highest possible variance. This is obtained by converting them to uncorrelated variables namely "principal components", which are ranked so that the first few contain the highest variance in all of the initial variables (Jolliffe, 2002). Among them, the first principal component contains the highest possible variance. Hence, for the wealth index, the first principal com-ponent is supposed to reflect the household wealth. The weight for each asset ownership variable can be determined as a factor score. By using these weights based on the first principal component, a household score is obtained (Tareq et al., 2021). The scores are then used to generate the cut-off points which determine three categories of the wealth index, namely low, middle, and high.

Table 11.1 presents valuable information about the characteristics of individuals represented in the L.I.T.S. I, L.I.T.S. II, and L.I.T.S. III by the utilization status of public healthcare.

Table 11.1 indicates that the average rate of individuals reporting the P.H.C.U. is 58.60% in 2006, 55.98% in 2010, and 27.93% in 2016. The rate of the P.H.C.U. among males also decreases from 60.27% to 26.14% over the years. Conversely, the rate of the P.H.C.U. among females follows a different pattern. The rate of females reporting the P.H.C.U. increases between 2006 and 2010; however, it decreases between 2010 and 2016. Nevertheless, the rate of report-ing the P.H.C.U. is higher for females than males except in 2006. The rate of the P.H.C.U. for individuals aged 18–24 years, 25–34 years, 35–44 years, and 55–64 years reflect an increasing trend, whereas the rate of the P.H.C.U. for individuals aged 45–54 years and aged ≥65 years rises between 2006 and 2010 and then falls between 2010 and 2016. Furthermore, among the age groups, the rate of the P.H.C.U. is the highest for individuals aged 18–24 years in 2006 (68.18%), for individuals aged ≥65 years in 2010 (60.00%), and for individuals aged 55–64 years in 2016 (33.62%). A sharp decline in the rate of the P.H.C.U. is observed for individuals with no degree, with secondary education, and with higher than secondary education for all years examined. The rate of the P.H.C.U. for individuals with primary education and with a bachelor's or post-graduate degree increases between 2006 and 2010; however, it decreases between 2010 and 2016. The rate of the P.H.C.U. is the highest for individuals with higher than secondary education in 2006 (77.78%), for individuals with no degree in 2010 (58.51%), and for individu-als with a bachelor's or post-graduate degree in 2016 (35.00%), considering the education level. Considering the categories of the asset index, it is observed that the rate of the P.H.C.U. for poor and rich individuals declines over the years. The rate of the P.H.C.U. for individuals in the medium category of the asset index reflects a pattern different from the others by initially increas-ing and then decreasing between 2006 and 2016. The rate of the P.H.C.U. is the highest for poor individuals in 2006 (64.03%) and 2016 (28.52%), while it is the highest for individuals in the medium category in 2010 (60.73%). The rate of the P.H.C.U. for individuals assessing their health as "bad" and assessing their health as "medium" reflects a decreasing trend. The rate of the P.H.C.U. for individuals assessing their health as "bad" and assessing their health as "medium" reflects a decreasing trend for all years examined. On the other hand, the rate of the P.H.C.U. for individuals assessing their health as "good" rises between 2006 and 2010 and then falls between 2010 and 2016. The rate of the P.H.C.U. is the highest for individuals assessing their health as "good" in 2010 (57.87%) and 2016 (29.12%), while it is the highest for individuals assessing their health as "bad" in 2006 (63.25%).

Table 11.1 Descriptive Statistics by the Status of P.H.C.U. (%)

Type of Factor		Variables	2006		2010		2016	
			Non-P.H.C.U.	P.H.C.U	Non-P.H.C.U.	P.H.C.U	Non-P.H.C.U.	P.H.C.U
Predisposing	Gender	Male	39.73	60.27	44.52	55.48	73.86	26.14
		Female	54.39	45.61	42.58	57.42	70.18	29.82
	Age	18–24	31.82	68.18	58.06	41.94	75.42	24.58
		25–34	36.11	63.89	45.79	54.21	73.15	26.85
		35–44	42.91	57.09	44.75	55.25	67.97	32.03
		45–54	41.36	58.64	40.70	59.30	75.93	24.07
		55–64	40.13	59.87	44.81	55.19	66.38	33.62
		≥65	50.00	50.00	40.00	60.00	75.00	25.00
	Education level	No degree	37.40	62.60	41.49	58.51	80.65	19.35
		Primary	47.35	52.65	42.62	57.38	69.48	30.52
		Secondary	36.76	63.24	43.55	56.45	73.91	26.09
		Higher than secondary	22.22	77.78	67.39	32.61	73.16	26.84
		Bachelor's or post-graduate	45.45	54.55	43.04	56.96	65.00	35.00
Enabling	Wealth index	Low	35.97	64.03	47.67	52.33	71.48	28.52
		Medium	49.78	50.22	39.27	60.73	71.91	28.09
		High	43.92	56.08	44.98	55.02	72.92	27.08
Need	Self-assessed health status	Bad	36.75	63.25	46.55	53.45	71.43	28.57
		Medium	42.28	57.72	47.46	52.54	76.92	23.08
		Good	43.21	56.79	42.13	57.87	70.88	29.12
		Total	41.40	58.60	44.02	55.98	72.07	27.93

Source: Author's calculations based on microdata from L.I.T.S. I, L.I.T.S. II, and L.I.T.S. III

Lastly, it can be argued from the descriptive statistics that there is a decreasing trend in the P.H.C.U. In addition, individuals with higher rates than the sample average of socio-economic characteristics for each year may have a higher possibility of P.H.C.U.

11.2.2 Methodology

Due to the discrete and binomial nature of the dependent variable of this study reflecting the choice of an individual whether to utilize public healthcare, a probit model is well suited for the estimation. A probit model is generally formulated using a latent variable *y*, which is stated in Equation (11.1).

$$y_i^* = x_i'\beta + \varepsilon_i \tag{11.1}$$

In Equation (11.1), β indicates the set of parameters and x_i indicates the set of independent variables. The latent variable y_i^* represents the probability of P.H.C.U. by an individual. If y_i^* takes on positive values, the individual will choose to utilize public healthcare, and the observed binary outcome is equal to 1. Conversely, if y_i^* does not take on positive values, the individual will choose to not utilize public healthcare, and the observed binary outcome is equal to 0. This process can be formulated as in Equation (11.2).

$$y_i = \begin{cases} 1 & if \quad y_i^* > 0 \\ 0 & if \quad y_i^* \leq 0 \end{cases} \tag{11.2}$$

Equation (11.2) can also be stated as in Equation (11.3).

$$P\{y_i = 1\} = P\{y_i^* > 0\} = P\{x_i'\beta + \varepsilon_i > 0\} = P\{-\varepsilon_i \leq x_i'\beta\} = F(x_i'\beta) \tag{11.3}$$

In Equation (11.3), F denotes the distribution function of $-\varepsilon_i$ or, in the common case of a symmetric distribution such as the normal distribution function, the distribution function of ε_i. The assumption for the normal distribution of ε_i results in the probit model. The probit model is generally estimated by the method of Maximum Likelihood (M.L.) estimation, which relies on the assumption that the distribution of the unobserved dependent variable is known, except for a finite number of unknown parameters. These parameters are estimated by taking those parameter values, giving the observed values the highest probability (Verbeek, 2017).

The marginal effects are important tools to determine how changes in an independent variable affect the probability of the dependent variable, holding other independent variables at specific values. For instance the marginal effect of the education level is the change in the probability of P.H.C.U. for a change in the education level, holding the other independent variables at the specific values. The marginal effects are appropriate measures for comparing the size of the effect of each independent variable on the dependent variable. They can be calculated at representative values of the independent variables or can be calculated by averaging the marginal effects computed at each observed value of the independent variables (Mize et al., 2019).

11.3 Results

Before the estimation of the model, the check of multicollinearity among the independent variables by employing the Variance Inflation Factor (V.I.F.) is a common method. The average V.I.F.

Table 11.2 Estimation Results of the Probit Model on the P.H.C.U.

Variables	2006		2010		2016	
	Coefficients	Marginal Effects	Coefficients	Marginal Effects	Coefficients	Marginal Effects
Male	0.39*** (0.132)	0.150*** (0.051)	−0.069 (0.096)	−0.027 (0.037)	−0.123* (0.07)	−0.041* (0.023)
25–34 years	−0.172 (0.296)	−0.065 (0.112)	0.308 (0.245)	0.116 (0.088)	0.048 (0.119)	0.016 (0.040)
35–44 years	−0.357 (0.294)	−0.135 (0.110)	0.334 (0.245)	0.126 (0.087)	0.226* (0.124)	0.077* (0.043)
45–54 years	−0.31 (0.297)	−0.117 (0.111)	0.439* (0.248)	0.162* (0.085)	0.013 (0.14)	0.004 (0.046)
55–64 years	−0.323 (0.303)	−0.123 (0.114)	0.351 (0.251)	0.131 (0.088)	0.359** (0.169)	0.128** (0.063)
≥65 years	−0.592* (0.309)	−0.224** (0.112)	0.452* (0.262)	0.166* (0.088)	0.131 (0.249)	0.045 (0.088)
Primary education	−0.225** (0.092)	−0.085** (0.035)	−0.083 (0.149)	−0.032 (0.057)	0.366 (0.276)	0.127 (0.098)
Secondary education	0.051 (0.174)	0.019 (0.065)	−0.139 (0.158)	−0.053 (0.061)	0.24 (0.276)	0.079 (0.090)
Higher than secondary education	0.614 (0.475)	0.205 (0.133)	−0.78*** (0.243)	−0.294*** (0.081)	0.275 (0.286)	0.095 (0.101)
Bachelor's or post-graduate degree	−0.238 (0.401)	−0.091 (0.154)	−0.134 (0.212)	−0.052 (0.083)	0.511* (0.298)	0.185* (0.113)
Low wealth	0.199* (0.102)	0.075* (0.038)	−0.114 (0.109)	−0.044 (0.042)	0.003 (0.087)	0.001 (0.029)
Medium wealth	−0.14 (0.115)	−0.053 (0.044)	0.124 (0.104)	0.048 (0.040)	0.028 (0.09)	0.009 (0.030)
Medium health	−0.176 (0.114)	−0.066 (0.043)	−0.005 (0.142)	−0.002 (0.055)	−0.012 (0.296)	−0.004 (0.098)
Good health	−0.209* (0.113)	−0.079* (0.042)	0.186 (0.137)	0.072 (0.053)	0.197 (0.29)	0.063 (0.089)

Notes: (1) Standard errors are reported in parentheses. (2) ***p < 0.01, **p < 0.05, *p < 0.1. (3) The reference categories for the independent variables are being female, being aged between 18 24 years, having no degree, being in the high category of the wealth index, and assessing the health status as "bad", respectively.

value taking less than 10 represents there exists no multicollinearity (Aregbeshola & Khan, 2024). The average V.I.F. values are 3.74, 3.57, and 5.17 for 2006, 2010, and 2016, respectively, indicating that there appears no multicollinearity.

Table 11.2 represents the estimation results of the probit model for 2006, 2010, and 2016. The coefficients for 2006 indicate that males have a higher probability of utilizing public healthcare than females. Among age groups, individuals aged 18–24 years are defined as the reference category. Individuals aged ≥65 years have a lower probability of utilizing public healthcare compared with those aged 18–24 years. Having no degree is determined as the reference category for the education level. Individuals who completed primary education have a lower probability of utilizing public healthcare compared with individuals having no degree in 2006. Individuals who are in the high category of the wealth index are defined as the reference category for this variable. Individuals who are in the low category of the wealth index have a higher probability of utilizing public healthcare compared with individuals who are in the high category. Individuals who assess their health status as "bad" are described as the reference category for this variable. Individuals who assess their health status as "good" have a lower probability of utilizing public healthcare compared with individuals who assess their health status as "bad" in 2006. As a consequence, it can be argued that predisposing, enabling, and need factors statistically significantly affect the probability of utilizing public healthcare in 2006.

The results for 2010 denote that the coefficients of variables follow a pattern different than in 2006. For instance gender has no statistically significant effect on the probability of utilizing public healthcare in 2010. Different from 2006, individuals aged 45–54 years have a higher probability of utilizing public healthcare compared to individuals aged 18–24 years. Individuals aged ≥65 years have a higher probability of utilizing public healthcare compared with individuals aged 18–24 years, while the reverse is true for 2006. Completing higher than secondary education becomes a statistically significant determinant, leading to a lower probability of utilizing public healthcare compared to having no degree. Different from 2006, neither wealth index nor self-assessed health status significantly affects the probability of utilizing public healthcare. As a result, the predisposing factors became the sole determinants of the probability of utilizing public healthcare in 2010.

The coefficients for 2016 first represent that males have a lower probability of utilizing public healthcare than females. Additionally, individuals both aged 35–44 years and aged 55–64 years have a higher probability of utilizing public healthcare than those aged 18–24 years. Also, individuals having post-graduate degrees have a higher probability of utilizing public healthcare compared with individuals having no degree. Lastly, neither wealth index nor self-assessed health status significantly affects the probability of utilizing public healthcare, similar to 2010. Consequently, in 2016, the predisposing factors are again the sole determinants of the probability of utilization of healthcare.

In addition to the coefficients, the marginal effects are reported in Table 11.2. The marginal effects for 2006, 2010, and 2016 have the same sign as the coefficients. The marginal effects are used to compare the level of impact of independent variables on the probability of P.H.C.U. In 2006, being aged ≥65 years has the highest marginal effect, which is followed by being male, completing primary education, assessing the health status as "good", and being in the low category of the wealth index. On the contrary, an education level which is higher than secondary education has the highest marginal effect in 2010. The highest marginal effect is followed by the marginal effects of being aged ≥65 years and being aged 45–54 years. The highest marginal effect stems from having a post-graduate degree in 2016. This is followed by being aged between 55 and 64 years, being aged between 35 and 44 years, and being male. Consequently, the highest marginal effects arise from the age and education level of individuals in 2006, 2010, and 2016. This again highlights the importance of the predisposing factors on the probability of P.H.C.U.

11.4 Conclusion

This study has revealed the determinants of P.H.C.U. in the aftermath of H.T.P. in Turkey, for the years 2006, 2010, and 2016 by employing data gathered from L.I.T.S. I, L.I.T.S. II, and L.I.T.S. III and using a theoretical framework of the behavioural model developed by Andersen (1968).

The results of this study show that gender as a predisposing factor creates statistically significant effects on P.H.C.U., albeit with opposite signs for the years 2006 and 2016. The result for 2006 reflecting the probability of P.H.C.U. higher for males as compared to females is consistent with the previous studies such as Mojumdar (2018) and Şenol et al. (2023) which focus on respectively India and Turkey. However, the result for 2016 reflecting the probability of P.H.C.U. lower for males as compared to females is consistent with most of the previous studies mentioned as expected excluding Mojumdar (2018) and Şenol et al. (2023).

Another predisposing factor, age, has statistically significant effects on P.H.C.U., which varies in opposite directions between 2006 and later. The result for 2006 reflecting the probability of P.H.C.U. lower for those aged ≥65 years compared with those aged 18–24 years is in line with that yielded by Kim and Lee (2016), Mojumdar (2018). On the contrary, the results for 2010 and 2016 reflecting the probability of P.H.C.U. higher for those older aged as compared to those aged 18–24 years are consistent with Blackwell et al. (2009), Tountas et al. (2011), and Şenol et al. (2023).

The results on the last predisposing factor used in this study, education level, indicate that having any education decreases the probability of P.H.C.U. for both 2006 and 2010, while the reverse is true for 2016. The results for 2006 and 2010 reflecting the probability of P.H.C.U. lower than those having no degree are in line with Kim and Lee (2016), Mojumdar (2018), and Sözmen and Ünal (2016). On the contrary, the result for 2016 reflecting the probability of P.H.C.U. higher for those having bachelor's or post-graduate degree compared with those no degree is consistent with Economou et al. (2008) and Tountas et al. (2011).

The enabling factor used in this study, the wealth index, significantly affects the P.H.C.U. only for 2006, neither 2010 nor 2016. The result for 2006 reflecting the probability of P.H.C.U. higher for those in the low category of the wealth index compared with those in the high category of the wealth index is consistent with Gan-Yadam et al. (2013) and Şenol et al. (2023).

The need factor used in this study, self-assessed health status, significantly affects the P.H.C.U. only for 2006, neither 2010 nor 2016. The result for 2006 reflecting the probability of P.H.C.U. lower for those who assess the health status as good compared with those who assess the health status as bad is in line with Economou et al. (2008), Blackwell et al. (2009), Gan-Yadam et al. (2013), Sözmen and Ünal (2016), and Şenol et al. (2023).

These results are evaluated together, which means that two predisposing factors, age and education level, create significant effects on P.H.C.U. in Turkey for all years examined, while enabling and need factors generate significant effects for only one year. Specifically, individuals' age or education level has the highest marginal effect for each year, reflecting the importance of these factors on P.H.C.U. in Turkey in the aftermath of H.T.P.

This study suggests some important policy implications. Policymakers should take into account predisposing factors in the case of designing policies on P.H.C.U. Policymakers would consider that the predisposing role of age may turn into a need factor in certain life cycles. Hence, the policies targeting specific age groups may be a key to the P.H.C.U. In addition, information campaigns which can create an effect similar to the increase in the education level of individuals and increase their awareness about health and health services can assist the policymakers. Moreover, considering gender differences in P.H.C.U. would be a crucial tool for designing and implementing policies.

This study reveals valuable information about the socio-economic determinants of the P.H.C.U. in the aftermath of H.T.P. in Turkey; however, it has several limitations. First, the dataset of this study does not include information on the utilization of different types of healthcare which results in not comparing them in terms of their determinants. Second, income is accepted as an important enabling factor for P.H.C.U., but data for income is only available in L.I.T.S. III. For the purpose of using all rounds of L.I.T.S., a wealth index is required to be created as a proxy of income in this study. Last, since the dataset used in the study contains data only up to 2016, it is not possible to examine the determinants of P.H.C.U. for the more recent period.

Further studies using different data sets and examining the influences of the socio-economic determinants on various types of P.H.C.U. in the aftermath of the H.T.P. in Turkey may expand the existing literature.

References

Andersen, R. M. (1968). *A behavioral model of families' use of health services*. University of Chicago Press.

Andersen, R. M., & Davidson, P. L. (2001). Improving access to care in America: Individual and contextual indicators. In: R. M. Andersen, T. H. Rice, & E. F. Kominski (Eds.), *Changing the U.S. health care system: Key issues in health services, policy, and management* (pp. 3–30). Jossey-Bass.

Aregbeshola, B. S., & Khan, S. M. (2024). Determinants of out-of-pocket health expenditure among older adults: Evidence from the Nigeria Living Standards Survey 2018–19. *Ageing International*, *49*, 450–466. https://doi.org/10.1007/s12126-023-09548-3

Başar, D., Öztürk, S., & Cakmak, İ. (2021). An application of the behavioral model to the utilization of health care services in Turkey: A focus on equity. *Panoeconomicus*, *68*(1), 129–146. https://doi.org/10.2298/PAN171121006B

Blackwell, D. L., Martinez, M. E., Gentleman, J. F., Sanmartin, C., & Berthelot, J. M. (2009). Socioeconomic status and utilization of health care services in Canada and the United States: Findings from a binational health survey. *Medical Care*, *47*(11), 1136–1146. https://doi.org/10.1097/MLR.0b013e3181adcbe9

Caner, A., & Cilasun, S. M. (2019). Health care services and the elderly: Utilization and satisfaction in the aftermath of the Turkish Health Transformation Program. *Gerontology & Geriatric Medicine*, *5*, 1–15. https://doi.org/10.1177/2333721418822868

Carrasquillo, O. (2013). Health care utilization. In: M. D. Gellman & J. R. Turner (Eds.), *Encyclopedia of behavioral medicine* (pp. 909–910). Springer. https://doi.org/10.1007/978-1-4419-1005-9_885

Cinaroglu, S., & Çalışkan, Z. (2022). Distributive pattern of health services utilization under public health reform and promotion in Turkey. *Value in Health Regional Issues*, *31*, 25–33. https://doi.org/10.1016/j.vhri.2022.01.005

Economou, A., Nikolaou, A., & Theodossiou, I. (2008). Socioeconomic status and health-care utilization: A study of the effects of low income, unemployment and hours of work on the demand for health care in the European Union. *Health Services Management Research*, *21*(1), 40–59. https://doi.org/10.1258/hsmr.2007.007013

European Bank for Reconstruction and Development [E.B.R.D.]. (2024). *Life in Transition Survey (LITS)*. https://www.ebrd.com/what-we-do/economic-research-and-data/data/lits.html

Gan-Yadam, A., Shinohara, R., Sugisawa, Y., Tanaka, E., Watanabe, T., Hirano, M., Tomisaki, E., Morita, K., Onda, Y., Tokutake, K., Mochizuki, Y., Matsumoto, M., Sugita, C., & Anme, T. (2013). Factors associated with health service utilization in Ulaanbaatar, Mongolia: A population-based survey. *Journal of Epidemiology*, *23*(5), 320–328. https://doi.org/10.2188/jea.je20120123

Hone, T., Gurol-Urganci, I., Millett, C., Başara, B., Akdağ, R., & Atun, R. (2017). Effect of primary health care reforms in Turkey on health service utilization and user satisfaction. *Health Policy and Planning*, *32*(1), 57–67. https://doi.org/10.1093/heapol/czw098

Hosseinpoor, A. R., Naghavi, M., Alavian, S. M., Speybroeck, N., Jamshidi, H., & Vega, J. (2007). Determinants of seeking needed outpatient care in Iran: Results from a national health services utilization survey. *Archives of Iranian Medicine*, *10*(4), 439–445.

Jolliffe, I. (2002). *Principal component analysis* (2nd ed.). Springer.

Kim, H. K., & Lee, M. (2016). Factors associated with health services utilization between the years 2010 and 2012 in Korea: Using Andersen's behavioral model. *Osong Public Health and Research Perspectives*, *7*(1), 18–25. https://doi.org/10.1016/j.phrp.2015.11.007

López-Cevallos, D. F., & Chi, C. (2010). Health care utilization in Ecuador: A multilevel analysis of socio-economic determinants and inequality issues. *Health Policy and Planning*, *25*(3), 209–218. https://doi.org/10.1093/heapol/czp052

Menon, R., Mollahaliloglu, S., & Postolovska, I. (2013). *Toward universal coverage: Turkey's Green Card Program for the poor*. UNICO Studies Series No. 18, The World Bank, Washington, DC.

Mize, T. D., Doan, L., & Long, J. S. (2019). A general framework for comparing predictions and marginal effects across models. *Sociological Methodology*, *49*(1), 152–189. https://doi.org/10.1177/0081175019852763

Mojumdar, S. K. (2018). Determinants of health service utilization by urban households in India: A multivariate analysis of NSS Case-level data. *Journal of Health Management*, *20*(2), 105–121. https://doi.org/10.1177/0972063418763642

Ökem, Z. G., & Çakar, M. (2015). What have health care reforms achieved in Turkey? An appraisal of the "Health Transformation Programme". *Health Policy*, *119*(9), 1153–1163. https://doi.org/10.1016/j.healthpol.2015.06.003

Sözmen, K., & Ünal, B. (2016). Explaining inequalities in health care utilization among Turkish adults: Findings from Health Survey 2008. *Health Policy*, *120*(1), 100–110. https://doi.org/10.1016/j.healthpol.2015.10.003

Şenol, V., Elmalı, F., Çetinkaya, F., Naçar, M., & Yalap, R. (2023). Change in utilization of health services and its affecting factors in Kayseri city center: A comparative population-based cross-sectional study in 2004 and 2017. *Turkiye Klinikleri Journal of Medical Sciences*, *43*(1), 49–63.

Tareq, M., Abdel-Razzaq, A. I., Rahman, M. A., & Choudhury, T. (2021). Comparison of weighted and unweighted methods of wealth indices for assessing SOCIO-ECONOMIC status. *Heliyon*, *7*(2), e06163. https://doi.org/10.1016/j.heliyon.2021.e06163

Tountas, Y., Oikonomou, N., Pallikarona, G., Dimitrakaki, C., Tzavara, C., Souliotis, K., Mariolis, A., Pappa, E., Kontodimopoulos, N., & Niakas, D. (2011). Sociodemographic and socioeconomic determinants of health services utilization in Greece: The Hellas Health I study. *Health Services Management Research*, *24*(1), 8–18. https://doi.org/10.1258/hsmr.2010.010009

Venkateswaran, S., & Singh, A. K. (2022). *Health system in Turkey: Reforms, transformations, and challenges*. CSEP Working Paper 36, Centre for Social and Economic Progress, New Delhi.

Verbeek, M. (2017). *A guide to modern econometrics* (5th ed.). John Wiley & Sons.

Chapter 12

Unmet Need for Mental Healthcare: A Comprehensive Prevalence and Determinants Investigation for Turkey

Kübra Coşar

Contents

12.1 Introduction

World Health Organization (W.H.O., 2022) defines mental health as;

> A state of mental well-being that enables people to cope with the stresses of life, realize their abilities, learn well and work well, and contribute to their community. It is an integral component of health and well-being that underpins our individual and collective abilities to make decisions, build relationships and shape the world we live in.

As it is clear by this definition, mental health determines an individual's way of thinking, lifestyle, and communication with the outside world. It affects all areas of interaction and communication

DOI: 10.4324/9781003539896-13

that exist within the life cycle of an individual, such as family relationships, work life, or relationship with the social environment. Therefore, social impacts and economic consequences are inevitable.

While there is no doubt that good mental health plays a key role in ensuring a healthy population and a healthy economy, mental and physical health are also inextricably linked, and their influence on each other is complex and profound (W.H.O., 2001). Studies have improved the understanding of the relationship between mental health and many diseases such as diabetes, cardiovascular disease, and many co-morbid somatic disorders (Robinson et al., 2013; Mensah and Collins, 2015; Vancampfort et al., 2016; Nielsen et al., 2021, Lemogne et al., 2021; Schuch and Vancampfort, 2021). In addition, mental health also has an impact on help-seeking, diagnosis, and treatment and has an influence on prognosis (Prince et al., 2007). While this situation may cause irreversible consequences for the health of individuals, it may also lead to increased health expenditures and creates burnout on the health system. Recent estimates show that the economic consequences of the cumulative global impact of mental disorder will be amount to US$ 16.3 trillion between 2011 and 2030 (W.H.O., 2021).

Mental health is an emerging issue that world leaders and policymakers are prioritizing as the importance of its economic and social impact is recognized. Mental disorders are the leading causes of disaster burden (G.B.D. 2019; Mental Disorders Collaborators, 2022) and are increasing rapidly due to natural disasters, epidemics, wars, and economic crises. According to the Institute for Health Metrics and Evaluation (I.H.M.E.), 12% of the world's population had a mental health disorder in 2019, and 28% more people experienced anxiety and depressive disorders in 2020 than in 2019 as a result of the COVID-19 pandemic. Moreover, the Health at a Glance 2023 Report stated that anxiety and depression have increased across all O.E.C.D. countries during the COVID-19 pandemic, with some countries, such as the United States, Canada, and Austria, experiencing levels more than twice as high as in 2019 (O.E.C.D., 2023). Despite the fact that mental disorders are driving force in the increase in disability and mortality worldwide, their high cost in terms of economic and social impact, and their high prevalence, they have not been put on the agenda as a health or development priority and not included in the Millennium Development Goals (U.N. and W.H.O., 2010; Vigo et al., 2016). With growing recognition in the international community, mental health has been included in the Sustainable Development Goals (S.D.G.s), adopted by the United Nations General Assembly in September 2015, under Goals 3: Ensure healthy lives and wellbeing for all at all ages, and Target 3.8.1 states: "achieve universal health coverage, including financial risk protection, access to quality essential health-care services and access to safe, effective, quality and affordable essential medicines and vaccines for all".

With the inclusion of mental health among the S.D.G.s and the recognition of its importance, the W.H.O. became a partner with the Comprehensive Mental Health Action Plan 2013–2030 to implement policies to protect and promote mental health. W.H.O. regards the good mental health and well-being as a fundamental human right that must be provided for the whole population. In line with the principle of 'no health without mental health', the Action Plan focused on reducing the treatment gap for people affected by mental disorders, improving the mental health of entire populations and reducing the contribution of mental disorders to the global burden of disease, and promoting and protecting the mental well-being of all (Patel et al., 2018; W.H.O., 2021). For this purpose, one of the Action Plan's six key cross-cutting principles and approaches is Universal Health Coverage (U.H.C.) (W.H.O., 2021):

> Regardless of age, sex, socioeconomic status, race, ethnicity or sexual orientation, and following the principle of equity, persons with mental disorders should be able to access, without the risk of impoverishing themselves, essential health and social services that enable them to achieve recovery and the highest attainable standard of health.

W.H.O. also announced the W.H.O. Special Initiative for Mental Health (2019–2023): Universal Health Coverage for Mental Health, which aims to ensure universal health coverage with access to quality and affordable mental healthcare for 100 million more people in 12 priority countries, with a budget of US$ 60 million over five years (W.H.O., 2019).

U.H.C. consists of two interrelated elements: The accessibility of the healthcare system and the protection against financial risks (Vega, 2013). Although Universal Health Coverage means ensuring accessible and equitable health system for all people, especially vulnerable and disadvantaged group without financial barriers, there is no doubt that there are still many people who could not reach healthcare because of financial districts in the world. When people do not have access to health services for reasons such as unaffordability, this situation is referred to as unmet health needs. The cost of mental health services has also been one of the major barriers to mental healthcare (Rowan et al., 2013).

It is important to identify risk factors, in addition to prevalence and reasons, in order to develop policy and implement strategies to prevent unmet needs and promote mental health and well-being. Epidemiological research has identified both structural and attitudinal barriers to care which led to unmet mental health needs, but reviewed literature has shown gaps in qualitative research on unmet mental health needs (Rens et al., 2020). Mental health and well-being have recently been raised as a global priority as a public health issue, so examining country-specific cases can make important contributions to the literature. This study aims to contribute to the literature by examining Turkey as an example of a middle-income country. Mental disorders such as depression and anxiety have been increasing in Turkey, and the problem is deepening with factors such as natural disasters, migration, economic downturns, and the COVID-19 pandemic in the world. According to the data of the Republic of Turkish Ministry of Health (M.o.H.), 17% of the population faces mental health issues. About 9 million people out of a population of 83 million seek help for mental health problems every year (W.H.O.). These statistics raise concerns about potential high levels of unmet needs for mental healthcare, which could contribute to increased prevalence of chronic mental and general illnesses, as well as excess mortality. In fact, in 2003, Turkey started to implement the Health Transformation Programme (H.T.P.) (Sulku et al., 2023). The main objective of this programme is the provision of universal health coverage for all citizens, especially socio-economically disadvantaged groups, to have equal access to health services (Atun et al., 2013). However, this does not guarantee that all health or mental health needs will be met. In this framework, to explore the effectiveness of the H.T.P. in accessing mental health services, this chapter will investigate the unmet needs for mental health due to financial reasons in the years 2014, 2016, 2019, and 2022. It is also important to identify the risk factors influencing unmet needs in order to develop and implement effective policies to address inequalities in access. Therefore, the first aim of this study is to examine the prevalence of unmet mental health needs by year and then to identify the demographic, socio-economic, and health correlates of unmet mental health needs using TurkStat Health Survey data via probit models.

12.2 Materials and Method

12.2.1 Data

In this study, Turkish Health Survey Micro Data Set was used for the years 2014, 2016, 2019, and 2022. The dataset was obtained from the Turkish Statistical Institute (TurkStat) in accordance with "Regulations on Procedures and Guidelines for Data Privacy and Confidential Data Security at Official Statistics" which came into force after publishing in Official Newspaper No.26204 and dated 20 June 2006 as described in the Turkish Statistical Institute's Decree No. 5429 and Law 13 as a nationally representative survey reflecting the whole country that also allows comparisons at national and international level. The dataset provides a wide range information on health indicators, including general health, chronic diseases, functional ability to perform daily activities, personal care, use of health services, use of medicines, vaccinations, and height and weight for individuals aged 15 years and over, enabling national and international comparisons. The data set was obtained through face-to-face interviews in households selected by stratified two-stage cluster sampling method. The sampling method is explained in detail on the official page of the Turkish Statistical Institute. The health survey was implemented for the first time in 2008 and was carried out in two-year periods until 2016. In this study, since the content of the questionnaire changed in 2014, the data set was used until 2022, which is the most recent year. The survey was carried out with a selected sample of 9,740, 9,470, 9,470, and 11,170 households for the years 2014, 2016, 2019, and 2022, respectively (TurkStat).

12.2.2 Methodology: Probit Analysis

In this study, due to the binomial structure of the dependent variable, unmet mental healthcare need, the probit model was used. Suppose the outcome variable, y, takes the value:

$$y = \begin{cases} 1 \text{ with probability p.} \\ 0 \text{ with probability } 1-p \end{cases} \tag{12.1}$$

Probit model corresponds to regression model for P. The regression model is formed by parameterizing to depend on an index function, where X is a regressor vector and β is a vector of unknown parameters. In standard binary outcome models, the conditional probability has the form

$$p_i = P\left(y_i = 1/x\right) = F\left(x'\beta\right) \tag{12.2}$$

where $F(.)$ is a specified parametric function of $x'\beta$, usually a cumulative distribution function (c.d.f.) on $(-\infty, \infty)$ to ensure that $0 \le p \le 1$. In probit model, $F(.)$ is a cumulative standard normal distribution function, which is written as follows:

$$F\left(x'\beta\right) = \frac{1}{2\pi} \int_{-\infty}^{x'\beta} e^{-z^2/2} dz \tag{12.3}$$

where z is standardized normally distributed variable with parameter (0,1), and to estimate parameter vector of β, Maximum Likelihood Estimation (M.L.E.) is used. M.L.E. maximizes the associated log-likelihood function:

$$\phi(\beta) = \sum_{i=1}^{N} \left[y_i \ln F\left(x_i'\beta\right) + \left(1 - y_i\right) \ln \left\{ 1 - F\left(x_i'\beta\right) \right\} \right] \qquad (12.4)$$

where N is the number of observations, then the M.L.E. is obtained using iterative methods and is asymptotically normally distributed (Cameron and Trivedi, 2005, p. 465).

12.2.3 Variables

Unmet need refers to a situation where an individual requires treatment to improve their health but does not receive available and effective care. This can happen for many reasons. Allin et al. (2010) conceptualize the unmet need in five categories, one of which relates to cost. This means that an unmet need arises when any need for healthcare services is not accessible because of any financial constraint, which may be the cost of treatments. This study examines the need for mental health services in spite of financial reasons, so the question 'Was there any time in the past 12 months when you needed mental healthcare (by psychologist or a psychiatrist for example), but could not afford it?' was considered to be a potential unmet need due to cost, so the dependent variable is constructed as follows: if the individual answered 'yes' to the questions, then the dependent variable takes the value of 1, representing the case of unmet mental healthcare need, and if the individual answered 'no' to the questions, then the dependent variable takes the value of 0. Those who answered 'No need for health care' were excluded from the study. It should be kept in mind that when this study refers to unmet needs, it actually refers to mental health services that cannot be met for financial reasons.

The independent variables were determined by following the literature on the identification of risk factors associated with unmet healthcare needs (Terzi et al., 2020; Başar et al., 2021; Tokatlioglu and Sulku, 2023). The independent variable's explanation and percentages of individuals experiencing unmet mental healthcare needs are given in Table 12.1.

Table 12.1 Independent Variables' Explanation and Percentage of Individuals experiencing Unmet Mental Healthcare Needs

Variable	Explanation	Category	Percentage (%)
Gender	Gender of the respondent	Male (base category) Female	67.26
Age	Age group of the respondent	15–24 (base category) 25–44 45–65 65 and over	13.08 44.68 34.12 8.12
Marital Status	Marital status of the respondent	Single, that is never married Married (base category) Divorced Widowed	68.56 16.33 7.96 7.15

Table 12.1 (*Continued*) Independent Variables' Explanation and Percentage of Individuals experiencing Unmet Mental Healthcare Needs

Variable	Explanation	Category	Percentage (%)
Education	The respondent's highest educational degree	Non-literate (base category) No formal education Primary Middle Secondary University High	17.55 6.82 42.49 13.16 13.40 6.01 0.57
Household Income	Information regarding household income level of the respondent (reported categorically)	1st 20% income group 2nd 20% income group 3rd 20% income group 4th 20% income group 5th 20% income group	47.77 19.66 14.22 10.80 7.55
Employee	Working status of respondent	Wage, salary, or casual employee Employer/ self-employed Working as unpaid family worker Other status (base category)	43.70 9.67 4.71 41.92
Insurance	Information regarding the insurance status of the respondent	Not insured (base category) Insured	14.56 85.44
General Health	Health in general of respondent	Very bad (base category) Bad Fair Good Very good	5.93 22.91 41.10 26.65 3.41
Chronic Illness	If the respondent has any physical chronic disease during 12 last months	No (base category) Yes	98.70 1.30
Depression	If respondent has depression during 12 last months	No (base category) Yes	56.21 43.79

12.3 Results

In the first stage of the analysis, unmet mental health needs' prevalence was measured by years 2014, 2016, 2019, and 2022 and is given in Figure 12.1. As it is seen clearly, the highest unmet need was observed in 2014 in the years examined within the scope of the study. In 2014, this rate was 6.5%, decreased to 2.93% in a short period of only two years, and remained almost at the same level in the following years.

Table 12.2 presents the results of probit model constructed to determine the unmet mental health needs. According to the results, being female has a positive effect on unmet mental health needs, meaning that women have more unmet needs than men, and this is statistically significant. The effect of age was analysed in four groups: 25–44, 45–64, and 65 and over, while 15–24 was the reference group. It is observed that unmet services decrease with increasing age, and this effect is the least for individuals aged 65 and over. Being single does not significantly affect unmet mental health needs. However, being divorced and being widowed have significant effects: being divorced

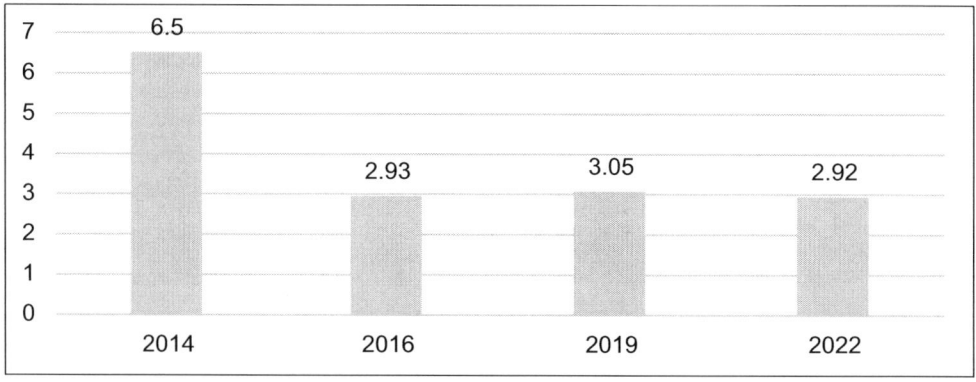

Figure 12.1   Rates of unmet mental healthcare needs by years.

Table 12.2 Probit Model Estimation Results

Variables		Coefficients	Marginal Effects
Gender	Female	0.1555*** (0.0382) [0.0807, 0.2303]	0.0089*** (0.0022) [0.0046, 0.0131]
Age Group	25–44	−0.0375 (0.0609) [−0.1567, 0.0818]	−0.0030 (0.0050) [−0.0129, 0.0068]
	45–64	−0.2685*** (0.0684) [−0.4026, −0.1344]	−0.0176*** (0.0051) [−0.0277, −0.0076]
	65+	−0.7252*** (0.0866) [−0.8950, −0.5555]	−0.0321*** (0.0049) [−0.0416, −0.0226]

Table 12.2 (*Continued*) Probit Model Estimation Results

Variables		Coefficients	Marginal Effects
Marital Status	Single	0.0459 (0.0556) [−0.0631, 0.1548]	0.0027 (0.0034) [−0.0039, 0.0093]
	Divorced	0.2716*** (0.0649) [0.1444, 0.3987]	0.0200*** (0.0059) [0.0084, 0.0317]
	Widowed	−0.1519** (0.0645) [−0.2784, −0.0254]	−0.0074*** (0.0028) [−0.0128, −0.0020]
Education	No formal education	−0.1629** (0.0702) [−0.3004, −0.0253]	−0.0137** (0.0057) [−0.0249, −0.0025]
	Primary	−0.2382*** (0.0498) [−0.3358, −0.1406]	−0.0187*** (0.0045) [−0.0276, −0.0099]
	Middle	−0.3924*** (0.0647) [−0.5191, −0.2656]	−0.0271*** (0.0050) [−0.0368, −0.0173]
	Secondary	−0.3459*** (0.0649) [−0.4731, −0.2187]	−0.0248*** (0.0051) [−0.0349, −0.0148]
	University	−0.4638*** (0.0771) [−0.6149, −0.3128]	−0.0301*** (0.0052) [−0.0404, −0.0199]
	High	−0.3707** (0.1790) [−0.7215, −0.0199]	−0.0261*** (0.0096) [−0.0448, −0.0073]
Income Group	Second 20%	−0.3055*** (0.0404) [−0.3845, −0.2264]	−0.0224*** (0.0030) [−0.0283, −0.0165]
	Third 20%	−0.2936*** (0.0456) [−0.3830, −0.2041]	−0.0217*** (0.0033) [−0.0282, −0.0153]
	Fourth 20%	−0.4031*** (0.0492) [−0.4996, −0.3067]	−0.0272*** (0.0032) [−0.0334, −0.0209]
	Fifth 20%	−0.4906*** (0.0580) [−0.6042, −0.3770]	−0.0307*** (0.0033) [−0.0372, −0.0242]

Table 12.2 (*Continued*) Probit Model Estimation Results

Variables		Coefficients	Marginal Effects
Employment Status	Wage, salary, or casual employee	0.1391*** (0.0384) [0.0639, 0.2144]	0.0081*** (0.0022) [0.0038, 0.0125]
	Employer/ self-employed	0.0926 (0.0575) [−0.0200, 0.2052]	0.0052 (0.0034) [−0.0014, 0.0118]
	Working as unpaid family worker	−0.2590*** (0.0695) [−0.3951, −0.1229]	−0.0101*** (0.0023) [−0.0146, −0.0057]
Insurance	Yes	−0.4407*** (0.0487) [−0.5360, −0.3453]	−0.0252*** (0.0028) [−0.0307, −0.0196]
Self-Assessed Health	Bad	−0.3293*** (0.0856) [−0.4971, −0.1614]	−0.0445*** (0.0139) [−0.0717, −0.0173]
	Fair	−0.4736*** (0.0836) [−0.6375, −0.3097]	−0.0578*** (0.0138) [−0.0849, −0.0307]
	Good	−0.8248*** (0.0875) [−0.9963, −0.6533]	−0.0787*** (0.0140) [−0.1061, −0.0513]
	Very good	−0.9560*** (0.1071) [−1.1659, −0.7460]	−0.0833*** (0.0141) [−0.1109, −0.0557]
Physical Chronic Illness	Yes	0.6712*** (0.1710) [0.3360, 1.0065]	0.0384*** (0.0098) [0.0191, 0.0576]
Chronic Depression	Yes	0.7528*** (0.0347) [0.6848, 0.8207]	0.0430*** (0.0022) [0.0386, 0.0474]
Year 2016		−0.2749*** (0.0320) [−0.3376, −0.2121]	−0.0157*** (0.0018) [−0.0193, −0.0121]
Year 2019		−0.2197*** (0.0719) [−0.3607, −0.0788]	−0.0126*** (0.0041) [−0.0206, −0.0045]
Year 2022		−0.1892*** (0.0658) [−0.3181, −0.0602]	−0.0108*** (0.0038) [−0.0182, −0.0035]

Table 12.2 (*Continued*) Probit Model Estimation Results

Variables		Coefficients	Marginal Effects
Constant		−0.2088* (0.1224) [−0.4487, 0.0310]	
		Observation = 28,436 Log likelihood = −4167.7374 Pseudo R^2 = 0.1768 Prob > chi^2 = 0.0000	

Note: Standard errors in parentheses, confidence intervals in brackets.***p<0.01, **p<0.05, *p<0.1

increases the probability of unmet mental health needs, while being widowed reduces it.In the education and income perspective, increase in the level of the education and income has a decreasing effect. In particular, graduating from university has the largest decreasing effect, and those with the highest incomes have less difficulty accessing mental health services. Furthermore, while wage, salary, or casual workers are more likely to have unmet mental health needs due to financial difficulties compared to non-workers, the situation is reversed for unpaid family workers. Being an employer/self-employed also has a positive effect, although it is not statistically significant. Having health insurance has a decreasing effect. From a health perspective, as people's self-perceived health improves, in other words as their general health improves, the likelihood of not being able to use mental health services decreases; on the other hand, if they have a chronic physical illness and chronic depression, which represents the mental state, the likelihood of encountering unaffordable health services increases. Finally, the coefficients of the year dummy variables are statistically significant and negative. This shows that time elapsed has a decreasing effect.

12.4 Discussion and Conclusion

With the inevitable increase in mental illness due to causes such as wars, economic crises, diseases, climate change, natural disasters, and the understanding of its socio-economic costs and importance, international organizations have focused on developing policies and strategies to protect and ensure mental health and also to improve the accessibility of health services that include everyone. Also, in Turkey, as in the world, new policies have been added to the agenda as health priorities. The Turkish Ministry of Health published the text of the National Mental Health Policy in 2006 (M.o.H., 2006), and the National Mental Health Action Plan (M.o.H., 2011) is based on the National Mental Health Policy, the implementation of which started in 2011. The Action Plan includes policies and strategies for building the mental health system, expanding community-based mental health services, and increasing the workforce (M.o.H., 2011). In addition, the Law on Disabled People, dated 1 July 2015 and numbered 5378, provides for the establishment of specially equipped sheltered workplaces, with technical and financial support from the state, to provide vocational rehabilitation for persons with mental disabilities and to create employment opportunities for those who are difficult to integrate into the labour market (European Commission, 2024). With this regulation, the access of individuals with mental health problems to health systems has been strengthened. According to our findings, the prevalence of unmet mental health needs is decreasing in parallel with all these policies.

When the factors impacting unmet mental health needs due to financial difficulties are analysed, it is observed that being a female has an increasing effect. Due to cultural values such as the gender perspective, women in Turkey are seen as reserve labour force, and their labour force participation rate is very low compared to men (Atasoy, 2017; Öztürk and Coşar, 2017). According to the World Bank, the female participation rate in the total labour force is 29.9, 31.2, 32.5, and 33.2 in 2014, 2016, 2019, and 2022 respectively. Although the figures have increased over the years, they are far below the world average. While women are in disadvantaged groups receiving lower wages, this problem deepens with the increase in women's labour force participation rate (Tokatlıoğlu and Doğan, 2021; Aldan, 2021). As a consequence of this situation, there is a disadvantage in terms of unmet mental health needs. Moreover, females have higher needs, utilization, and unmet needs rates in terms of mental healthcare than males (Kessler et al., 1981; Rhodes and Goering, 1994; Young et al., 2001). Başar and Öztürk (2020) supported this idea for Turkey in parallel with our findings.

Income is another important factor affecting unmet mental health needs. The probability of unmet mental health needs decreases as income increases. This result draws attention to the right to equal access to health services. In the context of the S.D.G.s, the aim is to provide equal access to the entire population, and in this direction, Turkey has initiated the Health Transformation Programme to ensure universal health coverage for all. According to our findings, having a health insurance reduces the probability of having unmet mental health needs. However, the fact that the individual is covered by general health insurance does not eliminate the inability to receive services from the health system due to financial difficulties (Başar et al., 2021).

The health status of the individuals was assessed by their self-assessed health, having a chronic physical illness and having chronic depression as an indicator of mental health status. It was found that while improving general health has a positive effect on the use of mental health services, people with chronic illness or chronic depression are more likely to have unmet mental health needs, even though they would need more than others. According to Yardim and Uner (2018), Terzi et al., (2020), Başar et al. (2021), and Tokatlioglu and Sulku (2023), these people are also disadvantaged when trying to access other health services, whereas these people are more fragile and vulnerable. The reason behind this situation may be the difficulties that people are already experiencing such as not receiving education, not being involved in social life, not working, or working in unskilled jobs with lower wages. As a result, these persons are more in need of financial protection.

First of all, the dataset only provides information on mental health services that cannot be covered due to financial difficulties. However, we know that there can be many reasons for unaffordable health services. Even from the perspective of financial difficulties alone, disadvantaged groups such as women, low-income individuals, those not covered by health insurance, and individuals with health problems are particularly vulnerable. Therefore, policymakers and administrators should produce more inclusive and protective policies for these individuals.

References

Aldan, A. (2021). Rising female labor force participation and gender wage gap: Evidence from Turkey. *Social Indicators Research*, *155*(3), 865–884. https://doi.org/10.1007/s11205-021-02631-9

Allin, S., Grignon, M., & Le Grand, J. (2010). Subjective unmet need and utilization of health care services in Canada: What are the equity implications? *Social Science & Medicine*, *70*(3), 465–472. https://doi.org/10.1016/j.socscimed.2009.10.027

Atasoy, B. S. (2017). Female labour force participation in Turkey: The role of traditionalism. *The European Journal of Development Research*, *29*(4), 675–706. https://doi.org/10.1057/s41287-017-0088-6

Atun, R., Aydın, S., Chakraborty, S., Sümer, S., Aran, M., Gürol, I., . . . & Akdağ, R. (2013). Universal health coverage in Turkey: Enhancement of equity. *The Lancet, 382*(9886), 65–99. https://doi.org/10.1016/S0140-6736(13)61051-X

Başar, D., & Öztürk, S. (2020). Assessing horizontal equity in the utilization of mental healthcare services in Turkey: A gender perspective. *Applied Health Economics and Health Policy, 18*(2), 299–309. https://doi.org/10.1007/s40258-019-00519-x

Başar, D., Dikmen, F. H., & Öztürk, S. (2021). The prevalence and determinants of unmet health care needs in Turkey. *Health Policy, 125*(6), 786–792. https://doi.org/10.1016/j.healthpol.2021.04.006

Cameron, A. C., & Trivedi, P. K. (2005). *Microeconometrics: Methods and applications.* Cambridge University Press.

European Commission. (2024). *Health and well-being: Mental health.* Retrieved from https://national-policies.eacea.ec.europa.eu/youthwiki/chapters/turkiye/75-mental-health (Accessed 28 June 2024).

GBD 2019 Mental Disorders Collaborators. (2022). Global, regional, and national burden of 12 mental disorders in 204 countries and territories, 1990–2019: A systematic analysis for the Global Burden of Disease Study 2019. *The Lancet Psychiatry, 9*(2), 137–150.

Institute for Health Metrics and Evaluation (I.H.M.E.). *Mental health.* https://www.healthdata.org/research-analysis/health-risks-issues/mental-health (Accessed 9 April 2024).

Kessler, R. C., Brown, R. L., & Broman, C. L. (1981). Sex differences in psychiatric help-seeking: Evidence from four large-scale surveys. *Journal of Health and Social Behavior, 22*(1), 49–64. https://doi.org/10.2307/2136367

Lemogne, C., Blacher, J., Airagnes, G., Hoertel, N., Czernichow, S., Danchin, N., . . . & Fiedorowicz, J. G. (2021). Management of cardiovascular health in people with severe mental disorders. *Current Cardiology Reports, 23*, 1–11. https://doi.org/10.1007/s11886-021-01553-7

Mensah, G. A., & Collins, P. Y. (2015). Understanding mental health for the prevention and control of cardiovascular diseases. *Global Heart, 10*(3), 221–225. https://doi.org/10.1016/j.gheart.2015.07.003

Ministry of Health of Turkey (M.o.H.). (2006). *Republic of Turkey national mental health policy.* Retrieved from https://extranet.who.int/mindbank/item/69 (Accessed 28 June 2024).

Ministry of Health of Turkey (M.o.H.). (2011). *The national mental health action plan (2011–2023).* Retrieved from https://extranet.who.int/mindbank/item/3866 (Accessed 28 June 2024).

Nielsen, R. E., Banner, J., & Jensen, S. E. (2021). Cardiovascular disease in patients with severe mental illness. *Nature Reviews Cardiology, 18*(2), 136–145. https://doi.org/10.1038/s41569-020-00495-5

O.E.C.D. (2023). Health at a Glance 2023: O.E.C.D. Indicators, O.E.C.D. Publishing, Paris, https://doi.org/10.1787/7a7afb35-en

Öztürk, S., & Coşar, K. (2017). İşgücüne katılmama kararında toplumsal cinsiyetin rolü. *Gazi Üniversitesi İktisadi ve İdari Bilimler Fakültesi Dergisi, 19*(2), 527–543.

Patel, V., Saxena, S., Lund, C., Thornicroft, G., Baingana, F., Bolton, P., . . . & Unützer, J. (2018). The Lancet Commission on global mental health and sustainable development. *The Lancet, 392*(10157), 1553–1598. https://doi.org/10.1016/S0140-6736(18)31612-X

Prince, M., Patel, V., Saxena, S., Maj, M., Maselko, J., Phillips, M. R., & Rahman, A. (2007). No health without mental health. *The Lancet, 370*(9590), 859–877. https://doi.org/10.1016/S0140-6736(07)61238-0

Rens, E., Dom, G., Remmen, R., Michielsen, J., & Van den Broeck, K. (2020). Unmet mental health needs in the general population: Perspectives of Belgian health and social care professionals. *International Journal for Equity in Health, 19*(1), 169. https://doi.org/10.1186/s12939-020-01287-0

Rhodes, A., & Goering, P. (1994). Gender differences in the use of outpatient mental health services. *The Journal of Mental Health Administration, 21*, 338–346.

Robinson, D. J., Luthra, M., Vallis, M., & Canadian Diabetes Association Clinical Practice Guidelines Expert Committee. (2013). Diabetes and mental health. *Canadian Journal of Diabetes, 37*, S87-S92.

Rowan, K., McAlpine, D. D., & Blewett, L. A. (2013). Access and cost barriers to mental health care, by insurance status, 1999–2010. *Health Affairs, 32*(10), 1723–1730. https://doi.org/10.1377/hlthaff.2013.0133

Schuch, F. B., & Vancampfort, D. (2021). Physical activity, exercise, and mental disorders: It is time to move on. *Trends in Psychiatry and Psychotherapy, 43*, 177–184.

Sulku, S. N., Tokatlioglu, Y., & Cosar, K. (2023). Receiving or not deemed necessary healthcare services. *BMC Public Health, 23*(1), 208. https://doi.org/10.1186/s12889-023-15135-7

Terzi, M., Kurutkan, M. N., Şahin, D., & Kara, O. (2020). Unmet medical care needs due to payment difficulty. *Sağlık Akademisyenleri Dergisi, 9*(4), 309–316.

Tokatlıoğlu, Y., & Doğan, N. (2021). Return of education for women across socio-economic status: Using quantile regression and Machado-Mata decomposition methods for Turkey. *Ege Academic Review, 21*(2), 93–110. https://doi.org/10.21121/eab.907367

Tokatlioglu, Y., & Sulku, S. N. (2023). The impact of the covid-19 outbreak on unmet health care needs in Istanbul. *Preventive Medicine Reports, 36*, 102400.

Türkiye Statistical Institute (TurkStat). *Türkiye health survey micro dataset.* Retrieved from: https://www.tuik.gov.tr/Kurumsal/Mikro_Veri (Accessed 29 June 2024).

U.N., W.H.O. (2010). *Policy analysis on mental health and development: Integrating mental health into all development efforts including MDGs.* United Nations, New York.

Vancampfort, D., Correll, C. U., Galling, B., Probst, M., De Hert, M., Ward, P. B., Rosenbaum, S., Gaughran, F., Lally, J., & Stubbs, B. (2016). Diabetes mellitus in people with schizophrenia, bipolar disorder and major depressive disorder: A systematic review and large scale meta-analysis. *World Psychiatry: Official Journal of the World Psychiatric Association (W.P.A.), 15*(2), 166–174. https://doi.org/10.1002/wps.20309

Vega, J. (2013). Universal health coverage: The post-2015 development agenda. *The Lancet, 381*(9862), 179–180.

Vigo, D., Thornicroft, G., & Atun, R. (2016). Estimating the true global burden of mental illness. *The Lancet Psychiatry, 3*(2), 171–178.

World Bank. *Labor force, female (% of total labor force) – Turkey.* Retrieved from: https://data.worldbank.org/indicator/SL.TLF.TOTL.FE.ZS?locations=TR (Accessed 28 June 2024).

World Health Organization (W.H.O.). *Supporting Turkish mental health policy and service delivery.* Retrieved from: https://www.who.int/about/accountability/results/who-results-report-2020-mtr/country-story/2020/supporting-turkish-mental-health-policy-and-service-delivery (Accessed 10 March 2024).

World Health Organization (W.H.O.). (2001). *The World health report: 2001: Mental health: new understanding, new hope.* Retrieved From: https://iris.who.int/handle/10665/42390 (Accessed 26 June 2024).

World Health Organization (W.H.O.). (2019). *The WHO special initiative for mental health (2019–2023): Universal health coverage for mental health.* https://iris.who.int/handle/10665/310981. License: CC BY-NC-SA 3.0 IGO

World Health Organization (W.H.O.). (2021). *Comprehensive mental health action plan 2013–2030.* Retrieved from: https://www.who.int/publications/i/item/9789240031029 (Accessed 26 June 2024).

World Health Organization. (2022, June 17). *Mental health: Strengthening our response.* https://www.who.int/news-room/fact-sheets/detail/mental-health-strengthening-our-response

Yardim, M. S., & Uner, S. (2018). Equity in access to care in the era of health system reforms in Turkey. *Health Policy, 122*(6), 645–651.

Young, A. S., Klap, R., Sherbourne, C. D., & Wells, K. B. (2001). The quality of care for depressive and anxiety disorders in the United States. *Archives of General Psychiatry, 58*(1), 55–61. https://doi.org/10.1001/archpsyc.58.1.55

Chapter 13

A Political Economy Analysis of Turkey's Health Transformation Programme

Jesse B. Bump and Susan Powers Sparkes

Contents

DOI: 10.4324/9781003539896-14

13.1 Introduction

Beginning in 2003, Turkey initiated a series of reforms under the Health Transformation Programme (H.T.P.) that has few – if any – parallels in scope and speed. Understanding the political economy of this process is important for the future of health reforms and Universal Health Coverage (U.H.C.) schemes.

Before the reforms, Turkey's aggregate health indicators lagged behind those of O.E.C.D. member states and other middle-income countries. Less than 70% of the population was insured, and even those with insurance did not have adequate access to timely health services (Akdag 2011). The health financing system was fragmented, with four separate insurance schemes and a "Green Card" programme for the poor, each with distinct benefit packages and access rules. Both the Ministry of Labour and Social Security and Ministry of Health (M.o.H.) were providers and financiers of the health system, and four different ministries were directly involved in the public healthcare delivery system.

Turkey's reform efforts were designed to rectify these problems, and virtually all aspects of the country's health system were affected, although the outcomes attributable to these changes have been debated even before the H.T.P. concluded. For example Atun et al. (2013) reported many positive effects of the H.T.P. and also attracted critical responses. Fourteen authors in ten letters questioned the reliability and interpretation of the data, arguing that the quality of Turkish data has declined (Aksakoglu 2014), that inequality has increased instead of decreased (Hamzaoglu 2014), that other data sources show a less favourable view of the H.T.P. (Pala 2014), that physician satisfaction has deteriorated under the H.T.P. (Tanik 2014), that the H.T.P. had the effect of privatizing healthcare (Civaner 2014; Kilic 2014), that the Atun et al. report systematically overlooked shortcomings of the H.T.P. (Aktan, Pala and Ilhan 2014), among other issues.

In part, these different views reflect the complicated political economy of health reform and wider disagreements about the future of Turkey. We focus on four political economy problems central to health reform and analyse the approaches used by the Minister of Health and his senior leadership team to overcome them. We do not analyse the effect of the reform on health indicators or outcomes; we analyse *how* the senior leadership of the M.o.H. navigated complex political economy challenges central to the reform. Our focus is on assessing these challenges in political economy terms to explicitly recognize the importance of both factors in shaping the distribution of resources for health. We discuss the basic dynamics of why these political economy challenges arise in health reform and then present our analyses of how they were overcome in the Turkish reform.

Following this introduction, we discuss our analytic methods and their limitations. We begin our analysis with an assessment of five contextual factors that were favourable to the reform, including Turkey's growing economy and young population. These factors provided a window of opportunity, of which the M.o.H. and the AK Party took advantage to adopt and implement reforms under the H.T.P. We then discuss four political economy challenges that were pivotal to the trajectory of the reform. These four challenges were identified though a review of the literature on health reform and an analysis of our interviews with stakeholders involved with Turkey's reform. We present them in roughly chronological order, although the sequences we describe overlap substantially. These challenges are (i) engaging beneficiaries to gain support for reform, (ii) managing the influence of opposing groups, (iii) managing the influence of the I.M.F. and World Bank on domestic politics, and covering the poor and unifying benefit packages. We provide an analysis of the strategies employed by the Turkish M.o.H. to overcome each of these challenges in the adoption and implementation the H.T.P. between 2003 and 2012. We then discuss some of the implications of the chosen strategies for the future of the Turkish health system and for countries studying this example.

Neither the evidence we gathered nor our method of analysis is intended to support a normative or ethical analysis of the policy design. All design choices have consequences, and where we clarify the effects of those choices it is to explain what happened and why; we do not evaluate whether policy choices were "good" or "bad" by any external standard.

13.1.1 Stakeholder Analysis

For this investigation, we employ stakeholder analysis, which is a structured method for assessing the "behaviour, intentions, interrelations, agendas, interests, and the influence or resources" of relevant actors concerning a particular policy or issue (Brugha and Varvasovszky 2000). An assessment of these factors can be used to map supporters and opponents and inform strategies for increasing the likelihood of success, for instance by identifying possible coalitions of supporters or opportunities to diminish the commitment of opponents. Stakeholder analysis typically involves specifying the players relevant to an issue – those engaged and those potentially engaged – evaluating their stance on the issue and forming judgements about their relative power to reach a calculus of political feasibility and develop strategies toward the desired aim (Reich 1995; Varvasovszky and Brugha 2000; Roberts et al. 2008).

We use stakeholder analysis retrospectively for historical analysis of the processes that govern success and failure in policymaking, as Akinci et al. (2012) have done with health reform in Turkey, and Bump and colleagues have done with diarrhoeal disease and the global health agenda (Akinci et al. 2012, Bump, Reich and Johnson 2012). In this study, we employ stakeholder analysis to assess the position, role, objectives, and strategies of relevant actors concerning the design and adoption of the H.T.P. between 2002 and 2004. We also conducted a separate stakeholder analysis on the expansion of the Green Card Program between 2003 and 2012, as it was identified as the key vehicle used to achieve U.H.C. in Turkey.

13.1.2 Data Collection and Analysis

We chose stakeholder analysis as our primary method because of its strengths in structuring and clarifying the complex politics of health reform and the welter of important contextual factors that shape the interaction of payers. We hypothesized that important stakeholders in the Turkish health reform would be roughly similar to the stakeholder groups important in other health reforms. Based on a literature review and experiences in other countries, we constructed a preliminary list of these stakeholders, which we then refined according to published articles on Turkey and advice from the General Directorate of Health Research of the M.o.H. in Turkey, at the World Bank offices in Ankara and Washington, D.C. The individuals and institutions identified through this process were asked to participate in key informant interviews. To help ensure consistency and completeness, we developed a semi-structured interview guide. We used the guide along with our stakeholder table in our interviews with informants. As we conducted our interviews and improved our understanding of the relevant actors, we adjusted the stakeholder table. In about half the interviews – particularly later ones – we shared a blank copy of the table with interviewees. Senior officials and academics agreed that the group of important actors represented on our table is accurate and reasonably complete.

We conducted our key informant interviews in Ankara and Istanbul, Turkey, in late March and early April of 2013. Interviews were conducted in English, in a mix of Turkish and

English, and in Turkish with professional interpretation, as dictated by circumstances. Each interviewee was informed of the purpose of the study, our intention to take detailed notes of each interview, and our process for handling interview data. Permission was requested to take notes and to report quotes attributed to a general affiliation. We pledged to share a draft report for comment with all interviewees and pledged not to quote any interviewee by name without obtaining specific permission. Detailed notes were taken during and immediately after each interview. Those interviewed included current and former government officials in the M.o.H., the Ministry of the Treasury, the Ministry of Labour and Social Security, the Ministry of Development Planning (formerly State Planning Organization), the Ministry of Family and Social Policy, the Turkish Statistical Agency, and Members of Parliament. We also interviewed representatives of non-governmental interest groups, including provider groups such as the Turkish Medical Association, the Turkish Midwifery Association, the Turkish Nurses Association, hospital administrators, university faculty, and university administrators. In May of 2013 in Washington, D.C., we interviewed current and former World Bank officials who had been involved with the reforms.

13.1.3 Limitations

Stakeholder analysis based on published articles and reports allows for the synthesis and evaluation of a great volume of qualitative information, but at the expense of fine detail, nuance, and contextual richness. This technique emphasizes actors at a particular point in time and is less suited to assessing structural factors, institutional procedures, and changes over time. Among the most important limitations of our methods is the choice of interviewees. In a process as large as health reform, there are many tens of millions of affected parties, and our method of selecting interviewees could not possibly capture all perspectives. Undoubtedly, we did not interview all of the most important players, nor did we cover all details in the interviews we did conduct. Our account is also limited by recall bias because it concerns events well in the past. Furthermore, our interviews were facilitated by the M.o.H. and included only central-level stakeholders and interest groups, both of which would influence the perspectives we obtained.

13.2 Contextual Overview

From the accounts of our interviewees and the written evidence we reviewed, we identified five contextual factors that were favourable to the political and economic viability of reform. First, in 2003, the M.o.H. was able to begin quickly because most components of the reform had already been developed, with existing work dating back at least to the early 1990s. Second, very high government spending on the social sectors was an important factor underlying the economic crises of 1999 and 2001, which created economic and political pressure to reform the health and pension systems. Third, the 2002 parliamentary elections delivered a legislative majority for the AK Party, ending decades of coalition governance. This majority was important because it limited the ability of other parties and special interest groups to block the process. Fourth, strong economic growth during adoption and implementation of the H.T.P. increased the fiscal space for health without imposing cuts elsewhere. Fifth, Turkey had a relatively young population with low expectations of the health sector. This meant the primary demand was for fewer and lower cost interventions than would be needed for an older population and that positive impressions of the reform were easier to create than would have been the case in a population with high expectations. These five factors were all favourable between 2003 and 2012, when the reforms took place.

13.2.1 A History of Health Reform

The AK Party acted quickly on health reform to capitalize on the popular support it enjoyed, following the 2002 elections. The M.o.H. reduced the time needed to develop its policies by drawing largely from health reform plans that had been devised and analysed throughout the 1990s. Previously, various coalition and military governments, working under World Bank loan agreements, had developed reform plans but had been unable to gain the broad support required to adopt and implement them (Tatar et al. 2011). Beginning with the 1990 Health Sector Plan, the M.o.H. and the State Planning Organization had proposed a health system model based on; (i) purchaser–provider split, (ii) universal health insurance, (iii) a rational policy for human resources and payment on the basis of performance, and (iv) the establishment of a family practitioner model (Tatar et al. 2011; Yasar 2011). These reform proposals had not been fully adopted under the coalition governments. Upon taking power in 2003, Minister Akdağ and his reform team embraced them for their own use. This reform team was in place from 2003 to 2013, when Minister Akdağ stepped down as Minister of Health (Atun et al. 2013). This team of trusted colleagues worked closely with the Minister on all aspects of the design, adoption, and implementation of the reform. According to interviews with current and former senior officials closely involved with the process, the reform team drew on the technical expertise of those who had devised these reforms and in parallel developed a politically viable communications strategy to present and promote the H.T.P.

13.2.2 Mounting Financial Pressure to Reform the Social Sectors

The financial crises of 1994 and 2000–2001 were caused in part by high government spending on the social sectors, but before the AK Party came into power, none of the coalition governments had been able to effect reform. The crises punctuated a decade of economic volatility, high and increasing public sector borrowing requirements, high interest rates, and increasing public sector deficits (Ertugrul and Selcuk 2001; International Monetary Fund 2002a, 2002b; Tatar et al. 2011). The weak economy undermined government efforts to provide resources for the health and the social security systems just as political fractiousness undermined attempts at reform. I.M.F. standby agreements highlighted inefficiencies and spending on the social security and health systems (International Monetary Fund July 2002). Prior to the 2002 parliamentary elections, ministerial leadership spearheaded by Minister of Economic Affairs and Treasury Kemal Derviş developed plans to address deficit issues, but the weak coalition governments could muster neither the leadership nor the political support to fully implement reforms (Boulton and Wolf 2002; Akyüz and Boratav 2003). The I.M.F. was concerned that the social security deficit was growing unsustainably, which in retrospect seems to have been accurate. The social security deficit grew from 1.9% of G.D.P. in 2000 to more than 4% of G.D.P. by 2005, the last year before reforms took effect in 2006 (World Bank 2006). Upon taking power, the AK Party inherited urgent problems in social security and health spending and also was bound by commitments made by previous governments with the I.M.F. to reduce government spending and stabilize the economy.

13.2.3 High Public Support for Reform

A wave of anti-government sentiments and public support for reform were important factors in the AK Party's victory in the 2002 elections. As political outsiders, the AK Party drew support from public dissatisfaction with the inaction of coalition governments, a series of high-profile corruption scandals, and economic instability, including the crisis of 2000–2001 (Heper 2003).

Crucially, the legislative majority won by the AK Party enabled it to pass reforms unilaterally, obviating the need to broker agreement between coalition partners.

After coming to power, the AK Party was under intense public pressure to act on two fronts. One was to reform the economy. The other was to improve health service delivery, particularly in rural and poorer regions of the country where the party's political base was centred. Inaction on either of these two fronts carried the risk of backlash in future elections (Özbudun 2006; Baris, Mollahaliloglu and Aydin 2011). Over the ten years of AK Party control covered by this report, health became an increasingly crucial element of the party's political success. According to interviews with current and former senior party strategists, they initially viewed health as a way to address equity issues and send resources to their political base. As the magnitude of problems in the health sector became apparent, they began to appreciate how many citizens were in need. They also became increasingly aware of how many votes could be garnered by improving peoples' access to quality health services. According to preliminary calculations, as many as 20 million people lacked basic services. Once the AK Party understood this need as votes in play, the party put its full weight behind the H.T.P.'s prompt adoption and implementation. As one interviewee formerly working as a senior strategist at the M.o.H. characterized the sequence, "In the beginning the politicians chose health, but by the end health chose the politicians".

13.2.4 Increased Fiscal Space for Health

Favourable economic conditions increased the availability of resources for health sector, which the AK Party used to fund and implement the H.T.P. Enabling much of this expansion of fiscal space for health was strong overall economic growth that increased G.D.P. by two-thirds in real terms, and real G.D.P. per capita by 70%, from US$5,952 to US$8,493 between 2002 and 2011 (Figure 13.1) (World Bank 2012). As the economy grew overall, the government also increased the share of G.D.P. spent on health, 5.4% to 6.7% between 2002 and 2011 (World Health Organization 2013). Calculated over the same period on a per capita basis in constant 2005 dollars (PPP), health spending grew by 265% (World Bank 2012).

13.2.5 Favourable Demographics and Low Expectations

The young Turkish population required relatively basic, primary care services as compared to expensive, hospital-based treatments for older populations. In 2002, 30% of Turkey's population

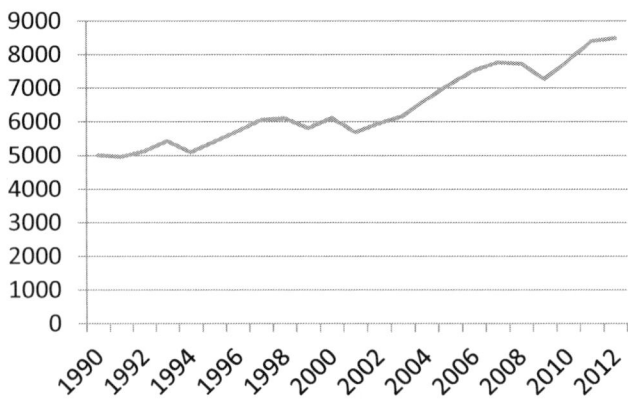

Figure 13.1 G.D.P. per capita in Turkey, 1990–2012 (constant 2005 US$).

was under 15 years of age, and only 6% was over 65 years of age (World Bank 2012). In addition to these favourable demographics, after years of failed attempts to reform the public health system, Turkish citizens had low expectations for the delivery of even these basic services. In 2003, only 39.5% of the population indicated that they were satisfied with the quality of care (OECD, WHO and World Bank 2008; Bleich, Özaltin and Murray 2009). This scenario gave the M.o.H. an opportunity to make quick gains in patient satisfaction with relatively small improvements to the system.

13.3 Political Economy Challenges in the Turkish H.T.P. (2003–2012)

Health reform is a politically charged process because it involves the reallocation of resources and responsibilities. Common goals of health reform are to increase equity, improve access for the poor, and to establish some minimum basket of services for all citizens. These goals all require the redistribution of resources, which raises the prospect that the process will generate winners and losers. Typically, groups that are well-off before the reform perceive discussions of policy change as potential threats to their benefits. This leads to a collective action problem because although a reformed system could become more efficient and provide more benefits for everyone, it is typically contested by small, well-organized groups whose interests would be impacted by a reform, including physicians, other providers, and groups with generous benefits such as civil servants. Those who have the most to gain from reform are those who receive few or no services, but these groups tend to be unorganized and unengaged in the reform process, even if they are large in number. As Mancur Olson (1971) wrote, a collective action problem arises because "rational, self-interested individuals will not act to achieve their common or group interests", unless the number of individuals in a group is small, or there is some incentive that makes individuals act in their common interest. Small groups will act towards a collective goal because they face relatively low costs to organize due to more uniform, individual interests and will reap high potential benefits per capita. Whereas large groups will face relatively high costs when seeking to organize for collective action, the potential benefits per capita may be small because they are distributed across many members.

In the subsections given next, we discuss four political economy challenges, including engaging beneficiaries to build support for reforms, managing the influence of opposing interests, managing the influence of the I.M.F. and World Bank on domestic politics, and covering the poor and unifying benefit systems.

13.3.1 Challenge #1: Engaging Beneficiaries to Build Support for Reforms

The basic political economy of reform favours opponents rather than potential beneficiaries because the costs tend to be concentrated on well-organized groups with high access to political and economic resources, which they can use to impede, dilute, or otherwise influence the process in their favour. By contrast, although potential beneficiaries tend to be far more numerous, they have few economic or political resources and are not likely to be engaged or organized in support of reforms. Successfully adopting and implementing reform require strategies for overcoming this challenge. In most settings, opponents include the urban elite: Physicians and other health workers whose rights, responsibilities, and pay are often directly affected by reform and formal sector workers, whose taxes can be used to finance services for the poor and whose benefits might be reduced accordingly. Potential beneficiaries are usually poor, reside in rural areas, and are underserved by the health system. The lopsided distribution of political and economic resources favours reform opponents in almost every way. A central challenge of reform is to somehow change or overcome this imbalance to generate sufficient popular support to overcome any remaining opposition.

In the Turkish Case: An important aspect of M.o.H.'s overall strategy was to quickly build support among the intended beneficiaries of reform, whose large numbers represented a potentially enormously powerful political force if organized behind the H.T.P. According to a World Bank official who developed estimates of the population in need, M.o.H. officials and other AK Party officials interrupted his slide show with applause when he presented a figure of 20 million citizens without insurance coverage. Although he initially believed that the appreciation was for his analysis, he later realized that the audience's enthusiasm reflected a new appreciation of the electoral potential of health reform. Those with no or limited access were the bulk of Turkey's citizens, living in the East and South in smaller cities and rural areas. Their support was important to the AK Party in general and would be required for more difficult aspects of the reform, which urban elites and organized interest groups would oppose, according to political analysis commissioned by the M.o.H. (Rossetti 2004). The same analysis also showed that in Turkey's recent past, political parties attempting reform had faced a backlash in subsequent elections; to avoid this fate, the AK Party would have to demonstrate results before the next general election, expected in 2007.

The M.o.H. built public support reform very quickly by focusing its early efforts on highly visible changes to the existing health system, acting first in the areas with the least services. Many interviewees with experience in the reform related this emphasis on immediate and noticeable improvements with the dual purpose of improving service delivery and patient satisfaction, while bolstering the political viability of the H.T.P. A recent World Health Organization report discusses the Minister of Health's approach as similar to how a team of medical doctors treats a trauma patient, first treating the most life-threatening problems before moving onto systemic and long-term issues (Johansen and Guisset 2012). For instance, among the first changes ordered by the senior leadership team was the abolishment of the unpopular practice of holding patients in facilities until their bills were paid. Holding patients as pawns until families could settle bills no doubt deterred some care-seeking, but this practice was employed *after* care was delivered, meaning that its primary consequences were probably in creating extremely negative feelings toward the health system and imposing financial distress on families. Ending the practice showed sensitivity to the moral and political dimensions of healthcare and not to the medical issues alone, as implied by the trauma team analogy. We emphasize this point because generating support for reforms inside the short election cycle required changes that could improve popular impressions immediately.

In fact, regardless of their public rhetoric on trauma teams, the senior leadership of the M.o.H. realized that citizen impressions of the health system were formed mainly by primary care experiences, rather than in secondary or tertiary care, according to the current and former officials who were engaged in formulating the H.T.P. strategy. Initial reform efforts sought to improve these impressions, for instance by refurbishing waiting rooms, conducting outreach activities to make patients feel welcome, and converting break rooms to exam rooms to increase the capacity to deliver services. As one senior M.o.H. official related as a generalized example, prior to the reform, a health facility might have had a staff of 30 health workers, but care would be provided in only three rooms. Other rooms were dedicated to other purposes, including separate break rooms for each type of employee – physicians, nurses, technicians, and others. Some were used as private offices, but M.o.H. calculations estimated that only 30% of employees were working regularly. These calculations indicated that far more of the demand for health services could be met in public facilities if the existing employees were encouraged to work there, and existing infrastructure were reoriented around care delivery as its primary purpose. The M.o.H. therefore concentrated initially on making more efficient use of its existing resources, which it could do quickly, and postponed the slower, more costly task of building new facilities. To overcome the resistance of some health workers, the Minister of Health and his team personally visited facilities and directly ordered the consolidation of break rooms and other space-saving measures to increase care delivery capacity.

The senior leadership also rapidly expanded emergency transport services, increasing the number of ambulances and extending the system's reach with specially equipped fixed- and rotary-wing aircraft to serve remote areas and afford fast transport for critical cases. A senior M.o.H. official involved in the design and implementation of the H.T.P. estimated that these enhancements led to three- to five-fold increase in the number of emergency transport vehicles in the country over the first ten years of reform. Again, this was a choice made on several grounds, only one of which was the technical consideration of bringing more people to care in times of need. Senior officials stressed to us that the ambulances were powerful, eminently visible symbols of a health system that cared for its citizens. Particularly for rural citizens covered for the first time, the emergency transport system was a compelling demonstration of the responsiveness of the M.o.H. and the AK Party. An interviewee involved in these policy decisions described the initial phase as capacity building. He said the leadership in the early stages did not want to build new infrastructure and focused instead on increasing capacity of the existing system.

These relatively simple changes improved public support for the reform and helped create the political momentum for more difficult, large-scale changes to the system planned for future years. Rapid and publicly visible changes to improve the accessibility of the system appear to be reflected in the percentage of people reporting problems, making an appointment for an examination or analysis, which dropped from 59.59% in 2003 to 29.30 in 2005 (Turkish Statistical Institute 2003–2012). Over the same period – the first two years of the H.T.P. – citizen satisfaction with health services overall rose from 46.17% to 55.27% (Turkish Statistical Institute 2003–2012). These satisfaction rates were reflected by an electoral support for the AK Party in both the 2007 and 2010 parliamentary elections. In these elections, the AK Party continued to build on its electoral majority by placing its health reform achievements as a centrepiece of the party platform (Bryant 2010).

13.3.2 Challenge #2: Managing the Influence of Opposing Interest Groups

Interest groups, including physicians and beneficiary groups, tend to exercise strong influence on reforms because they are well organized, have high access to political and economic resources, and are usually closely engaged in the process because it directly affects their interests. Physicians tend to view government insurance programmes as a threat to their autonomy, and therefore they are likely to oppose such reforms using their political influence and their authority within the health system (Immergut 1990). Trade unions and formal sector workers typically have health benefits under pre-reform systems. Often, health reform threatens their interests because extending coverage to low-income groups means redistribution, which might be expressed as a reduction in their benefits or a diversion of their funds. For instance formal sector workers in Ghana were initially opposed to health reform in 2003 because an increased access for the poor was partly funded through a 2.5 percentage point diversion of their pension contributions (Rajkotia 2007). Organized beneficiary groups also tend to oppose the integration of other health insurance schemes into their own because theirs is typically the best funded, and unification therefore means a dilution of resources available for their uses. Unifying benefit systems can be desirable from an efficiency perspective because it has the potential to simplify administration and reduce overhead, which would free more resources for the provision of services. But the political economy of unification is extremely difficult because its redistributive elements impose immediate costs on small, organized, and powerful interest groups. On the other side, the benefits are abstract, would occur in the future, and would accrue to the poor, who, in most cases, are not organized to provide support because they have few economic and political resources and are not likely to be engaged in the process. Organized interest groups often pose significant opposition to reforms, as they have in the United States and Mexico, for example (Hacker 1998; Lakin 2010).

In the Turkish Case: In the initial stages of the H.T.P., the Minister of Health and his senior leadership team identified groups important to the reform and developed strategies to persuade or overcome those expected to oppose it. Plans to manage this opposition were then incorporated into the reform strategy. After delineating stakeholder groups, the Minister of Health and his senior leadership team began to engage opposition groups to gauge the possibilities to win their support. In some cases, the reform plans were adapted to accommodate concerns. In other cases, the M.o.H. and AK Party leadership worked to neutralize the influence of opponents by splintering their support or delegitimizing their views.

Political analysis played an important role in the management of opposition groups. Several interviewees directly involved with the reform mentioned the influence of a stakeholder analysis report and a then-recently published book, *Getting Health Reform Right*, which stresses the importance of politics in determining both the trajectory and outcome of reform (Rossetti 2004; Roberts et al. 2008). The authors note that "astute policy developers begin political analysis early in the policy cycle". The M.o.H. also had the book translated into Turkish so it would be more accessible to a greater proportion of its staff. The stakeholder analysis was commissioned in 2003 to provide a roadmap to the politics of the reform in Turkey and a guide to dealing with opposition. The report analysed the positions and influence of stakeholders involved, assessed future electoral ramifications, and proposed strategies to manage interest groups during the implementation phase of the reform (Rossetti 2004). The report identified public providers, members of the social security institutions, and the central government bureaucracy and civil servants as key actors opposed to the H.T.P. By understanding the influence opponents were expected to have and the reasons for their positions, the government could plan how to manage the politics of policy adoption and implementation.

Trade unions were one of the most influential beneficiary groups opposed to reforms. Senior Government staff, including representatives from the Ministry of Labour and Social Security, held a long series of meetings with union representatives to discuss how the reforms would affect the benefits of their membership. The M.o.H. prepared numerous analyses to forecast benefits under various assumptions to reassure representatives that in no case would benefits decrease under the H.T.P. and that in most cases benefits would increase. Several informants involved in designing the reform reported that the inter-ministerial working group had initially planned a basic benefit package with options for supplementary care. However, as the group continued its discussions, equity emerged as an increasingly important consideration. In its final form, the reform's long-term goal objective was to provide all citizens with the same benefits as retired civil servants, who had the most generous of all pre-reform packages. This strategy dramatically increased the resources required for reform, but it helped ensure that most organized beneficiary groups would not oppose the reform. To address financial sustainability, the reform included cost control in the form of a family physician gatekeeper and capitation system. These mechanisms were expected to reduce the potential for physician-induced demand and limit overuse of secondary and tertiary care. However, the M.o.H. was only able to implement the capitation system. The gatekeeper function was not implemented due to public opposition, as well as a shortage of family physicians available in the country. Once beneficiary groups understood the benefits they would gain, they began supporting the reform and influenced its design to enhance their benefits.

A second influential opposition group was white-collar civil servants, who opposed the reform for two general reasons. First, as the beneficiaries of the most generous entitlement package, they feared that reform would diminish their benefits. Second, most of these elite civil servants were secularists and tended to oppose the AK Party politically. They were also concerned about the implications of the concurrent social security reform, particularly for the retirement age, which stood at 48 years of age for women and 52 years of age for men. The M.o.H. and Ministry of Labour and Social Security leadership first deployed a persuasion strategy in an attempt to convince the white-collar civil servants that their benefits would not decrease. But the attempts were not successful, and elite civil servants appealed to President Sezer to block the reform. To overcome their opposition, the M.o.H. and Ministry of Labour and Social Security decided to exempt all existing civil servants from reform, agreeing to apply new rules only to those hired in the future.

Health workers are typically among the most influential groups in health reform because they are called upon to deliver health services, are well organized, have an influential position in society, and usually have access to political resources (Immergut 1992). The role of health workers in reform was identified in the political analysis report and likely was intuitive to the Minister and senior officials because almost all of them had long experience in the health system. The Minister and his team engaged in dialogue with health workers in the early stages of the H.T.P. and devised strategies to manage their interests. The participation of health workers in the planned reforms was essential to improving service delivery, as health workers are the ones who actually deliver the services. But one of the biggest problems in increasing delivery was a shortage of trained professionals; for instance Turkey's ratio of physicians per population was only about one-third the EU average when the H.T.P. began (Tatar et al. 2011). For the reform to succeed, the workforce would have to operate at higher capacity. The M.o.H. provided incentives for health workers to deliver more services by linking pay with the quantity of services provided and patient satisfaction. This system dramatically increased the salaries of physicians providing services in the public sector. The pay-for-performance scheme was used as a way to allocate additional pay to physicians and nurses and had the additional advantage of avoiding the cumbersome bureaucracy associated with adjusting pay under the formal civil service regulations. The M.o.H. also brought more delivery capacity into the public sector facilities by ending so-called dual practice arrangements, under which physicians would not only spend some of their time in public facilities but also see patients in private practices. The increased pay available under the pay-for-performance scheme was intended to compensate physicians for the remuneration they could no longer earn in private practice, draw them into public service full time, and incentivize them to provide more care. In the view of senior officials we interviewed, the pay-for-performance scheme was an important motivating factor for health workers who have faced heavy workloads under the increased demand created by the H.T.P. Some interviewees also referenced the policy as a critical factor in decreasing dual practice even before the M.o.H. was able to pass the Law on Full-Time Practice, which prohibited M.o.H. physicians from also working in the private sector.

The pay-for-performance system pleased physicians primarily engaged in service delivery, but it did not change the opposition of all physicians or other health workers. With groups that remained opposed, the M.o.H. worked to marginalize their influence. These opponents included the Turkish Medical Association (T.M.A.) and the Turkish Nurses Association. The government accomplished the reform without the support of these powerful groups by fracturing their membership and swaying popular opinion against their leadership. Remaining opposed were the medical elite – far fewer in number and limited to specialized facilities in major cities. Although the membership of the T.M.A. was unified in opposition at the beginning of the reform, much of its membership was primarily engaged in service delivery and became supportive because of the incentives available under pay for performance. The organization's leadership, those in specialized roles, and members of the academic elite remained opposed but were relatively few in number. A senior T.M.A. official observed that the "30,000" specialists in staunch opposition had had little influence on the reforms, citing vast public support for the Ministry's plans and publicity campaigns against the medical elite. Our interviews with senior officials at these organizations and in academic medicine revealed intense dissatisfaction with the reform and a deep distrust of the M.o.H. leadership. As the pay-for-performance system does not include allowances for teaching or research, those interested in these activities felt personally punished in the assessment of those we interviewed. These people expressed dissatisfaction with personnel allocation policies, as well. After graduating from medical school, all new physicians perform two years of public service. Before the reforms, the best students with academic interests were assigned to leading medical schools as assistant professors. But under the reforms, nearly all graduates are now assigned to public facility roles, to M.o.H. hospitals, or to new medical schools with close relationships to the M.o.H. As a result, there are few younger faculty trained in what were formerly the most prestigious places. Specialist physicians we interviewed explained their discontent with a long list of problems. Because of M.o.H. cost controls, they are not always able to procure the supplies they need to serve patients, they said. Because the M.o.H. scheduling system makes appointments that are 15 minutes in length, there is too little time to adequately diagnose problems or provide lifestyle guidance, we were told. Because of these and other problems, many faculty have left – some for private practice, some for other countries, and some to retirement. The capacity to perform complex procedures at leading medical centres has been severely reduced, we were told. Our interviewees also expressed concerns for the quality of care under the H.T.P. because quality assurance rests on patient satisfaction, but in many cases, patients are not well informed about what care is appropriate. As complaints from patients to the M.o.H. constitute a serious issue for providers, the physicians we interviewed expressed concerns for the loss of autonomy and a compromised doctor–patient relationship.

To neutralize the threat to the reforms posed by opposition groups, the AK Party created a new union of health workers to draw supporters away from existing professional associations and undermine their support base. By creating factions within health workers, they reduced the power of T.M.A. and Turkish Nurses Association to act as a united voice for all providers. A similar strategy was employed to counter resistance from Y.Ö.K. – the organization responsible for supervising all Turkish universities and which, at the beginning of the H.T.P., was still controlled by appointees of previous governments and distrusted the AK Party. Interviewees from elite universities voiced concern that the reforms had channelled resources away from their institutions, as a political tool by the AK Party leadership to undermine their influence. The government worked around this opposition until 2008, when the newly elected President Gül was able to appoint a new head of YÖK friendly to the AK Party. These tactics allowed the M.o.H. and AK Party to overcome the resistance from previously strong interest groups that remained in staunch opposition to the reform.

The M.o.H. ensured that the central components of the H.T.P. were adopted and implemented by engaging those groups likely to oppose the reforms. Some they persuaded to support the reforms and others they neutralized or overpowered.

13.3.3 Challenge #3: The I.M.F., the World Bank, and Domestic Politics

By choice or necessity, many countries engage the I.M.F. and World Bank in policy reforms, but the relationship between these institutions and domestic political economy processes can be complicated. The power dynamics can be especially complex at times of crisis when countries are at the most need of assistance. The I.M.F.'s role in economic stabilization and fiscal reform as a lender of last resort gives it very high political and economic power. The World Bank's engagement is particularly notable in social sector reform because of its strengths in project design and implementation, as well as its role in discussions between various ministries, including both those that provide finances and those that deliver services. Both international institutions become involved in the policy reform process through their lending activities and technical expertise. Middle-income countries can strategically use financial and technical resources available from both the I.M.F. and World Bank. However, there is the potential for tension between the policies and advice of the international institutions and the direction of the domestic policy agenda.

In the Turkish Case: The Turkish Government sought support from the World Bank and I.M.F. over the course of the H.T.P. (2003–2012). Both institutions were closely engaged in the Turkish economy and health sector when the AK Party took office in late 2002, including through I.M.F. standby agreements relating to the economic crises of 2000/2001 (International Monetary Fund July 2002). As part of these agreements, Turkey had pledged to reduce inflation and bring its public sector debt under control (Alper and Alper 2003). The M.o.H. had a long-standing relationship with the World Bank dating to the first health policy loan agreement in 1990. These ties strengthened under the AK Party government; in 2004, the M.o.H. signed a US$ 75M loan agreement for hiring technical expertise in the design and implementation of the H.T.P. (Republic of Turkey and International Bank for Reconstruction and Development 2004). The M.o.H. was able to benefit from the financial and technical resources as well as crucial political support for the Washington institutions, while maintaining its own leadership over the full course of the reform's design, adoption, and implementation. The M.o.H. drew on the Bank's support to improve the reforms' legitimacy in domestic politics, and the AK Party government relied on the I.M.F.'s approval of domestic budgets and financial affairs to help calm markets at home and abroad.

AK Party leadership and several ministries relied on I.M.F. standby agreements to stabilize the economy and public support by I.M.F. representatives to reassure financial markets. As part of these agreements, I.M.F. representatives were intimately involved in policy discussions that surrounded expenditures and revenues. One of Turkey's most important pledges under the I.M.F. standby agreements was to control social sector spending. A major part of the underlying fiscal problem was uncertainty that had resulted from several years of incorrectly low forecasts and subsequent actual expenses that were far higher, which led to budget overruns and large deficits. The Minister of Health and his team worked to convince I.M.F. officials of the fiscal soundness of the health reform proposal by presenting detailed forecasting models of the potential for long-term cost saving under a U.H.C. system that promoted primary care, even if some short-run costs might be higher. These discussions could be highly contentious because of divergent interpretations of the forecasts and because of the potential conflict between providing universal coverage and reducing the country's high public sector debt. In these discussions, Minister Akdağ relied on the strong support of the Prime Minister for the H.T.P. to advance the reform proposal despite reservations by some parties.

The M.o.H. had a long-standing relationship with the World Bank and continued to work closely with it over the course of the reform. The Minister and his team collaborated with World Bank officials in designing and implementing the H.T.P. The well-established working relationship with the World Bank on health system improvements allowed the Minister of Health and the inter-ministerial working group to quickly access flexible, external resources as needed. Working group members interviewed for this study recalled that the Government agreed to a relatively small World Bank loan (US$ 75M) specifically to gain access to the expertise of the Bank's staff and its international network of consultants. The capacities gained this way were augmented by hiring into the Ministry many of the consultants who had worked for the World Bank in support of health projects in the 1990s. Many of our interviewees recalled the importance of advice and strategies contributed from these sources, including about a dozen background papers funded by Japan via a World Bank trust fund. One of these papers analysed the politics of the proposed reform, the stakeholders involved, its future electoral ramifications, and proposed strategies to manage interest groups during the implementation phase of the reform (Rossetti 2004). The M.o.H. used the loan proceeds to commission reports and implement programmes to support the design and implementation of the H.T.P. with much greater flexibility than would have been possible with government revenues.

Interviewee accounts referenced the largely, positive working relationship between the M.o.H. and World Bank throughout the reform process. However, at times, M.o.H. plans did not fit within typical World Bank timelines or processes or procedures. In these cases, staff members of the M.o.H. and the World Bank worked together to find mutually acceptable solutions. For instance Minister Akdağ proposed hiring teams of Field Coordinators to directly manage the implementation of the H.T.P. in each of Turkey's 80 provinces. The purpose of these teams would be to communicate directly with the Minister, providing him with detailed and timely information from the front lines of the reform. As recounted by several interviewees directly familiar with the establishment of the Field Coordinating Teams, the hiring process was politically complex. Each team was to be led by an advisor personally known and trusted by the Minister, a requirement designed to limit local influence on the information, which might have downplayed problems or overly emphasized progress. The Minister was particularly concerned about obtaining accurate information to ensure that local committees were distributing Green Cards and following other directives according to M.o.H. policy. This was potentially contentious because it asserted M.o.H. authority over a process that had in some cases been a local patronage opportunity.

But there were significant challenges to hiring the Field Coordinators as envisioned by the Minister. First, he needed to entice trusted staff to take leave from their current jobs in Ankara to work in outlying provinces. Second, he needed a way to ensure that Field Coordinators would still have jobs available to them when their tenure was over. Third, he needed to work within World Bank procurement guidelines to place both qualified and loyal staff in these positions. The basic tension arose between the Turkish government regulation that civil service slots could be held open indefinitely only for employees leaving for international agencies and the World Bank's standard guidance against sole-source, or non-competitive contracting, which was preferred by the Ministry because of its concern for hiring trusted and loyal Field Coordinators. Ultimately to introduce the Field Coordinators into the health system and overcome these obstacles, the Minister and his leadership team succeeded in negotiating these bureaucratic constraints with a creative mixture of funding and hiring through different multilateral agencies. Putting loyal staff in a front-line monitoring role extended the Ministry's centralized authority deep into the field with accurate information from the local level, and a much greater ability to intervene when complexities or problem threatened the reform's progress.

The Minister of Health and his team learned from the history of interactions between the I.M.F., World Bank, and the Turkish Government to use the institutions' valuable resources to their utmost advantage. Their leadership skills are demonstrated by their resolute commitment to the central objectives of the H.T.P. and figuring out mechanisms to effectively achieve them, as well as their willingness to accept and benefit from the technical expertise of the World Bank.

13.3.4 Challenge #4: Covering the Poor and Unifying Benefit Systems

Many countries have attempted to create U.H.C. systems by expanding entitlement programmes for low-income groups, but in recent years, only Turkey has succeeded in integrating the entitlement programmes into a unified system covering all citizens. Ghana, Mexico, and Thailand, for instance, have all undertaken reforms to move toward U.H.C. These countries have all been successful in expanding coverage, particularly for the poor. But merging the subsidized programmes for low-income households with the existing schemes for formal sector workers has remained elusive (Hughes and Leethongdee 2007; Agyepong and Adjei 2008; Knaul et al. 2012). Combining coverage plans for the poor with those for formal sector employees is very difficult because it represents an enormous challenge of political economy. Formal sector workers tend to be well organized and influential politically and usually enjoy the most comprehensive benefit package, at least in part because they usually contribute the most resources to the system. Formal sector workers therefore have high economic and political power. Reform usually threatens their interests because the redistribution required to cover low-income groups implies a potential reduction in their own benefits and/or the use of some of their contributions for others. Formal sector beneficiaries have resisted integration efforts for these reasons. Low-income groups whose members stand to benefit from reform tend to have relatively little economic power and are usually not engaged in the electoral process, where their large numbers could constitute substantial political power. This generic political economy is thus very unfavourable for reform because its likely opponents have direct interests at stake and have access to political and economic resources, while potential proponents are likely to be unorganized, disengaged, and have limited access to either political or economic resources.

In the Turkish Case: To expand coverage and move towards a unified U.H.C. system, the M.o.H. worked around obstacles to postpone or avoid potential opposition. We highlight three important steps: First, the M.o.H. decided to use the existing Green Card Program as its primary vehicle for scaling up coverage for low-income households in part because modifying a programme did not require parliamentary approval, whereas starting a new programme would have. The M.o.H. simply adapted the Green Card Program to fit the policy objectives of the H.T.P. under its own authority. Second, the Minister of Health and his senior leadership team brought the Green Card Program under the Ministry's auspices so they could control it completely. Third, they stimulated demand for the Green Card Program by expanding the benefits' package, increasing the number of Green Cards in circulation, and making concurrent supply-side improvements. Throughout this process, the M.o.H. carefully monitored the programme's progress in implementation. This progress towards expanding coverage was embraced by low-income households in rural areas of Turkey. As the benefit package expanded and the cost of the programme grew, both factors reduced the potential for opposition to the M.o.H.'s plan for an integrated social security system. Potential opposition from existing beneficiaries declined the discrepancies between benefit plans was shrinking. Potential opposition from and financing authorities declined because the marginal cost of expanding benefits was also shrinking.

Once U.H.C. was identified as the primary objective of the H.T.P., senior leaders at the M.o.H. debated several policy options before settling on the Green Card, according to several interviewees who participated in the process. They chose to work with an existing programme, rather than creating an entirely new scheme for low-income households, which would have required legislative approval. The Green Card Program was chosen because it was the only part of earlier attempts to create a universal, general health insurance scheme that had been passed by the parliament and implemented. But before the H.T.P., the Green Card Program had significant limitations. It provided coverage for low-income households only for inpatient expenses incurred in public facilities, and it was widely regarded as unsuccessful because of corrupt enrolment procedures, a limited benefit package, and poor public service quality (Karadeniz 2012; Menon, Mollahaliloglu and Postolovska 2013). Estimates based on the 2003 Household Budget Survey show that there were only 2.5 million beneficiaries, and of those households enrolled, only 31% were in the poorest decile (Aran and Hentschel 2012). But these problems aside, the Green Card Program did exist in law and did operate, even if imperfectly, both of which gave the Minister of Health and his leadership team an avenue for delivering services, expanding entitlements, advancing their policy goals, and generating public support without having to enter the parliamentary process and sustain the attendant delays.

As a second step, the M.o.H. drew on the strong support of the Prime Minister to bring the budget and administration of the Green Card Program under its own auspices. Prior to the reforms, Social Solidarity Foundations under the Prime Minister's Office ran the Green Card Program. In 2004, the M.o.H. requested direct control of the programme so that it could then oversee its expansion efforts and work to address bottlenecks in implementation without needing approval from other ministerial entities. Because the Social Solidarity Foundations were under the Prime Minister's control, he was able to easily transfer the Green Card Program to the M.o.H. based on the Minister's request. Interviewees involved in this process reported that a first step in gaining administrative control of the Green Card Program was to replace the "Green Cards" with new "green booklets" as a mechanism to make all enrolees report to local authorities, where they could be counted.

The M.o.H. gained administrative and budgetary control of the Green Card Program in 2004; however, they avoided creating local opposition by initially refraining from changing any enrolment procedures, which would have affected patronage relationships at the local level between local committees and enrolees. Local committees continued to be responsible for processing applications; however, the M.o.H. had direct monitoring and reporting mechanisms to ensure that their policy objectives were followed. In doing so, they avoided opposition from local committees, which were accustomed to making eligibility determinations. Instead, the government waited and incorporated eligibility determination into the Ministry of Family and Social Policies' IT system in 2012 only after enrolment abuses arose in the public discourse (Hurriyet Daily News 2010).

Once the administrative arrangements for Green Card reform were in place, the M.o.H. worked to increase demand for the programme by expanding the benefits' package and improving the public sector delivery system. The M.o.H. expanded the benefit package, adding coverage for outpatient services in 2004 and coverage for outpatient medicines in 2005 (Menon, Mollahaliloglu and Postolovska 2013). The M.o.H. needed to increase demand for the Green Card Program to power the enrolment required to raise coverage rates and ultimately to secure the requisite electoral support for the reforms from low-income households residing in rural areas. Many key informants described an explicit M.o.H. policy to distribute as many Green Cards as possible to bring more people into the health system. This was both technically and politically expedient because it provided more benefits to citizens, empowered local committees to facilitate the process, and increased the electoral support for the AK Party among its base. Their efforts to stimulate demand proved successful as the number of Green Card holders increased from 2.5 million in 2003 to 9.1 million in 2011 (Figure 13.2) (Hurst, Scherer and Chakraborty 2008; Ministry of Health Turkey 2012).

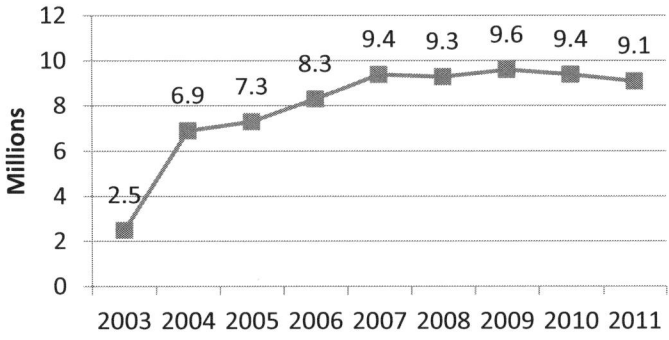

Figure 13.2   Number of Green Card beneficiaries, 2003–2011.

These expansion efforts required additional funding. A member of the senior leadership team reported that by gradually expanding both the benefits and beneficiaries of the Green Card Program, the M.o.H. was able to desensitize those within the government responsible for financing the reform. But viewed over several years, expenditure on the Green Card Program increased dramatically – from 3.8% of public health expenditures in 2003 to 10.8% in 2007 and 8.4% in 2009. Green Card expenditures as a percent of total public expenditures increased from 0.4% in 2003 to 1% in 2009, and from 0.2% of G.D.P. in 2003 to 0.4% of G.D.P. in 2009 (Menon, Mollahaliloglu and Postolovska 2013).

Concurrent with efforts to maximize Green Card enrolment, the M.o.H. also invested in improvements to the public health delivery system. It focused its efforts on rural and poorer areas of the country, where Green Card eligible individuals resided. In an interview, Minister Akdağ explained that providing financial protection for poor households was not enough and that the M.o.H. also had to ensure they had access to health services (Baris, Mollahaliloglu and Aydin 2011; Johansen and Guisset 2012). The family medicine programme, conditional cash transfers for maternal health services, pay for performance scheme, and merging the S.S.K. hospitals into the M.o.H. system were all reforms that directly benefitted Green Card enrolees. These supply-side efforts, combined with the expanded benefit package, were used as enticements to increase the demand for the Green Card Program.

By the time the Ministry of Labour and Social Security and M.o.H. required approval by the Turkish Parliament to merge the social security institutions and create a unified social security scheme in 2006, the M.o.H. had already greatly expanded the benefits and increased the number of Green Card beneficiaries. Despite this progress, unification and integration efforts were still delayed. First, the Ministry of Labour and Social Security and M.o.H. had to overcome a Constitutional Court challenge to the unified system from President Sezer, who generally opposed AK Party initiatives, on the grounds that it would disadvantage civil servants. Once provisions were made to ensure that current civil servants could keep their existing benefits, delays in integrating the Green Card Program were caused by difficulties in creating a rigorous means-tested eligibility determination system. Several interviewees reported abuse in the enrolment system and the lack of capacity within the M.o.H. and Ministry of Labour and Social Security to effectively implement an income-determination system. There had also been popular backlash against the Green Card Program based on news reports of abuse and over-enrolment. The M.o.H. responded with promises to reform the system and conduct more rigorous income tests (Hurriyet Daily News 2010). Interviewees reported that in response to this public outcry, the M.o.H. began a formal review of Green Card enrolees to reduce abuse in the system and worked to ensure that premium support was provided only to eligible households.

By the time actual integration of Green Card holders into the General Health Insurance System commenced in January 2012, the hard work of increasing benefits, expanding coverage, and standardizing enrolment systems had already been done. On 1 January 2012, the newly formed Ministry of Family and Social Policies took over the responsibility for determining the eligibility for premium support from the M.o.H. (Menon, Mollahaliloglu and Postolovska 2013). Green Card beneficiaries had 12 months to reapply to receive premium support, which led to the official abolishment of the Green Card Program. In the first year of the new system, 7.5 million people were eligible for full premium support, and an additional 4.5 million were eligible for reduced premium payments (Ministry of Family and Social Policy May 2013). Under this new system, the Ministry of Family and Social Policy determines eligibility, the Ministry of Finance pays the premiums for beneficiaries directly to the Social Security Institution, the Social Security Institution pays for the health services, and the M.o.H. delivers the health services to the beneficiaries.

This incremental approach to expanding coverage and unifying all health coverage schemes allowed the M.o.H. to provide benefits and get the support of low-income households for the health reform without stirring up opposition from financing agents over the programme's fiscal implications. As we discuss under contextual factors, it certainly helped that the Turkish economy grew during the reforms. Exempting the highest entitlement group from reform neutralized their opposition. Resistance from other high-benefits groups lessened and then ceased as the reformed benefits expanded to narrow and eventually close the gap with the best plans.

13.4 Discussion

In this section, we discuss some of the most significant strategies used by the M.o.H. to overcome the four political economy challenges as identified through our interviews and in our subjective judgement. We organize our discussion according to the political economy challenges we identified earlier. In addition to this, we discuss four areas in which design and implementation choices were likely to create challenges.

13.4.1 Implementation Strategies

Building support among beneficiaries: To build support among beneficiaries of the reform, M.o.H. leadership prioritized service delivery improvements for underserved populations over investments in other areas of importance to the health system. For instance the quality of care, research, teaching, and specialized medicine did not receive the attention or resources dedicated to primary care. In the short run, the redistribution of resources was designed to address inequities in the system and build political support for the reforms, although the relative neglect of specialists and academic medical centres poses grave risks to the future of the system, as we mention in the next section. Building support among beneficiaries required improving popular attitudes toward the health system and attracting more people to public facilities. Recast, the problem was to encourage citizens to consume more health services. The success of the H.T.P. in increasing patient visits and citizen satisfaction testifies to the efficacy of these efforts. However, no country has been able to provide as many health services as are demanded by citizens. The imbalance of unlimited demand for health services and finite resources is addressed through rationing systems.

As the demand for health services continues to rise, fiscal concerns will require Turkey to consider ways to limit the care-seeking or ration care provided – problems that arise because of the H.T.P.'s success and whose solution is essential to the long-term financial sustainability of the system.

Managing the influence of opposition of groups: The M.o.H. succeeded in winning the support of some of the groups that initially opposed the H.T.P., but even ten years into the reforms, some groups remain vehemently opposed. Specialist physicians, the elite ranks of nurses and midwives, and some other health workers have been marginalized, and our interviews reveal highly negative feelings among some of these professions toward the M.o.H. and the policies that guide the health system. Satisfaction surveys of urban physicians, for instance, show very negative views of current job satisfaction and low expectations for future improvements (Tanik et al. 2013). These sentiments may undermine the profession by discouraging physicians from staying in practice and deterring students from entering medical school. Similarly, among nurses, midwives, and other health professionals low satisfaction threatens the performance of current workers and may diminish the number of people choosing to train in these areas. These dynamics threaten the supply and quality of services the system can provide.

Managing the influence of the World Bank and I.M.F. on domestic politics: The M.o.H.'s strategic management of its relationships with the I.M.F. and World Bank carries risks and reflects the importance of negotiating a united front between ministries. The M.o.H. is not typically a strong ministry in domestic politics and therefore tends not to have as much leverage as others in its negotiations with International Financial Institutions, particularly not with the I.M.F., which focuses on macroeconomic issues. The Ministry of Finance and Treasury are usually the ministries with the most bargaining power in these interactions due to their role in the fiscal affairs of their country. The creation of an inter-ministerial working group to devise the H.T.P. comprising members from the financially oriented ministries, as well as those most concerned with service provision, gave the M.o.H. a far stronger position compared with planning on its own. This ministerial coordination, along with the complete support of the Prime Minister, allowed the Minister of Health and his team to take an aggressive position with both organizations to fully leverage their resources in support of the H.T.P.

Covering the poor and unifying benefit systems: The sequenced approach taken to expanding the Green Card Program shows one way to incorporate a targeted entitlement programme for low-income groups into a unified U.H.C. social security system covering the whole population with a harmonized benefit package. The M.o.H.'s decision to use the existing Green Card Program as the key vehicle to achieve U.H.C. allowed it to avoid legislative delays or roadblocks associated with creating an entirely new social security scheme for low-income households. The gradual expansion of benefits and coverage built public support and momentum behind the concept of U.H.C. so that the unified system was politically palatable by the time Green Card beneficiaries were to be integrated with the Social Security Institution. By the time the Green Card Program was replaced by the premium assistance scheme and fully integrated with the Social Security Institution in 2012, political opposition and the prospect of increased expenditure were not impediments to reform. These obstacles had already been overcome by the incremental approach to expanding coverage.

13.4.2 Trade-Offs and Challenges

Redistribution of resources: The political importance of acting quickly and the technical decision to greatly increase benefits for most citizens led to the practical imperative to redistribute existing resources and also increase total allocations for health. In general, resources were diverted away from elite urban institutions and devoted instead to the provision of health services in secondary cities and rural areas. In the short run, this choice increased the availability of inexpensive, basic services, which have a high return on investment and tend to benefit younger populations, as compared to the high-cost interventions typically required later in the life cycle. The reform also targeted resources towards Green Card beneficiaries, which helped enrol low-income households that had had little or no coverage in the past.

Although this redistribution addressed inequities, it appears to have weakened some parts of the health system. For example the rapid establishment of the family medicine model and a robust primary care system was achieved in part by channelling resources away from tertiary care centres in major urban areas. These centres did not receive their customary allocation of assistant professors because those physicians were assigned to public hospitals in service delivery roles. Unless remedied, the development of fewer highly trained specialists will endanger the quality and availability of tertiary care. Additionally, the pay for performance system encourages the reallocation of time toward service delivery but does not reward teaching, mentoring, or research – all crucial activities for academic medical centres that provide the most advanced services, develop new techniques, conduct research, and train specialists. As the H.T.P. continues to unfold, resources will be required for research, specialized care, and specialist training. Reinvigorating these areas is essential for the long-term performance of the health system and is also important for Turkey's goal of becoming a medical tourist destination.

Quality of care: The H.T.P. focused in large part on increasing the use of the public healthcare system. The next phase of health reform will need to focus on quality and safety in healthcare to both maintain demand and continue to improve the health of the Turkish population (Ministry of Health Turkey 2012; Atun et al. 2013). The pay-for-performance system is designed to encourage greater service delivery, but it is not well suited to evaluate the quality of those services. The system should be re-evaluated to include more mechanisms to ensure high-quality care. Patient feedback systems partially address this concern, but patients are not necessarily able to accurately judge the quality of care they receive. Over-reliance on patient perception as a quality indicator can undermine the quality of services by reducing provider authority and compromising the clinician–patient relationship.

Financial sustainability: The financial sustainability of the health system will be an ongoing concern as Turkey's population ages, the prevalence of chronic diseases increases, and economic growth forecasts weaken. The initial design of the H.T.P. included checks on future health spending, but these have yet to be implemented. H.T.P. planners included way to limit the growth of government spending on health by using a family physician gate keeping system, and offering a basic guaranteed benefit package that could be supplemented with additional insurance, but both of these measures were abandoned as politically unviable. Without these mechanisms, the decision to offer extensive benefits through the General Health Insurance Scheme carries with it long-run cost pressures. Thus far, policymakers have prioritized coverage expansion, improved service delivery, and equity over concerns about cost increases under the H.T.P. As the demand for higher-cost services rises, the politically difficult task of introducing some form of rationing will be required to permit long-term sustainability.

The pay-for-performance system carries additional financial risks due to its potential to promote induced demand. The financial incentives for clinicians encourage the excess provision of medical services, and patients are typically willing recipients because they usually want more care. The H.T.P. set out to increase demand for health services among citizens who previously had not met their needs through the public system. As the health system transitions from focusing on the quantity of services to also emphasizing the quality of care, the M.o.H. will need to manage utilization patterns to ensure effective and efficient care-seeking behaviour.

Dissatisfaction among medical specialists: The expansion of service delivery and increases in utilization both translated to greatly increased workloads for healthcare providers. For physicians satisfied to work in service delivery roles, the pay-for-performance system has yielded generously commensurate pay increases. However, these pay increases have not fully assuaged all provider groups. Many providers do not want the majority of their salaries to be derived from performance bonuses (Tanik 2014). Dissatisfaction remains extremely high among specialists and academicians, and tensions between these groups and the M.o.H. are very high regarding professional autonomy, institutional independence, dual practice laws, compensation policies, and other areas. Also, nurses, midwives, pharmacists, and other provider groups have not received pay increases as large as those for physicians, and wage-related dissatisfaction is acute for some of their members. The dissatisfaction among providers – particularly specialists – is an extremely important threat to the integrity and capacities of the health system because it drives top performers into private practice, curtails research, and weakens teaching capacity, all of which can have negative influences on the future because they have the potential to push new college graduates to choose other professions. The M.o.H. will need to work with provider groups to improve relations and restore cooperation in all areas of the health system. It should also carefully monitor the numbers and quality of students choosing health and/or medical education and where they choose to practise during their careers.

13.5 Conclusion

We have attempted to shed light on how the Minister of Health and his leadership team addressed political economy conflicts at the heart of Turkey's comprehensive reforms. Our analysis complements many previous studies of the technical aspects of Turkey's reform and its results by showing how political economy challenges are inherent in different aspects of health reform and explicating the approaches used in this case to address them. We believe that although the specific presentation of these challenges does reflect factors particular to Turkey at the time of the reforms, the basic conflicts are likely to arise in many settings because they reflect groups and interests common in societies around the world. Similarly, we believe that the core elements of the solutions employed by the Minister and his leadership team could be adapted to other settings because they reflect forces common to politics in most places. Building support quickly; persuading, neutralizing, or marginalizing opposition groups; asserting domestic priorities in engagements with the IFIs; and carefully sequencing reforms to avoid or limit potential problems are sufficiently general propositions as to be relevant in most democracies. These conclusions, however, do not guarantee success in all cases. For instance the speed and scope of the Turkish reforms reflect many capacities developed over decades and required substantial monetary resources, even by the standards of a G20 economy. Turkey's reforms were based largely on redistribution and took place at a time of economic expansion, which presents different challenges than does resource creation or reforms undertaken in worse economic conditions.

References

Agyepong, I. and Adjei, S. (2008). "Public social policy development and implementation: A case study of the Ghana national health insurance scheme." *Health Policy and Planning* **23**: 150–160.

Akdag, R. (2011). *Turkey Health Tranformation Program evaluation report 2003–2010*. Ministry of Health.

Akinci, F., Mollahaliloglu, S., Gursoz, H. and Ogucu, F. (2012). "Assessment of the Turkish health care system reforms: A stakeholder analysis." *Health Policy* **107**(1): 21–30.

Aksakoglu, G. (2014). "Health-care reform in Turkey: Far from perfect." *The Lancet* **383**(9911): 26–27.

Aktan, A. O., Pala, K. and Ilhan, B. (2014). "Health-care reform in Turkey: Far from perfect." *The Lancet* **383**(9911): 25–26.

Akyüz, Y. and Boratav, K. (2003). "The making of the Turkish financial crisis." *World Development* **31**(9): 1549–1566.

Alper, C. E. and Alper, Z. Ö. (2003). "Emerging market crises and the I.M.F.: Rethinking the role of the I.M.F. in light of Turkey's 2000–2001 financial crisis." *Canadian Journal of Development Studies/ Revue canadienne d'études du développement* **24**(2): 267–284.

Aran, M. A. and Hentschel, J. S. (2012). *Protection in good and bad times? The Turkish Green Card health program*. Policy Research Working Paper 6178. World Bank, Washington, DC.

Atun, R., Aydın, S., Chakraborty, S., Sümer, S., Aran, M., Gürol, I., Nazlıoğlu, S., Özgülcü, Ş., Aydoğan, Ü., Ayar, B., Dilmen, U. and Akdağ, R. (2013). "Universal health coverage in Turkey: enhancement of equity." *The Lancet* **382**(9886): 65–99.

Baris, E., Mollahaliloglu, S. and Aydin, S. (2011). "Healthcare in Turkey: From laggard to leader." *British Medical Journal* **342**.

Bleich, S. N., Özaltin, E. and Murray, C. J. L. (2009). "How does satisfaction with the health-care system relate to patient experience?" *Bulletin of the World Health Organization* **87**(4): 271–278.

Boulton, L. and Wolf, M. (2002). *Turkey's ailment: The country's chances of controlling public debt and securing economic recovery could be jeopardised by the ill-health of the prime minister*. Financial Times, London.

Brugha, R. and Varvasovszky, Z. (2000). "Stakeholder analysis: A review." *Health Policy and Planning* **15**(3): 239–246.

Bryant, S. (2010). "Erdogan seeks re-elections as Turkish healthcare plan trumps headscarves." *Bloomberg News*.

Bump, J. B., Reich, M. R. and Johnson, A. M. (2013). "Diarrhoeal diseases and the global health agenda: Measuring and changing priority." *Health Policy and Planning* **28.8**(2013): 799–808.

Civaner, M. M. (2014). "Health-care reform in Turkey: Far from perfect." *The Lancet* **383**(9911): 26.

Ertugrul, A. and Selcuk, F. (2001). "A brief account of the Turkish economy, 1980–2000." *Russian & East European Finance & Trade* **37**(6): 6.

Hacker, J. S. (1998). "The historical logic of national health insurance: Structure and sequence in the development of British, Canadian, and U.S. medical policy." *Studies in American Political Development* **12**(01): 57–130.

Hamzaoglu, O. (2014). "Health-care reform in Turkey: far from perfect." *The Lancet* **383**(9911): 27.

Heper, M. (2003). "The victory of the justice and development party in Turkey." *Mediterranean Politics* **8**(1): 127–134.

Hughes, D. and Leethongdee, S. (2007). "Universal coverage in the land of smiles: Lessons from Thailand's 30 baht health reforms." *Health Affairs* **26**(4): 999–1008.

Hurriyet Daily News. (2010). *Turkey to halve number of green card holders by 2012*. Hurriyet Daily News. Istanbul.

Hurst, J., Scherer, P. R. and Chakraborty, S. (2008). *Turkey – Organization for economic co-operation and development (OECD): Reviews of health systems* [Turkiye – Ekonomik isbirligi ve kalkinma orgutu (OECD): saglik sistemi incelemeleri]. World Bank.

Immergut, E. M. (1990). "Institutions, veto points, and policy results: A comparative analysis of health care." *Journal of Public Policy* **10**(4): 391–416.

Immergut, E. M. (1992). *Health politics: Interests and institutions in Western Europe*. Cambridge, New York: Cambridge University Press.

International Monetary Fund. (2002a). *Turkey Article IV Consultation*. Washington, DC.

International Monetary Fund. (2002b). *Turkey: Request for standby agreement*. I.M.F. Country Report No. 02/136. Washington, DC.

Johansen, A. and Guisset, A.-L. (2012). *Successful health systems reforms: The case of Turkey*. World Health Organization Europe, Copenhagen.

Karadeniz, O. (2012). "Extension of health services coverage for needy in Turkey: From social assistance to general health insurance." *Journal of Social Security* **2**: 103–123.

Kilic, B. (2014). "Health-care reform in Turkey: Far from perfect." *The Lancet* **383**(9911): 28–29.

Knaul, F. M., González-Pier, E., Gómez-Dantés, O., García-Junco, D., Arreola-Ornelas, H., Barraza-Lloréns, M., Sandoval, R., Caballero, F., Hernández-Avila, M., Juan, M., Kershenobich, D., Nigenda, G., Ruelas, E., Sepúlveda, J., Tapia, R., Soberón, G., Chertorivski, S. and Frenk, J. (2012). "The quest for universal health coverage: Achieving social protection for all in Mexico." *The Lancet* **380**(9849): 1259–1279.

Lakin, J. (2010). "The end of insurance: Mexico's Seguro popular, 2001–2007." *Journal of Health Politics Policy and Law* **35**(3).

Menon, R., Mollahaliloglu, S. and Postolovska, I. (2013). *Towards universal coverage: Turkey's Green Card program for the Poor.* World Bank, Washington, DC.

Ministry of Family and Social Policy. (May 2013). *Premium support eligibility 2012 and 2013.* Government of Turkey, Ankara.

Ministry of Health Turkey. (2012). *Strategic plan 2013–2017.* Ankara.

OECD, WHO and World Bank. (2008). *OECD reviews of health systems: Turkey.* Paris.

Olson, M. (1971). *The logic of collective action: Public goods and the theory of groups.* Cambridge, MA: Harvard University Press.

Özbudun, E. (2006). "From political Islam to conservative democracy: The case of the justice and development party in Turkey." *South European Society and Politics* **11**(3–4): 543–557.

Pala, K. (2014). "Health-care reform in Turkey: Far from perfect." *The Lancet* **383**(9911): 28.

Rajkotia, Y. (2007). *The political development of the Ghanaian health insurance system: Lessons in health governance.* Bethesda, MD: Health Systems 20/20 Project, Abt Associates.

Reich, M. R. (1995). "The politics of health sector reform in developing countries: Three cases of pharmaceutical policy." *Health Policy* **32**(1–3): 47–77.

Republic of Turkey and International Bank for Reconstruction and Development. (2004). *Loan agreement: Health transition project.* Loan number 4737 TU.

Roberts, M., Hsiao, W., Berman, P. and Reich, M. R. (2008). *Getting health reform right: A guide to improving performance and equity.* New York: Oxford University Press.

Rossetti, A. G. (2004). *Republic of Turkey health transformation program: Strategic options for the implementation of the health sector transformation in Turkey.* Ankara: Ministry of Health and The World Bank.

Tanik, F. A. (2014). "Health-care reform in Turkey: Far from perfect." *The Lancet* **383**(9911): 28.

Tanik, F. A., Bilaloğlu, E., Özçelik, Z. and Okman, U. (2013). "Th e greatest motivation: Assurance of practicing the profession with dignity. Motivational state of physicians in Turkey." *World Medical Journal* **59**(3).

Tatar, M., Mollahaliloglu, S., Sahin, B., Aydın, S., Maresso, A. and Hernández-Quevedo, C. (2011). *Turkey health system review.* Health Systems in Transition **13**(6): 1–186. EOoHSaP.

Turkish Statistical Institute. (2003–2012). *Life satisfaction survey.* Government of Turkey. Ankara.

Varvasovszky, Z. and Brugha, R. (2000). "A stakeholder analysis." *Health Policy and Planning* **15**(3): 338–345.

World Bank. (2006). *Turkey public expenditure review.* Report No. 36764-TR. Washington, DC: World Bank.

World Bank. (2012). *World development indicators.* Washington, DC: World Bank.

World Health Organization. (2013). *Turkey national health accounts – health expenditure series.*

Yasar, G. Y. (2011). "'Health transformation programme' in Turkey: An assessment." *The International Journal of Health Planning and Management* **26**(2): 110–133.

Chapter 14

Capital Accumulation and the Restructuring of the Turkish Health System

Aziz Küçük

Contents

14.1 Introduction

Since the 1980s, the Turkish healthcare system has undergone fundamental transformations under the influence of neoliberal market-oriented policies and reforms. The Health Transformation Programme (H.T.P), which was launched in 2003, brought significant changes to service delivery, organization, resource management, and financing in the Turkish health system. This programme, which was prepared with the support of the World Bank, restructured public healthcare in line with the expansion of market forces, reflecting the definition of the state as an important catalyst for the healthy functioning of the market.

To better understand the nature, composition, regulation, and role of the health field, one must understand its political and economic context as a whole. In other words, to comprehend the relationship between capitalism and health services, an analysis should be conducted through the lens of the

DOI: 10.4324/9781003539896-15

state's role in the capital accumulation process. The capitalist state form cannot be considered independently of the capital relationship because the stability of capitalism relies on the stability of capital accumulation, which, in turn, relies on state facilitation and direct state intervention in economic affairs (Singh and Tiwana, 2020). Although capital accumulation may take different forms during the development process of capitalism, the state always continues to provide and protect the conditions for capitalist accumulation. The role of the state is essentially the reproduction of the system based on capital accumulation (Gülalp, 1988). In this context, healthcare usually has an instrumentalism that meets the economic and political needs of the capitalist system as a whole. Today, the field of health, which has become a subject from being an integrative part of commodity production, is being restructured in harmony with the requirements of the capitalist accumulation process. The field of healthcare consists of different capital accumulation processes ranging from service delivery to health insurance, from pharmaceutical and medical equipment production to medical research. In parallel, the state is organized to support the capital accumulation process in healthcare.

In the study, it is argued that healthcare in Turkey was aimed at providing the prerequisites for capital accumulation until the 1980s, but under the influence of neoliberal policies, it became the subject of capital accumulation after the H.T.P. Therefore, it is pointed out that health sector reform means more than improving health and healthcare services. In this regard, this study seeks to answer the following questions: What are the functions of healthcare historically since the development of the modern state? How and according to what dynamics are the delivery and organization of healthcare shaped within the capitalist mode of production? In other words, what does the phenomenon of transformation occurring within the framework of the principle of historicity in the field of health mean in terms of the relationship between the state and capitalism? What is the importance of the health reforms implemented in Turkey in terms of the capital accumulation process?

14.2 Debates about the Capitalist State and Capital Accumulation

To ensure the essential prerequisites for sustaining the profitability of capitalism, an apparatus separate from market forces is required to fulfil the collective requirements of capital as a whole, namely, the state. According to Wallerstein (1983), who stated that the modern state's development was closely connected to the emergence of capitalism, "it is idle to speculate whether capitalism could have flourished without the active role of the modern state". The role of state organization within the capitalist system is to facilitate and enhance the reproduction of capital.

Capitalist state theorists generally agree that the fundamental prerequisites necessary for sustaining capitalism include accumulation, legitimacy, and reproduction (Przeworski, 1990; O'Connor, 1973; Offe, 1975). The magnitude and scope of state activities are closely connected to the positive development of the economy. State activities are financed by revenues collected from the profits and wages realized in the economy through taxes, loans, and public borrowing. This dependence of state activities and resources on the overall health of the economy is evident in the state's current fiscal crises. For example it is known how welfare services such as social security and health are negatively affected in economic crisis situations. If the economy worsens, tax revenues and loan repayments decrease. As a result, since state resources are dependent on capital accumulation, a continuous and smooth process of capital accumulation is extremely important for the expansion of the state.

The inner logic of capitalism is the continuity of accumulation, which is the production of surplus value for the accumulation of capital or the process that Marx (1967) termed "accumulation for accumulation's sake, production for production's sake". According to the regime of accumulation and style of regulation, while the function and importance of the process of capital accumulation have historically varied, it has always been linked to state regulation (Hirsch, 2011). The role of the state here is to reproduce the system based on capital accumulation. Therefore, concerning the distinction between the public and private spheres of capital accumulation, it can be argued that the state is positioned in the public sphere to provide the general conditions for capital accumulation carried out by the capitalist class in the private sphere (Gülalp, 1988).

In debates on the capitalist state, the state is understood as a complex social relationship of many different levels. The main levels are largely classified around three main approaches based on Marxist state debates: 'Class-theoretical' (Lenin, Miliband, Poulantzas, etc.); 'capital-theoretical' (Altvater, O'Connor, Offe, Harvey, etc.); and 'state-theoretical' (Jessop, etc.). Liberal state practices and the structure of their institutions have not been given much attention in Classical Marxism (Marx, Engels, Lenin, and Gramsci). The Marxist understanding of the state, based primarily on class contradictions, views the existence of state organizations as a result of irreconcilable class contradictions created in capitalist society. Structuralist Marxists such as Althusser and Poulantzas argue, after initially claiming that capitalism encompasses a distinct institutional division of the economic and political spheres, that the economy is ultimately not the sole determinant and hegemonic factor (Boucher, 2012). According to Poulantzas (2000), in terms of the relationship between the state and the economy, capitalist production relations allow relative autonomy to the state from the economic sphere (capital accumulation and surplus value production), which also forms the basis of the organizational structure and functionality of the state. Because the structure of these capitalist production relations shapes the separate positions and new areas of both the state and the economy.

O'Connor and Offe have attempted to create a synthesis by addressing the accumulation and legitimacy problems of the capitalist state in a framework that does not lead to economic and political reductionism. O'Connor (1973), who seeks the reasons for the state's financial crisis in capitalist accumulation conditions, has argued that financial crises emerge as a necessary condition for the sustainability of capitalist accumulation. The function of "accumulation" inherent in the nature of the modern state as a capitalist state is conceptualized by Offe in line with the classic historical–materialist analyses presented by Marx. According to Offe (1975), the state is neither a "servant" nor an "agent" of a single class. The capitalist state seeks to fulfil and protect the collective interests of all members of a class society dominated by capital. This understanding is a combination of the organizational and functional definition of the state. At the most general level, although excluded from production and capital accumulation, the capitalist state is dependent on production and accumulation as a "tax state". However, it must also maintain its neutral image and therefore its necessary legitimacy.

Representatives of the "school of derivation of the state", including Altvater, Hirsch, Holloway, and Piccioto, articulate objections to conceptualizing the state solely as a "structure" designed to serve the imperative needs of capital or as a mere "instrument" crafted to safeguard the interests of the bourgeoisie. This approach derives the functional necessity of the state from the analysis of the capitalist mode of production. Some characterize the state as an "ideal collective capitalist", while others attempt to derive the state from the logic of "class struggle" (Clarke, 1991).

Jessop has prominently emerged in recent debates on the capitalist state by utilizing a strategic-theoretical method, forming a synthesis of capital-theoretical and class-theoretical approaches to explain the capitalist state. Jessop's (2002) notable contribution to Marxist theory lies in his analysis of the evolving capitalist state in the post-Fordist era. He posits that the Schumpeterian workfare post-national regime (S.W.P.R) is supplanting the traditional Keynesian National Welfare State due to its inadequacy in sustaining social cohesion and fostering capital accumulation over time. Jessop has tried to show how the dynamics and functions of state forms are shaped by changes in capital accumulation. S.W.P.R is described as a modern situation that highlights the development of the supply side of the economy through competition, flexibility in the labour process, technological change, innovation, and promoting efficiency. Jessop (2002) argues that the role of the state tends to focus intensively on intervening in the reproduction of labour power (such as health, education, transportation, housing) and the valorization process of capital (such as scientific research, technological innovation, industrial restructuring), rather than ensuring the continuity of the general political and ideological conditions of capital accumulation.

14.3 The Function of Healthcare in the Capitalist State

The health industry in capitalist society has four interconnected economic functions: Capital accumulation, provision of investment opportunities, absorption of surplus value, and reproduction of labour power (Rodberg and Stevenson, 1977). Medicine and health institutions reproduce the physical conditions of labour power by ensuring people's health. Furthermore, expenditures on health services are often considered an investment in human capital, as they enhance a person's ability to work.

Healthcare supports capital accumulation in three ways. First, many diseases that reduce labour productivity can be treated or cured. Second, medicine is an important ideological tool for the ruling class in maintaining social balance and domestic peace necessary for production and profitability. Finally, the health industry itself has become an important area for investment and profit (Himmelstein and Woolhandler, 1984). While the first two of these roles have a long history in healthcare, the last one has become a driving force in the growth of healthcare after 1980. Prior to 1980, emphasis was placed on the biological and ideological dimensions of healthcare. However, with the commodification of healthcare, the primary objective shifted towards profit rather than the promotion of health.

During the Fordist accumulation regime starting in the 1920s, one of the sectors that experienced significant expansion was the health sector. This growth was driven by the establishment of university hospitals and the rapid development of the pharmaceutical industry. In this period, a notable integration emerged among education, research, innovation, and service delivery, following the production chain model of the Fordist system (Hernández-Álvarez et al., 2020). Thus, the state increasingly abandoned its traditional role as a "decommodifying agent" and replaced it with the role of the "commodifying agent" during the neoliberal era (Cerny, 1999).

Leys (2001) emphasizes that four conditions must be fulfilled for the commodification of healthcare: First, the services provided must be capable of being broken down and reconfigured into standardized units that can be priced and sold; second, the public must be persuaded to want these services as commodities; third, the existing labour force of service providers must be redefined and remotivated to become wage workers producing a surplus for shareholders, with the further consequence that previous organizational formats and incentive structures become increasingly weakened and ineffective; and fourth, the change to for-profit provision involves substantial investment and some risk, which private capital generally requires the state to absorb.

Since the establishment of the medical–industrial complex in the 1960s, healthcare has been shifting away from the Fordist industrial model towards financialization and cognitive capitalism amidst changes in the accumulation regime of contemporary capitalism (Jessop, 2002). The phenomenon of health financialization, which entails the transformation of publicly owned social services such as healthcare and social security into financial assets, has resulted in substantial structural changes within the sector. These include the formation and growing presence of financial funds, the concentration of capital, and mergers and acquisitions that have increased the degree of internationalization of the healthcare sector. Herman (2010) claims that one of the driving forces behind the transformation in the health sector is multinational health companies and large-scale financial institutions, seeking profitable investment opportunities in health services. While demand decreases can be seen in other sectors, there is always a need for patient treatment regardless of the economic situation worldwide. Therefore, what makes the healthcare sector so attractive to private investors is its stable commercial structure that does not fluctuate. In this context, the opening of the healthcare sector to foreign companies wishing to invest in areas such as insurance, hospital services (including the P.P.P. financing model), consulting, and R&D has ensured the internationalization of healthcare. The industrial aspect of healthcare services, encompassing sectors such as health tourism, medical complexes, health information systems, pharmaceutical and medical device technologies, and biotechnology, is progressively expanding in size.

14.4 Development of Healthcare in Turkey in Terms of Capital Accumulation (1920–2002)

In Turkey, during the Early Republican period, the function of constructing social order through organizing for the fight against epidemic diseases, environmental health, and public health measures came to the forefront. The institutionalization efforts of the Ministry of Health (M.o.H.), which is one of the first ministries established in 1920, were influenced by public health activities perceived as a prerequisite for capital accumulation by imperialist states in search of markets. As seen in the establishment of both the General Directorate of Health for Borders and Coasts and the Institute and School of Public Health, the development of basic healthcare infrastructure emerged as a necessity for opening up new areas of accumulation, both nationally and internationally. While the responsibilities assigned to Special Provincial Administrations and municipalities in the management of healthcare continued, especially with the enactment of the General Public Health Law in 1930, the state's supervisory and regulatory role began to gain prominence. Thus, the state undertook the task of filling the infrastructure gap by providing public healthcare necessary to ensure the material conditions for production.

Turkey, which entered the process of integration into the restructured global economy post-1945, approached health reform and the promotion of health as integral parts of its national development process. The planning processes in the field of health, such as the First Ten-Year National Health Plan, National Health Program, and Socialization Program, which emerged after World War II, were used as technical tools in the production and reproduction of international capital accumulation processes. After 1950, the opening of rural areas to markets, rapid urbanization, and the emergence of new opportunities for accumulation led to certain sections of trading capital transforming into industrial capital through direct and indirect collaboration with foreign capital. These years also marked the beginning of the development of private capital in the field of health. The establishment of an organization in rural areas, in accordance with development objectives, was commenced following the enactment of Socialization Law No. 224 in 1961. Emphasis was placed on promoting labour reproduction through population planning, health education, maternal and child health policies, and social equilibrium. As a result, a holistic healthcare services model has been adopted since the 1960s post-socialization era. This model effectively combines preventive, supportive, and therapeutic services within a cohesive administrative framework.

Since 1980, there has been a notable shift towards marketization and commodification within the realm of health services. During this period, an organizational structure emerged that placed a greater emphasis on accumulation rather than preventive medicine services and the reproduction of labour power. The transition in policy direction towards cost reduction and the minimization of health expenditures until the 1990s marked a substantial evolution in both service delivery and organizational frameworks subsequent to the enactment of the "Health Services Basic Law" in 1987. This legislation aimed to establish an administration model rooted in the fundamental principles of managerialism. Although the health reforms in Turkey throughout the 1990s, guided by World Bank-sponsored "project loans", fell short of complete privatization, they did create an environment conducive to the more seamless introduction of privatization. Despite efforts to introduce reform initiatives within this context, progress was impeded by political and administrative instabilities as well as class conflicts exacerbated by recurrent financial crises.

14.5 Turkish Health Transformation Programme

The AK Party Government, established in light of the economic and political consequences of the 2001 crisis, prepared the Health Transformation Programme in 2003 with the objective of restructuring the healthcare sector. This programme, which includes an extensive array of reform components implemented in the 1990s and supported by financing from World Bank projects, represents the convergence of the healthcare system's organizational, financial, and operational structure with the goals of the nascent economic landscape. The H.T.P consists of eight components crafted to organize, finance, and deliver healthcare in a manner that is effective, efficient, and equitable.[1]

14.5.1 Accumulation through Commodification of Healthcare

During the initial phase of the H.T.P., the predominant emphasis was on implementing policies aimed at improving governance, efficiency, and patient and employee satisfaction and ensuring the long-term financial sustainability of the healthcare system.

14.5.1.1 General Health Insurance Gathering Everybody Under a Single Umbrella

The social insurance component of the Turkish social security system exhibited a fragmented structure concerning both the institutional framework and social insurance laws. In 2006, through the H.T.P., five pre-existing insurance schemes were consolidated into a mandatory General Health Insurance Scheme with a unified payer. This reform was designed to create a comprehensive health insurance system and to separate the institutions that provide and purchase the service. According to Cebeci (2013), the change in the structures of the M.o.H. and Social Insurance Institutions (S.I.I.s) in order to open the health field to the accumulation process in Turkey started with the separation of the actors who provide and purchase healthcare. Thus, S.I.I. hospitals, which previously provided services for use-value for SII members, and the S.I.I., which was the consumer of the service produced, were separated from each other.

The separation of healthcare provision and financing, the consolidation of healthcare financing under a single entity, the integration of healthcare services, and the enhancement of healthcare accessibility represent coordinated reforms. In 2005, through Law No. 5283, public hospitals managed by entities such as the Social Security Institution (SII), the Directorate General of Security, the Post and Telegraph Corporation, the Directorate General of State Railways, and the Turkish Electricity Distribution Corporation (TEDAŞ) were unified under the auspices of the MoH. Subsequently, in 2010, both Red Crescent hospitals and select municipal hospitals were brought under the purview of the MoH. Lastly, in 2016, military hospitals were also transferred to the MoH. As a result, all public health services, excluding university hospitals, came to be administered by the MoH, reinforcing the Ministry's role in health system planning, regulation, and oversight.

This new model, based on a contractual relationship between institutions purchasing and providing services, focuses on the management and control of expenditures through an efficiency-driven, competitive, and managerial approach. Public resources, also known as public funds, serve as the foundation for the emergence and expansion of private capital within the sector. A classic illustration of the evolution of private capital with public financing is the signing of contracts between private medical centres, hospitals, and SSI for service provision to eligible individuals.

As illustrated in Table 14.1, the rise in treatment costs has resulted in an increase in both public health expenditure and the allocation of funds from the public budget to the healthcare sector. Concurrently, the private health and insurance sector has experienced rapid growth. This growth has challenged the notion of a "sustainable financing structure", a fundamental tenet of the H.T.P, and has not adequately addressed the deficit in the social security system. Nonetheless, as noted by Gough (1975), the expansion of public spending does not conflict with the accumulation of private capital; rather, it is a crucial prerequisite for such accumulation.

Table 14.1 Examples from Social Insurance, Private Insurance, and Expenditure Data

	2002	*2011*	*2022*
Ratio of general government health expenditure to total health expenditure (%)	70.7	79.6	76.4
Total public and primary voluntary health insurance coverage	69.8	97.6	98.8
Ratio of treatment expenses to total expenses of S.S.I. (%)	37	57	66
The ratio of private health institutions in S.S.I.'s treatment expenses (%)	14	29	11
Ratio of M.o.H. hospitals in S.S.I.'s treatment expenses (%)	--	52	68
Illness/health insurance company	35	34	50
The ratio of private health expenditures to total health expenditures (%)	29.3	20.4	23.6
Number of private health insurers	558 thousand	2.8 million	2.6 million + 3.6 million people with complementary health insurance

Source: Insurance Association of Türkiye Sector Report (2022), OECD (2024), TURKSTAT (2023).

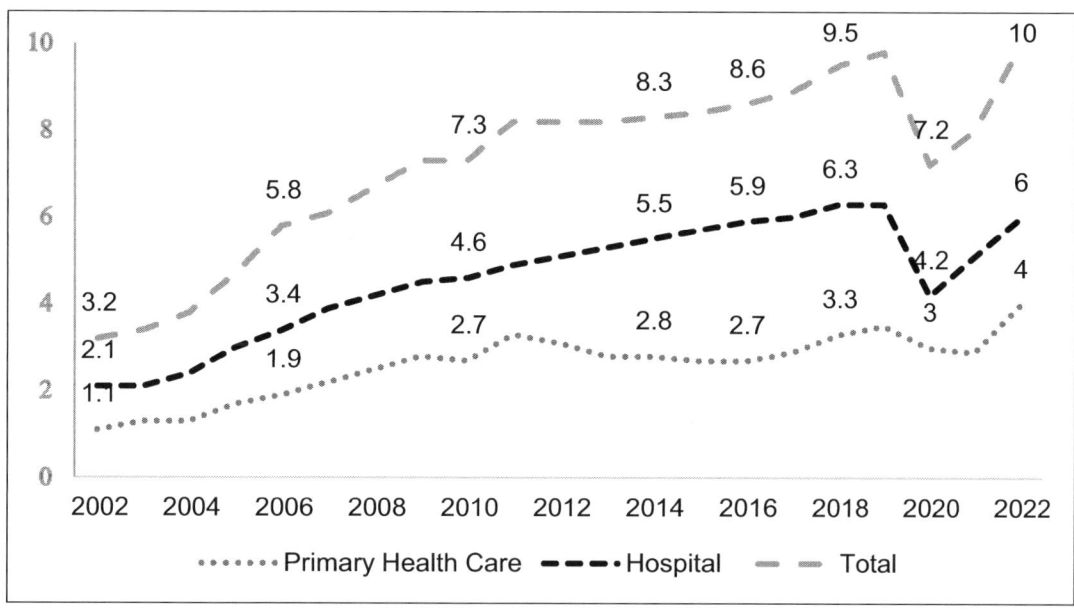

Figure 14.1   Total number of per capita visits to physician in healthcare facilities by years, Turkey (2002–2022).

14.5.1.2 Widespread, Easily Accessible, and Friendly Healthcare System

The H.T.P is committed to establishing a comprehensive, easily accessible, and user-friendly healthcare system to effectively meet the increasing demand for medical services. Patients are encouraged to view health services as a commodity to foster their engagement in seeking medical care. The state and public entities have organized the marketization of health services based on the standardization principle, which forms the essential foundation of commoditization. Proficient tools such as treatment protocols, clinical guidelines, total quality management, accreditation systems to classify healthcare facilities and services, health insurance payment notifications (such as the Health Implementation Communiqué), evidence-based medical practices, Central Physician Appointment System (MHRS), and home healthcare have been employed in this initiative (Ulutaş, 2011; Küçük, 2018a). Despite the proposal of a referral chain policy aimed at reducing healthcare expenditure, its implementation remains pending. The impact of these advancements is evidenced by the increased number of patients seeking medical care at healthcare institutions. As depicted in Figure 14.1, the per capita rate of physician visits has progressed from 3.2 in 2002 to 7.3 in 2010 and further to 10.0 in 2022 (MoH, 2002–2022).

An additional aspect of the commodification of health services pertains to the willingness of employees to embrace change. They have been integrated into this process through various mechanisms, such as the performance-based supplementary payment system, high-wage employment policies in regions facing challenges in recruiting personnel as per Law No. 4924, and the implementation of the family medicine model.

14.5.1.3 Strengthened Primary Healthcare and Family Medicine

The inception of family medicine practice in 2004 under Law No. 5258 on Family Medicine Pilot Practice represented a significant advancement in the commoditization of primary healthcare services. Initially introduced as a pilot programme, family medicine practice was later expanded nationwide by 2010. This model of care offers primary healthcare and preventive services, with primary care classified into community-based and individual-based categories. Various entities were designated specific roles such as Community Health Centres and Family Medicine. Service provision remained fragmented, with family health units operating independently within the same centre, each catering to approximately 2,000 individuals (Zencir, 2012). Family medicine practice entails the reorganization of primary healthcare delivery under a new liberal ideology. Competitive remuneration packages were implemented to encourage physicians to adopt this practice, facilitating the engagement of general practitioners in contractual roles.

14.5.2 Organization for Direct Capital Accumulation: Decree Law No. 663 and beyond

After the 2008 crisis, the state assumed the responsibility of actively steering the development of new industrialization and employment policies in close partnership with capital. The main aim of this shift is to strengthen international competitiveness by prioritizing industrial investments and enforcing new regulatory measures over labour. The state adeptly turned the crisis into an opportunity in terms of the enduring patterns of capital accumulation and the mechanisms governing the accumulation process (Oğuz, 2011).

In 2011, Decree Law No. 663 was implemented, signifying a notable advancement in the healthcare industry through the successful integration of long-awaited modifications in health services. The MoH has adopted a regulatory and overseeing role, subsequent to the reorganization of its main directorates to evolve into an agency-style entity. As a part of this reorganization effort, public hospital unions have been established, and administrative roles such as branch manager and chief have been phased out. This transformation depicts a shift from a vertical hierarchical setup to a horizontal organizational arrangement. The technical regulations demonstrate a shift by the state towards creating an organizational framework that facilitates the accumulation of capital in the health sector within the context of managerialism.

14.5.2.1 The Ministry of Health as the Planner and Controller

Decree Law No. 663 has empowered the MoH with regulatory and oversight duties. The General Directorate of Health Information Systems, a crucial unit under the Ministry's purview, is assigned the pivotal responsibility of "information collection". Meanwhile, the General Directorate of Health Services is mandated with the critical tasks of "regulation and oversight" over both public and private healthcare facilities. Service delivery responsibilities are designated to established agencies. The MoH, with a strategic focus on steering rather than operational implementation, is dedicated to strengthening audit capabilities, enhancing policy and planning procedures, setting up performance monitoring benchmarks, and emphasizing the vital roles of information gathering and rule-making within the state's organizational framework. The stewardship role and institutional configuration of the MoH fulfil a dual purpose. The organizational structure described before symbolizes the complex relationship between the organization of the state and capital, skilfully obscuring the fundamental nature of the capitalist state. It also portrays the state's role as a regulator and overseer vis-à-vis capital, thus preserving its relative autonomy.

14.5.2.2 Health Enterprises Having Financial and Administrative Autonomy

Between 2012 and 2017, 89 "Public Hospital Unions" (P.H.U.s) were established in 81 provinces as provincial organizations affiliated with the Public Hospitals Administration of Turkey, with Decree Law No. 663. It was envisaged that public hospitals would be operated with a managerial approach since the Basic Health Services Law No. 3359 was published in 1987. The P.H.U.s model aims for hospitals to benefit from economies of scale and ensure the decentralization of hospitals by increasing their administrative and fiscal autonomies. Additionally, professional contractual management was adopted with this model, which foresaw working in public hospitals with private sector management techniques based on economic efficiency and high service quality (Küçük, 2018b). Later, it was observed that this structural separation between central and provincial organizations harmed strategic capacity and institutional development and resulted in coordination problems, duplication, and even waste issues. The P.H.U.s model was terminated with Decree Law No. 694 in 2017, and the command and control model of the MoH was reinstated. New Public Management (N.P.M.) reforms led to the fragmentation of a previously monolithic public sector, and these policies of decentralization, autonomy, and marketization were merely a response to the changing requirements of capital accumulation.

14.5.2.3 Education and Science Institutions Supporting the System

In the restructuring of the health industry in line with the needs of capital accumulation, the state turned to financial and organizational solutions "through institutional adaptation" (Loeppky, 2010). In particular, the need for knowledge capital (R&D) and human capital, which are necessary for accumulation, has brought to the agenda the necessity of establishing TUSEB and the University of Health Sciences, which are two important organizational reforms simultaneously in Turkey.

14.5.2.4 Health Institutes of Turkey (TUSEB)

In 2014, the Health Institutes of Turkey (TUSEB) was established by Law No. 6569 to operate in the field of health science and technologies, to support planned and sustainable development. TUSEB is a private budget organization with public legal personality, scientific, and administrative autonomy. TUSEB, which has offices and centres on Ankara and Istanbul campuses, is structured as the relevant organization of the MoH. TUSEB is made up of nine research institutes, established in line with the requirements of health science and technology (TUSEB, 2024):

- Turkish Biotechnology Institute
- Turkish Maternity, Child and Adolescent Health Institute
- Turkish Cancer Institute
- Turkish Public Health and Chronic Diseases Institute

- Turkish Traditional and Complementary Medicine Institute
- Turkish Healthcare Quality and Accreditation Institute
- Turkish Health Policies Institute
- Turkish Vaccine Institute
- Turkish Health Data Research and Artificial Intelligence Applications Institute

Through these institutes, TUSEB aims to ensure the production of new products and the development, localization, and nationalization of existing ones. They maintain that studies on the development of medical products and technologies needed by the Turkish healthcare system, especially drugs, vaccines, medical devices, biomaterials, and diagnostic kits, are brought from the R&D stage to the production stage and transformed into products that can be used in the clinic. The institutes aim to encourage R&D, clinical research, and technology development studies in the public and private sectors and to provide a scientific environment and funding for researchers. Lastly, they aim to lead in the development of health science and technology culture and ecosystems.

One of the recent advancements in this sector involves the establishment of Turkey Health Valley, following the Presidential Decree published in the Official Gazette on 25 May 2024. This initiative aims to develop an integrated health system that encompasses R&D, clinical research, and production readiness in the pharmaceuticals and medical technologies field. Turkey Health Valley's primary objective is to enhance the nation's capabilities in health-related education, R&D, biotechnology, and informatics. This upcoming enterprise, led by TUSEB, will deliver services via prototype production facilities, a significant data research hub, and centres of excellence.

Pharmaceutical and innovative biomedical R&D studies, which are one of the mandatory prerequisites for the sustainable development of the health sector, are carried out in a wide range as a result of the post-Fordist accumulation regime. Public organizations taking on such an identity, as stated by Jessop (2002), show that states support information infrastructures and social innovation systems at different scales and promote movement away from national utility structures with universal supply obligations suited to an era of mass production and mass consumption to more flexible, differential, multiscale structures suited to a post-Fordist era. Additionally, this organization aims to intervene to restructure research in universities to bring it more closely into alignment with the perceived needs of business and to encourage the management and exploitation of intellectual property through spin-offs, licencing, partnerships, science parks, technology parks, industry parks, and so on.

The healthcare sector, including medical research, drugs, medical technologies, hospitals, and health insurance regulations, plays a crucial role in the bio-economy through biotechnology. State support for research and development is essential for the advancement of bio-industrial complexes. The establishment of research institutes as shared resources for the healthcare industry signifies a socialized form of capital accumulation strategies. Therefore, there is a desire to develop a national growth model centred on R&D to facilitate the integration of domestic and international capital within the healthcare sector

14.5.2.5 University of Health Sciences

On 15 April 2015, the University of Health Sciences (SBU) was established by the MoH under the authority of Law No. 6639. SBU comprises 63 training and research hospitals affiliated with the MoH, in addition to five institutes and 22 faculties. In response to the evolving production structures in the health sector driven by capitalism, the establishment of this organizational structure has been motivated by the imperative to cultivate human capital in healthcare, tailoring it to meet the dynamic requirements of the labour market. The MoH's engagement in education and research activities through SBU is strategically aligned with the contemporary demands of the market economy, characterized by innovation, knowledge-driven practices, entrepreneurship, and adaptability. SBU's dedicated focus on research, supported by a robust research and development division aimed at enhancing local pharmaceuticals, vaccines, and medical devices production, highlights the importance of jointly analysing it with the TUSEB (University of Health Sciences, 2024). The coexistence of TUSEB and SBU, operating under two complementary regulatory frameworks, reflects the symbiotic relationship between knowledge capital and human capital.

14.5.2.6 *P.P.P Model and City Hospitals Projects*

A Public–Private Partnership (P.P.P.) is a financing model where investments and services are carried out under public obligations, with costs, risks, and profits shared between the public and private institutions through a long-term contractual agreement (Hodge and Greve, 2017). Although the legal foundations of the P.P.P model in Turkey are based on Law No. 5396, adopted in 2005, a new regulation was enacted in 2013 with Law No. 6428, eliminating implementation deficiencies. The P.P.P. model, designed with the build-operate-transfer method, entails radical changes in the delivery, organization, and financing of health services (Küçük, 2018a). According to the legislation, contracts are formed for a period not exceeding 25 years, excluding the fixed investment term, and the lands of the campuses to be built are given to the companies free of charge by the Ministry of Treasury and Finance. The model's financing is covered by the general budget. In the projects, financing, construction, equipping, maintenance-repair, delivery of non-clinical services, and operation of hospitals are entrusted to private investors. The financing model of the project is based on using 20% equity and 80% debt. By 2024, 18 city hospitals with a bed capacity of 28,650 have been built using the P.P.P. model, with the total investment amount for these hospitals calculated as $13.08 billion (S.B.B., 2024).

Due to neoliberal restructuring and the marketization of healthcare, hospitals are being developed as large industrial complexes, thereby catalysing the growth of local and regional economies. In terms of the capitalist economy, large-scale hospitals offer various tools for accumulation in many areas, especially production, investment, and employment. In this context, city hospitals constructed under the P.P.P. model were designed as "new industrial spaces or regions" in line with the post-Fordist production model. The P.P.P. model aims to advance capital accumulation by coordinating the public and private aspects of the accumulation process. Higgott et al. (2000) additionally observe that the collaboration between public and private actors represents an emerging approach to advancing capitalist accumulation within the context of worldwide structural transformations. The construction of hospitals with the P.P.P. model is one of the important neoliberal accumulation dynamics with its policies and practices that encourage privatization, dispossession, and marketization. Harvey's (2003) concept of accumulation by dispossession offered a useful conceptual framework for understanding the P.P.P. model. Particularly, privately funded P.P.P.s facilitate spatial as well as temporal displacement by means of the accumulation by dispossession mechanism. This model, which contributes to the resolution of overaccumulation crises through spatio-temporal "fix", opens new markets, new production capacities, and new resources through temporal displacement with long-term contracts (25–30 years) and through spatial displacement by relocating hospitals to new geographical areas for the private sector.

14.5.2.7 USHAŞ International Health Services Inc

International Health Services Inc. (USHAŞ) was established by Law no. 7146, which was adopted on 26 July 2018. USHAŞ, the relevant institution of the MoH, is responsible for promoting the services offered in the field of international health services in Turkey and for supporting and coordinating the activities of the public and private sectors regarding health tourism. USHAŞ began operating on 4 February 2019, with an initial capital of ten million Turkish liras, and its headquarters is located in Ankara. All of its shares belong to the Ministry of Treasury and Finance.

The establishment of USHAŞ was driven by the recognition of health tourism as an economic opportunity following the impact of the 2007–2008 world economic crisis. Throughout history, such entities have functioned as instrumental tools in the advancement of market economies. Despite their status as public institutions, their incorporation of private interests within their joint-stock structure enables them to facilitate private firms and their international partners in market liberalization. USHAŞ emerged as a response to the growing foreign exchange need amid the crisis triggered by the balance of payments in Turkey, amplified by the global economic downturn. The institutionalization of USHAŞ underscores the shift towards a marketing-oriented health system, with a focus on catering to foreign patients and the development of city hospitals under the P.P.P. model – serving as integral components of these strategic objectives (Somel, 2020). This integration of the P.P.P. model, establishment of state-of-the-art health campuses offering enhanced hotel services, and the promotion of health tourism is poised to generate substantial added value, fostering a multiplier effect on capital accumulation. In 2023, Turkey welcomed a total of 1,538,643 visitors seeking healthcare services, generating a revenue of 3 billion US dollars (TURKSTAT, 2024).

Decree Law No. 663 introduced a significant regulation allowing for the potential establishment of "free healthcare zones" in Turkey. As outlined in Article 49 of Decree Law No. 663, the MoH has been granted the authority to create such zones in accordance with the regulations of Law No. 3218 concerning free zones. The key aims of these free healthcare zones include attracting greater foreign investment; developing the area into a prominent health tourism destination (encompassing medical tourism, thermal tourism, and elderly tourism); facilitating the rapid integration of advanced medical technologies; enhancing employment opportunities; and attracting skilled healthcare professionals to the nation. Despite the presence of the necessary legal framework, the implementation of the free healthcare zones initiative has not materialized as expected.

14.6 Conclusion

The capitalist economic thought represents a perpetual and potentially limitless mechanism of capital accumulation. The imperative for growth within the capitalist economy, also known as its unquenchable thirst for capital accumulation, positions the modern state as a capitalist entity reliant on the functional necessities of this accumulation process. Consequently, the state is obligated to consistently intervene in order to ensure economic prosperity, mitigate economic downturns, and address potential barriers to sustained growth. In Turkey, the H.T.P. and its various components are the result of a structured framework established to meet the state's requirements for capital accumulation. The managerial, organizational, and financial reform initiatives of the H.T.P encompass state regulations intended to facilitate direct capital accumulation. Through regulations governing the restructuring of healthcare services, such as the establishment of city hospitals under the P.P.P. model, public hospital unions, health free zones, USHAŞ, and TÜSEB, the healthcare sector assumes a critical role in promoting capital accumulation by restructuring capitalist production relationships. The enforcement of Decree Law No. 663 has made advancing capital reproduction within the healthcare sector a core priority.

The current pursuit of reorganizing state and health services is crucial in enhancing economic efficiency and fostering capital accumulation. It is crucial to note that the state's focus on supporting and expediting capital accumulation while turning public resources into commodities through allocation to accumulation-driven policies should not be viewed as the sole or optimal measure of rationality. Indeed, choices such as the abandonment of P.H.U.s and P.P.P. models, or avoidance of regulations that would increase the labour-capital contradiction, underscore the critical role played by political and administrative control mechanisms within the state.

In the realm of healthcare, the state plays a pivotal role in influencing the trajectory of the healthcare industry at a large scale through its policy determinations and strategic investments. The rise in public healthcare expenditures underscores the importance of focusing on the strategic allocation and prioritization of public funds, rather than solely emphasizing cost reduction. Paradoxically, despite the adoption of initiatives such as "decentralization", "service procurement", and "autonomy" in healthcare restructuring endeavours since the 1990s, they have often led to heightened central oversight and increased public expenditure. Hence, it is desired that the state offer infrastructure support and financial incentives, rather than engaging in operational activities directly. As a result, it is anticipated that the fiscal incentives and the economic-regulatory duties of the state will broaden in the upcoming years.

Note

1 These components are (i) The MoH as the Planner and Controller; (ii) General Health Insurance Gathering Everybody under the Single Umbrella; (iii) Widespread, Easily Accessible, and Friendly Healthcare System (Strengthened Primary Healthcare and family medicine, Effective and Staged Referral Chain, Health Enterprises Having Financial and Administrative Autonomy), (iv) Health Manpower Equipped with Knowledge and Competence and Working with High Motivation, (v) Education and Science Institutions Supporting the System, (vi) Quality and Accreditation for Qualified and Effective Healthcare, (vii) Institutional Structure in the Management of Rational Medicine and Equipment (National Medicine Institution, Medical Devices Institution), (viii) Access to Effective Information in Decision-Making Process: Health Information System.

After the 2007 elections, three more titles were added to these eight titles: (i) Health Promotion and Healthy Lifestyle Programs for a Better Future, (ii) Multisectoral Health Responsibility for the Mobilization of Parties and Intersectoral Cooperation, (iii) Cross-Border Healthcare that will increase the Country's Power in the International Arena (Akdağ, 2008).

References

Akdağ, R. (2008). *İlerleme Raporu: Sağlıkta Dönüşüm Programı Ağustos 2008*. Sağlık Bakanlığı Yayın No:749, Ankara.

Boucher, G. (2012). *Understanding Marxism*. New York: Routledge.

Cebeci, A. (2013). 2000'li Yıllarda Türkiye'deki Kamu Yönetimi Değişimini Çözümlemek. *Marmara Üniversitesi İ.İ.B. Dergisi*, XXXV(II), 175–206.

Cerny, P.G. (1999). Reconstructing the Political in a Globalizing World: States, Institutions, Actors and Governance, in F. Buelens (ed.), *Globalization and the Nation-State*. Cheltenham: Edward Elgar, pp. 89–137.

Clarke, S. (Ed.) (1991). *The State Debate*. Hampshire: Macmillan.

Gough, I. (1975). State Expenditures in Advanced Capitalism. *New Left Review*, I(92), 53–92.

Gülalp, H. (1988). Capital Accumulation and the State, in M. Williams (ed.), *Value, Social Form and the State*. London: Palgrave Macmillan.

Harvey, D. (2003). *The New Imperialism*. Oxford: Oxford University Press.

Hermann, C. (2010). The Marketisation of Health Care in Europe, *Socialist Register*, 125–144.

Hernández-Álvarez, M., Eslava-Castañeda, J.C., Henao-Kaffure, L., Orozco-Díaz, J., & Parra-Salas, L.E. (2020). Universal Health Coverage and Capital Accumulation: A Relationship Unveiled by the Critical Political Economy Approach. *International Journal of Public Health*, 65(7), 995–1001. https://doi.org/10.1007/s00038-020-01437-9

Higgott, R.A., Underhill, G.R.D., & Bieler, A. (Eds.) (2000). *Non-State Actors and Authority in the Global System*. London and New York: Routledge.

Himmelstein, D.U., & Woolhandler, S. (1984). Medicine as Industry: The Health-Care Sector in the United States, *Monthly Review*, 35(11), 13–25.

Hirsch, J. (2011). *Materyalist Devlet Teorisi: Kapitalist Devletler Sisteminin Dönüşüm Süreçleri*. İstanbul: Alan Yayıncılık.

Hodge, G.A., & Greve, C. (2017). On Public–Private Partnership Performance: A Contemporary Review. *Public Works Management & Policy*, 22(1), 55–78.

Insurance Association of Türkiye. (2022). *Insurance Association of Türkiye Annual Report 2022*. Istanbul.

Jessop, B. (2002). *The Future of the Capitalist State*. Cambridge, UK: Polity Press.

Küçük, A. (2018a). *Capitalism, State, Health and Türkiye*. Ankara: Akademisyen Publishing. (in Turkish).

Küçük, A. (2018b). Public Hospital Reform in Turkey: The "Public Hospital Union" Case (2012–2017). *The International Journal of Health Planning and Management*, 33(4), e971–e984. https://doi.org/10.1002/hpm.2574

Leys, C. (2001). *Market Driven Politics: Neoliberal Democracy and the Public Interest*. London: Verso.

Loeppky, R. (2010). Certain Wealth: Accumulation in the Health Industry, In L. Panitch & C. Leys (eds.), *Socialist Register 2010: Morbid Symptoms: Health under Capitalism* vol. 46, Merlin Press: London, pp. 59–83.

Marx, K. (1967) *Capital*. New York: International Publishers.

MoH. (2002–2022). *The Ministry of Health of Türkiye Health Statistics Yearbook 2002–2022*. Republic of Türkiye Ministry of Health, Ankara.

O'Connor, J. (1973). *The Fiscal Crisis of the State*. New York: St. Martin's Press.

OECD. (2024). *Health: Health Expenditure and Financing*. https://stats.oecd.org/Index.aspx?ThemeTreeId=9, 23.01.2024

Offe, C. (1975). The Capitalist State and The Problem of Policy Formation, in L.N. Lindberg (ed.), *Stress and Contradiction in Contemporary Capitalism*. Lexington, Mass.: D.C. Heath, p. 125–144.

Oğuz, Ş. (2011). Krizi Fırsata Dönüştürmek: Türkiye'de Devletin 2008 Krizine Yönelik Tepkileri. *Amme İdaresi Dergisi*, 44(1), 1–23.

Poulantzas, N. (2000). *State, Power and Socialism*, Translated by Patrick Camiller, Finland: Verso.

Przeworski, A. (1990). *The State and the Economy Under Capitalism*. London: Routledge.

Rodberg, L., & Stevenson, G. (1977). The Health Care Industry in Advanced Capitalism. *Review of Radical Political Economics*, 9(1), 104–115.

Singh, P., & Tiwana, B.S. (2020). The State and Accumulation under Contemporary Capitalism. *World Review of Political Economy*, 11(1), 76–94.

Somel, A. (2020). Ekonomik kriz ve sağlık turizmi: Uluslararası Sağlık Hizmetleri Anonim Şirketi neden kuruldu? *METU Studies in Development*, 47(2), 205–255.

Strateji ve Bütçe Başkanlığı (S.B.B). (2024). *Yatırımlar, Kamu Yatırımları: KÖİ Proje Göstergeleri*. https://www.sbb.gov.tr/koi-gostergeleri/, 11.02.2024

TURKSTAT. (2023). *Health and Social Protection: Health Expenditure Statistics*. https://data.tuik.gov.tr/Kategori/GetKategori?p=Saglik-ve-Sosyal-Koruma-101, 31.12.2023.

TURKSTAT. (2024). *Education, Culture, Sports and Tourism, Tourism Statistics-2023*. https://data.tuik.gov.tr/Kategori/GetKategori?p=Egitim,-Kultur,-Spor-ve-Turizm-105, 12.02.1024

TUSEB. (2024). *Corporate: About Us*. https://www.tuseb.gov.tr/en/corporate/about-us, 12.03.2024

Ulutaş, Ç.Ü. (2011). *Proleterleşme ve Profesyonelleşme Tartışmaları Işığında Türkiye'de Sağlık Emek Sürecinin Dönüşümü*. Ankara: Notabene Yayınları.

University of Health Sciences. (2024). *About Us: Mission & Vision*. https://www.uhs.edu.tr/about-us/mission-and-vision, 11.02.2024

Wallerstein, I. (1983). *Historical Capitalism*. Thetford, Norfolk: Verso.

Zencir, M. (2012). Sağlık Reformların Arka Planı: Sağlık Hizmetlerinin Sermaye Birikim Sürecine Doğrudan Katkısı. *Türk Tabipleri Birliği: Mesleki Sağlık ve Güvenlik Dergisi*, 12(45–46): 49–58.

Chapter 15

Evaluation of Turkey's Health Transformation Programme in Terms of Medical Ethics

Nüket Örnek Büken

Contents

15.1 Introduction

Significant changes have been made in the organizational structure of the Ministry of Health in Turkey since the Justice and Development Party (A.K.P.) came to power in 2002. These reforms, neoliberal in nature, have taken place under what is called the Health Transformation Programme (H.T.P.).

The H.T.P., announced by A.K.P. in 2003, in its very first article, defines the functions of the Ministry of Health as solely planning and supervision. The restructuring of the Ministry this has necessitated was implemented in subsequent years by gradually withdrawing the Ministry from providing healthcare services (Pala, 2023).

With this neoliberal reform, the Ministry of Health was tasked with "defining health policies and overseeing and guiding the sector in terms of capacity building" (Republic of Turkey Ministry of Health, 2005). The tasking of the Ministry with "guiding the sector in terms of capacity building" clearly demonstrated the role the Ministry would be taking in the commercialization of the health sector.

The H.T.P., a World Bank project, transformed healthcare workers into intermediaries for the sale of services, while transforming service recipients into consumers and "patient rights" into "consumer rights".

DOI: 10.4324/9781003539896-16

The services to be received by individuals are no longer determined by their needs but by their ability to afford them. Those who can pay are granted the right to choose, and the quality of service is now measured by "customer" satisfaction rather than medical criteria. The practice of informed consent, theoretically aimed at enabling patients to participate in decisions about their own lives and health, has been transformed into a kind of sales contract within this system (Civaner, 2023).

Alongside the H.T.P., policies that contributed to the transformation of healthcare services into objects of trade have had various effects on health service recipients, providers, and ultimately on the ethics of the profession and professional values.

Politicians and policies have designated physicians as the responsible party for the structural problems in the system. This, combined with their conscious effort to discredit physicians in the public eye, has transformed the attitudes of physicians towards their patients and towards their profession. Physicians feel unsafe under increasingly precarious working conditions and threats of violence. This prompts them to be more protective of their jobs, their respectable place in society, and, above all, their safety. This protective response is evident in the significant increase in the desire of physicians, especially prospective physicians, to migrate to other countries.

15.2 Changes in Primary Healthcare Services and Ethical Issues Arising from These Changes

One of the most important pillars of the H.T.P. is the transition to the "family medicine system" (general practitioner) in primary healthcare services. The "family medicine system", presented as the Turkish Model, is actually a system shaped by the World Bank in the past 30 years, which separates service buyers from providers, establishes contracts based on market mechanisms, relies on consumer choice, is service-oriented, and is characterized by the deregulation and precariousness of labour in healthcare (Çiçeklioğlu and Şevik, 2023). The transformation from the "Health Centre" system into the "family medicine system" in Turkey reflects a 20-year adventure in the privatization of healthcare and its negative consequences.

With the implementation of the H.T.P., "Health Centres" previously established by the Law No. 224 were gradually shut down, starting from 2007. All centres were gone by 2010, and "Family Health Centres" established in their place. The "Health Centres" had been medical and social institutions providing health services to residents in designated geographic areas. These centres integrated preventive and primary curative services in line with the science and art of public health. Various health services, such as the fight against diseases like malaria, syphilis, leprosy, trachoma, and tuberculosis, or services for different population groups such as maternal health and child health were provided in Health Centres with a comprehensive service delivery approach in a narrow area. The "Health Centre" was a good horizontal organizational model (Pala, 2021).

The "family medicine model" the H.T.P. has brought was prepared with an approach that disregards physician visits to homes/schools/workplaces and expects citizens to apply to "Family Health Centres". Thus, the contemporary approach to health service delivery, which adopted bringing health services to the doorstep of individuals, even if they did not apply themselves, was abandoned, focusing instead on curative services, and a competitive medical approach model quickly spread.

By closing down Health Centres, which were a service unit embodying a holistic approach to preventive and primary curative services for individuals and community-oriented health services, and by establishing two different institutions under the names of "Family Health Centre" and

"Community Health Centre", health services for individuals and community and environmental health services were separated.

When evaluating preventive health services within primary healthcare in our country – categorized under infectious diseases, non-infectious diseases, and reproductive health – the outcomes of this programme become evident. The COVID-19 pandemic has clearly revealed all the deficiencies of the existing primary healthcare services system, particularly in terms of the early detection, surveillance, and identification of sources of infectious diseases.

Primary healthcare services, particularly for chronic diseases, have been shown to prevent hospital admissions, reduce the risk of complications, and avoid the progression to more serious illnesses through early intervention. There is ample evidence that treatments for five chronic diseases (diabetes, chronic obstructive pulmonary disease, asthma, hypertension, and congestive heart failure) can be provided through outpatient care or community care. These diseases are referred to as "outpatient-responsive diseases", and hospital admissions due to these reasons are defined as "preventable hospitalizations". While the share of preventable hospital admission days for five chronic diseases (diabetes, hypertensive diseases, heart failure, C.O.P.D., and asthma) is on average 5.8% in 30 O.E.C.D. countries, it is 11.8% in Turkey, which unfortunately ranks first in the list (O.E.C.D., 2020).

The ineffectiveness of both individual and societal preventive services for non-communicable diseases and the likely transformation of the integration plan presented as a new structure with healthy life centres into a consumption-based, market-oriented programme due to neoliberal policies are evident.

Although preventive health services for reproductive health have been quantitatively increased, it has been found that the quality of services has not improved. The failings in services that are not part of performance-based-payment have worsened health outcomes and increased inequalities (Çiçeklioğlu and Şevik, 2023).

Similar to universal health coverage, the Health Transformation Programme is focused on a health system based on insurance, and, essentially, it has transformed the organization of primary care to a large extent. Along with health transformation policies, traces of global neoliberal health policies, especially the emphasis on quantity rather than quality, have been reflected in reproductive health services. It has been frequently reiterated that preventive maternal and child health services have been improved with the H.T.P.; however, there is a need to closely evaluate the quality of this improvement and the changes that have taken place over the years (Kaya et al., 2019).

A rights-based approach should be prioritized in reproductive health service delivery rather than global neoliberal policies that emphasize individualism and demand. However, statements such as *"the individual benefiting from the service should be placed at the centre of the service, and services should be based on the needs, demands, and expectations of these individuals as a principle"* (Akdağ, 2012) oppose the rights-based discourse by prioritizing individualism and demand, disregarding states' obligations regarding reproductive health and sexual rights.

15.3 Emerging Ethical Issues in Secondary and Tertiary Healthcare Services

The Ministry of Health's withdrawal from secondary and tertiary healthcare services in line with the directives of the World Bank was realized with the establishment of "Public Hospital Unions" by Decree Law No. 663 which came into force in 2011. In the new structure, units such as the General Directorate of Maternal and Child Health and Family Planning, Malaria Control Department, Tuberculosis Control Department, and Cancer Control Department are not placed in the central organizational structure of the Ministry of Health.

Public Hospital Unions were part of the privatization initiative in the health sector. With the recommendation of the World Bank, a public–private partnership model that would later be named City Hospitals began to take place on the agenda as an innovative way to control costs in the construction and management of public hospitals and to enhance services (World Bank, 2003) and as a means of transferring new and large resources to global capital.

It is known that hospitals which were established and which operate on the public–private partnership model erode the healthcare services system and offer private and profit-oriented services, and the focus of healthcare services provided in these hospitals is not on human health but on profit to be gained.

The inability of university hospitals to achieve a balance in the educational-service-research functions can be considered a structural problem in Turkey. The abandonment of a tiered health service approach within the healthcare system and the abolition of the referral system after 2007 have deepened this structural problem. Overall, the preference for a hospital-focused health system over the past 20 years has led university hospitals to become the first point of contact, when their capacity and equipment are designed for them to be a step in the healthcare system and not the place of initial application.

The health reform and Health Transformation Programme having created a hospital-centred system where university hospitals depend on revolving fund revenues for the purchase of material, the procurement of services, and additional payments to personnel has deeply affected these hospitals. This dependence of public hospitals and especially university hospitals on revolving fund revenues also negatively affects medical education (Yavuz, 2023).

15.4 Conclusion

With the H.T.P., initiatives were launched to reduce the effectiveness of public health service delivery, followed by legal regulations and financial support packages put into effect to open the health sector to private actors. In order to ensure the right to health, a basic human right, there is no other option but for the public sector to effectively provide health services at every level and to meet the health needs of all citizens without them having to face obstacles such as inability to afford or access services. In this context, the Ministry of Health must play a key role. Unless the organizational structure and functions of the Ministry of Health are changed to provide public, high-quality health services to everyone, everywhere, and at all times, the right to health cannot be ensured.

It is important to remember that although the three main subheadings of health policies – financing, organization, and management – seem to be determined by political preferences, each of these preferences are fundamentally a moral choice. Medical ethics is related to health policies in terms of fair allocation of limited resources, prevention of the devaluation of the physician identity, development of intra-professional solidarity, and the arrangement of work environments leading to the best quality of service. Therefore, it is important to reiterate that health policies fall within the scope of medical ethics.

Health policies directly concern the professional independence, professional responsibility, working life, health environment, and service delivery of health workers. Therefore, it is natural for health workers to develop an attitude towards health policies in terms of their professional and social responsibilities.

With the Health Transformation Programme, the provision of health services, which is the primary duty of the state, has been privatized, and the job security of health workers has been put at risk. Due to the prioritization of the individual over the community in service delivery, the limiting of service to individual demand and purchasing power, the focusing of health service delivery on disease/treatment, and the replacement of fair distribution with cost-effectiveness, inequalities have increased.

Turning health services into a tradable commodity has distanced the relationship between providers and recipients from being based on trust. It has transformed health institutions into businesses and patients into customers. Patient rights have been reduced to consumer rights. The right to choose one's physician, granted to patients, aimed at creating competition rather than patient benefit, has had a negative impact on service quality, resulting in the erosion of professional values.

It is necessary to re-emphasize that it is a right to receive health services according to needs and that it is one of the fundamental duties of the state to guarantee the fulfilment of this right. Health services should be provided through general taxes and within the framework of social justice. In the determination of health policies and the sharing of resources, the principle of justice will continue to form the fundamental ethical dimension of the issue. In this context, it should be strongly emphasized that rather than the "economic criteria", principles of a social state must be taken into consideration in determining which service is provided to whom, based on what principles, and how service costs are shared.

The current roles of university hospitals within the health system must be changed, and they should be quickly returned to their actual functions as research and application centres of universities. This necessitates the implementation of a tiered referral system, and for structural financial arrangements to be made. Market dynamics will continue to negatively affect medical education so long as reforms fail to prioritize public health services.

Ultimately, Turkey should adopt a national health system that is inclusive, financed through general taxation and aligned with the principles of a social state committed to public welfare. Priority must be given to preventive health services to reduce unnecessary health expenditures, which have been excessively increased and redirected to the private sector. It is essential to establish a team of qualified health management professionals. By prioritizing national health policies over external and market-driven strategies, Turkey can ensure a fairer and more efficient healthcare system for everyone.

References

Akdağ, R. (2012) *Turkiye Health Transformation Program Evaluation Report (2003–2011)*. Ankara: Ministry of Health publications, 43–439. https://sbu.saglik. gov.tr/Ekutuphane/Yayin/453

Çiçeklioğlu, M., Şevik, I. (2023) Sağlıkta Dönüşüm Programı'nın 20. Yılında Birinci Basamakta Koruyucu Sağlık Hizmetleri, *Toplum ve Hekim*, Cilt: 38 Sayı: 2, syf: 133–144.

Civaner, M. (2023) Sağlıkta Toplum Sözleşmesi Temellerini Kaybediyor, *Toplum ve Hekim*, Cilt: 38 Sayı: 3, syf: 235–240.

Kaya, Ç., Akman, M., Ünalan, P., Çifçili, S., Uzuner, A., Akdeniz, E. (2019) Comparison of Preventive Health Service Provision Before and After Reorganization of Primary Care in Turkiye: A Communitybased Study, *Primary Health Care Research & Development*, Cilt: 20, syf: E119. https://doi.org/10.1017/S1463423619000069

OECD. (2020) *Realising the Potential of Primary Health Care*. OECD Health Policy Studies, OECD Publishing, Paris. https://doi. org/10.1787/a92adee4-en.

Pala, K. (2021) Dönüşen Sağlıkta Pandemi, in Elbek, O., Pala, K. (eds.) *Pandeminin Düşürdüğü Maskeler COVID-19 Salgınının Muhasebesi*. İletişim Yayınları.

Pala, K. (2023) Ministry of Health in the Years of AKP, *Toplum ve Hekim*, Cilt: 38 Sayı: 2, syf: 126–132.

Republic of Turkey Ministry of Health. (2005) *Sağlık 2005*. Ankara. https://ekutuphane.saglik.gov.tr/Yayin/163.

Yavuz, C.I. (2023) Son 20 Yılda Mezuniyet Öncesi Tıp Eğitimi, *Toplum ve Hekim*, Cilt: 38 Sayı: 4, Syf: 254–263.

World Bank. (2003) *Private Health, Policy and Regulatory Options for Private Participation*. Viewpoint. https://openknowledge.worldbank.org/handle/10986/11295.

Concluding Remarks

Dilek Başar and Selcen Öztürk

Turkey's health reforms have brought transformative changes across the healthcare system, with the Health Transformation Programme (H.T.P) serving as a crucial element of the country's health policy. These reforms have aimed to enhance accessibility, efficiency, and the quality of healthcare services, prompting significant interest from both academic and policy circles. However, a comprehensive academic analysis has been missing from the discourse. This book addresses that gap, offering a cohesive evaluation of the reforms' impact on different stakeholders and the broader economy, providing a more complete understanding of Turkey's healthcare transformation.

The primary aim of this edited volume is to offer a comprehensive and critical analysis of Turkey's H.T.P. Bringing together contributions from leading scholars and practitioners, it examines the programme's impact from diverse perspectives. The book evaluates the H.T.P.'s impact on various perspectives. By synthesising these insights, it aspires to be a key resource for policymakers, academics, and students engaged in health economics, public health, and policy analysis.

The book examines H.T.P. from multiple angles. *Part I* evaluates the government's perspective, revealing that while the H.T.P. improved health indicators, its impact on consumption inequality was minimal. It also highlights positive outcomes in health spending and access but stresses the need for domestic drug production. *Part II* focuses on healthcare providers, identifying diagnostic challenges for refugees and inefficiencies in private hospitals. *Part III* looks at healthcare users, noting high satisfaction overall but a decline for private services, while also discussing household health expenses and the rise of e-health. *Part IV* analyses healthcare utilisation, finding that reforms have not significantly reduced inequalities, especially for children and mental health services. *Part V* addresses the political economy and ethics, stressing the role of the H.T.P. in capital accumulation and advocating for publicly funded healthcare to reduce inequality.

This book offers valuable recommendations for both political decision-makers and academic researchers. From a policy perspective, it highlights the need for targeted strategies to address gaps in equity, such as improving healthcare access for marginalized groups like refugees and those with unmet mental health needs. It also suggests that domestic drug production and investment in healthcare infrastructure are crucial to maintaining efficiency and sustainability. For future academic research, the book underscores the importance of analysing the long-term socioeconomic impacts of healthcare reforms, encouraging further study into the relationship between health policy, economic inequality, and the evolving needs of diverse populations. By integrating these insights, both policymakers and scholars can build on the lessons from Turkey's Health Transformation Programme to shape more equitable, efficient, and effective health systems moving forward.

DOI: 10.4324/9781003539896-17

INDEX

Note: Page numbers in *italics* indicate a figure and page numbers in **bold** indicate a table on the corresponding page.

9781032885230